TONGUES OF THE SPIRIT

A STUDY OF PENTECOSTAL GLOSSOLALIA
AND RELATED PHENOMENA

TONGUES OF THE SPIRIT

A STUDY OF PENTECOSTAL GLOSSOLALIA
AND RELATED PHENOMENA

CYRIL G. WILLIAMS

CARDIFF
UNIVERSITY OF WALES PRESS
1981

British Library Cataloguing in Publication Data

Williams, Cyril Glyndwr
Tongues of the spirit.
1. Glossolalia
2. Pentecostal churches
I. Title
248'. 29   BL54
ISBN 0-7083-0758-2

PRINTED BY THE CAMBRIAN NEWS (ABERYSTWYTH) LTD.

I goffadwriaeth fy rhieni

DAVID WILLIAMS

HANNAH WILLIAMS

PREFACE

The phenomenon of glossolalia or 'speaking with tongues' is a feature of the Pentecostal and Neo-Pentecostal movements of this century. It has been regarded by some as nothing more than the emotional extravagance of unstable eccentrics, while Pentecostals themselves see in it the resurgence of a Biblical phenomenon to be attributed to the work of the Holy Spirit. In this book I have examined, briefly, various interpretations of glossolalia and raised the question of seemingly related phenomena in other religious contexts, both undertakings, in my view, being pre-requisites of theological appraisal.

The task has occupied me for several years since it could be performed only intermittently as other duties permitted. During this time I have seen interest in the subject grow and the phenomenon itself spread rapidly over five continents and across denominational barriers. Inevitably, developments have outpaced publication. A case in point is the news of the impending closure of the Fountain Trust which came too late to refer to it in the chapter on Neo-Pentecostalism. Notwithstanding the changing scene, the questions raised here are basic to any investigation and evaluation of this phenomenon.

Many persons, on both sides of the Atlantic, have helped to make this book possible, particularly individuals of diverse religious backgrounds who kindly gave me interviews. I am especially indebted to former students of my class on the Hebrew Prophets at Carleton University, Ottawa, who discussed aspects of this investigation with me and helped in the distribution of a questionnaire. The demands of final preparation for publication have been lightened by the co-operation of colleagues at Aberystwyth. I am particularly grateful to the Reverend Islwyn Blythin who kindly undertook to read through the typescript and prepare the indexes and to the Reverend S. I. Enoch who read the typescript and undertook the laborious task of proof reading in all the stages of preparation. I am indebted, in addition, to both these friends for many useful comments for the improvement of this work. I must also express my thanks to Mrs Beryl Jenkins who did most of the typing for publication and for correspondence in connection with it.

I should like to take the opportunity to place on record my gratitude to my revered teacher Emeritus Professor A. R. Johnson, F.B.A., for his interest in my work but above all for the inspiration of his friendship over the years. At the same time I must hasten to add that he is in no way responsible for any of the views expressed here.

viii

My sincere thanks are due to the Drummond Trust and to the Catherine and Lady Grace James foundation for grants in support of publication, to the University of Wales Press for publishing and to the Cambrian News, Aberystwyth, for all the care and patience shown in printing.

Finally, I must add a special word of thanks to my wife, who, as always, rescued me from several chores with characteristic cheerfulness. All the inadequacies and the errors that remain in the book must be claimed as mine alone.

University College of Wales   Cyril Glyndwr Williams
Aberystwyth.

CONTENTS

ACKNOWLEDGEMENTS

I wish to acknowledge with gratitude the permission received from the following to quote from their publications: Fountain Trust; The Apostolic Church; William B. Eerdmans, Publishing Company, Grand Rapids, Michigan; Logos International; Charisma Books; Gospel Publishing House. I am also indebted to the following publishers for permission to use extracts from the works indicated: Paulist Press, New York-K. and D. Ranaghan, *Catholic Pentecostals*, copyright Paulist Press; Hodder and Stoughton Limited—J. P. Kildahl, *The Psychology of Speaking in Tongues*, S. Durasoff, *Bright Wind of the Spirit, Pentecostalism Today*, J. L. Sherrill, *They Speak with Other Tongues*; Cambridge University Press—S. G. Wilson, *The Gentiles and the Gentile Mission in Luke —Acts*; Eastern Pentecostal Bible College, Peterborough, Ontario—G. F. Atter, *The Third Force*; Basil Blackwell Publisher, Oxford—E. Haenchen, *Acts of the Apostles*; Evangelical Press —E. Evans, *The Welsh Revival of 1904*; George Allen and Unwin—N. Bloch-Hoell, *The Pentecostal Movement*, J. Blofeld, *Mantras* (Mandala Books); Macmillan Publishing Co.—R. B. Y. Scott, *The Relevance of the Prophets* revised edit. (copyright 1944 by Macmillan Publishing Co., Inc., renewed 1972 by R. B. Y. Scott. Copyright © 1968 by R. B. Y. Scott), William J. Samarin, *Tongues of Men and Angels* (Copyright © 1972 by William J. Samarin); S. C. M.—G. von Rad, *The Message of the Prophets*, W. J. Hollenweger, *The Pentecostals*; The University of Chicago Press—F. Goodman, *Speaking in Tongues* (© 1972 by the University of Chicago), R. Werblowsky, 'Mystical and Magical contemplation: The Kabbalists in Sixteenth Century Safed' in *History of Religions* i (i) (1961).

Permission was obtained to include some Scripture quotations from the Revised Standard Version of the Bible, copyrighted 1971 and 1952 by the Division of Christian Education of the National Council of the Churches of Christ in the U.S.A.

All the authors whom I approached readily allowed me to employ quotations from their works. These include: Professor Morton T. Kelsey, University of Notre Dame, Indiana, from his book *Tongue Speaking* (Doubleday and Company); Dr. Ian Stevenson from his work *Xenoglossy: A Review and Report of a Case* (The University Press of Virginia); Professor Rengt Sundkler, (Uppsala and the International African Institute) from *Bantu Prophets in South Africa*; Professor H. Newton Malony, Fuller Theological Seminary, Dr. Virginia H. Hine and the Society for the Scientific Study of Religion Inc., University of Connecticut, from articles in *J.S.S.R.*; Professor Luther P. Gerlach, University of Minnesota from published papers; Dale K. Fitzgerald, New School for Social Research, New York, from 'Prophetic Speech in Ga Spirit Mediumship' a paper of the Language Behaviour Research Laboratory, University of California; Professor Gary B. Palmer, Associate Professor, University of Nevada, from unpublished papers and thesis; Dr. L. M. Vivier, Pretoria, South Africa, from his Doctor of Medicine dissertation in the Department of Psychiatry and Mental Hygiene, University of Witwatersrand; Dr. Jerry L. Sandidge, Director University Action, Eurasia, from his unpublished thesis 'The Origin and Development of the Catholic Charismatic Movement in Belgium', Katholieke Universiteit Te Leuven, (I am indebted to the Reverend John Stuart Roberts, B.B.C. Wales, for calling my attention to this work).

By kind consent, excerpts are included from E. Mansell Pattison, 'Behavioral Science Research and the Nature of Glossolalia', *Journal of the American Scientific Affiliation* 20 (1968) copyright held by the American Scientific Affiliation, an organisation of Christian Men and Women of Science, 5 Douglas Ave., Elgin, Illinois, U.S.A. Routledge and Kegan Paul kindly allowed me to reproduce my article 'Glossolalia as a religious phenomenon' from *The Journal of Religion and Religions* 5 (1975) and the University of Wilfrid Laurier Press, similarly, the article 'Ecstaticism in Hebrew Prophecy and Christian Glossolalia' which appeared in *Studies in Religion Sciences Religieuses* 3: 4 (1974). I am indebted to Professor W. J. Samarin for copies of several papers; Mrs. Yvonne Haddad, Colgate University, for much information on Islamic mysticism; Mr. Erin Hewitt, Carleton University for reporting on his research work; and Principal Omri Bowen, Bible College, Penygroes, for guidance to literature on The Apostolic Church.

PRINCIPAL ABBREVIATIONS*

A.J.S.	*American Journal of Sociology*
A.J.S.L.	*American Journal of Semitic Languages and Literatures*
Arch.Psy.	*Archives de Psychologie*
B.W.	*British Weekly*
D.B.	*Dictionary of the Bible* ed. J. Hastings (1909)
Enc. Brit.	*Encyclopaedia Britannica*
E.R.E.	*Encyclopaedia of Religion and Ethics* ed. J. Hastings (1908)
E.T.	*Expository Times*
E.Tr.	English Translation
F.G.B.M.F.I.	Full Gospel Business Men's Fellowship International
H.T.R.	*Harvard Theological Review*
Hum. Biol.	*Human Biology*
I.D.B.	*Interpreter's Dictionary of the Bible*
Int. J. Psa.	*Internatinal Journal of Psycho-Analysis*
Int. Psych.	*International Psychiatry Clinics*
J.A.S.A.	*Journal of the American Scientific Affiliation*
J.A.S.P.R.	*Journal of the American Society for Psychical Research*
J. Belge de Neurol. et de Psychiat.	*Journal Belge de Neurologie et de Psychiatrie*
J.Enc.	*Jewish Encyclopaedia*
J. Nerv. Ment. Dis.	*Journal of Nervous and Mental Diseases*
J.S.S.R.	*Journal of the Scientific Study of Religion*
J.T.S.	*Journal of Theological Studies*
N.E.B.	New English Bible
N.T.	New Testament
N.T.S.	*New Testament Studies*
O.T.	Old Testament
P.S.P.R.	*Proceedings of the Society for Psychical Research*
R.S.V.	Revised Standard Version
R.H.R.	*Revue de l'historie des religions*
S.V.T.	Supplements to *Vetus Testamentum*
V.T.	*Vetus Testamentum*
W.C.C.	World Council of Churches
Z.A.W.	*Zeitschrift für die alttestamentliche Wissenschaft*
Zeitsch. für Psychol.	*Zeitschrift für Psychologie*

*Articles at the beginning of titles have been omitted.

Chapter i

THE ECSTATIC ELEMENT IN HEBREW PROPHECY AND CHRISTIAN GLOSSOLALIA

The ecstatic theory of Hebrew prophecy was very much in the forefront of interest in Old Testament studies in the early decades of this century. The work of Gustav Hölscher[1] and T. H. Robinson[2] may be viewed as representing this emphasis. Subsequently, interest in this area abated, partly because of lack of confidence in the ability of the psychological approach to reveal the inner experience of the prophets, but primarily because other aspects of O.T. studies claimed the attention of scholars, such as the cultic role of the prophets, the question of literary form and transmission, and more recently the structure of prophetic books. Recently, however, great advances have been made in anthropological research in the phenomenology of religion, in the behavioural sciences, and not least in sociolinguistics. There has also been in the last decade a remarkable resurgence of glossolalic[3] occurrence outside Pentecostalism, in traditional churches both Catholic and Protestant. Once again, therefore, in my view, the psychology of prophecy calls for reappraisal.

One should not assume *a priori* that there is no generic connection between modern glossolalia and ecstatic prophecy or that glossolalia can be dismissed as pathological indulgence, and the research that has hitherto been undertaken on modern glossolalia has convinced this writer that our understanding of prophetic experience would be advanced if studies of modern glossolalia were taken into account.[4] This is not by any means to minimize either the importance of working from within the biblical texts or the need for a due appreciation of ancient modes of thought both Hebrew and Greek, but rather to enter a plea for the correlation of such basic studies with empirical field and clinical studies of dissociated states of consciousness as well as with data provided by phenomenological studies.

Of course, there are enormous difficulties in the way, the paramount one arising from the seemingly impossible task of ascertaining the core prophetic utterance from the basic structures of prophetic speech, with their obvious elaboration in traditional moulds. Here the work of Claus Westermann must be regarded as the

1

foundation of future inquiry.[5]   He shows the weakness of approaches which trace back the speeches of the prophets to private experience or to a general category of revelation, and argues for recognition of the prophets as basically messengers who speak in the style of messages employing traditional formulas, speech forms, and speeches which have been handed down.   It is not possible, for instance, to distinguish between the true words of Yahweh and the prophet's words simply on the basis of introduction by the messenger formula.   Westermann complains that the ecstatic theory isolated and emphasized the 'reception' of the word, while the present phase of prophetic investigation places too much importance upon the 'delivery' of the word.[6]   He argues that what comes in between, namely transmission, has been neglected.

Even so, the question of the authorizing of the prophet as speaker remains and H. W. Wolff is in my view right in stressing the importance of the call in this connection.[7]   This is not to argue for a uniformity of pattern nor to ignore the rich variety of prophets and the diversity of prophecy which embraces for instance the valuable contribution of anonymous cultic prophets as well as that of canonical prophets.   But where even a little information is provided concerning the life of an individual prophet, and at best it is meagre, the call-experience seems to be of key significance.   Wolff, however, argues against an ecstatic interpretation of prophetic experience, since the accounts depict a clear I-Thou relationship, and the messenger's speech establishes an alert personal relationship to the surrounding world.[8]   What Wolff has not sufficiently recognized is the range of ecstatic experience which can accommodate both a trance state with a high degree of dissociation and a state in which normal consciousness is intensified to a new pitch but in which the relation aspect is not only retained but accentuated.   Even in the accounts of the call there is a certain amount of stylization,[9] and very little information can be gleaned as to the psychical condition of the prophet or the actual content of the visions received.   What is clear is that inspiration came to the prophet sometimes unexpectedly (1 Kings 13:20),   sometimes after long expectation (Jer. 42:7), and that, in many cases at least, the reception of revelation had somatic effects.   As Von Rad says, 'when it is told of a prophet that the hand of Yahweh came upon him or fell upon him (1 Kings 18:46; Ezek. 8:1), or when a prophet himself even says that the hand of Yahweh seized him (Isa. 8:11), there is every reason for believing that behind these brief notices lie experiences which not only shook his soul but caused bodily disturbances as well.   Ezekiel relates how he sat on the ground awe-struck and unable to speak a word for seven days after his call (Ezek. 3:15). Daniel, too, says that all the blood drained from his face, that he fell to the ground (Dan. 10:8f) and that after one such experience he lay sick for some days (Dan. 8:27).'[10]

R. B. Y. Scott advances the interesting claim that most of the prophets received at least their first impulse to speak in some form of prophetic ecstasy, in the course of which a 'Word from Yahweh' emerged in their consciousness and demanded utterance.[11] This experience of the welling up of the 'Word' within the prophet was not restricted to the call of the prophets (cf Isa. 8:11; Jer. 20:9), and Scott holds that there are indications that it became articulate in their minds 'as a brief enigmatic sentence or phrase, or even as a single word.' Such instances he calls 'embryonic oracles'; I shall return later to a consideration of this aspect.

Despite difficulties and uncertainties, I suggest that the literature as it stands provides some clues and circumstantial evidence on the basis of which it is legitimate to make deductions about the psychological conditions of prophecy, and, furthermore, that the time-cultural gap does not make comparisons between the psychological conditions of prophecy and glossolalia invidious, provided that they are made with circumspection within the limitations imposed by the availability of 'lead' descriptions.[12] The question which I pose is whether, and if so in what way, the ecstatic features associated with Hebrew prophecy can be related to what has been observed of the experience and behaviour of glossolalists.

The history of prophetic interpretation shows a wide range of application for the term 'ecstatic', from states of frenzied group behaviour to exalted states of creative activity.[13] For T. H. Robinson, the most thoroughgoing British exponent of the ecstatic theory, and one whose views still merit attention as they anticipate, in emphasis, an interest in the role of the unconscious in states of dissociation, the ecstatic condition is one in which the unconscious ripens into consciousness.[14] He maintains that the deeper ranges of spiritual life which lie far below the level of normal consciousness represent the real point at which the self-revealing divine impinges on the human soul. The general tendency since Hölscher and T. H. Robinson, however, has been to exaggerate the divergence between the canonical prophets and their forerunners. It has been widely held that, while the early *nebhî'îm* were subject to frenzied behaviour, incoherent cries, and trancelike states, these features almost totally disappear in the canonical prophets. This attitude is well illustrated in Mowinckel's early position. Of the canonical prophets, he writes:

3

In them the ecstatic substratum, i.e. the mental concentration upon a single idea, a single passion, has assumed more tranquil forms. On the whole little remains of the ecstatic element, apart from that which is the sound psychological substratum and core of religious ecstasy: the all predominating, all exclusive consciousness of having been called by Yahweh to deliver a religious and moral message. All external stimuli such as dancing and music have been abandoned. True, the state in which they deliver that message is 'elevated', but it is also characterized by spiritual clarity and reasoned judgement. The utterances are in a finished artistic form; to the solemn words of judgment they generally add a clear, reasoned, moral and religious exposition, and their words do not come to them as wild stammering glossolaly—as involuntary, unconscious words accompanied by unconscious reflex actions—but as moral and religious apprehensions of inexorable facts, apprehensions which 'rise up' in them from the depths of the subconscious to attain lucidity, merging into their moral and religious personality. Apart from the occasional visions and auditions to which they allude, there is nothing about the reforming prophets suggestive of any markedly ecstatic experience in the old frenzied forms.[15]

This statement represents the main stream of interpretation in this century. Two things need to be noted: the recognition of the role of the subconscious and of the 'elevated' state of the prophet in delivering his message. Can this 'elevated' state still be described as ecstatic, or should one, like Micklem, confine the term ecstatic to states where there appears to be almost total loss of self-control on the part of the subject, or where we have mechanical utterances of words which show no trace of conscious thought?[16] R. B. Y. Scott describes this elevated prophetic condition as one in which the prophet feels the presence within his mind of a light which raises to a new level his awareness and understanding, but Scott retains the term ecstasy: 'Such intensity and exaltation of spirit resulting from a recognized divine impulsion, is then a *new kind* of prophetic ecstasy, related to the concentration and absorption of the mystic, the artist and the genius, but different because of its action element.'[17] It differs, too, says Scott, in that it expresses itself in a new kind of ecstatic speech, clearly intelligible, direct and radical, and charged with strong emotional force.

What emerges among interpreters of prophecy is an awareness, not yet however satisfactorily articulate, of grades of ecstasy which

4

may very loosely be described as 'lower' where there is suppression of normal consciousness and 'higher' where there is a quickening of normal consciousness. Very few interpreters have made even this broad kind of distinction in their usage of the term 'ecstatic'. There have been, however, some exceptions where bolder classification has been attempted. Hölscher, for example, has distinguished between what he calls 'sthenic' and 'apathetic' ecstasy. The former is characterized by involuntary movements of limbs and loud cries which give birth to song and dance,[18] a state seemingly akin to what Felicitas Goodman in her observations on glossolaly describes as the 'hyper-aroused' state of dissociation.[19] By 'apathetic' ecstasy Hölscher means an abnormal state where the ecstatic is subject to hallucinations and where a fearful obsession paralyses the whole organism and consciousness.[20] Some features of what Hölscher associates with the sthenic prophetic condition, Goodman, on the basis of empirical studies, finds true of the glossolalic state, except that she also finds hallucinatory elements in it. For her the glossolalic state is one of hyperarousal, an altered state of consciousness with obvious somatic agitation.[21] In describing the prophetic experience, Hölscher similarly has ascribed the physical and psychical phenomena accompanying it to an exceptional intensifying of the emotions which changes the normal conditions of consciousness, but he goes on to say that this turns the prophet into a psychopathic case, characterized by delirium and madness. In this state, Hölscher claims, the prophet experiences a sense of compulsion to speak or to act; this, he interprets as a quasiphysical coercion due to loss of control over the play of the muscles. The physical effects, in other words, are automatically produced.

Hölscher might have given a more restrained account had the scientific study of glossolalic parallels, such as those described by Goodman, been available to him. She discovers a certain ebb of energy discharge in glossolalists of long experience,[22] analogous, one would suggest, to the refinement of the prophetic condition after the initial experience of the call. Furthermore, we have accounts of glossolalic utterances given in a relaxed atmosphere,[23] and this writer knows several glossolalists who can 'exercise their gift' at will[24] with deliberation and with no untoward or perceptible physical change. Goodman would insist that even in such cases there is a mild form of dissociation, undetected by the untrained observer, and that the subsequent utterance is superimposed upon this altered state of consciousness. What I suggest, then, is that, while Hölscher weakens his interpretation by insistence upon the psychopathological excesses of prophecy, he is right, in part at least,

5

n the role he allows the non-rational and unconscious factors. His distinction of sthenic and apathetic is only partially valid, for hallucinations can attend both kinds of experience described, as, indeed, they can accompany experiences where normal consciousness is elevated with an enhancement of mental faculties. In such a 'higher' ecstatic state the interplay of the non-rational unconscious and the rational conscious is of a more sensitive nature than usual, in that the association of ideas with words, for example, is more readily made, and in that sounds, words, or ideas incubating under the threshold, in the deeper levels of personality, may emerge with concomitant or resulting physical effects.

J. Mauchline has advanced another kind of distinction, listing three types of prophetic ecstasy: self-induced ecstasy; passive ecstasy in which the ecstatic state is produced in the subject by the psychological influence of the group, or by a group leader; and individual ecstasy.[25] This circumstantial classification could be applied as readily to glossolalists as to the prophets. The role of the leader and the 'learning' experience mediated by the group are typical of glossolalist events, while individual utterance in private worship is also a common occurrence.

It may be presumptuous to define any prophetic state *per se*, and one can legitimately ask what some O.T. scholars mean by a passive state of ecstasy. Does it mean that the subject's normal consciousness is completely extinguished, that the senses lose their normal function, and that self-control is lost? Here glossolalist experience may afford a useful parallel, if one speaks in terms of an altered state of consciousness with varying degrees of dissociation from the normal environment. Prophetic conditions similarly appear to range from a trance-like state, with loss of self-consciousnes and surrender to subconscious suggestion, through an indistinct borderland condition of being half awake, to one of active consciousness.[26] It would be easier, of course, to make distinctions on the basis of differences in the conceptual systems of ecstatics than on the basis of a psychological appraisal. We might speak, for example, of transportation ecstasy, where, as in shamanism, the experience is associated with belief in the passage of the soul beyond the body; of absorption ecstasy, to borrow Lindblom's term,[27] in the case of some mystics whose ultimate achievement is transcendence of the ego in the all-embracing oneness with the deity (in theistic contexts) or the universal All (in monistic contexts); or of relational ecstasy where, as in prophecy or indeed glossolalia, there is a deepened sense of rapport with the deity or the Holy Spirit. Within this last category, however, there is still room for psychological classification depending upon the degree of dissociation of the subject.

6

Most interpreters prior to Hölscher rejected any abnormality whatsoever in the canonical prophets, claiming them to be rational, fully conscious, profound, and creative thinkers. This was to minimize the visionary and auditory elements in the accounts of the prophetic call, e.g., in the case of Isaiah, not to mention the undoubtedly ecstatic features of much of Ezekiel's activity. In this writer's view, the ecstatic susceptibility of the canonical prophets must be accepted, but the extent of the suppression of normal consciousness in any instance can only be conjectured. Guillaume maintains that a feature which stands out in Hebrew visions and ecstasies, in sharp contrast to the ecstasies of the Neoplatonic and Muslim schools of mystics, is the prophet's intense consciousness of himself. Generalizations in this area are fraught with dangers, and the boldness of this assertion is mitigated by Guillaume's own enigmatic description of the consciousness of the prophet as 'an unconscious self-consciousness'.[28] What is meant is that the consciousness functions as in a dream, merely recording or watching the film of the subconscious screen.[29] This would seem to have a parallel in glossolalic utterance, where the speaker cannot choose the sound or word, but there is a major distinction in that the glossolalic generally cannot subsequently recall or repeat what he has uttered,[30] and may not even recognize his own 'tongue' when it is played back to him on tape.[31]

The degree of alienation from normal surroundings varies considerably in the case of glossolalics. That some continue to speak, disregarding the bell employed to call them to 'surface' in some religious services,[32] indicates the depth of the suppression of normal consciousness. On the other hand, as indicated earlier, the glossolalist can experience tongues in a relaxed atmosphere, and, in the case of an experienced 'speaker', turn to it at will and so demonstrate control over his charismatic powers. In both glossolalic and prophetic conditions there would seem to be a whole range of intensity of feeling and degrees of awareness. It is noteworthy that A. W. Knobel, one of the earliest investigators of prophecy in the last century, recognized a progression of degrees within the ecstatic state.[33] At one moment, it is only an elevated emotional feeling and attitude; at another time it rises to a lively moment of spiritual life and at yet another time, it grows to a violent upheaval and finally passes over into ecstasy or rapture: 'Diese ist die höchste Stufe derselben und überhaupt der höchste Grad der Geistesregsamkeit; sie ist die Steigerung der geistigen Lebendigkeit zur höchsten Potenz.'[34]

Knobel adds that, when such an extreme state of spiritual

7

upheaval sets in, it is bound to exercise a strong influence over the functions of the whole human organism and to produce changes in it. Later interpreters have adduced many examples of these physical effects. Pedersen, for instance, mentions stammering exclamations (Isa. 28:10); the actions of a madman (1 Sam. 21:14 EVV. 13); tremblings and shakings (Dan. 10: 10, 11); dumbness (Dan. 10: 15; Ezek. 3:26; 24:27; 29:21; 33:22); falling to the ground stunned (Ezek. 1:28; 3:23; cf Dan. 10:9); staring (Ezek. 3:15).[35] Gunkel regarded the actions of the prophets as outward manifestations of their inner ecstasy. These actions, he maintains, could be of a convulsive nature (1 Kings 18:26), sometimes without the prophet's knowledge or will (1 Kings 18:12), and sometimes akin to symptoms of drunkenness even in the case of a calm personality like Jeremiah (Jer. 23:9).[36] Philo long ago had in fact described the prophetic inspiration as a divine intoxicating (*theia methē*) 'more sober than sobriety itself'. His description of the physical concomitants of the experience of divine possession (*'e'ntheos katokōchē*) might well be a description of many examples of modern glossolalic behaviour too: 'When grace fills the soul, that soul thereby rejoices and smiles and dances, for it is possessed with a frenzy (*bebákcheutai*), so that to many of the unenlightened it may seem to be drunken, crazy, and besides itself.' The term *bebákcheutai* could be taken to indicate the kind of behaviour associated with physical intoxication at the festivals of Bacchus or Dionysus, but Philo stresses that it is only a surface resemblance since this is 'sober intoxication' (*méthe nēphalios*)![37]

Physical manifestations of glossolalic ecstasy[38] provide striking parallels to prophetic behaviour and suggest that we are dealing with inner conditions which have strong psychological affinities. What has not been sufficiently allowed for in studies of prophecy, however, is the possibility that an individual may progress through a whole range of subjective ecstatic states. If we consider our glossolalist parallel in this case, following Goodman, we find that once a person has learned to dissociate, subsequent events are initiated more and more easily, some of the organizational pattern becomes eroded, and intensity and dissociational levels drop.[39]

The writer himself has observed extraordinary changes among glossolalists. Some, who at one time had obviously manifested a hyperaroused state with kinetic mobility, were able years later to speak with tongues in what seemed to be a perfectly normal condition with no outward sign of dissociation. Even the content of the utterance evolves: the incoherent, inarticulate bablings of a 'beginner' develop into more phonologically structured pulses and 'sentences' which, while still linguistically unintelligible, have the general characteristics of highly charged rhythmic speech, and, if Goodman is right, a discernible intonational pattern.[40]

The all-important difference between glossolalic utterance and the prophetic oracle would seem to be that the latter, even in its primary embryonic forms, has articulate sounds and identifiable words which later can be elaborated in a comprehensible manner.[41]   But it must be remembered that the glossolalic utterance too is meant to be accompanied by intelligible interpretation for the edification of the community.   The exercise of glossolalia in the early Christian community was discouraged unless it was accompanied by interpretation, which this writer understands not as 'translation' but as a function, just as charismatic as glossolalic utterance, and sometimes practised in a residual dissociation state by the same individual.[42] Modern examples of charismatic interpretation may demonstrate the same rhythmic quality of utterance as the unintelligible utterance of glossolalia and are often presented in an archaic scriptural literary style.   What is striking in glossolalic interpretation is that sometimes persons of little or no educational background, whose only language is the vernacular, have spoken in the most sublime and refined of terms with a beauty of diction that they would not possess in their normal condition.   On other occasions, however, grammar and coherence of thought are neglected.[43]

Modern Pentecostals attribute glossolalic utterance to the charismatic impartation of the Holy Spirit.   One exponent of the faith claims that tongues-speaking is a

> manifestation of the mind of the spirit of God employing human speech organs.   When man is speaking with tongues, his mind, intellect, understanding are quiescent.   It is the faculty of God that is active.   Man's will, certainly, is active, and his spirit, and his speech organs; but the mind that is operating is the mind of God through the Holy Spirit.[44]

This readiness to acknowledge the role of the Holy Spirit is understood in a way which would seem to parallel that of the *ruach* as the vehicle of inspiration in Hebrew prophecy, except that in the higher range of ecstatic condition the mind of the prophet need not be quiescent but may be quickened to a more intense degree than usual, so that he can make associations of words and ideas and see relations in the religious and political scene hidden from most. Many O.T. scholars, however, have held that, while the early pre-canonical prophets understood inspiration as invasion by the spirit (*ruach*),[45] the canonical prophets placed less emphasis on the spirit,

9

staking their reputation on possession of the word (*dhābhār*). One should not overemphasize this distinction, for none of the prophets would repudiate the activity of the spirit,[46] which, while it might occasion ecstatic behaviour of the eruptive kind, could also issue in 'those temperate qualities which characterize the ideal servant of Yahweh and specifically His vice-regent upon earth'.[47]

What I claim, then, is that those who recognize ecstatic features in Hebrew prophecy, both pre-canonical and canonical, are probably right, but that the degree of dissociation involved may differ, not only from individual to individual, but also in the history of the religious experience of the individual. As Eliade has observed, 'Not only can a community consciously or unconsciously practise many religions, but the same individual can have an infinite variety of religious experiences from the "highest" to the most undeveloped and aberrant.'[48] Even critics who wish to dissociate the canonical prophets from ecstatic conditions feel obliged to concede that some abnormal features occur. Isaiah's call, for example, seems a genuine ecstatic experience with a high degree of dissociation and hallucinatory elements. Yet the vision is described in the first person singular, indicating that the condition is not one of mystic absorption but of prophetic relationship and one furthermore in which normal consciousness seems to have been raised to a new intensity. The relational aspect in this case does not preclude a condition of abnormal excitation.[49] Von Rad cites Isaiah 21:1-10 (which is not from the prophet Isaiah) as a passage which 'lets us see as no other does something of the prophet's very deeply agitated and tormented state as he received a "stern vision" '.[50] Again certain passages of Jeremiah strongly suggest a state of hyperecstatic experience. The degree of dissociation in this case does not seem as pronounced as in Isaiah's call, and self-consciousness is retained in spite of the overwhelming nature of the experience. In Jeremiah 20: 7-9 (R.S.V.), for instance, the utterance, in this case of course intelligible, comes with irresistible force:

> O Lord, thou hast deceived me,
>   and I was deceived;
> thou art stronger than I,
>   and thou hast prevailed.
> I have become a laughing-stock all the
>   day;
>   every one mocks me.

10

For whenever I speak, I cry out,
  I shout, 'Violence and destruction!'
For the word of the Lord has become
  for me
  a reproach and derision all day long.
If I say, 'I will not mention him,
  or speak any more in his name,'
there is in my heart as it were a burning
  fire
  shut up in my bones,
and I am weary with holding it in,
  and I cannot.

On the other hand, in most of Jeremiah's utterances, as in the case of Isaiah, there is no hint of abnormality.[51]   The interpretation of Ezekiel's prophetic activity is controversial, but most critics have recognized ecstatic features in his behaviour, even though they have not accepted such an extreme position as Hölscher's, who held that Ezekiel was subject to cataleptic fits and who found evidence of unintelligible speech in Ezekiel 7 and 21.[52]   Here I would agree with Micklem that the term $m^e sh\bar{a}lim$ is not the Hebrew for glossolaly (Ezek. 21:5 [EVV, 20:49]),[53] and that the passage provides no support for Hölscher's statement that Ezekiel was unintelligible. What one can, perhaps, find in Ezekiel is what I described earlier as transportation ecstasy (Ezekiel 3:14; 40:2, 17; 37:1-10).

Watson E. Mills says one should not make the mistake of linking earlier appearances of ecstaticism into a lineal descent which leads ultimately to first century glossolalia.[54]   I am not arguing for a lineal development from early Hebrew prophetic conditions to modern-day glossolalic experience.   In fact, as I now hope to show, there is no evidence of glossolalia *per se* in the Old Testament, but nevertheless many psychological features associated with the glossolalist experience are present, as well as similarities in the conception of the role of the spirit.   What I am urging is due recognition for the respectable role of the non-rational in religious experience, a factor which is more readily evident in ecstaticism than in normal religious behaviour.   I contend, in fact, that varying degrees of ecstatic dissociation are present in Hebrew prophecy and that the psychological conditions may parallel the variety of states encountered in modern glossolalic behaviour, making a distinction, of course, between the state or condition and the utterance which derives from it.[55]   Ecstatic elements in both Hebrew prophecy, glossolalia ancient and modern, and indeed in other religious cultures, are, I believe, generically related psychologically,[56] but differ, among other things, to the extent that conceptual systems affect subjective states, and in all cases in the degree of dissociation involved.

Let us then consider whether there is in the O.T. any hint of glossolalic utterance, which by virtue of its unintelligibility can be distinguished within the more general category of ecstatic utterance.[57]   One would not expect a transcript of such an utterance —even the New Testament does not provide that and modern examples are not by any means plentiful, but there could be some covert clues.   J. Pedersen believed that the very term $n\bar{a}bh\hat{i}$' is perhaps derived from the ecstatic incoherent cries of the prophet.[58] Some have regarded nb' as a weakened form of $\sqrt{nb^c}$ (to bubble forth).[59] It seems more likely, however, that the term is related to the Accadian $Nab\bar{u}$ (to call, name) and the Arabic $naba$'a (to utter a sound, to inform, announce).[60]   H. H. Rowley states that there can be no certainty as to what the primary meaning of the word was,[61] yet the same cautious writer allows that on the philological side the Niph'al and Hithpa'el verbal forms commonly mean 'to behave in an uncontrolled manner'.[62]

Gunkel found echoes of the stammering and stuttering of the canonical prophets in certain mysterious words and combinations of words such as Jezreel, Loammi, Loruhama, Immanuel, Shear-jashub, Maher-shalal-hash-baz, Rahab-hammosh-bath.   These terms are intelligible, however, especially if viewed in the light of prophetic symbolism.[63]   As already indicated, Hölscher discovered evidence of unintelligible utterance in Ezekiel 7 and 21.   But these chapters similarly are more fittingly interpreted as relating symbolic activity.   Ezekiel's howling and crying (21:6, 7) is, in this case, not so much a spontaneous ecstatic outburst, or a release of private feelings of sadness, as a part of his predictive enactment of the grief to occur in Jerusalem.   The utterances that follow, while they may have been released in a state of hyperarousal, are by no means unintelligible as in glossolalic utterance.

Jeremiah 23:30, 31 (R.S.V.) might appear to be a reference to something akin to glossolalic behaviour on the part of the false prophets:

> Therefore, behold, I am against the prophets, says the Lord, who steal my words from one another.   Behold, I am against the prophets, says the Lord, who use their tongues and say, 'Says the Lord' (n^{e}'um-$Yhwh$).

It has been suggested that the passage implies the imitation of prophetic intonation—the characteristic of ecstatic speech.[64]

12

Scott suggests that there was something peculiar and characteristic about n^{e}'um and the manner of uttering it, which the false prophets imitated. He further suggests that for hallōq^{e}him we should read hā'ill^{e}gīm bil^{e}shōnām, 'who speak inarticulately with their tongues', 'stammer' (cf. Isa. 32:4; 33:19).[65] This is a plausible supposition, and one might consider the parallel imitative quality of glossolalia, where members of a group unconsciously mimic the utterance forms of the group leader, and also bear in mind the importance of the intonational pattern for the study of glossolalia. There the parallel ends, since in Jeremiah it is not so much the unintelligibility of the false prophets that is condemned as their lack of originality. Two passages in Isaiah invite attention. The first is Isaiah 28:11 (R.S.V.):

> Nay, but by men of strange lips
> and with an alien tongue
> the Lord will speak to this people.

Since these words are cited in a crucial passage on tongues in the Corinthian epistle (1 Cor. 14:21), it is all the more important to offer a comment upon it. St. Paul's rendering is a loose one and does not follow the LXX closely.[66] The immediate background is that of false prophecy. Both priest and prophet who speak in the stupor of intoxication are condemned (v.7). They in turn mock the prophet, and v.10 (R.S.V.) is possibly in mimicry of his stammering utterance:

> For it is precept upon precept, precept
> upon precept,
> line upon line, line upon line,
> here a little, there a little.

The taunt of Isaiah's opponents is significant if it indicates the form of stuttering utterance associated with the prophet, but it offers no evident ground for assuming the utterance to be glossolalic. On the contrary, it must have been intelligible, for the prophet in retort warns them that soon they will indeed hear the judgement of God from the lips of a strange people in a foreign tongue, a reference to the threat of Assyria. That word will come and will be as unintelligible as Isaiah's had been overtly simple. There is no evidence here of glossolalia, notwithstanding the suggestion of stammering and the repetitiveness[67] of the prophet's utterances, which of course may well have been given in a hyperaroused state.

The other Isaiah passage (R.S.V. 33:19) which refers to obscure speech is a prophecy of weal promising the abatement of foreign oppression:

> You will see no more the insolent people,
>> the people of an obscure speech which
>>> you cannot comprehend,
>> stammering in a tongue which you
>>> cannot understand.

It has no significance for our purpose, except that we may note that speech in an uncomprehended tongue seems like 'stammering' to those who do not understand it.[68]

In the Ezra-Apocalypse there is one passage which might be thought to offer a closer parallel for glossolalia. iv Ezra (2 Esdras) 14: 40-1 describes how Esdras is bidden to drink from a full cup and how, as a result, his heart uttered understanding:

> And I took it and drank; and when I had drunk
>> My heart poured forth understanding,
>>> wisdom grew in my breast,
>> and my spirit retained its memory.[69]

If the cup is to be understood literally, it could be an example of a physically induced hyperaroused state of ecstasy. If, on the other hand, it is interpreted metaphorically as the cup of inspiration, physical inducement need not be assumed. Esdras attains a state in which consciousness is heightened, not subdued, and certain faculties exceed their normal function.[70] Understanding is enhanced and memory strengthened, the latter being a claim made also by some persons in revivalist settings.[71] The passage is also interesting for its account of the role of the five amanuenses who 'wrote what was dictated in order, in characters which they knew not' (v.42). We are informed that 'the Most High gave understanding unto the five men', and their function in transcribing the words of Ezra in a new Hebrew script which they did not know may be intended to suggest a miraculous charismatic quality, resembling in a way the function of the oral interpreter in a Christian community.[72] At least there is a slight possibility that this is the case, and studies in automatic writing[73] do not weaken the feasibility of such an explanation.

We referred earlier to Scott's attractive thesis that 'embryonic oracles' become articulate in the minds of the prophets as a short saying or even a single word. These emotion-charged utterances were the primary form of subsequent literary elaboration, but sometimes they were published in writing (cf. Isa. 8: 1; 30: 8-9; Hab. 2: 2-4) or as names given to children (cf. Isa: 7: 3, 14; 8: 3; Hos. 1: 4, 6, 9). Scott suggests that possibly Isaiah's own name came to him in a moment of 'the higher prophetic ecstasy'.[74] Some of these core utterances are what he calls 'primary oracles of assonance' where, as in Amos 8: 2, the idea of *qēç* is suggested by *qāyiç*, a word similar in sound which enters the mind by chance. Other primary oracles such as Isaiah 5: 7 represent a play on similar words, in this case *ç dhāqāh-çᵉᶜāqāh*. In these and other examples he finds certain common characteristics:

> they are brief, striking, enigmatic and marked by strong rhythm, verbal symmetry, paronomasia, assonance and a preponderance of sibilant and guttural sounds. All contain the quintessence of longer oracles. It seems probable that they preserve the prophet's first articulation of the Word which Yahweh was putting into his mind and on his lips.[75]

If this was, indeed, the way in which primary oracles were formed, then, while there is some resemblance to glossolalic utterance in the occurrence of assonance and strong rhythm, there is also a marked difference. Here the words have an idea association as well as a 'sound' appeal, and it is the idea that is subsequently elaborated. In glossolalia, the utterance which is ejaculated appears to have some numinous association and is often powerful in affecting others, but it has no idea content except when extraneous words interrupt the flow. It is in this sense an undeveloped utterance awaiting interpretation, but the psychological process involved may be akin to that in primary oracles, in that both occur in an ecstatic condition. In prophetic oracles, where there is an idea content, the normal consciousness seems to have been heightened to an intense degree of alertness and sensitivity where associations are more readily perceived than in normal conditions. In glossolalic ecstasy, on the other hand, the normal consciousness is often subdued and the resultant utterance is more mechanical and devoid of intelligible content.

While there is no direct evidence of unintelligible glossolalic utterance in Hebrew prophecy then, the ecstatic susceptibility of the prophets cannot be denied. In this, they are psychologically akin to glossolalists in both the modern and the apostolic setting, and the affinity is even more pronounced if it be conceded that some intelligible utterances may be classified as glossolalia. This is by no

15

means a derogatory appraisal of the prophets. It is now a well-attested fact that glossolalists are no more abnormal in their emotional life than others,[76] nor need they be from an inferior educational background, as some have claimed. When I say that the prophets are susceptible to ecstatic states, I mean that they experience hyper-aroused conditions with varying degrees of dissociation, ranging from trancelike states to those in which the consciousness is heightened to a pitch of unusual sensitivity and perceptivity. In most cases physical concomitants would accompany these states, but in itself somatic kinetic behaviour is no indication of the nature of the experience. This is why it is ultimately impossible for the outside observer to distinguish between true and false prophet. What is facilitated by the psychophysical condition depends upon the conceptual assumptions of the individual and the depth of the relational quality of his personal life—'relational' here meaning his awareness of being in relationship with a personal god or his spirit and the extent to which he shares in the divine pathos. His utterances in the hyperaroused state, however, would have a different emotional effect upon others than words uttered in a calm rational condition. They would be uttered in a rhythmic fashion recognized by the listeners as having prophetic quality. This is not to deny that spurious prophecy would exist, and the problem of distinguishing true and false has a parallel in the discerning of the spirits demanded in the N.T. The physical expression seems to be an energy release for the power generated by the welling up of the unconscious into consciousness. At this meeting point of forces, the prophet is both active and passive, but he himself would be at a loss to say which, ascribing the whole event to the 'hand of Yahweh', the 'Spirit of the Lord' or the 'Word of God', or whichever terminology is most contemporary. Glossolalia in the N.T. is also such a meeting point where even the linguistic utterance is an energy release for the power at work in the unconscious and attributed to the Holy Spirit. By acknowledging the role of the unconscious[77] I do not wish to deny a theological explanation; in fact, I would suggest that it makes a theological explanation more intelligible. Just as dream images may have archetypal significance, I suggest that primal numinous sounds[78] may be released in glossolalia. This, however, is a question demanding separate treatment.

In the next chapter I shall consider the nature of glossolalia in the New Testament.

1. *Die Profeten* (Leipzig: Hinrichs 1914).
2. *Prophecy and the Prophets in Ancient Israel* (London: Duckworth 1923).

16

3. Glossolalia is 'speaking in tongues', by which I mean, ordinarily non-cognitive utterances which are lexically non communicative. There may be exceptional cases, however, where intelligible utterances have all the stress and intonational features associated with glossolalia. See F. Goodman *Speaking in Tongues: A Cross-Cultural Study of Glossolalia* (Chicago: University of Chicago Press, 1972), 110. Nils Bloch-Hoell, *The Pentecostal Movement* (London: Allen and Unwin, 1964), 142f., groups glossolalia into four types or degrees: (1) inarticulate sounds or utterings; (2) articulate sounds or pseudo-language, alliterations and reiterations being very common in this group; (3) articulated and combined language-like sounds, art or fantasy language; (4) automatic speech in a real language (which he calls xenolalia; I use the term xenoglossia for this category). Whether glossolalia can take the form of xenoglossia will not be considered in this chapter. Here I shall continue to understand by glossolalia, in the strict sense, non-cognitive utterance.

4. I should note here the radical differences in the way glossolalia is interpreted in academic studies. W. J. Samarin, for instance, declares that it is not by definition a concomitant of an altered state of consciousness or some kind of automatic behaviour, 'The Linguisticality of Glossolalia' *The Hartford Quarterly* 8:4 (1968), 70n. He regards it as a form of pseudo-language, and, as such, accessible to everyone; see 'Forms and Functions of Nonsense Language' *Linguistics* 50 (1969), 72. Goodman op. cit. 8, on the other hand, regards glossolalic utterance as an artifact of a hyperaroused state—the surface structure of a non-linguistic deep structure, that of the altered state of consciousness. It will be apparent to the reader that I incline to Goodman's view except that I would hold that in some glossolalic events, in the case of those who have long practised 'speaking with tongues,' there need be no outward sign of an abnormal state.

5. C. Westermann, *Basic Forms of Prophetic Speech*, E. Tr. H. C. White (Minneapolis: Augsburg Publishing House 1967). See, now however, A. R. Johnson, *The Cultic Prophet and Israel's Psalmody* (University of Wales, 1979) 151f.n.

6. Westermann, ibid., 103.

7. 'Hauptprobleme alttestamentlicher Prophetie', *Evangelische Theologie* (1955), 446-68.

8. 'Die Begrundung der prophetischen Heils-und Unheils spruche' *Zeitschrift für die alttestamentliche Wissenschaft* 52:1 (1934), 1ff., cited by Westermann.

9. See G. Von Rad, *The Message of the Prophets*, E. Tr. D. M. G. Stalker (London: SCM, 1968), 34.

10. ibid., 39.

11. R. B. Y. Scott, 'The Literary Structure of Isaiah's Oracles' in H. H. Rowley ed., *Studies in Old Testament Prophecy* (Edinburgh: T. and T. Clark, 1950), 34.

12. Clearcut ideas concerning the psychophysical state cannot be given, but there are sufficient indications of abnormal features, from a wide range of experiences, including visionary and auditory features. cf., e.g., Isa. 17:12ff.; 30:27f.; Jer. 4-6; or the description of Eliphaz's experience in Job 4:12-17. The theological assumption is that the *ruach* speaks in the prophets, and the conceptual system in this respect is similar to the views of modern glossolalists concerning the role of the Holy Spirit.

13. For a summary of earlier investigations see H. H. Rowley 'The Nature of Old Testament Prophecy in the Light of Recent Study' in *The Servant of the Lord* (London: Lutterworth, 1952), 91-128.

14. T. H. Robinson in *Expository Times* 48 (1963/7), 182, idem., 'The Ecstatic Element in Old Testament Prophecy' *The Expositor*, 8th series, 21 (1921), 217-38

15. S. Mowinckel, 'The "Spirit" and the "Word" in the Pre-Exilic Reforming Prophets' *Journal of Biblical Literature* 53 (1934), 209. In a postscript in *J.B.L.* 56 (1937), 261-5, Mowinckel feels he ought to have stressed the

ecstatic element even less. cf. *Die Erkenntnis Gottes bei den alttestamentlichen Profeten* (Oslo 1941), 13.

16. N. Micklem, *Prophecy and Eschatology* (London, 1926), 118.
17. R. B. Y. Scott, *The Relevance of the Prophets*, rev. ed. (Toronto: Collier-Macmillan, 1968), 93-4.
18. The references given are Ezek. 6:11; 21:19 EVV 14; Jer. 6:11; 4:19; 20:8,9.
19. Goodman, op. cit., 59ff.
20. Hölscher, 13: 'Ein plötzlichen Reiz, der entweder ausserordentlich stark ist oder Vorstellungen von einer Gefahr unbekannten Art weckt, fuhrt einen Schreck herbei, der auf ganzen Organismus und auf des Bewusstsein.' The following references are given: Gen. 15:9ff.: Dan. 10:7ff; Job 4: 12-16; Dan. 7:28; Ezek. 3:26; 24:27; 33:22; Acts 9:8-17.
21. Goodman, op. cit., 96: '..when a person goes into dissociation he will also utter glossolalia. I want to contend that, conversely, when he utters glossolalia, he is also in hyperarousal.'
22. Goodman, op. cit., 95.
23. cf. the report of a special episcopal commission appointed by the Bishop of Chicago to investigate recent glossolalic events in his diocese: 'There is no sign of disorder or even excitement' (cited by G. F. Atter, *The Third Force* 3rd ed. (Peterborough, Ont. 1970), 234). The mood is often one of quiet expectation; cf. Kevin Ranaghan and Dorothy Ranaghan, *Catholic Pentecostals* (Toronto: Paulist Press, 1969), 68, reporting the experience of Tom Noe: 'There were several others in the room also waiting, and so I prayed silently, moving my lips to the prayers. I was very quiet and meditative throughout, and the only out of the ordinary thing that happened was that after I had finished the last prayer, my lips decided to keep moving, and rearranged themselves into a confusion of p's, k's and l's. I was just about to start speaking out loud in tongues when I remembered that there were ignorant bystanders around who might be quite upset to witness such an outburst.' It is to be noted that the 'speaker' could resist the urge to yield, which illustrates the ability to choose whether to utter in tongues or not, and he also refrained from using tongues in the presence of others. Presumably, he would not therefore regard them as a 'sign for unbelievers'.
24. cf. the statement of Felipe, a minister of the Utzpak, Yucatán, congregation: 'I am now able to speak in tongues; when I want to, I can control it, and if I don't want to, then I can contain myself. I can also control whether I speak loudly or quietly' (Goodman, op. cit., 84).
25. 'Ecstasy' *Expository Times* 49 (1937/8), 295-9. Mauchline defines ecstasy 'as the name applied to those types of experience in which the experient becomes temporarily alienated from the physical and sensible world, and enters into rapport with a whole field of consciousness which is denied him in the normal state.' Such a state would correspond to Goodman's state of hyperarousal, an altered state of consciousness. However, we need to determine, where this is possible, in which way it is altered, since ecstasy can be associated with a state of stupefaction as well as a state of exaltation. cf. N. W. Porteous, 'Prophecy' in *Record and Revelation* ed. H. W. Robinson (Oxford, 1938), 228: 'It is the appropriate term to employ when an overmastering emotion of whatsoever kind produces a state of exaltation or stupefaction in which the mind is obsessed by a single idea or group of ideas to the exclusion of all other ideas, or one or more of the senses are abnormally stimulated, with accompanying suspensions of the other bodily functions. Complete aphasia in certain directions is characteristic of the ecstatic condition.'
26. Johs Pedersen, *Israel: its life and culture* i-ii, E.Tr. Mrs. A. Möller (Oxford, 1926), 159 describes the esctatic state as one in which the soul bursts its frame: 'The consciousness of self disappears altogether and the violent movement in the forces of the soul find expression in strange gestures.'

By way of contrast is the view of I. P. Seierstad, one of the strongest critics of the 'ecstatic' interpretation, that if the consciousness of the ego is lost, the ecstatic state falls outside the usual range of personal mental-life activity. He finds no evidence of such a state in the call experience of Amos, Isaiah, and Jeremiah. See *Die Offenbarungserlebnisse der Propheten Amos, Jesaja und Jeremia* (Oslo: Dybwad 1946). This contrast illustrates the tendency to think in terms of either/or, whereas in my view the prophets were subject to a variety of states ranging from 'lower' kinds of ecstatic behaviour where self-consciousness might appear to be subdued or lost to 'higher' ecstatic states where the 'relational' nature of the experience was in the forefront of the prophet's mind. W. Gruehn, *Religionspsychologie* (1926), cited by Seierstad 71, n.2, offers a threefold division of the main states of consciousness:

    A   die unterwachen Zustände;
    B   das Normalwachsein;
    C   die Uberwachen Zustände.

This broad division is acceptable, but not Gruehn's specific examples within these classes. For instance, under C he includes Entzuckung (Excitation), Entruckung (Exaltation), and Aussersichsein (Ekstase, Nirvana). Some forms of ecstasy could be thus placed, but not all, and Nirvana transcends all states of consciousness.

27.   J. Lindblom, 'Einigen Grundfragen der alttestamentlichen Wissenschaft' in *Festschrift für Alfred Bertholet* (Tubingen 1950), 325 ff. See also 'Die Religion der Propheten and die Mystik' in *Z.A.W.* NF 42 (1939) 54-74. Lindblom distinguishes 'absorption ecstasy', in which the personality is lost in the Godhead, and 'concentration ecstasy', wherein there is a deep concentration of the soul on a single notion or feeling.

28.   A. Guillaume, *Prophecy and Divination* (London: Hodder and Stoughton, 1938), 294.

29.   When I speak of the consciousness as recording, I do not suggest that it is completely passive; indeed in the prophets its activity may involve evaluation (cf. Jer. 15:19).

30.   There is some amount of recall in some cases. See Ranaghan and Ranaghan, op. cit., 68.

31.   Goodman, op. cit., 93.

32.   Goodman, op cit., 70.

33.   A. W. Knobel, *Der Prophetismus der Herbäer I* (Breslau, 1837).

34.   ibid, 155.

35.   Pedersen, op. cit., 158ff.

36.   H Gunkel, 'The Secret Experiences of the Prophets' *Expositor*, 9th series, 1 (1924), 356-66.

37.   H. W. Wolfson, *Philo* 2 (1962), 50.

38.   Among the various somatic effects accompanying dissociation noted by Goodman are: falling down (6), trembling and shaking (5, 127), rocking back and forth (63), stuttering (81, 94), flushing of the face (64), profuse perspiration (64, 82, 127), jumping (217), yelling (65), tightly closed eyes (96), rhythmical movement (126). Of ways to facilitate dissociation the following are mentioned: fasting (77), repetition of words (80), rapid deep breathing (83), rhythmic clapping of hands and singing (78), arhythmical walking, clapping and manipulations of the body (79). Perusing such a list, and similar ones from other observers, or accounts of revivalist meetings, one might be tempted to think that glossolalists are mentally unbalanced subjects and that glossolalia could be dismissed as pathological (cf. W. Sargant, *The Battle for the mind* (Harmondsworth: Penguin 1957), 105; D. W. Burdick, *Tongues : to speak or not to speak* (Chicago; Moody Press 1968), 75. Before arriving at such a conclusion, however, one should also consider the beneficial results claimed by glossolalists who frequently mention joy, the dissolution of anxiety, changes in interpersonal relationships, increased capacity for love towards others, and

concern for others. The evidence does not support an explanation of glossolalia as pathological; see Virginia H. Hine, 'Pentecostal Glossolalia: Toward a Functional Interpretation' *Journal for the Scientific Study of Religion* 8 (1969), 217; cf; E. B. Fiske, New York Times, 2 May 1971, reporting on the findings of the Lutheran Medical Centre of Brooklyn that persons who engage in glossolalia are no more or less emotionally healthy than other persons.

39. F. D. Goodman, 'Phonetic Analysis of Glossolalia in Four Cultural Settings' *J.S.S.R.* 8(1969),138.

40. *Speaking in Tongues* 110. W. J. Samarin, on the basis of careful linguistic analysis, find significant patterns recurring. ('Variation and Variables in Religious Glossolalia,' paper given at the 69th annual meeting of the American Anthropological Association, San Diego, 22 November 1970. I appreciate receiving this paper and others from this author). Samarin also refers to the development of skill in the production of glossolalia and in a more refined control of its use. He rejects Goodman's position that glossolalia is an artifact of trance and claims external evidence that an altered state of consciousness is rare in the experience of Christian glossolalists. The views of such a competent authority in sociolinguistics must be heeded, but while I feel that Goodman has gone too far in practically making hyperaroused dissociation and glossolalia synonymous, and while I have observed that dissociation is not at all discerned in some cases, yet I cannot agree that an altered state of consciousness is as rare as Samarin asserts. In my view there is a strong parallel between the variety of conditions in the experience here and in prophecy which subsumes the wild behaviour of the early pre-canonical prophets, visited by the divine *ruach*, as well as the condition which produced the insights of the major prophets.

41. I am aware that on occasion highly charged utterances in glossolalic settings may be intelligible and yet have a stress and intonation pattern similar to unintelligible glossolalia (Goodman, *Speaking in Tongues*, 110 provides such an example). The distinction between this and ecstatic praise in an exalted state must be a very fine one, but, where there is sustained intelligibility, I would hesitate to employ the term glossolalia for that utterance. Glossolalia is always predominantly unintelligible and the intelligible words which occasionally intrude are minimal. See, however, G. B. Cutten, *Speaking with Tongues* (New Haven: Yale University Press, 1927), 169ff. Cutten finds a progression in the outward expression of speaking with tongues: namely (1) inarticulate preglossolalic sounds (2) pseudo language or articulate sounds which simulate words and (3) fabricated or coined words. He adds a fourth form: speaking of some words in a foreign tongue, perhaps not consciously known by the speaker, but always one with which he has come in contact and reproduced through exalted memory due to his abnormal condition.

42. Goodman, *Speaking in Tongues*, 159. G. C. Joyce, *The Inspiration of Prophecy* (Oxford, 1910), 159 writes: 'the interpreter was not so much a translator of words. . as a revealer to the assembled company of the mental processes which lay behind the utterance of the speaker'.

43. Goodman, ibid., 4n.

44. Harold Horton quoted in C. Brumback, *What Meaneth This?* (Springfield, Mo. 1947), 129; cf J. T. Nichol, *The Pentecostals* (Plainfield, NJ: Logos International, 1966), 11f.

45. It is beyond the scope of this chapter to trace the development in the application of the term *ruach*, but the importance of such a study needs to be recognized in dealing with the thought background of prophecy and glossolalia. While in the O.T. it came to be applied to normal activities, it was so used mainly when the ordinary possessed a degree of unusualness. The main association of the *ruach* is with the extraordinary, particularly the impulse which led the prophet to a special kind of utterance re-

garded as the manifestation of a non-human power. The way in which the conception of the spirit developed in moral depth is traced in E. Bevan, *Symbolism and Belief* (London: Collins, Fontana Library 1962), 150ff. Bevan maintains that the ideas attached to the term 'Holy Spirit' in the first days of Christianity 'have been shaped not only by the traditional Old Testament associations of the term 'Holy Spirit' but by new actual experiences within the primitive community-that apparent control by a Power not themselves, sometimes coming upon believers abruptly at particular moments and impelling them to abnormal utterance, sometimes simply quickening their thoughts and supplying words in controversy or exhortation or prayer.' To accept the idea of newness of experience in the early Christian community is not to my mind to deny the continuity of charismatic activity, or the similarity of the basic non-linguistic substructure of the experiences.

46. H. H. Rowley, *Harvard Theological Review* 38 (1945), 20; idem., *The Servant of the Lord*, 111.
47. A. R. Johnson, *The Vitality of the Individual in the Thought of Ancient Israel* 2nd ed. (Cardiff: University of Wales Press, 1964), 34.
48. M. Eliade, *Shamanism: Archaic Techniques of Ecstasy*, E. Tr.   W. R. Trask (New York: Random House, 1964), xviii.
49. cf. Von Rad, *The Message of the Prophets*, 41. Contrast H. W. Wolff in *Ev. Theol.* (1955), 455f.
50. ibid., 39f.
51. It is salutary, however, to bear in mind that our penchant for the orderly and rational should not determine our interpretation. In the ancient world, the uncontrollable did not offend, and in ancient Israel, the abnormal was understood in terms of possession by the *ruach* of Yahweh.
52. Hölscher, op. cit., 303.
53. For a study of this term see A. R. Johnson, in *Wisdom in Israel and in the Ancient Near East*, ed. M. Noth and D. W. Thomas, Supplements to *Vetus Testamentum III* (Leiden: Brill 1955), 162-9.
54. 'Glossolalia and Ecstaticism: Parallel Phenomena?', a paper read at a meeting of the American Academy of Religion at Atlanta, Georgia, October 1971. I am grateful to Dr. Mills for providing a copy of his paper.
55. Goodman, *Speaking in Tongues, passim* thinks in terms of glossolalic utterance being superimposed upon the altered state of consciousess. I find the word 'superimposed' too strong, suggesting deliberation, and would prefer simply to say that the utterance derives from, or, indeed, accompanies the state.
56. cf. W. Jacobi, *Die Ekstase der alttestamentlichen Propheten* (München, 1920), 7 who finds parallels in the behaviour of dervishes, N.T. 'speaking in tongues', and the more fervent evangelical sects where music is employed to heighten feeling and to induce 'ecstasy'.
57. Too often, glossolalia is indiscriminately claimed without proper examination of the texts; e.g. L. M. Vivier, 'The Glossolalic and His Personality' in *Beitrage zur Ekstase*, ed. Th. Spoerri, *Bibl. psychiat. neurol.* 134 (1968), 153-75 who cites among non-Christian examples Moses (Num. 11:7); Miriam (Num. 12:1-2); Isaiah (Isa. 28:10-13); and the sons of the prophets (1 Sam. 10:1-13, 19:18-24). cf. the confident assumption in E. M. Pattison and R. L. Casey, 'Glossolalia: A Contemporary Mystical Experience' in *International Psychiatry Clinics* 5 (1969), 134. They refer loosely to glossolalia practised by 'the prophets of the ancient religions of the Near East' and to reports of xenoglossia among 'prophets and mystics of Assyria, Egypt and Greece'. Then they add 'The Hebrew prophets appear to have similarly engaged in ecstatic states and practised glossolalia'.
58. J. Pedersen, *Israel: Its Life and Culture, III-IV* (Oxford 1940), 111. T. H. Robinson, similarly, understood the word to bear an ecstatic significance: *Expositor*, 8th series 21 (1921), 224.

59. A. Kuenen, *The Prophets and Prophecy in Israel*, E. Tr. A. Milroy, (London 1877), 42: B. Stade, *Biblische Theologie des Alten Testaments* (Tübingen, 1905) I, 132; S. Mowinckel, *Psalmenstudien I* (Kristiana: Dybwad, 1921), 16; H Hackmann 'Die geistigen Abnormitaten der alttestamentlichen Propheten' *Nieuw Theologisch Tijdschrift* 23 (1934), 42.
60. A. R. Johnson, *The Cultic Prophet in Ancient Israel*, 2nd ed. (Cardiff: University of Wales Press 1962), 24.
61. Rowley, *The Servant of the Lord*, 97.
62. The use of the Hithpāʿel is not in fact common in the canonical prophets. In Jer. 26:20 it is used for the activity of the unfortunate Uriah, extradited from Egypt, and put to death by Jehoiakim. He is undoubtedly regarded as a true prophet, but there is nothing to indicate the nature of his prophetic experience and behaviour. In Shemaiah's letter of protest from exile, the Hithpāʿel form, occurs for both the raving prophets and for Jeremiah (Jer. 29:26, 27), but the source of the letter is not irrelevant in considering the choice of verbal form, coming as it did from those opposed to the prophet. The other instances in Jeremiah (14:14; 23:13) are in reference to false prophets. Another occurrence is in the account of Ezekiel's vision of the valley of dry bones (Ezek. 37:10). Niphʿal forms occur more frequently and are used for the activity of both false prophets and canonical prophets. They offer no illumination as to the psychology of prophecy. I must then agree with those who find etymological arguments unconvincing.
63. cf. Pedersen, Israel I-II, 112.
64. J. Skinner, *Prophecy and Religion* (Cambridge, 1922), 193.
65. Scott, 'The Literary Structure of Isaiah's Oracles', 178.
66. C. K. Barrett, *The First Epistle to the Corinthians* (London: Black, 1968), 322f. says there is some evidence (Origen, *Philocalia* ix. 2) that Paul may have used here a version known also to the later O.T. translator Aquila. I find no reason to demur at his finding that 'it was probably the word "men of other tongues" that caught his eye and suggested the application of the passage to his discussion of "tongues." It is this, rather than the historical setting of the prophecy, in which Isaiah threatens his people, who have failed to listen to his words, with the foreign speech of Assyrian invaders, that is in Paul's mind.'
67. Glossolalia is repetitious in the sense that the same basic sounds recur in a particular 'glossa'. See W. J Samarin, 'The Linguisticality of Glossolalia' *The Hartford Quarterly* 8:4 (1968), 61 who adds that 'a preference for certain sounds gives to glossa its exotic flavour'.
68. J. G. Davies, 'Pentecost and Glossolalia' *The Journal of Theological Studies* n.s. 3 (1952), 228-31 points out that this passage is not an isolated instance of a foreign tongue understood as a sign of retribution. (cf. Deut. 28:49 and Jer. 5:15). This is a valid statement, but then he goes on to compare this theme with St. Paul's argument in 1 Cor. 14 that glossolalia is a sign of judgement upon unbelievers, and that, against such a background, it is reasonable to assume that St. Paul understood glossolalia to be talking in foreign languages. This is not, in my opinion, a reasonable assumption. The obvious point of comparison is the unintelligibility which the foreign tongue shares with glossic utterance.
69. As in R. H. Charles, *The Apocrypha and Pseudepigrapha* (Oxford, 1913) q.v.
70. Charles, ii, 623: 'The effect of ecstasy was often such that the subject of it lost consciousness and memory. In Ezra's case, however, the natural faculties are immensley strengthened and intensified. This is inspiration, so our passage seems to imply, in its highest form.'
71. David Morgan, the major figure in the Welsh revival of 1895 (and incidentally the one who baptized Dr. Timothy Richard of China in 1860), describes the visitation of the Holy Spirit as effecting a strange and mysterious change in him in which he was aware with awe of a marvellous illumination of his faculties, especially of his memory: 'I awoke about

four in the morning remembering everything of a religious nature that I had ever learnt or heard.' See E. Evans, *The Welsh Revival of* 1904 (London: Evangelical Press, 1969), 66ff.

72.   cf. Samarin op. cit., 58, who says there is no *a priori* reason why a glossolalic utterance may not be written, and I would add that there is no forbidding reason why the work of the amanuenses here is not meant to be understood as a miraculous achievement.

73.   See F. D. Goodman, 'Glossolalia and single-limb trance: some parallels' *Psychotherapy and Psychosomatics* 19(1971), 92-103.

74.   Scott, op cit., 86.

75.   cf. Philip Orth's account of his spiritual experience in Ranaghan and Ranaghan, 102f: 'God was working within me. I could feel a distinct tingling in my hands, and immediately I became bathed in a hard sweat that seemed to pop out of every pore. Also, at that moment, a word came into my mind that I cannot ever recall hearing before-*Rasheim*.'

76.   Goodman, *Speaking in Tongues* xvii, in criticism of those who describe glossolalists as schizophrenics, epileptics, or hysterics.

77.   cf. C. G. Jung, *Collected Works* (London: Routledge and Kegan Paul, 1953) IX: 1, 55:XI, 162f, 184 Jung regards speaking in tongues as one evidence of a breakthrough of the objective psyche, or deep collective level of the unconscious.

78.   In the nature of the case this is a speculative statement, but it is not unreasonable to suppose that, before articulate language, phonetic inventiveness brought into being 'a whole imaginary universe by its sonorous explosion'. (M Eliade, *A History of Religious Ideas* i (London: Collins, 1979), 27).

At a later stage, when utterance has been assigned meaning, particularly as among the Semites, where the elemental cry itself is preserved as a name, the exclamation will be an outlet of the feeling of the numinosum. (See J. Lindblom, *Prophecy in Ancient Israel* (Oxford, 1962), 9 and R. Otto, *Aufsätze das Numinose betreffend* (Gotha: L. Klotz, 1929),11f.).

Thus Buber, speculating concerning the prehistoric use of the name YHVH, follows Duhm's suggestion that 'the name is in some degree only an extension of the word *hu*, meaning he.'. (M. Buber, *Biblical Humanism* edit. N. H. Glatzer (London: Macdonald, 1968), 56). The original form of the dervish cry *Ya-hu* (O He) may have been Ya-huva, a form which may also have produced *Yahvah* and *Yahveh*. Elsewhere, Buber suggests that the name *Yah* or *Yahu*, if reflected in it was the primitive Semitic pronoun '*Ya*', was an exclamation, a 'numinous primal sound'. (M. Buber, *The Prophetic Faith*. E. Tr. C. Witton-Davies (New York: Harper and Row 1960), 28.

The origin of the divine name will probably remain elusive, but what is beyond doubt is that rhythmic exclamation of this kind can exercise a powerful effect, which could be described in terms of a strong numinous discharge, particularly when the oral character of the primitive exclamation is itself identified as the divine name. This numinous association could well carry over into later more sophisticated circles, when ethical and rational features come more forcibly and clearly into play in employing the divine name.

It is interesting in this connection to call attention to the frequency of the emphatic use of the pronoun 'He' (*Hū*) for Yahweh in the worship of ancient Israel, the significance of which is brought out by A. R. Johnsou in his recent *tour de force*, *The Cultic Prophet and Israel's Psalmody* (Cardiff: University of Wales, 1979), 19f. In Psalm 95 for instance, there are two examples, and it is Johnson's view that in both cases 'the associations of this personal pronoun as used by the God of Israel would be such that it could be expected to carry certain overtones for His worshippers, reminding them of the full significance of the name "Yahweh" or "Yahu" (originally the cultic cry "O He!") as denoting the divine Being who is over and above all others and, as such, is the "Holy One" *par excellence*.' See also by the same author, *The Vitality of the Individual in the Thought of Ancient Israel* 2nd edit. (Cardiff: University of Wales, 1964),108n.4.

In Sufi circles the effect of chanting a form of the divine name is well known (see below pp. 195f.). In their case, a sense of the beyond which is within is attained. In ancient Israel, however, while it is not inconceivable that such chanting could occur in cultic circles, and the frequent references to music and musical instruments would seem to indicate various forms of rhythmic expression, the goal would not be mystical unity. While it may be possible to find indicators of a whole range of experiences in the Hebrew Scriptures, the main current of thought in cultic worship, particularly as reflected in the Psalms, is, in my terminology, relational, that is, the sub-ject-object relationship in the divine encounter is not transcended. It encourages a vital concern for social responsibility on the basis of a true relationship with the Holy One.

CHAPTER II

GLOSSOLALIA IN THE NEW TESTAMENT

The main question posed here is whether the Lukan account of tongues at Pentecost (*lalein heterais glōssais*—'to speak in other[1] tongues', Acts 2: 4) refers to a phenomenon identical with the Corinthian experience described by Paul (*lalein glōssais* 'to speak in tongues', 1 Cor. 14: 5, cf. 1 Cor. 12: 30; 1 Cor. 14: 6, 18, 23, 27, 39). The Corinthian phenomenon has been most frequently interpreted as ecstatic utterance[2], while the account of Pentecost in Acts 2 is thought to describe the miraculous ability of the Apostles on that occasion to speak in real languages proper to the country in which their listeners were born. The most widely accepted view finds expression in this confident statement written very early in this century:

> It is admitted on all hands that what St. Luke describes in Acts 2 is a divinely bestowed power of speaking in foreign languages; whereas the glossolalia of 1 Corinthians 12-14 seems to have been rapt ecstatic utterance, unintelligible and needing interpretation—but not necessarily involving the use of foreign languages.[3]

In short, the Corinthian phenomenon is designated glossolalia and the Pentecost phenomenon is what is referred to in curent terminology as xenoglossia. These have become key terms in any discussion of this subject and it is proper to define their usage. By glossolalia, I mean unintelligible, non-cognitive utterance which may vary in sound from inarticulate to articulate. Occasionally some words which are recognizable, or simulated words, unconsciously introduced, may interrupt the flow of incoherence.[4] To the speakers it is a real language which has religious significance but since it is lexically non-communicative, even though it may have language features such as word-like or even sentence-like structures, it bears no resemblance to any known human language and is not a language in the accepted sense.[5] Xenoglossia, on the other hand, is utterance in a foreign tongue, not known by the speaker and unlearned by him, but intelligible to those with knowledge of the language.[6] The rejection of traditional interpretations by two modern exegetes highlights the complexity of the problem of understanding the New Testament phenomenon. J. G. Davies[7] and R. H. Gundry [8] maintain that references to speaking in tongues at Pentecost and Corinth do not signify glossolalia. They insist that neither Paul nor Luke meant 'ecstatic utterance' when referring to normative Christian speaking in tongues, but that, on the contrary, what is described as occurring at both Corinth and Jerusalem is speaking in used foreign languages.

Gundry observers that the use of the term *glōssa* for intelligible language far exceeds its use for obscure speech in Biblical Greek and contends that only very strong evidence can overthrow the natural understanding of speaking in tongues as speaking in used human languages. Taken in isolation this etymological argument is not convincing. Paul employed *glōssais* for the tongues of angels (1 Cor. 13: 1) while 'he who speaks in a tongue' (*glōssē*) is said to address God, not men, and furthermore no one understands him (1 Cor. 14: 2). It is highly unlikely that tongues signify known languages in these contexts. The term *glōssa* may indicate the physical organ, known languages, dialects or sub-dialects, but also the incoherent utterance of certain forms of spiritual fervency.[9] The meaning therefore needs to be localised in each instance. Normal usage is not the only criterion when the subject of investigation is what appears to be a new phenomenon or at least one that is unfamiliar in a particular context. In such cases a term in common currency may be given an extension of connotation and sometimes the new meaning establishes a technical application. This seems to have happened in the Corinthian context where 'speaking with', or 'in tongues'—tongue talk—clearly refers to what Samarin calls 'anomalous verbal behaviour'.[10]

One meets a similar unwillingness to deviate from normal usage in Davies's examination of *hermēneuein* and its cognates. He finds that, apart from seven occurrences in 1 Cor. 12 and 14, of the twenty-one other instances in the LXX and the New Testament, eighteen have the primary meaning of translation, and on the basis of this evidence claims that the word used by St. Paul of interpreting glossolalia carries with it the strong suggestion of translating a foreign language. Gundry found this line of reasoning convincing and he adds that '. . . the term interpret(ation) (διερμηνεύω), used frequently in connexion with glossolalia in 1 Corinthians, normally refers to translating a language when used in such a context'.[11] This seems to me a circular argument since appeal is made to normal

26

usage 'in such a context' when this is precisely the object of inquiry. Philological evidence of the use of terms in their primary connotation elsewhere does not necessarily rule out a more technical usage in this context. St. Paul could employ the terms *glōssa* and *hermēneuō* to indicate a new kind of 'tongue' and a new kind of 'translating'. Both tongues and their interpretation were regarded as manifestations of the powers of the Spirit in the New Age and as God's charismatic gifts to the church (1 Cor. 12: 28-30). To pray with a 'tongue' is to pray in the Spirit (1 Cor. 14: 14, 15) and the utterance is unintelligible to the listener (1 Cor. 14: 16) It is for this reason that Paul stresses the communicative function of intelligible interpretation but this does not mean that we are to understand by *hermēneuein* or its cognates a formal translation of the actual utterrance, or by *glōssa* a real language. It is the whole event that is being interpreted, namely, the utterance and the experiential context in which it is produced. I believe that what is involved was explained with insight and sensitivity in a book which still merits attention, although published seventy years ago. I refer to G. C. Joyce, *The Inspiration of Prophecy* (Oxford, 1910). Joyce writes:

'Incoherent, or more properly speaking, inarticulate the sounds of tongues may have been; but such incoherence or inarticulateness is not to be confused with absence of meaning. Behind the mere sounds were, we believe, definite thoughts and feelings in the mind of the speaker, which the interpreter was capable of making known to the rest of the congregation, thus giving them the opportunity of sharing in the exaltation of spirit of which the tongue was the outcome. The ability to do so was a special power distinct from the gift of tongues in itself, though the two gifts might co-exist in the same person. When speaker and interpreter were two different persons, then psychologically the power of interpretation was akin to that of thought reading. To the thoughts and feelings in the mind of the speaker the mind of the interpreter responded so vividly and so accurately that he was able to put them into language. What part the actual sounds played in the process it is not possible to determine. Nor is it necessary. We have already seen that the sounds in themselves were probably meaningless, except so far as they may have conveyed rough indications of the state of mind of the speaker. And, if so, the interpreter was not so much a translator of words—words probably there were none to translate—as a revealer to the assembled company of the mental processes which lay behind the utterance of the speaker.'[12]

One might add that while the psychological explanation need not be accepted as the total explanation—which would be sheer reductionism—it may commend itself as indicating the charismatic channels whose source eludes investigation.

In discussions of 'tongues' at Corinth the paraphrase of Isa. 28: 11, 12 (LXX) in 1 Cor. 14: 21 has received much attention.[13] C. K. Barrett suggests that what attracted Paul to this passage was the expression 'men of other tongues'[14] and Gundry maintains that it is not ecstasy but probably the use of *laleō* in the Isaiah prophecy which caused the predominance of *lal-* in 1 Cor. 14. These views are acceptable enough; on the other hand, expositors are often tempted to read too much into the citation of this Old Testament passage in relation to tongues. Davies, for instance, argues that in the original context the 'unintelligible' foreign language of the Assyrian conquerors is associated with divine judgement and retribution, and since the same kind of association is made in Isa. 33: 19, Deut. 28: 49 and Jer. 5: 15 while, furthermore, St. Paul describes glossolalia as a sign of judgement upon unbelievers, it is reasonable to assume that St. Paul understood glossolalia to be talking in foreign languages. In which case, of course, the phenomenon at Corinth would be basically similar to that of Pentecost.

As G. G. Findlay observed long ago,[15] the analogy of the Assyrian tongue lends no support to the notion that the tongues of Corinth were foreign languages. If St. Paul introduced this passage *ad hoc* (but this is by no means certain,[16]) he might have simply appropriated the text by virtue of the association mentioned by Barrett above. The real point of the citation according to Findlay, comes out in *hōste hai glōssai eis sēmeion* . . . There appears to be a perplexing ambiguity, however, in understanding the sign value of 'tongues' and an apparent inconsistency between the words of vs. 22 and the possible impact on unbelievers described in vs. 23. The former reads 'Clearly then these "strange tongues" are not intended as a sign for believers but for unbelievers' (NEB). Yet according to vs. 23 the effect of strange tongues on unbelievers is to make them regard the speakers as mad, which hardly constitutes 'tongues' as a sign,[17] while vs. 24 affirms the efficacy of prophecy as a means of conviction of unbelievers. Grundy's view is that the undesired impact of speaking in tongues on unbelievers foreseen by Paul,

'. . . stems solely from the Corinthian failure to require accompanying translation at all times, with the result that what Paul regarded as genuine human languages sounded to unbelievers like meaningless successions of syllables similar to the ecstatic speech in Hellenistic religions familiar to the hearers . . .'[18]

In other words, where there is translation there is no fear of causing an impression of madness. (Gundry's explanation of Acts

28

2 is consistent with this, for, with respect to that account, he argues that the charge that the Apostles were drunk came from Palestinian Jews who did not understand the languages spoken, while the non-Palestinian Jews understood them and were amazed.)[19] This thesis is attractive for its clarity, and, if accepted, the question of reconciling the function of glossolalia as a sign for unbelievers with the charge of madness by the uninstructed and unbelievers (vs. 23)[20] poses no problem. But others have sought this reconciliation without insisting that the Corinthian phenomenon was xenoglossia. In fact, it is a widely held view that Paul demonstrates that while speaking in tongues performed in orderly fashion and with accompanying interpretation is a sign for unbelievers, exercised in a disorderly manner and with extravagance it can give the impression of madness. Whatever solution is advanced, it must sufficiently acknowledge a basic contrast in Paul's thought. As C. K. Barrett rightly observes, throughout the chapter (1 Cor. 14) up to the quotation from Isaiah, Paul has been concerned to contrast speaking with tongues with prophecy.[21] This contrast involves the test of intelligibility. Tongues are unintelligible, prophecy is intelligible, but tongues when interpreted could, in fact, perform the function of prophecy. There is no need to underplay the force of *mainesthe* 'you are mad' in vs. 23 or to accept Barrett's view that here it indicates a state of possession by a supernatural force, though madness was often thought to be symptomatic of possession. In the O.T. for instance, the term *mᵉshuggāᶜ* (madman) occurs in reference to prophets.[22] In 1 Cor. 14: 23, however, *mainesthe* could simply mean something like 'You are crazy' as in the charge laid against Paul himself by Festus: '*Mainē, Paule* . . .' (Acts 26: 24).

The view advanced here is that the original *Sitz im Leben* of Isa. 28: 11, 12 has little if any import in this context, in other words that Paul in employing this passage is not thinking particularly of tongues as a sign of judgement upon unbelievers, but has simply brought in, by virtue of the reference in it to 'strange tongues' and 'the lips of foreigners', what may have been a proof text for tongues speaking, but more probably, in my view, a Pauline *ad hoc* quotation. To extract significance from every detail of this loose quotation would be misleading. More significant is the new context of its application by Paul. Hitherto he has been speaking in terms of the unintelligiblity of tongues and his aim in view of Corinthian excesses is to play down their role in comparison with intelligible prophecy. Nevertheless he does not wish to deny the divine source of tongues as manifestations of the Holy Spirit. The thought of judgement does not seem to be in his mind, but more likely the fact that the

Corinthians had regarded tongues as a sign for believers, a view he wants to correct.[23]   The Isaiah passage ostensibly provides him with support for the counter-view that, if anything, they are a sign for unbelievers, but, even as such, they are not effective, and he reinforces this estimate with his future construction 'and even then they will not listen to him'.[24]   For the Corinthians, on the contrary, 'tongues' were *the* sign to believers of the manifestation of the Spirit.[25]

The problem of the obscurity of vs. 22, it must be confessed, remains perplexing, but what is clear is that in the Corinthian context Paul goes to great lengths to extol prophecy.   He has shown that within the worshipping community tongues without interpretation, while they can express a person's thanskgiving, are of no help to convict the plain man and do not build up the church, because of their unintelligibility.   Having said this of their function within the community, then he considers their merit in relation to the mission of the church to the outsider.   Here if they are thought of as a sign, without interpretation they are not only ineffectual but may confound unbelievers.   Prophecy, on the other hand, is efficacious as a sign to convert unbelievers.   On both counts in fact, the inner building-up of the community and the witness to outsiders, intelligible prophecy is more effective.   Yet Paul certainly does not deny a place to unintelligible glossolalia for the individual who communicates with God (vs. 28), or who has his utterances interpreted whether by himself or by another.   Without building too much on it we may note, that, while the term *sēmeion* 'sign' does not occur frequently in the Pauline epistles, where it is found, it is not necessarily negative or coupled with the idea of retributive judgement,[26] a connexion required in the context of 1 Cor. 14 by those who maintain that Paul cited the Isaiah passage for its historical significance, the import of which is that the threat of foreign tongues is a threat of divine judgement upon the unbelieving.[27]

I discover no compelling reasons to abandon the widely held view that the Corinthian phenomenon is unintelligible glossolalia, which in this case was attended by excessive and uncontrolled behaviour. Paul's call for orderliness in public worship clearly shows that the excesses of the Corinthians were not necessary features of the glossolalic event, and, indeed, he is quite specific in his instructions how glossolalia must be made subject to control.[28]   The interpretation of 1 Cor. 14 is not a simple choice of regarding tongues as either ecstatic incoherent utterances or speaking in real languages.   Ecstasy is is much too vague a term to employ unless it be abundantly qualified to make clear that there are many degrees of it, ranging from mild dissociation to extreme uncontrollable rapture.[29]   Here, empirical data from contemporary observations are not without relevance. In modern glossolalia the degree of dissociation will vary enormously, say from the incipient stage of glossolalia, often attended by physical symptoms, to that in which the speaker through long experience has acquired fluency in one or more 'glossa' and can in many instances produce his glossolalia at will. It is, however, fair to recall once more that W. J. Samarin, a redoubtable authority in this field, will not allow that glossolalia is the product of an altered state of consciousness at all and, therefore, will not agree to the use of the term ecstatic, if it includes dissociation as one of its features.[30] While I cannot share Samarin's view, he does highlight the problem with a term like 'ecstasy'.

That the Corinthian phenomenon is not xenoglossia seems clear from 1 Cor. 14, 10-11, yet Gundry comes to a conclusion which is directly opposite. He writes: 'Finally, Paul's writing in the middle of his discussion about tongues, "There are doubtless many different languages in the world, and none is without meaning; but if I do not know the meaning of the language, I shall be a foreigner (βάρβαρος, speaking a foreign language) to the speaker and the speaker a foreigner to me" (xiv. 10f.), should clear away any vestige of doubt that he thinks of the gift of tongues as miraculous speaking in unlearned human languages.'[31] This conclusion is unwarranted, for here Paul obviously is engaged in making an analogy between speaking in tongues and speaking in foreign languages—a redundant exercise if, in fact, the Corinthians were indeed speaking foreign languages.[32]

What then of Luke's account of Pentecost in Acts 2? There can be no question of Luke's intention. He relates how the Apostles[33] had spoken real languages identified by (some of the?) Jews present as the language of their native lands. Is it then clearly established that the phenomenon at Pentecost is xenoglossia—a view so widely accepted?[34] By no means: at the risk of presumption, my contention is that at Jerusalem as at Corinth, the phenomenon with which we are concerned is glossolalia, a phenomenon which, in spite of the vast cultural separation in time, is in fact basically similar to modern manifestations in Pentecostal and more recently neo-Pentecostal circles, which share Luke's emphasis on the Spirit of God as power.[35] Luke's purpose is best served by emphasizing the miraculous effect of the Holy Spirit and in this respect xenoglossia would have a higher rating than glossolalia. Or it may be simply a case of his characteristic concreteness of thought which enables him readily to accept claims that the inspired languages heard were in fact real foreign languages. It is virtually impossible to get behind Luke's typological ingenuity[36] and theological purposiveness to determine the facts, yet there may be pointers in the account to sustain the view that the Pentecost phenomenon in reality was identical with that at Corinth, or for that matter at Ephesus (Acts 19: 6), Caesarea (Acts 10: 46) or presumably Samaria (Acts 8:17). At Caesarea (Acts 10: 46) there is no hint of 'foreign languages', yet when Peter reports the events at Caesarea to the Jerusalem brethren he claims that the Holy Spirit fell upon the Gentiles 'just as upon us at the beginning' (Act 11: 15) and further declared that 'God gave them no less a gift than he gave us' (Acts 11: 17). These passages may represent a pre-Lucan tradition but it is abundantly clear that the writer wants to identify the manifestation among the Gentiles with the Pentecost phenomenon, whose most striking feature was speaking in other tongues (Acts 2: 3f.).

The familiar account of Acts 2 reports how in Jerusalem 'devout Jews drawn from every nation under heaven' (vs. 5) were bewildered when 'each one heard his own language spoken' by Galileans (vss. 6, 7.). There follows the impressive list of peoples and places to indicate their purported countries of origin and mother tongue. Most likely, adjustments have been made to an original list, but this does not affect the salient problem.[37] What is pertinent is whether these Jews were temporary visitors from other areas of the Middle East who had come to Jerusalem for Pentecost, or were in fact domiciled in Jerusalem. Haenchen is most emphatic that the Jews in question had become residents of Jerusalem and that Luke is *not* thinking of pilgrims at the feast.[38] It is, however, reasonable to assume that three types of Jews would be found at Jerusalem at Pentecost, namely habitual dwellers in Jerusalem, Jews of the Diaspora who had come originally from other countries but were now dwelling in Palestine, and non-residents who were merely temporary visitors. The distinction between *kat-oikountes* 'permanent residents' and *epidēmountes* 'temporary dwellers' was not always made.[39] Peter, in his address (vs. 14), seems to imply such a distinction, since presumably 'Fellow Jews' refers to all Jews present and 'You who live in Jerusalem' to established residents.[40]

J. G. Davies regards the account of Pentecost in Acts 2 as dependent upon the LXX account of the Babel (Gen. 11: 1-9), Pentecost being the reversal of Babel.[41] God's action is emphasized in each case, but whereas in the Babel narrative the result is that men cannot understand each other's speech, at Pentecost inspired utterance is intelligible. It is quite possible that the author intended it to have the symbolic meaning of the 'unbabbling of tongues' signifying the end of confusion and ignorance.[42] If such was the author's intention, as already intimated, to give maximum value to this miracle of speaking in unlearned foreign languages would suit his purpose. Whether the reversal of the Babel motif is present or not, it is clear that the author intends the Pentecost happening to be understood as a miracle of xenoglossia. Yet, while it is no longer possible to get behind the interpretative account to historical fact, claims of xenoglossia in modern settings may provide some pertinent insights relevant to certain features of the Lukan narrative. Samarin for instance, makes a simple but telling observation:

> As in the Biblical account . . . glossolalists do not themselves claim to have spoken such-and-such a foreign language (or do so rather uncommonly) ... Generally, it is someone else who identifies the supposed language.[43]

The view advanced here is that the experience at Pentecost was, indeed, a public eruption of glossolalia. The utterances were not directed to the human audience but rather towards God.[44] This, of course, poses several problems: would the writer deliberately misrepresent glossolalia as xenoglossia? If this cannot be countenanced, had he, then, but little, if any, knowledge of the nature of glossolalia which would account for his version? Neither distortion nor ignorance on the part of the author sounds convincing. It is hardly likely that Paul's companion[45] would not have witnessed the baptizing of converts in the name of the Lord Jesus with results like those at Ephesus (Acts 19: 6), or, if not himself a witness, had not been informed in detail of such occurrences. The seven disciples at Tyre who, 'warned by the Spirit, urged Paul to abandon his visit to Jerusalem' (Acts 21: 4), communicate a message brought through prophecy. It is not inconceivable that the prophecy might have been an interpreted 'glossa'. While Luke may not have given charismatic prophets a very high rating in relation to church leaders in matters of authority, he allows a prominent role to Spirit inspired prophets in the earlier 'ideal' Church.[46] In this incident at Tyre he emphasizes the agency of the *pneuma*, but gives no indication how the revelation had been mediated to the group. The fact that they were a *group*, and urged Paul as a group, would heighten the possibility that more than one had been instruments of the divine communication and that glossolalia and interpretation could be the source of their prophecy. All in all, it is as hard to believe that Luke was insufficiently informed of a phenomenon acknowledged as the work of the Spirit as it is to believe that glossolalia was an uncommon experience in the early Apostolic Church.[47]

In modern glossolalic circles, if comparison be permitted, as I think it should, claims of utterances in foreign languages are sometimes made. Even if these claims could be scientifically authenticated, which is not yet the case in any single instance, this would not mean that all glossolalic utterances would be of this character. Similarly, in the early Church, claims of xenoglossia would be advanced and there is no doubt that Luke makes such a claim for Pentecost and, in making it, would not consider that he was in any way contradicting or misrepresenting Paul's understanding of glossolalia. Yet this is no ground for insisting that for Luke every instance of speaking in tongues is an instance of xenoglossia.

It may occur in modern glossolalic utterance that interspersed with what is otherwise unintelligible, sounds or phonetic combinations are produced which resemble, or, in some cases, may be identical with word forms in known tongues. Some such examples, but by no means all, may be explained psychologically in terms of cryptomnesia. It was said, for instance, that the glossolalia of some Irvingites contained 'many Greek and Latin radicals and with inflections also much resembling those of the Greek language'.[48] One George Pilkington[49] claimed by virtue of his facility in several languages to understand tongue speakers in the Irvingite circle and advanced translations. Thus 'gthis dilemma sumo'was rendered 'I will undertake this dilemma'; 'Hozequin alta stare' as 'Jesus in the highest'; 'Holimoth holif awthaw' as 'Holy, most holy father'; and 'Casa sera hastha caro' as 'the house will be in my care'.[50] Admittedly this is a somewhat unusual sample of glossolalia and echoes of English, Latin and Spanish are fairly obvious. It should be noted, however, that contemporary glossolalists have on occasion assigned meaning to certain 'words' and 'phrases' in their glossas, particularly recurring utterances. Yet as Samarin points out, frequent occurrence alone is not enough to make glossolalic expression take on meaning, 'what is necessary is an emotional state that is significant or meaningful to the speaker.'[51] Again, '. . . a glossolalic discourse alludes to meaning rather than specifies it.'[52] Normally, the utterance of the glossolalists is lexically unintelligible to himself and to others, and when interpretation is given in the assembly it is not an exercise in grammar or a translation of the 'words' but an interpretation of the whole event. In quantitative terms the interpretation may be much longer or much shorter than the glossolalic utterance which in itself indicates that translation, in the sense of conveying the meaning of what has been expressed in one language in another language, is not what cccurs. L. Christenson[53] says it is not an exact 'translation' but a rendering of the content or 'gist' of the utterance of tongues. My own view is that more is involved and I would suggest that the clue lies in the sense of deep rapport at the experiential level between speaker and interpreter,[54] and that the latter feels under strong compulsion to utter the interpretation for one particular glossa of several which may have been heard on a given occasion. Between them there is an affinity of mood and both verbalisations, in my view, are upsurges from the depth of personality, like the welling up of the 'Word' of Yahweh in the ancient prophets (Jer. 20: 9). Thus, the view expressed by Lapsley and Simpson[55], that glossolalia is purported to be understandable by those who have the gift of interpreting such speech, needs qualification.

Where a similarity, or indeed identity, exists between glossolalic units and words in known tongues, the explanation may be a simple matter of statistical probability that 'some consonant-vowel combinations occuring in a glossolalia utterance may also be a meaningful unit in some language'.[56] When claims of xenoglossia are made it may well be that an association is made by the listener on the basis of the similarity of certain sounds to those in a tongue with which he has some knowledge or familiarity. These claims occur not infrequently among modern glossolalists, particularly among Pentecostals of various description, who believe that the gift of glossolalia may enable speakers to communicate with listeners in their own tongue, although normally glossolalia is not communicative in that sense. For example, a sermon given by Pastor Andrew Turnbull of Glasgow at the Convention of the Apostolic Church at Penygroes, Wales, in August 1919 opens with these remarks:

> The Holy Ghost makes us acquainted with everybody, with the people of every nation. Down in Sunderland, at one of my meetings, there the Holy Ghost had spoken through me, and an old man came up to me and said 'You speak Welsh, are you a Welshman?' On another occasion I travelled with three negroes. My heart was yearning for them: the Holy Ghost came upon me, and I spoke in tongues, and one of my black brothers said, 'You speak Congo language!'[57]

Turnbull adds, 'The Holy Ghost can link us to every nation', meaning that a person with the charismatic gift may speak in unlearned languages, a conviction which in some instances is an important component of the commitment to engage in missionary work.[58] The sincerity with which such beliefs are held cannot be doubted but the stubborn fact remains that substantial verification is notoriously elusive since reports are invariably based upon subjective impressions or secondary sources.[59] Samples of glossolalia are now available on tape, but, so far, none bears more than an occasional resemblance to any known language, and no case of xenoglossia in current Neo-Pentecostalism has been verified by competent linguists.[60] Those who accept as factual Luke's account of Pentecost as reported in Acts 2 will not be convinced by these observations, but, in fact, those among them who would insist that modern glossolalia is continuous with the phenomenon in the Early Church would be on stronger ground if they regarded the utterances at Pentecost not as manifestations of xenoglossia but of glossolalia as at Corinth. It is suggested here that what may well be the case in the event reported by Luke is that some glossolalic utterances called to mind to the hearers languages or dialects of their place of origin.[61] If, indeed this were so, the endowment of the Jewish listeners with *hermēneia* to account for the intelligibility claimed for the utterances would be unnecessary. In any case, not being of the faith they would not be so endowed.[62] If the Jews were residents in Jerusalem, as Haenchen insists, then by this time they might, in any case, only have vague knowledge of the vernacular of their purported native countries. As W. L. Knox observes: 'In reality it is most unlikely that any Jew of the Dispersion would have understood such native dialects as survived in the remoter regions of the Middle East, since the Jews of the Dispersion were almost entirely city dwellers.'[63] If, on the other hand, there were Jewish pilgrims from these areas, they would most certainly be able to speak Greek or Aramaic and so would require no miracle of xenoglossia for communicating purposes. Luke's intention, however, did not involve a concern for communication, but was theologically determined, and xenoglossia heightened the miracle of the event. He sought to emphasize the role of the Spirit as the power guiding the missionary expansion of the Church.[64] Xenoglossia generated amazement and wonder (2: 7) (presumably greater than what unintelligible speech would have achieved), and listeners were prompted to enquire about the source of this manifestation (2: 8, 12).

It is my view that sounds uttered by the speakers seemed to some Jewish hearers as identifiable words in languages dimly recalled.[65] It is even possible that interspersed among inarticulate utterances would be actual identifiable words. This occurs sometimes in modern glossolalia, and Moffat hints at an analogue from the ancient world also when he reminds us of the jumble of incoherent ejaculations mixed up with native and foreign titles of deities in magical papyri of the second and third centuries.[66] Whether the recognized words

36

were actual foreign terms or only resembled such, once the association had been made even by one or two persons, others in the atmosphere of intense excitement would discover their own associations, and subjective impressions became rapidly diffused conviction Against such a view it may be argued that *ēkouon* (ADK) in Acts 2: 6 describes a hearing of some duration[67] but, as in the case of modern claims for xenoglossia, a claim for the identification of part of an utterance could easily be extended to the whole through auditory illusion. Whatever the actual facts, the miraculous attraction of xenoglossia served Luke's theological purpose which links the mission of the Spirit with the Jewish feast of Pentecost,[68] but there is no reason to doubt that it was Luke's genuinely-held belief that his report not only had symbolic significance but corresponded to fact.

Most who have written of the Corinthian and Pentecost phenomenon have thought in terms of a simple choice between two alternatives: glossolalia or xenoglossia, the former often being described as babbling, gibberish or globbledegook.[69] The use of such epithets not only betrays insensitivity to the glossolalic event viewed *in toto* but fails to recognize the variety of glossolalic manifestation which can take even the form of harmonious singing where several persons participate, or can be produced in private in quiet surroundings, or indeed can be engaged in the mind alone.[70] While, as a theoretical convenience, one may separate the verbal from the experiential in the glossolalic event, to begin to understand involves viewing it as a totality. The separation of utterance from its existential context, while convenient for linguistic analysis purposes, is not in the best interests of interpreting the phenomenon as a whole.[71] Likewise, to regard glossolalia merely as a verbal manifestation rather than as a total experience within a religious culture leads not only to the isolation of verbalisation,[72] but possibly to a disregard of the creative potential of glossolalia in terms of personal therapy and conduct. If glossolalia has any creative aspects, then it is probably to the areas of personal and communal life that we should look for clues.[73] For this reason, the communities and their beliefs which generate this type of behaviour, and, above all, the impact it exercises upon those who practise it, as well as their understanding of it, must be taken fully into account, while comparison with so-called parallels in mystery cults or elsewhere can only be done with adequate information of the total setting in each case.[74]

In the writer's view, what evidence there is suggests modern glossolalia has a strong biblical basis[75] and, moreover, that glossolaalists can claim to be in an apostolic tradition.[76]

Having considered the Biblical evidence, this study will focus next on the manifestation of glossolalia in the present century. This does not imply that the phenomenon has been entirely unknown throughout the intervening centuries, but, whereas previously eruption has been exceedingly sporadic, in this century its growth has been truly remarkable. In addition, while the information that has been amassed concerning present-day glossolalia is still inadequate, it is naturally much more accessible, extensive and factual than any study of the past could provide.

As for the past, it is generally accepted that glossolalia can be included as one of the manifestation of ecstatic phenomena within Montanism in the second century A.D.[77] Opinion is divided as to whether the continuation of glossolalia is confirmed by ambiguous references in Ireneaus (ca. A.D. 130-200)[78] and Tertullian (ca. A.D. 160-220).[79] By the fourth century, judging by the writings of Chrysostom (ca. A.D. 345-407), there was no glossolalia in the Eastern Church and according to Augustine (A.D. 354-430) it was absent from the Western Church also.[80]

We can say that from apostolic times until the pietistic revivals of the seventeenth and eighteenth centuries the incidence of glossolalia was minimal, although some of the saint missionaries of the mediaeval period are credited with the ability to speak in unlearned tongues.[81] This power is also claimed for the Huguenot peasants of the Cevennes region of South France, also called Camisards, who share many features in common with the earlier Montanists. Their children became prophets who, so it is said, during the persecutions ca. 1685 to the early 1700's spoke in unlearned foreign languages, their utterances deriving from a higher Power which spoke through them. In the eighteenth century dissatisfaction with the sterility of the rational approach in religion led pietists to seek more direct contact with God and this resulted in various manifestations of 'enthusiasm' including glossolalia. It manifested itself among early Quakers,[82] Methodists, Jansenites in France, Irvingites in England, and a little later in America it was associated with the Shakers and the early Mormons.[83]

But never before in the history of the whole Christian Church or in any part of it, has glossolalia erupted with such vigour and in so widespread a manner as in this century. It came to the fore as a central feature in Pentecostalism, and my next task is to examine it in that context. To do that it will be necessary, however briefly, to give some account of Pentecostalism itself and the manner of its development.

1. *heteros* can mean different or foreign. Luke employs the word 'tongue' six times only in Acts (in chapter 2, 10 and 19) and commentators are by no means unanimous that he is describing the same thing in each case, see B. L. Smith, 'Tongues in the New Testament' in *The Churchman* 87 (1973), 283. Other references in the New Testament to the phenomenon of tongues are restricted to Mark 16:17 and 1 Cor. 12-14, but there may be veiled references in 2 Cor. 12:12, 3; Rom 15:18, 19; 1 Thess. 5:19 and Rom. 12:11. See J. M. P. Sweet, 'A Sign for Unbelievers, Paul's attitude to Glossolalia' in *N.T.S.* 13 (1966-67), 240-257.

2. The translators of the New English Bible employ this very phrase or similar words, but in fact '*ekstasis* is never used in the Greek New Testament to describe a speaker in tongues. Yet it appears often in descriptions of the activity of the Spirit subsequent to New Testament times, particularly in the Montanist revival. See R. Knox, *Enthusiasm* (Oxford, 1950), 25-49.

3. D. Walker, *The Gift of Tongues and Other Essays* (Edinburgh, 1906), 3. The same writer, however, concedes that speech in foreign languages may have been manifested at Corinth too (79). A useful discussion of the views of earlier exegetes is found in A. D. Palma, 'Glossolalia in the Light of the New Testament and Subsequent History', Unpublished B.S.T. thesis, Biblical Seminary, New York (1960).

4. See previous chapter nn.3 and 41.

5. True, many claims have been made in modern glossolalic circles that speakers in tongues have spoken in foreign languages, but no case has been scientifically authenticated, and there is no doubt that the normative characteristic of glossolalia is unintelligibility. See further W. J. Samarin, *Tongues of Men and Angels* (London: Collier-Macmillan, 1972), 227.
   The term is used here for the religious phenomenon of talking in tongues, but it should be noted that speakers in tongues in contemporary glossolalic circles often demonstrate a development from inarticulate mumbling to speech which may conform to exterior aspects of ordinary language. See further W. J. Samarin, 'Evolution in Glossolalic Private Language' in *Anthropological Linguistics* 13 (1971), 58. In this invest-igation, glossolalia signifies both 'embryonic' utterance and articulated verbal behaviour within the religious context. The term is used sometimes for pseudo-language in non-religious contexts, but this usage does not concern us here. For types of glossolalia cf. E. Lombard, *De la glossolalia chez les premiers chretiens et des phénomènes similaires* (Lausanne: 1910). For the view that in the New Testament no single definition will suffice, since the phenomenon 'was as varied as it was diffuse', see R. A. Harrisville, 'Speaking in Tongues—Proof of Transcendence?'in *Dialog* 13 (1974),11-18.

6. The term *xénoglossie* in French was invented by Charles Richet who published a report on the case of a French woman, who, so it was claimed, had the capacity to write Greek, a language she had not learned, *Pro-ceedings of the Society for Pyschical Research* 19 (1905-07), 162-194.

7. 'Pentecost and Glossolalia' in *J.T.S.* ns. 5 (1952), 228-31.

8. ' "Ecstatic Utterance" (NEB)?' in *J.T.S.* ns. 17 (1966), 299-307.

9. W. F. Arndt and F. W. Gingrich, *A Greek-English Lexicon of the New Testa-ment and other early Christian Literature* (Cambridge, 1957). J. H. Moulton and R. Milligan, *The Vocabulary of the Greek New Testament* (London, 1930), 128.

10. Samarin, *Tongues of Men and Angels*, 235.

11. Gundry, *J.T.S.*, 300.

12. Joyce, op. cit., 159.

13. C. K. Barrett, *The First Epistle to the Corinthians* (London: A. and C. Black, 1958), 313 renders 1 Cor. 14:21: 'It is written in the Law, I will speak to this people by men of strange tongues and by the lips of strangers (rejecting *eterois* in favour of *heterōn*) yet even so they will not listen to me saith the Lord'.
   Paul's words are not in agreement with Isa. 28:11, 12 LXX, and the prophet's third person is turned into the first, appropriating the words

to God. He also omits the first part of verse 12. The relevant portion of the Isaiah passage reads in LXX: '*die phaulismon cheileōn dia glōssēs heteras, hoti lalēsousi tō laō toutō . . . kai ouk ēthelēsan akouein*' - 'Because they will speak to this people through despised lips, by a strange tongue . . . and they were (sic) not willing to understand' (trans. in J. Héring, *The First Epistle of Saint Paul to the Corinthians* (London: 1962), 152. Héring, with others, raises the question whether Paul is quoting from memory, and suggests a possible source in an ancient translation, used later by Aquila, since Origen claims to have discovered the Pauline wording in the Greek version of the Old Testament by Aquila.

14. C. K. Barrett, *First Corinthians*, 322-3.
15. In W. R. Nicoll, edit. *The Expositor's Greek Testament* 2 (New York: Dod, Mead and Co., 1901), 910.
16. Paul rounds off the quotation with *legei kurios*, 'saith the Lord'. This quotation might be an *ad hoc* introduction, on the other hand, many *legei kurios* texts were already in stereo-typed form when Paul used them. See E. E. Ellis, *Paul's Use of the Old Testament* (Edinburgh, 1957), 111. He suggests (107) that here Paul may be adapting to his purpose a 'testimonium' of early Christian anti-Jewish polemic, and he is followed by J. M. P. Sweet, op. cit., For the judicial significance of tongues see A. Robertson and A. Plummer, *First Epistle of St. Paul to the Corinthians* (Edinburgh, 1911), 316.
17. There is no problem here for modern Pentecostal writers. Donald Gee, a renowned authority within Pentecostalism, wrote of glossolalia: 'Although its chief purpose was for communication with God in prayer and praise, yet it could also provide an arresting sign to unbelievers if any were present. Divine providence could add to the impressiveness of the sign by causing the language uttered to be the mother-tongue of the unbeliever, as on the Day of Pentecost. This was apparently incidental, however, and was not inherent in the gift.' *Concerning Spiritual Gifts* (Springfield, Missouri, n.d.), 58.
18. One ought to mention, in view of the reference to ecstatic speech in Hellenistic religions, that while it was no doubt a feature, to claim parallels to glossolalia among the religions of the first century, as many writers do, would be to exceed the evidence. See E. Andrews, 'Tongues, Gift of,' *I.D.B.* R-Z, 671. Watson E. Mills, ('Glossolalia and Ecstaticism: Parallel Phenomena?' a paper read to the American Academy of Religion, Atlanta, Georgia (1971)) mentions that sources dating from the first and second centuries, such as Strabo, Plutarch, Pausanias and Philo, indicate the communication of contemporary oracles in intelligible language. Strabo gives an account of such features as the effect of percussion instruments in the worship of Dionysius, Cybele and others, and describes the chants 'evah' and the stamping of feet (Strabo, Geography, X iii, 13, 15). Mills's conclusion is that the classical sources seem to seriously challenge the dogmatic equation of glossolalia with the oracles of the Greek religion. G. Delling, *Worship in the New Testament* (Philadelphia; Westminster Press, 1962), 31, holds that Christian glossolalia did not involve many of the orgiastic features of its pagan parallels, The fact is that the whole question of parallels is a subject which has not hitherto been adequately researched, and a great deal of obscurity remains. cf. for instance, the comments of T. K. Oesterrich on the Delphic oracle in *Possession: Demonical and Other* (New York, 1930), 312.
19. Gundry, op. cit., 304.
20. There is no apparent significant difference here between *idiōtai* 'outsiders' and *apistoi* 'unbelievers'. See H. Conzelmann, *Der erste Brief an die Korinther* (Göttingen, 1969), 286. It has been suggested that *apistoi* are rejectors of the faith but that *idiōtai* are persons unacquainted with Christianity and here receiving their first impression of it (Findlay, op. cit.).
21. *First Corinthians*, 323.

22. Hos. 9:7; Jer. 29:26; 2 Kings 9:21; 1 Sam. 21:16 EVV. 15 (*mešuggācīm*)..
23. J. M. P. Sweet's speculation has much to commend it. He says it is unlikely that the sign value of tongues is an original contribution of Paul's and thinks it probable that Paul is taking up a Corinthian slogan (from their letter to him?): *hai glōssai eis sēmeion eisi tois pisteuosin*, op. cit., 240. In that case, Paul radically changes the slogan and makes tongues a sign not for believers, as the Corinthians would have it, but for unbelievers. Following upon this suggestion, the trend of thought could be traced as follows. Confronted with the Corinthian excesses and their over confidence in tongues as a sign, Paul shows that if tongues are to be considered as a sign, at all, they must be thought of as a sign to unbelievers, not believers. Yet, even as a sign to unbelievers, they are less effective than prophecy and more likely to confound unbelievers rather than to convict them.
24. cf. F F.. Bruce, 1 *and* 2 *Corinthians* (Oliphants: New Century Bible, 1971), q.v.
25. This would be reasonable enough. Believers would defend tongues as a touchstone of the authenticity of the speaker's experience of the Holy Spirit. cf. F. F. Bruce's comments on Acts 10:46 'Apart from such external manifestations, none of the Jewish Christians present, perhaps not even Peter himself, would have been so ready to accept the fact that the Spirit had really come upon them', Bruce, *Commentary on the Book of Acts* (London: Marshal Morgan and Scott, 1954).
26. *sēmeion* only occurs eight times in Paul. On three occasions the traditional category *sēmeia kai terata* is employed (Rom. 15:19; 2 Cor 12:12 and 2 Thess 2:9). In 1 Cor. 1:22, Paul is critical of the Jews because they seek a sign, *sēmeion aitousin*, implying a rejection of the demand that he should prove his authenticity as an apostle sent to speak for God with signs. See H. K. Rengstorf in *Theological Dictionary of the New Testament* 7 (Eerdmans, 1971), 259. All that we can safely say, on the basis of the sparse examples of Paul's use of *sēmeion*, is that there is an ambivalence of connotation, and that the term is not necessaritly associated with threats of judgement but can have a positive significance.
27. e.g. F. F. Bruce, 1 *and* 2 *Corinthians*, interprets Isa. 28:11 as a sign of divine judgement and maintains that 'Paul's point is that a divine communication in strange tongues addressed to the deliberately disobedient will confirm them in their disobedience: they will remain all the more *unbelievers*'. Rengstorf says that speaking in tongues is a' σημεῖον to ἄπιστοι because it shows that they are unbelievers and separated from God. It presents itself in some sort as an argument or ground by which to know their own unbelief'. Héring, *First Corinthians*, 152 implies that there is a snatch of glossolaly in the Massoretic text of Isa. 28:10 since the prophet goes on to speak of Jews 'who refused to believe and who were not even impressed by it'. In fact, it is somewhat presumptuous to take Isa. 28:10 and the quotation from Isa. 28:11, 12 in this way. There is no firm ground for associating Isa. 28:10 with glossolalia although *saw lā-sāw, qaw, lā-qāw* in Isa. 28:10 have been explained as a childish repetition of the letters of the alphabet or imitations of glossolalic utterance. Bruce, *First Corinthians*, 132 refers to 'baby-talk'.
28. In modern glossolalia, control may be exercised by speakers, whether to speak or not, but not over what is said. cf. Diocese of California, Division of Pastoral Services, Study Commission on Glossolalia, *Preliminary Report* (1963), 6.
29. Observers of modern glossolalia find that the glossolalic event may occur in a setting of tranquillity as well as in fervent revivalist groups. For example, it is claimed that in Catholic Pentecostalism 'the emotionalism and demonstrativeness that have been so typical of the worship services in Pentecostal denominations have been replaced by a quieter spirit of deep conviction and deep feeling, which loves silence as well as language

as a medium for praising God', E. D. O'Connor, *Pentecost in the Catholic Church* (Dove, 1971), 24. St. Paul was well aware of the variety of glossolalic expression, note *genē glōssōn* in 1 Cor. 12:28.

30. W. J. Samarin, *Tongues*, 204.
31. Gundry, op. cit., 306.
32. cf. W. Baird, *The Corinthian Church—A Biblical Approach to Urban Culture* (Abingdon, 1964), 124.
33. *pantes* in 2:1 is ambiguous. Some say it refers to the 120 brethren (e.g. R. P. C. Hanson, *The Acts of the Apostles* (Oxford, 1967)) but most restrict it to the Twelve Apostles.
34. For a summary of traditional interpretations, see W. Mills, *Understanding Speaking in Tongues* (Grand Rapids, 1972), 30. These can be broadly classified as those which hold (a) that tnogues here are intelligible foreign languages, e.g. A. Wright, *Some New Testament Problems* (London: Methuen, 1898); (b) that glossolalia at Pentecost was interspersed with foreign words, e.g. Kirsopp Lake in F. J. Foakes-Jackson and Kirsopp Lake, *The Beginnings of Christianity: The Acts of the Apostles* 5 (New York: Macmillan, 1920-1933), 120; (c) that the Pentecost narrative represents a miracle of hearing, e.g. G. B. Cutten, *Speaking with Tongues: Historically and Psychologically Considered* (New Haven: Yale, 1927); (d) that the validity of the narrative must be challenged e.g. A. von Harnack, who thinks in terms of a conflation of two or more sources. A. von Harnack, *The Acts of the Apostles* (New York: Putnam, 1909), 179-183, 188-189.
35. Mills, 34-5, insists that the understanding of glossolalia is tied to Luke's purpose which emphasizes the role of the Spirit in the early Christian community.
36. F. F. Bruce, *Commentary on Acts*, 59 calls attention to the interesting Midrashic comment on the giving of the Law: 'and every people received the law in their own language' (Midrash Tanchurma 26c). 'So now, on the reputed anniversary of law-giving, people from every nation under heaven "heard the praises of God", every man . . . in his own language!'
37. E. Haenchen, *Acts of the Apostles* (Oxford, 1971), 169-70, believes that the list in its original form must have contained twelve names: 1. Parthians; 2. Medes; 3. Elamites; 4. Mesopotamia; 5. Cappadocia; 6. Pontus; 7. Asia; 8. Phrygia; 9. Pamphylia; 10. Egypt; 11. Libya Cyrenacia; 12. Rome. He adds, 'It is no accident that the list ends, like Acts itself, with Rome, for Luke did not just write the list down "anyhow" but adapted it to his purposes. In place of the Persians he introduces the Parthians, whose name was at that time on everyone's lips. It is likely, on the other hand, that he took the Medes and Elamites, those erstwhile Great Powers from LXX, in order to name the remotest peoples "from the ends of the earth". But all the twelve peoples must speak foreign languages; thus the Greeks and the Jews themselves (hence Hellas, Palestine and Syria) were ruled out as usable names . . . We do not know where Luke found this list, presumably his source contained names only of countries, not of signs of the zodiac. It is therefore advisable, when seeking to understand Luke's list, not to think exclusively in terms of a tradition, but to make due allowance for a theological writer's sense of effective "composition".' Some authors would retain Judea in vs. 9, others regard it as a scribal error. 'Jews' is missing in ℵ. S. G. Wilson, *The Gentiles and the Gentile Mission in Luke-Acts* (Cambridge, 1973), 122 says: 'There is very little manuscript evidence for omitting it, and variations like Chrysostom's "Indian" and Tertullian's "Armenian" are best explained as attempts to resolve the tension with v. 5. The inclusion of Judea is best explained as a rough way of saying that all nations were present.' Wilson also thinks that the inclusion of Judea can be justified on the grounds that they may have spoken a dialect different from the Galilean dialect of the Twelve. See F. F. Bruce, *Commentary on the Book of the Acts*, 62 for other variants.

38. Haenchen, op. cit., 169n.; cf. H. Conzelmann, *Die Apostelgeschichte* (Tubingen, 1963), 25-6.
39. F. J. Foakes-Jackson and K. Lake, *The Beginnings of Christianity* IV 19.
40. Against any such distinction, see Haenchen, 178n.
41. J. G. Davies, *J.T.S.* 228-9.
42. So J. N. Lapsley and J. H. Simpson, 'Speaking in Tongues' in the *Princeton Seminary Bulletin* 58 (1965), 3-4. Other writers state that for Luke, Pentecost was the beginning of the new Covenant, see J. G. Dunn, *Baptism in the Holy Spirit* (S.C.M. 1970), 46.
43. Samarin, *Tongues*, 110.
44. c.f. B. L. Smith, 'Tongues in the New Testament' in *The Churchman*, 87 (1973), 285.
45. Here I follow C. S. C. Williams, *A Commentary on the Acts of the Apostles* (London, 1957) 3: 'Of Paul's companions mentioned in his epistles and in Acts, Luke is most probably the one who wrote Acts or part of it.' See there also a discussion of conflicting views. B. L. Smith, op. cit., writes '. . . the facts that Luke was a companion of Paul and that they both talk about "tongues" (*glōssai*) should restrain us from distinguishing too sharply (if at all) between their various descriptions.'
46. cf. H. Conzelmann, *The Theology of Luke* (New York: Harper and Row, 1960), 208-18; M. E. Boring, 'How we may identify oracles of Christian Prophets in the Synoptic Tradition? Mark 3:28-29 as a Test case' in *J.B.L.* 91 (4) (1972), 506, 508.
47. See, however, Ira J. Martin 3rd, *Glossolalia in the Apostolic Church*, (Berea, Ky., 1960), 61, where it is held that Luke did not know the phenomenon of glossolalia personally and therefore completely misunderstands and misinterprets its true nature. On the extent of glossolalia in the Apostolic Church, see L. Christenson, *Speaking in Tongues and Its Significance for the Church* (Minneapolis, 1968), 92.
48. *The Morning Watch*, cited by A. L. Drummond, *Edward Irving and his Circle* (James Clarke n.d.), 169.
49. Author of a pamphlet *The Unknown Tongues* (1831).
50. See Drummond, op. cit., 73; Joyce, op. cit., 61.
51. Samarin, *Tongues*, 92.
52. ibid., 93.
53. Christenson, 116.
54. cf. Joyce, 159: 'Only in the presence of the speaker, and under the influence of the mysterious spiritual bond which brought one mind into touch with another, could the task of interpretation be accomplished.' Of course, as Joyce observes, psychologically, the case was different when a person interpreted himself, but his explanation of such interpretation begs several questions which cannot be raised here.
55. 'Speaking in Tongues', op. cit.
56. F. D. Goodman, *Speaking in Tongues: A Cross-Cultural Study of Glossolalia* (Chicago, 1972), 150.
57. Reported in *The Riches of Grace* i (8), 7. Pentecostal literature contains many claims of xenoglossia. See e.g. C. Brumback, *Suddenly . . . from Heaven: A History of the Assemblies of God* (Springfield, Missouri, 1961), 117-8; J. L. Sherrill, *They Speak in Other Tongues* (Hodder and Stoughton, 1965), 98 196-211; 'A Moslem Student Finds Christ'. *The Pentecostal Evangel* (August 9, 1959), 32, cited by Palma, 73.
58. For comments on this evangelistic function of glossolalia, which in the terminology of this treatise should more precisely be termed xenoglossia in this context, see Samarin, *Tongues*, 111.
59. cf. Samarin, ibid.
60. F. Farrell, 'Outburst of Tongues: The New Penetration' in *Christianity Today* 7 (24), 3-7.
61. This view is to be clearly distinguished from the so-called miracle of hearing, namely that it was the crowd who were empowered, each to

hear in his own tongue what the Galileans voiced whether in their ordinary words or in a mysterious spirit language (*'Geistsprache'*). See on the miracle of hearing, F. Godet, *Commentary on St. Paul's First Epistle to the Corinthians* (Edinburgh, 1898), 320. A. Wickenhauser, *Die Apostelgeschichte* (Regensburg, 1961), 37. M. T. Kelsey, *Tongues Speaking* (Doubleday, 1968), 150, reminds us that this explanation was suggested and rejected by Gregory of Nazianzen as early as 350 A.D. Walker's suggestion is an interesting one: 'the authorities in Palestine sanctioned the use of any language whatever in repeating the Shema, the Eighteen Benedictions, and the Grace at Meals. Probably on many former occasions the Apostles and other Christians had heard these Jews of the Dispersion using these doxologies and offering praise to God in the language of the country in which they sojourned. These forms of worship, falling on their ears, without any conscious attention on their part, had become a portion of their mental possession or property. When, through the irresistible rush of the Spirit's power, they were thrown for the time into a state of, practically unconscious, ecstasy, the outburst of adoration came flooding to their lips in forms supplied from the resources of a memory abnormally quickened and lacking normal control, and so they "began to speak with other tongues as the Spirit gave them utterance".' (Walker, op. cit., 60-61; Palma, op. cit., 28).

62. Haenchen, op. cit., 169.
63. W. L. Knox, *The Acts of the Apostles* (Cambridge, 1948).
64. G. W. H. Lampe, *The Seal of the Spirit* (1915), 65.
65. cf. C. S. C. Williams, *A Commentary on the Acts of the Apostles* (London: A. and C. Black), 63: 'But anyone who has been present when others have been subject to strong emotional and spiritual or even alcoholic (cf. 2:15) pressure or stimulus may have observed that words of complete gibberish together with words suggesting a foreign tongue are mixed up when the censors of the psyche are removed'.
66. J. Moffatt, *The First Epistle of Paul to the Corinthians* (London, 1938), 213.
67. Haenchen, op. cit., 169, B א E have *ēkousen*, meaning came to hear.
68. D. L. Gelpi, *Pentecostalism: A Theological Viewpoint* (New York, Toronto, 1941), 70.
69. e.g. I. Stevenson, in *Journal of the American Society for Psychical Research* 60 (1966), 300-303.
70. cf. Kelsey, op. cit., 145-6; 'I now find that I use this phenomenon almost entirely within my mind, that is to say that I hardly ever speak in tongues, but "think" the activity in the same way that I am now thinking in English as I type this information.'
71. A general observation on the relationship of language and experience is not inappropriate here. J. Laffal, 'Language, Consciousness and Experience' in *The Psychological Quarterly* 36 (1967), 61, writes: 'Formulations which treat language and experience as if they were separated and as if one could precede the other are lacking in that they do not identify the link within the individual that joins the two.'
72. See J. R. Jaquith, 'Toward a typology of Formal Communicative Behaviour: Glossolalia' in *Anthropological Linguistics* 8 (1967), 1-7.
73. See A. W. Sadler, 'Glossolalia and Possession: An Appeal to the Episcopal Study Commission' in *J.S.S.R.* 4 (1964), 84-90.
74. This is not to deny that there can be common psychological features between religious glossolalia and related phenomena, nor is it an endorsement of the view that because it is capable of a psychological interpretation it must be spurious. What I am arguing for is due regard for the total situation lest what is distinctive may be ignored in a process of reductionism. The claim that there are parallels need not necessarily lead to a disclaimer of the transcendental quality of glossolalia. The source will certainly elude investigation but its field and method of operation may be accessible to observation.

On the question of parallels, as one would expect there is a cleavage of opinion. There are those who believe that to admit parallels would be a denial of transcendence, e.g. the Lutheran, L. Christenson, op. cit., the Episcopalian, M. T. Kelsey op. cit., cf. too the protective stance of the Lutheran, Arnold Bittlinger, *Gifts and Graces, A Commentary on 1 Corinthians 12-14*, trans. H. Klassen, (London, 1967). On the other hand phenomenologists, historians of religion and scholars generally do not share this aversion to speaking of parallels. Conzelmann goes so far as to insist that it is only by recourse to comparative materials in Greek religion that even a definition of glossolalia is possible, H. Conzelmann, *Der erste Brief an der Korinther, Kritisch-Exegetishcer Kommentur über das Neue Testament* (Göttingen, 1969), 276 cf., J. Behm, 'Glossolia 'q.v. and E. Schweitzer, 'Pneuma, Pneumatikos' q.v. in G. Kittel, *Theologisches Wörterbuch zum Neuen Testament* (Stuttgart, 1959).

75. cf. D E. Rosage, *Retreats and the Catholic Charismatic Renewal* (Dove, 1971), 26.

76. The Pentecostal emphasis on the experience of the Spirit is justified on the New Testament evidence, and older traditional Protestant exegetes were wrong to think that the charismata had ceased with the Apostles. See J. D. G. Dunn, *Baptism in the Holy Spirit* (S.C.M. 1970), 225.

77. In the second century, there was a revival of Pentecostal phenomena among a group of Christians in Asia Minor led by Montanus. It is said of him that he raved and talked nonsense, 'prophesying in a way that conflicted with the practice of the Church handed down generation by generation from the beginning'. Eusebius, *History of the Church* V.16. 6-10; See also V. MacDermot, *The Cult of the Seer in Ancient Middle East* (London: Welcome Institute of the History of Medicine, 1971),60.

78. A. Roberts, edit. *The Ante-Nicene Fathers* (N.Y., Scribner, 1926)I, 409.

79. ibid., II, 447.

80. A. A. Hoekema, *What about Tongue-Speaking?* (Grand Rapids: Eerdmans, 1966), 10 ff.

81. Cutten, op. cit.. 42 ff. who warns us against the embellishments in these reports.

82. In fact it is not absolutely clear whether glossolalia occurred among the early Quakers. R. Knox, *Enthusiasm*, 551 does not allow that glossolalia occurred among either Quakers or Methodists, and he is followed by J. R. Williams, *The Pentecostal Reality* (Logos, 1972), 43n. See however the contrary view in P. Schaff, *History of the Christian Church* 1, 237.

83. Knox, ibid, 558ff.

CHAPTER III

THE ORIGINS AND DEVELOPMENT OF THE PENTECOSTAL MOVEMENT

Pentecostalism is a twentieth century separatist movement which has made more dramatic and rapid advance than any other branch of the Christian Church. It is the largest single group within what has been described as the Third Force in Christendom.[1] The latter is seen as an addition to Catholic-orthodox and pan-Protestant types of Christianity and it has been claimed to represent a revolution in our day comparable in importance with the establishment of the original Apostolic Church and with the Protestant Reformation.[2] This may prove to be an exaggeration but it serves a useful purpose in calling the attention of students of religion to a development which most certainly cannot be ignored.

Pentecostalism exhibits many particular idiosyncrasies which vary from group to group, so that any one description will hardly meet with universal assent. Yet all would agree in saying that the generating power of the movement from the beginning has been its enthusiasm of the spirit which has often reached revivalist intensity in the past. The action of the Holy Spirit is held to become manifest in what one can say is a constituent element in the structure of Pentecostalism, namely, speaking in tongues.[3] 'Tongues' are regarded as one of the divine charismata to the church and they are identified with the phenomena of the Early Church. Indeed one writer claims that what characterises Pentecostals generally is the insistence that all of the supernatural gifts of the Apostolic Age are available today.[4] Most Pentecostals speak of Jesus as the source of these gifts[5] and He is also referred to as the one who baptizes men 'in the Holy Ghost'. For these and other reasons the sects can be said to be Jesus-centric.

Pentecostal writers almost invariably stress the central importance of speaking with tongues. One writer says it is 'the truth which made the movement'[6] and another calls it the heart of the Pentecostal Revival.[7] J. T. Nichol links it with other charismatic gifts and the practice of divine healing as the distinctive characteristics of Pentecostalism.[8] In similar vein, the former Pentecostal

46

leader Donald Gee insists that Pentecostalism can only justify its name by offering a testimony to a definite spiritual and personal experience based on the significance and story of the Day of Pentecost.[9] Most Pentecostals would agree with a statement issued by the movement in Denmark rejecting the doctrine that regeneration and Spirit baptism are the same thing. According to the statement, it is the belief of Pentecostals that the Spirit baptism is a special experience, subsequent to conversion[10] and accompanied by the manifestation of tongues.[11] Spirit baptism is not some vague indeterminable thing but an experience which finds outward expression in speaking with tongues.[12] Not all who belong to Pentecostal churches have arrived at this experience, and not all who have this initial manifestation of tongues, continue to speak in tongues subsequently. Where the ability is retained, it is regarded as a vehicle for praising God in worship, and, also, when used collectively, for the benefit, or as they say, the edification of the church, it is regarded as a 'gift', but more of that presently.

As previously stated, while glossolalia has been for the most part conspicuously absent in Christendom since Apostolic times it has recurred, albeit exceedingly sporadically over the centuries. As indicated, it has been associated with the Montanists in second century Italy, the Albigenses in twelfth century France, the mendicant friars of the thirteenth century, the Jansenites, possibly the early Quakers, the Wesley[13] and Whitfield revivals, the little prophets of the Cévennes at the end of the seventeenth century, the Irvingites early in the last century, the Shakers, the Mormons, the Mennonites of Eastern Canada, Khlysti a sect of flagellants in seventeenth century Russia, the Pryguni in the nineteenth century[14], the Smorodintsi and the Murashkovtsi, Russian sects named after their leaders in the present century.[15] Several isolated instances were reported in the United States in the latter half of the last century.[16] In England, it is said that some spoke in tongues during the mission of D. L. Moody in Sunderland in 1873.

In the present century the phenomenon has appeared outside the Pentecostal Movement, as, for example, in Father Divine's sect in the United States. During the last two decades, however, glossolalia has been prevalent in what has come to be designated as Neo-Pentecostalism or The Charismatic Renewal. This comprises independent groups, with participants drawn from several denominations, and some without any previous religious affiliation; groups within what have come to be known as main-line churches, both Protestant and Catholic, and campus groups.

Historical reviews of glossolalic occurrence in the past are not too numerous, perhaps because the hard evidence is rather scant. In fact the most frequently cited source is still G. B. Cutten, *Speaking with Tongues* (New Haven, 1927).[17] Accounts of non-religious forms of glossolalia are even more scarce. This is not the case with Pentecostalism nor with Pentecostal glossolalia, for there is a growing output of books and articles on both, by Pentecostals themselves and by outside observers. This is true also of Neo-Pentecostalism. The history of Pentecostalism over a world-wide spectrum has now been accomplished in admirable fashion[18] so that, for my purpose, only a brief résumé is required of the events which brought the Pentecostal movement to the forefront in this century. A topic like glossolalia must be discussed against its background, and nowhere has glossolalia occupied such a central role as in twentieth century Pentecostalism. What this chapter offers then is a brief outline of the emergence of what is now referred to as 'classical' Pentecostalism in North America and in Europe with some comments on the interacting influences.

Revivalism prior to Pentecostalism

The Pentecostal movement has no single founder and while its source is often traced to the Revival which began at Los Angeles in April 1906[19] there were in fact many events and personalities on both sides of the Atlantic which it may be claimed played a part, some more directly than others, in preparing the ground for the Californian revival. For instance the influence of evangelists like Charles Finney, D. L. Moody and R. A. Torry, on both sides of the ocean, should be taken into account. Indeed, many independent and separate evangelical stirrings in both Europe and North America can be regarded as antecedents of the Azura St. eruption.

B. R. Wilson[20] is no doubt right that revivalism was a technique inherited from the evangelicals of the nineteenth century (and one appropriate to a mass society). In North America many of the early Pentecostal leaders were products of nineteenth century Holiness groups, and these groups themselves were offshoots of Methodism.[21]

W. W. Menzies has viewed the emergence of Pentecostalism in the U.S.A. against the background of religious and social changes at the turn of the century and saw Fundamentalism and the Holiness Movements counteracting the erosion of the religious world. He asserts that 'It was largely out of the spiritual concern generated in this segment of the church that the yearning for a new Pentecost was born.'[22] But why could not the evangelical segment as it was meet this need? H. A. Goss attributes the appeal of the new

48

Pentecostal movement to the infectious joyousness of gospel singing which he reckoned compensated for the austere holiness code of the Holiness movement.[23]   The Holiness Movement in turn had been 'a Puritan reaction against a supposedly stiffening institutionalism and secularism in the greater American churches',[24] and the same tensions could be observed in Europe before the advent of Holiness churches on that continent.   The introduction of the American Holiness Movement to Keswick in England is attributed to Robert P. Smith, and he saw it spread from there to the continent where it exercised great influence on the German Gemeinschaftbewegung.[25]

The Holiness Groups emphazised the total sanctification of the believer and this sanctification was thought of in terms of an identifiable experience independent of, and subsequent to, conversion. For them, this experience was baptism by the Holy Ghost.   Some groups, to the left as it were of the Movement, departed from the main stream in that they looked for evidence of this experience of sanctification in some 'supernatural' sign such as a vision or dream or 'speaking in tongues'.[26]   In J. T. Nichol's view this wing was destined to become the Pentecostal movement.   He specifies a number of doctrinal and behavioural emphases which Pentecostalism inherited from the ideology of these Holiness groups viz:

(1)   that there is a blessing to be sought and to be received subsequent to and distinct from conversion.

(2)   that one must seek to be led by the Spirit in all the affairs of life.

(3)   that revivals and camp meetings ought to be utilized for the purpose of winning converts and rejuvenating the spiritual lives of the faithful.

(4)   that believers should maintain a vibrant hope in the imminent return of Christ, and

(5)   that one ought to forsake the world and shun all manifestations of 'worldliness'—amusements, jewelry, use of cosmetics, luxury.[27]

There is no mention of speaking with tongues in this list, but glossolalia was practised among deviationists within the Holiness Churches.   In fact, since the middle of the last century there had been sporadic isolated instances of glossolalia in some Holiness groups in the United States.   For instance, The Gift Adventists of southern New England had practised speaking with tongues and the interpretation of tongues since 1854 and their leader also exercised the gift of healing.[28]   The main Holiness tradition was not in favour of tongues and so a rift with deviationists was inevitable. Though the link between minority Holiness Groups who practised tongues and the new Pentecostalism which was to emerge can be convincingly established, nevertheless one must not forget the contribution of the parent Holiness Churches. They brought to the fore a doctrine which was to assume centrality in Pentecostalism namely 'baptism in the Holy Spirit'. As stated, the Holiness Groups associated this with what they termed the blessing of sanctification which they regarded as a second work of grace. Pentecostals, on the other hand, maintained that speaking in tongues was a sign of baptism in the Holy Spirit, a view rejected by the Holiness Groups. Pentecostals, too, on the whole tended to regard sanctification in terms of process rather than as a specific act of grace.

At the turn of the century glossolalia occurred in a small group in Tennessee known as Christian Union, but it was not unknown in other evangelical circles outside the revivalist activities of some Holiness Churches. For instance it was in evidence among a group of Swedish Mission Christians at Moorhead Minnesota in the 1890s and it was not unknown in Baptist circles either, although there it would be quite the exception. W. Jethro Walthall, a Baptist minister, who spoke in tongues in 1879, was later ejected from that denomination and founded the Holiness Baptist Association. Another Baptist minister, the Reverend Robert R. Singleton, led a revival in Greenvale S.C. in 1905 and a number of converts spoke in tongues.[29] A revival with charismatic healing and tongue speaking occurred in Galena, Kansas (1903) and this spread to Texas during the years 1904-06. All in all, then, one can say that there was a great deal of revivalism towards the end of the last century, and that it was very largely the product of the Holiness movement. Speaking in tongues, however, was a peripheral phenomenon and there was little indication as yet of the central role it would play in Pentecostalism.

The eruption of fervent revivalism at Los Angeles in 1906 needs to be viewed against this background of several local stirrings over a very wide area of the American scene. There were, of course, more immediate and direct links, particularly the events at Charles F. Parham's Bethel Bible College, Topeka, Kansas City in the winter of 1900-01. Parham, a Methodist preacher is regarded as the founder of American Pentecostalism.[30] Forty students joined him in his quest for the key to the spiritual power in the early Church. A seminar held by a group of these students drawn from several denominations discussed an assigned topic: 'Baptism in the Holy Spirit'. Their study led them to conclude that the Scriptures

50

clearly indicated that the evidence for baptism with the Holy Spirit was 'speaking with other tongues'. At a watch-night service on December 31, 1900, Parham 'laid hands' on a student named Agnes N. Ozman, and she, so it is claimed, spoke in Chinese. For three days subsequently she was unable to speak in English and could only write in Chinese characters! With the advent of the New Year a new era of spiritual power dawned and this has been hailed as the beginning of the modern Pentecostal movement.[31] The interesting feature of this event is that Parham himself at that time had not experienced glossolalia. Three days later he did, and subsequently so did many of the other students, but Parham had little success in his early efforts until his faith-healing campaign in Galena, Kansas in 1904. He went on to hold many successful campaigns after this and he also founded a second Bible School, this time at Houston Texas. It was one of Parham's Houston students, namely W. J. Seymour, who subsequently became the central personality of the Los Angeles revival. Seymour did not speak with tongues prior to coming to Los Angeles although he had experienced at Houston what Bloch-Hoell describes as 'an ecstatic experience without motoric speech'.[32] Seymour came to Los Angeles to be associate pastor of a small Nazarene mission in the Holiners tradition, but his 'Pentecostal' teaching led to ejection from the pastorate. However, he continued to conduct services in people's homes and at these gatherings many began to speak with tongues. Growing congregations made it necessary to find a building to accommodate them. This is how they came to be in a former Methodist church at 312 Azusa St., an address which became internationally known as the cradle of the Pentecostal movement in America.

Turning to Europe, one can with hindsight see similar preparations underway for the emergence of Pentecostalism. The untiring transatlantic journeyings of that pre-jet age is quite extraordinary. In fact there was a constant interflow back and forth across the Ocean and the one continent influenced and was influenced by the other. This can be illustrated in the case of the Welsh Revival of 1904-05 which, more than any other event in the British Isles, prepared the way for Pentecostalism in Britain.[33] The Welsh Revival had its roots in native soil in nineteenth century revivals of both local and general impact. The most significant of these was the revival of 1859 mainly associated with the name of David Morgan, Ysbyty Ystwyth.[34] The '59 revival in Wales had been within what is now referred to as a main-line tradition, but other influences from revivalist circles led up to what is known in Wales as Evan

Roberts's Revival (1904-05). One could, for instance, mention the evangelistic campaigns of D. L. Moody and Ira D. Sankey and the energetic evangelism of Scot Alexander Dowie and others; conferences aimed at the deepening of the spiritual life such as the Keswick Conventions; the American Holiness Movement with camp meetings and missions, and as stated, brought to England by Robert Parsall Smith.[35]

One Holiness Movement in England founded by Mr. Reader Harris K. C. and known as the 'Pentecostal League' had direct links with Wales and the 1904 revival. A Welsh draper in London, Mr. David Thomas, was converted at one of the League's meetings by a Dr. Watson from Boston. Thomas eventually formed his own International Holiness Mission in 1907 with its headquarters at Battersea. It is interesting to note that both Reader Harris and Thomas were on a joint mission to Carmarthen in West Wales some months before the Great Revival of 1904. Thomas had been brought up in the area and could be said to be on home ground. An evaluation of the mission by the distinguished divine, the Reverend Keri Evans, is illuminating. He wrote: 'I well remember the mission conducted by Mr. David Thomas, assisted by Mr. Rees Thomas, and for one day by the late Mr. Reader Harris, K.C. in Carmarthen, about a year before the Welsh Revival of 1904-05. When I say "well remember", I do not mean that all the details are clear in my mind, but that the mission stands out among many such as an event of real significance for the religious history of the time.'[36] Evans goes on to refer to the special stress at these meetings on the work of the Holy Spirit and the need for complete surrender to the Will of God. In his view these were neglected truths in the Church at that time, but they became 'live' in the Revival. 'The insistent emphasis with which they were preached prepared the mind and heart of many in Carmarthen—myself for one—for the wonderful outpouring of the grace of God in the great Revival that soon followed.'[37]

In fact, there were many local missions of a similar nature which can now be seen as harbingers of the Great Revival. One was the evangelistic campaign of John Pugh in Cardiff in 1891, which later led to the founding of the Forward Movement. Further afield was the industrious evangelism of Alexander A. Boddy, vicar of All Saints Parish Church, Sunderland. Boddy had led a spiritual revival in North-East England since 1866 and in 1904 he journeyed to Wales to work with Evan Roberts.[38] Further afield still one can look to transatlantic influences such as the return of a Welsh minister who had experienced revivalist outbursts in his church at Scranton, Penn. in 1896.[39] In turn the Welsh Revival itself made its contribution to the happenings in Los Angeles.[40] Joseph Smale, pastor of the First Baptist Church in Los Angeles returned from Wales in 1905 enthused by the Revival. He later conducted his own campaign in Los Angeles after resigning from the Baptist Church.[41] Frank Bartleman, a Holiness minister, attracted by Smale's account of the Welsh Revival, corresponded with its charismatic leader Evan Roberts. In his diary, Bartleman wrote of the effect upon him of hearing of the Welsh Revival: 'My soul was stirred to its depths and I then and there promised God He should have full right of way with me, if He could use me'.[42] Bartleman's evangelistic endeavours in Los Angeles paved the way for the Pentecostal Movement.[43] He met W. J. Seymour in 1906 and in fact became one of the key figures in the Azusa St. revival.

Of course, I am not suggesting that the Los Angeles Revival was the outcome of the revival in Wales, for, as I have stated, the Pentecostal Movement was already astir in North America before the events in Wales. In fact, as Sherrill has observed, the Movement sprang up simultaneously in several countries and in his view no influences of one group upon another can be traced.[44] I still contend, however, that certain links between the Welsh Revival and the Los Angeles awakening can be established.[45] At the same time, in one very important respect, the former differed from the Pentecostalism which was to follow, for the Revivalist Evan Roberts, like many Holiness leaders before him, discouraged speaking with tongues. To what extent glossolalia had actually been manifested in Wales at that time is not at all clear. Some writers claim that it was a feature of the 1904 revival.[46] Harper for instance is quite specific: 'there were manifestations of the Spirit, including speaking in tongues, during the revival of 1904-05'.[47] Synan goes even further and claims that Tongues were prevalent in the Welsh revival citing as his authority *The Yorkshire Post* of 27 December 1904.[48] This source had also been cited in the well known Vivier dissertation on glossolalia.[49] I cannot accept, however, that the newspaper source refers specifically to tongues. What the *Yorkshire Post* actually found to be remarkable was that young people who lived in Anglicised areas in Wales, and had no facility in their parents' Welsh tongue, spoke in that language in revival meetings. They did this, according to the report, as if they were familar with it. The phenomenon described, in my view, is neither glossolalia nor xenoglossy. These young people, it seems, had been brought up in homes where Welsh was spoken and that language would also be the medium of worship in the chapels which many of them had attended in childhood. What is remarkable is that somehow in the revivalist atmosphere they were able to hold forth in a tongue in which they had little or no competence, although they would have been familar with hearing it spoken. The *Yorkshire Post* recognised this as a psychological problem. The report reads: 'These young Welshmen and Welshwomen who know little or no Welsh, and who certainly cannot carry on a sustained conversation in their parents' tongue, and who are supposed to have derived little or no benefit from the Welsh services, now, under the influence of the revival, voluntarily take part in public prayer—but the language employed is almost invariably, not the familar English, but the unknown, or supposed to be unknown, Welsh. Biblical phrases, and the peculiar idiomatic expressions connected with a Welsh prayer which they never used before, and which they were supposed hitherto not to be able to understand, trip off their tongue with an ease and an aptness which might be supposed to indicate long and familiar usage . . .

. . . How is this to be accounted for? How can we explain the fact that a youth or maiden who cannot speak a dozen words in Welsh in ordinary conversation, can nevertheless engage for five or ten minutes in public prayer in idiomatic Welsh? Do these young people really know Welsh without being conscious that they do know it? Have the religious services of the past after all appealed to an intelligence the existence of which they themselves never suspected?'

The present writer has heard Welsh speakers abandon the vernacular for sublime, if archaic, Biblical expressions while giving 'interpretation of tongues', as if they unconsciously realised that that was sacred work demanding a sacral language. In these cases, however, it was known that they were users of the Welsh tongue as their first language in normal conversation. What happened in these examples was that they replaced their every-day tongue with a more polished literary version. The *Yorkshire Post* is describing another category, namely, those who had little or no command of Welsh. How do these come to give an impression of familiarity with a supposedly unknown language? My own view is that, just as in certain mystical states there is a 'return' to primal vividness and clarity in thought images, so in revivalist settings there can be a resurgence of primal sound currents, but this question will be taken up again in chapter nine. Suffice here to say that these young people had probably retained far more impressions from childhood, more than they realized, and that cryptomnesia may be the clue to the events described. Whatever the explanation, there is no substantial evidence for Synan's firm contention that the Welsh revival provides 'striking examples of the practice' of glossolalia.

So far, I have found no explicit reference to glossolalia in any first hand report, either in Welsh or in English, dealing with that eventful period. Perhaps there is a veiled reference in the diary to Seth Joshua, one of Evan Roberts's chief helpers. Describing a revivalist scene in 1904, Joshua writes: 'We held another remarkable meeting tonight. Group after group came out to the front seeking the full assurance of faith. What was wonderful to me was the fact that every person engaged in prayer, without one exception The tongue of fire came upon each. We lost all sense of time in this service.'[50] The reference to the 'tongue of fire' may be merely an echo of Scriptural usage, but need not necessarily signify glossolalia. On the other hand, why should the leader discourage it unless there had been some eruption of tongues? By itself, the expression 'tongue of fire' is not explicit evidence, no more than the expression 'baptism of fire' which was also frequently on the lips of the revivalists. The latter indicated an intense spiritual occasion, but one which did not necessarily involve speaking with tongues.[51] Evan Roberts himself gave a central place to the Holy Spirit and says of his first meeting at Moriah, Loughor, that he 'urged them to prepare for the baptism of the Holy Spirit',[52] but there is no evidence that baptism in the Holy Spirit was associated in his mind with speaking with tongues, as it would be in the case of later Pentecostals. Roberts in fact was keenly aware of the suceptibility of 'tongues' to abuse and welcomes its absence at that time since 'until the spiritual sections of the Church of Christ are more acquainted with the counterfeiting methods of the spirit of evil, and the laws which give them power of working, any testimony to such experience as true, cannot be safely relied upon'.[53] It is likely that the charismatic leader had become aware of an incipient stage of glossolalia both in his own case and that of others. Many of the revivalists, overpowered by the affective nature of their experience, uttered repeatedly some word or phrase as if normal expression was inadequate to discharge the intensity of inward feeling. We have a report of intense spiritual excitement experienced by Evan Roberts himself at a meeting on the threshold of the Revival:

> I cried out, 'Bend me! Bend me! Bend us.! Oh! Oh! Oh! Oh!' As she was wiping my face, Mrs. Davies said 'O amazing grace.'[54]

If the Welsh Revival did not encourage glossolalia, it had the other features of revivalist enthusiasm to a remarkable degree, and it may be reckoned at least as one of the occurrences which prepared the way for the Pentecostal movement. On the other side of the ocean the Azusa St. Revival of 1906 can be seen as the beginning of Pentecostalism in America, yet one must not forget those other influences in the last century, and in the first decade of this century, which also contributed to the climate in which that movement emerged.

Pentecostals themselves are reluctant to associate the Movement with a single founder. Thus Donald Gee said that some of the leaders had been powerfully used to extend the border of Pentecost, and that some had been founders of particular sectional organizations within it, but he emphasized that the outstanding leaders of the Pentecostal Movement were themselves the products of the movement. Even so, the history of the movement is largely the story of these vigorous and dedicated evangelists. Within Pentecostalism itself attempts have been made to recognize founder father figures, such as W. J. Seymour, who brought the spark to the West Coast of America, A. J. Tomlinson who established the Church of God, Cleveland, Tennesee; Charles F. Parham, who announced himself 'The Founder and Projector of the Apostolic Faith Movement'[55] and the brothers George and Stephen Jeffreys of the Elim Church in Britain. It is clear then that, while the movement would prefer to minimise the role of historical founders, leadership is of supreme importance. Those who came to Pentecostalism came in response to revivalist leaders, who did not aim initially to establish a sect but rather to 'revive Christendom'. Inevitably, perhaps, their work led to fragmentation and the proliferation of sects.[56]

Early Pentecostalism in North America
Pentecostal ideas spread from Los Angeles to other parts of the United States and the Movement spread to Canada. There, also, Holiness Groups had paved the way, as did the immigrant Irvingite groups who had arrived in the nineteenth century and founded churches such as the church at Kingston, Ontario. Speaking in tongues was not unknown in these circles. The first Pentecostal Assembly in Canada was established in the Ottawa Valley in 1911 by R. E. Mc.Alister, a young Holiness preacher who had witnessed the Los Angeles Revival. He published a monthly magazine entitled the *Good Report* and worked enthusiastically for the spread of Pentecostalism in Eastern Ontario. In Central Ontario, however, the focus of the Movement was an independent mission run by a Pastor and Mrs. Hebden. The mission apparently had no direct links with Los Angeles, but it may not be without significance that it was

November 1906 when the Pastor's wife first experienced glossolalia, that is a few months after the eruption of the Revival at Azusa St. The influence of the Hebden group spread through the central part of the province. One of their converts was Aimee Semple McPherson who in 1923 became the founder of the International Church of the Foursquare Gospel in Los Angeles, and she has been described as the most famous 'American' (sic) revival preacher of her age.[57]

The revival came to Manitoba in 1907 through the agency of A. H. Argue a young Winnipeg business man who had been introduced to Pentecostalism by W. H. Durham at Chicago. These early leaders recognized the importance of using the most effective means of communication to reach a wide audience. At that time it was the printed page, but later Pentecostals have used the modern media dexterously and can teach a great deal to the traditional churches in this respect. Both Argue and Durham had their publications; Durham published *Pentecostal Testimony* which has been described as a 'journalist sledge hammer',[58] and Argue published a paper called *The Apostolic Messenger*, which appeared in two issues in 1908 with a distribution of 70,000 copies. As in Ontario, the movement spread rapidly through the Prairie province and produced leaders of influence, such as Frank Small who in 1921 founded the Apostolic Church of Pentecost, a group which grew significantly in Western Canada, and A. G. Ward who introduced the Pentecostal emphasis to a branch of the Mennonites at Kitchener, Ontario, called the Mennonite Brethren in Christ.[59] The Winnipeg Revival spread further west when the Reverend Hugh Cadwalader, an evangelist from Texas, had considerable success in Saskatchewan. Further west still, progress was chequered in the early days but by today there are Pentecostal churches in almost every village of note along the west coast. The same is true of the maritime provinces of the eastern seaboard, but of all the Canadian provinces the most Pentecostal is Newfoundland where five per cent of the population belong to Pentecostal churches. The 1961 census showed an astounding growth during the previous decade and the Pentecostal advance has been sustained since.[60]

The Los Angeles awakening spread to other countries and strengthened the spiritual stirrings in Britain and Europe. Los Angeles was well located to attract visitors from all over the globe and the events which occurred there were given prominent press coverage at the time. One feature which attracted attention was the importance the revivalists attached to speaking in tongues. This emphasis, however, led to controversial debate within the churches of the various Holiness Groups. The latter had never really arrived at a clearly articulated and unequivocal position regarding speaking in tongues, although the majority had disapproved, some vehemently. Now, a distinct cleavage emerged. As noted already, the Holiness Churches had emphasized a post-conversion experience, namely, that of complete or entire sanctification. They attributed this experience to baptism with the Holy Ghost and Fire, and taught that it was every believer's privilege and obligation to receive the blessing of sanctification. The revivalists, on the other hand, did not claim complete sanctification and understood the Baptism of the Holy Ghost in terms of 'power from on high' given for service and witness.[61] This Baptism, they maintained, was accompanied as in New Testament times by outward evidence, the most persistent being speaking with tongues. The Holiness groups insisted that sanctification is a genuine experience irrespective of Tongues and caimed the authority of no less than Wesley, the founder of Methodism, for their doctrine. Since so many Pentecostals had been nourished in this Perfection teaching the division brought poignant heart searching in both Holiness Churches and Pentecostal groups.

W. H. Durham, an Azusa St. convert since 1907 and subsequently pastor of the North American Mission of Chicago, came out strongly in 1911 against the teaching that a second work of sanctification was necessary in addition to the work of conversion. This was also the position accepted by congregations which later formed the nucleus of what grew to be numerically the strongest wing of Pentecostalism, namely the Assemblies of God. Durham found himself in opposition to W. J. Seymour, by then leader of the Azusa St. Mission, as well as to groups such as the Church of God, the Pentecostal Holiness Church and the Apostolic Faith Association. According to Brumback[62], Durham's position had been misrepresented by those who insisted that he restricted sanctification to the time of the individual's regeneration. There seems to be some justification for this understanding of his position for at one stage this appears to have been his teaching, but later he modified his earlier position and viewed sanctification as a growing process expressed in holiness of life. Of greater significance was what Brumback discerns as another perceptible shift in his teaching, namely, from a faith centred upon a subjective experience to what is described as the objective—subjective—relationship of Cross and believer. Durham argued that 'By accepting sanctification as a work which is based on the finished work of Calvary the believer *starts* on a high plane of holy living, and can maintain it by abiding in Christ. In this manner the object of our faith is not in an experience of sanctification but in the Lord Jesus Christ "who of God is made unto us . . . sanctification" '.[63] These doctrinal distinctions and particularly the differences concerning the significance of Tongues led to a major cleavage within the Holiness Churches. The Church of the Nazarene and most congregations of the Christian and Missionary Alliance aligned themselves against the acceptance of Tongues as evidence of Baptism in the Holy Spirit. Other Holiness Churches, such as the Fire Baptist Holiness Church, founded by B. H. Irwin, the Pentecostal Holiness Church, the Church of God and The Church of God in Christ simply accommodated Revivalist teaching alongside their other cardinal doctrine and in some cases a three stage pattern of doctrinal emphasis emerged viz.: conversion, sanctification *and* 'baptism of Fire'.

In spite of adverse criticism and contempt, the Azusa St. Mission continued to attract leaders of other revival fellowships. These returned to their own communities revitalised, with new will and enthusiasm. In this way the movement gave added impetus to revival missions in North Carolina, Chicago, Akron Ohio and spread to many other states including Missouri, Arizona and Indiana.

The Revivalists found their converts not in Holiness Groups alone, but also among the more traditional denominations such as Episcopalians, Baptists, Methodists, Presbyterians etc. Yet the Holiness and Methodist background of most of the revivalists left an unmistakable influence upon Pentecostalism generally. It could be seen, for instance, in the informality of the services, in their evangelical phraseology and the austerity of their places of worship, although neither Holiness Group nor Methodism can claim exclusive association with any one of these.

The movement also aroused reaction, and, in fact, tensions between enthusiasm and discretion increased and led to divisions and fragmentation. Charles Parham, who had expressed distrust of the excesses of the Los Angeles revival, was rejected in 1909 by the group known as 'The Apostolic Faith'.[64] Parham also seems to have possessed strong racial prejudices and these became manifest in his avid support of the Ku Klux Klan, an attitude repugnant to Pentecostals generally. Soon the Apostolic Faith group changed its name to 'Pentecostal'. Even at this early stage some felt the need for a greater degree of uniformity among the various revivalist groups and worked for a measure of organisation. This led to a kind of merger of the Pentecostal groups in the South-Western states with those in the South-Eastern states. In the Fall of 1909 H. G. Rogers, who convened a conference at Dothan, Alabama,

59

was elected moderator of the new organisation which adopted the name 'Church of God', unaware that this designation had already been adopted by a group in Cleveland, Tennessee. The organisation also appointed J. W. Ledbetter as secretary. Licensed ministers were ordained and application made to the Southern Clergy Bureau for their recognition. Early in 1912 'The Church of God' formed an association with the black 'Church of God in Christ' and adopted the latter designation. These trends towards denominationalism and organisation were not by any means universally welcomed. There were also doctrinal disputes. Some opposed the trinitarianism of the vast majority within Pentecostalism and 'unitarian' groups emerged who made their slogan 'Jesus only' fairly familiar. One such group was known as 'The United Pentecostal Church'. It forbad baptism in the name of the Trinity maintaining that Jesus alone was the Godhead. In 1919 a 'Jesus only' wing of the Assemblies of God uner G. T. Hayward formed a movement known as 'The Pentecostal Assembly of the World', but Pentecostalism in general retained its central emphasis upon the work of the Holy Spirit, and remained trinitarian.

Within the main movement of Pentecostalism the trend towards more organisation was inevitably opposed for it was seen as a threat to the working of the Holy Spirit. A storm of protest had broken out when the General Committee of 'Pentecostal saints' and 'Churches of God in Christ' was announced for the Hot Springs Arkansas, April 2-12, 1914. Opponents of any move towards centralization in Church Government described it as the 'first step to Popery'.[65] Those who urged organisation sought to bring some order into the chaotic conditions which prevailed, if only to provide guidance on legal matters concerning ownership of property. Indeed, one of the purposes of the Convention was to consider the disregard for order:

> Many of the saints have felt the need for chartering the Churches of God in Christ, putting them on a legal basis, and thus *obeying the laws* of the land as God says (See Rom. 13). We confess we have been 'slothful in business' on this point, and because of this many assemblies have already chartered under different names as a *local* work, in both home and foreign lands. Why not charter under *one Bible name*, (2 Thess. 2-14) thus eliminating another phase of division in Pentecostal work? For this *purpose also* let us come together.[66]

The argument's appeal to both expediency and scriptural authority becomes a feature of much Pentecostal disputation, but it is not always attended with the same success as happened in this first convention. The latter brought delegates from all over the States apart from the West Coast, and these discovered a sense of solidarity in fellowship over-riding their differences. Brumback describes the three days of this convention as 'the epitome of the basic theme of the Assemblies of God: "a voluntary cooperative fellowship" '.[67] The general designation 'Assemblies of God' was officially adopted and local churches were encouraged to adopt the new name. It was not, however, until 1927 that a constitution was set out formulating the policy of the Assemblies of God, and the General Council incorporated. Henceforth it was this Council which issued credentials to 'worthy ministers within the Pentecostal, Apostolic Faith and Church of God in Christ groups'.

Early Pentecostalism in the British Isles
In Britain the Holiness Movement did not play such a prominent role in preparing the way for Pentecostalism as was the case in the United States. But here also there was opposition from Holiness groups such as Reader Harris's 'Pentecostal Mission'. Speaking in tongues was even described as a 'satanic counterfeit'.[68] The Welsh Revival of course was a major influence in the background of Pentecostalism in the British Isles but a more immediate one was the work of the dynamic 'European Apostle' T. B. Barratt. An English methodist minister, Barratt had toured the U.S.A. in 1906-07 and he had also corresponded with W. J. Seymour the Los Angeles leader. Barratt became engrossed in the work of the revivalists and he himself experienced glossolalia at a Pentecostal type meeting in New York in 1906. He returned to Europe to labour with tremendous success in Norway, Finland and Sweden, and he is hailed as the harbinger of Pentecostalism in these and in other European countries.[69]

Alexander Boddy, the vicar of All Saints, Sunderland, went especially to Norway to observe Barratt's mission at first hand and was even more impressed than he had been with the Welsh Revival which he had witnessed at Tonypandy.[70] He invited Barratt to England, and Barratt's visit in 1907 led to a dramatic and rapid expansion of revivalism in the north-east. All Saints, Sunderland, became as important a centre for Pentecostalism in England as Azusa St. in America, and it was this spiritual awakening in the north-east as much as any that led to the inception of the Pentecostal Movement in Britain.

Apart from minor bodies like the Full Gospel Testimony,[71] Bible Colleges, some independent churches, and some small independent groups of churches, the three main bodies of Classical Pentecostalism in Britain are the Elim Church, The Assemblies of God and The Apostolic Church. Only a brief word can be included concerning each of these three developments.

Before the Pentecostal Movement had aspired to any organisation, in fact as early as 1909, a Missionary Union was formed and missionaries took the Pentecostal message abroad to Africa, China, India and elsewhere. These missionaries went more often than not with only very slender support from a local church and most went without training, apart from those who were given some training in the Missionary Training School of the Pentecostal Missionary Union. There was great activity from 1911-20, and revival techniques were perfected. It was the period which saw the birth of the Elim Pentecostal Movement as the result of the labours of the brothers George and Stephen Jeffreys of Maesteg in South Wales. Stephen, a miner, with no formal theological training, became a powerful and eloquent revivalist. He could make his delivery effective whether he addressed congregations in the London Convention, Kingsway, centres in North America, or on his home ground in the Welsh valleys. While conducting a campaign in Island Place Mission Hall, Llanelli, on a Sunday night in July 1914 it was reported that a 'vision' of a lamb appeared on the wall behind the revivalist who had preached on 'the fellowship of His sufferings'. The 'vision' later changed into the face of a suffering Christ. In retrospect, it was taken to be a sign of the great misery of the First World War, for War was declared just two weeks after the appearance of the 'vision'.

In 1915, George Jeffreys received an invitation to conduct a mission in Monaghan, in Northern Ireland, and it was there that the first Elim Evangelistic Band was formed in that year, when a young Irishman, named Ernest Darragh, became the officially designated 'evangelist'. In October 1918, the legal title 'Elim Pentecostal Alliance' was adopted by the Movement and its headquarters was established in Belfast. George Jeffreys launched campaigns in England and in Wales in the early twenties with much success. The movement next adopted the name 'The Elim Foursquare Gospel Alliance of the British Isles', and this ascription was retained until 1966 when it was changed once more to the Elim Pentecostal Churches. The 'Foursquare' in the title was to signify that the movement stands foursquare on Holy Scripture. In 1940 a rift had occurred in the Elim movement in Britain, the outcome of which was that George Jeffreys founded The Bible Pattern Church. He had urged local congregations to become owners of their own property rather than allow the Elim Property Trust to manage their affairs. He had shown ability as an expositor and also as organiser but the Pattern Church never met with the success of the parent wing of the movement. Elim Churches, however, have maintained their ground and their publication *The Elim Evangel* has a circulation of 6,000 and is distributed among 325 assemblies in the British Isles.

The distinctions between the Elim Movement and the Assemblies of God are mainly in matters of church government and administration. 'The Assemblies of God in Great Britain and Ireland' is a Fellowship of several Pentecostal groups formed in 1924 with the object of preserving 'the testimony of the full Gospel, to strengthen the bonds of fellowship between like minded believers, and to engage in aggressive evangelism at home and abroad.' The Elim Group became somewhat 'Presbyterian' in organisation while the Assemblies could be said to be more in the 'Independent' or 'Congregational' tradition with their insistence upon the autonomy of the local church This autonomy, however, did not reach to doctrinal matters and there had been some uneasiness as to the doctrinal emphases of some independent Pentecostal churches. The Welsh Pentecostal Assemblies were aware also of the pressure of the Apostolic Church in Wales and, since there seemed to be no move towards a union of the assemblies in England, some of the Pentecostals in Wales sought membership as a Welsh District Council of the Assemblies of God of the U.S.A.! As Donald Gee remarks 'this stung the English brethren into action'[72] and the outcome was the birth of an organised fellowship namely the 'Assemblies of God in Great Britain and Ireland', an organisation quite independent of the U.S. As in the case, say, of the Non-Conformist Independent Churches, the Assemblies, while autonomous, nevertheless, cultivated a fellowship of interest, purpose and activity, which in fact extended to the wider Pentecostal movement as well. Consequently, soon after the Second World War, the British Pentecostal Fellowship was formed, and one practical result was the publication of a common hymn book, namely, *the Redemption Hymnal* which has been widely used ever since by most, if not all, Pentecostal groups. Like the Elim Churches, and Pentecostalism generally, the Assemblies of God regard missionary activity as a *sine qua non* of the Church. They are in the tradition of great evangelists like Wesley and Spurgeon, and revivalists such as Finney, Moody and Torrey.[73] This wing of Pentecostalism has over five hundred assemblies and its official organ *Redemption Tidings* has a weekly circulation of over 10,000 copies.

The most highly organised Pentecostal group in Britain stemmed from the Apostolic Church of Wales. It was founded in 1917 at Penygroes in Dyfed under the leadership of a local miner D. P. Williams, and in this case links with the Welsh Revival can be historically identified. Evan Roberts the Revivalist 'laid hands' on D. P. Williams at Moriah Chapel, Loughor on Christmas Day 1904.[74] There were other links as well, since a Pentecostal group within an interdenominational 'Mission' at Penygroes were largely products of the Revival. It was from this nucleus that the Apostolic Church emerged. The 'Pentecostals' within the larger revivalist group in the village were 'led' to purchase a plot of land and 'directed by divine guidance' to erect a building upon it and to name it 'Pabell y Cyfarfod' (Tent of Meeting). This Pentecostal cell had already shown 'Apostolic' traits in its reliance upon the guidance given through prophetic utterance in the congregation. W. O. Hutchinson had already established his version of the 'Apostolic Faith Church' at Winton, Bournemouth, and his visit to Penygroes strengthened the conviction of the local group in the validity of their interpretation of the New Testament. Hutchinson consecrated the two brothers D. P. and W. J. Williams to the offices of Apostle and Prophet respectively. While Hutchinson's own movement floundered when many of the faithful forsook him, the Penygroes church flourished and grew from strength to strength, until it is now a body of some two hundred and fifty churches in Britain alone, and has spread to very many other countries.

Its spiritual descent from the Welsh Revival is acknowledged in the opening words of the Constitution of the Apostolic church: 'Whereas in consequence of the visitation of God popularly known as the "Welsh Revival of 1904-05", and by subsequent revelations to Daniel Powell Williams, Thomas Jones, Andrew Turnbull, Edgar Frank Hodges, Herbert Victor Chanter and diverse other ministers of God through the Holy Spirit, by the Word of God Written, and by the Word of God spoken, through numerous channels . . .' .[75] The ending of this same first item of the Constitution is also interesting in terms of its recognition of an emerging national consciousness, a feature which does not seem to have taken deep root in the movement subsequently. The constitution reads: . . . and there were established assemblies for the purpose of spreading and propagating those Evangelical Tenets and the truths concerning the Order of the Church (as revealed and taught by the Apostles in the Early Church and set forth in the Acts and Epistles of the New Testament) in the Principality of Wales, in England, Scotland and in Ireland, as more particularly related in the literary annals of the said Apostolic Church; and the title 'The Apostolic Church of Wales' was used and the assemblies in England, Scotland and Ireland were described as 'other assemblies in co-operation and fellowship with the above'.

Very soon, however, all the assemblies in the movement, irrespective of location, adopted the truncated designation 'The Apostolic Church'. In 1922 a 'Conference of the Denomination' was held at Bradford and that city became the home of the Missionary Headquarters of the Apostolic Church. Later the movement's Printing Press—The Puritan Press—was based here. In 1934 Glasgow became the Finance Centre of the movement but Penygroes continued to be the General Headquarters for governmental and doctrinal matters. It also provided the site for the Apostolic Church Bible School. The Apostolics claimed divine guidance in the choice of location for all these institutions.

The movement has not been as vigorous or prolific as the Elim Group or The Assemblies of God but it has had a wide outreach nevertheless. As stated, it has spread to many countries including Australia, Canada,[76] the United States and Africa, being particularly successful in Nigeria. The account of the travels and achievements of the two brothers, D. P. and W. J. Williams, is told by T. N. Turnbull in *Brothers in Arms*,[77] and he also outlines the success of the denomination. In 1920 the Apostolic Church could claim only fifty assemblies; in 1930 the number had risen to about one hundred and fifty in Britain and a further fifty abroad; by 1947 there were one thousand two hundred and fifty assemblies throughout the world and by 1962 this number had risen to well over two thousand.[78]

The Apostolic Church shares most of the fundamental beliefs of the other two main groups in British Pentecostalism but claims to be more thoroughly Pentecostal than either of the other two groups. It insists that it is more scriptural in ordering church leadership. The five offices which it recognizes are to be identified with those specified in Eph. 4:11, namely Apostles, Prophets, Evangelists, Pastors and Teachers. An Apostle is 'discovered' by the revelation of a call to the Apostleship disclosed to an 'ordained' Prophet or by a 'direct revelation to the Apostleship at a General Council'.[79] A prophet is recognized as such by the Apostleship, the latter being a number of Apostles acting in concert by authority of the council *or* the whole council of Apostles. They are 'guided by the depth of revelation coming through the channels concerned'.[80] The Apostolic Church, while it has by no means despised gifts for organisation and church government, has sought to function in accordance with its understanding of divine will as revealed in Scripture and as mediated directly to its prophets. It is not surprising, therefore, that the interpretation of glossolalic utterance is an important feature of church life in the Apostolic community.

World-wide Pentecostalism

Having looked briefly at the emergence of Pentecostalism in North America and the main groups in Britain, to give a complete picture one would have to think globally since the phenomenon spread far and wide. Here only a few observations can be made but fortunately the reader can now be referred to the work of Hollenweger as a mine of information.[81] A study of that work shows that Pentecostalism indeed does now represent a strong component within the Third Force in Christendom. In fact, the progress made in Britain is not to be compared with the huge strides made in Scandinavia, for in Norway and Sweden, Pentecostalism is stronger than any other Protestant denomination. Harper attributes the comparatively slower progress in Britain to uncertain leadership in the early stages: 'There was no one with the skill of Barratt or Pethrus to lead the movement in its earlier stages.'[82] Pentecostalism is growing more rapidly than any other religious group in France, while in Germany the movement is now overcoming the result of the setback suffered during the Nazi regime. Before and during the Second World War Pentecostal Assemblies in Germany had to be nominally identified as Baptist causes in order to survive. In the post-war period the Arbeitsgemeinschaft was formed and comprises some one hundred and fifty churches. In Italy, the Assemblies of God are the most flourishing group of Pentecostals with a membership of some one hundred thousand. The remarkable success of Pentecostalism in the U.S.S.R. is due in no small measure to the labour and courage of Ivan Voronaer who founded hundreds of Pentecostal churches during the 1920's. The story of his struggle with the Baptists, as well as with the political authorities, is told by Steve Durasoff.[83] An estimate of the number of Pentecostals in the Soviet Union at present gives a total of two hundred thousand. It is said that twenty thousand of these are seeking emigration.

Pentecostalism has by now become firmly rooted in all five continents. The Indian Pentecostal Church was founded in 1923 by a former ordinand of the Syrian Church. In relation to the total population of the sub-continent of six hundred million, one hundred thousand Pentecostals would appear to be insignificant, but in a land with so many ancient indigenous faiths, perhaps it is surprising that there are even that many. On the other hand its fervency might be expected to appeal to the more enthusiastic *bhakti* sects. South Africa has five Pentecostal organisations and the movement represents four per cent of the total population. The Pentecostal Church of Australia was founded in 1925 and merged with other groups in 1937 when the Assemblies of God in Australia came into being. The Pentecostal Church had been formed in New Zealand a year prior to Australia and the Assemblies of God General Council of New Zealand was established a little later. Here the Assemblies of God as elsewhere were strongly missionary orientated and their witnesses worked in Japan, the Pacific Islands, New Guinea and elsewhere in the Antipodes. Pentecostalism has also attracted many in Africa, especially in Ghana and Nigeria. One of the most prominent and successful leaders in Africa has been the Zulu Nicholas Bhengu and in 1962 be became the chairman of the African section of the Assemblies of God. The results of his charismatic ministry have been remarkable and his diplomacy in dealing with leaders and governments both black and white has not gone unrecognised.[84] But, of all the world's regions, the most flourishing for Pentecostalism is South America particularly Chile where, out of a population of over seven million, one in seven is a Pentecostal. While other churches decline, the Pentecostal movement continues to advance, and its phenomenal growth can be appreciated when one is reminded that there were only 10,000 Pentecostals in Chile in 1932 while now there are over a million. Progress has been equally remarkable in Brazil.[85]

As one would expect, a movement which has had to adapt to very many diverse cultures in different parts of the world, will not present an absolutely uniform structure. Local conditions give rise to differences of Pentecostal expression in Scandinavia, Germany, Britain, the Commonwealth, the United States and elsewhere. Time, too, brings changes even in the most conservative of religious traditions, and the Pentecostal movement is no exception. For instance, the early converts were drawn mainly from previous church fellowships and were grounded in Biblical tradition. Subsequently, converts seem to have a weaker background and to be less committed to moral and doctrinal standards. In the early years, the revivalists could forego the need for offices and an established ministry, but this, of course, changed quite rapidly, and bureaucratization became increasingly apparent. The tension between institutionalism and inspirationalism will remain an inevitable condition of Pentecostalism.

In spite of these changes, brought about through the contingencies of historical development or the accident of geography, Pentecostalism has been remarkably consistent in its basic emphasis.

The most anomalous of the deviations was perhaps the Jesus unitarianism in some forms of Pentecostalism in the United States, already mentioned, and the Smorodintsi in Russia. Overwhelmingly, however, Pentecostals have subscribed to the fundamental assertions of the Apostles Creed although their services do not require credal recitation. What characterizes Pentecostal groups universally is the central place given to charismatic functions in the church. 'Their only distinctive doctrines and practices centre round being Pentecostal in that they believe in the baptism in the Holy Spirit as a definite experience for Christians, received subsequent to conversion, accompanied by manifestations of the Spirit as inaugurated by the Grace of God on the Day of Pentecost, and still possible in the Church.'[86]

Glossolalia is the recognised sign of baptism in the Spirit, and at this point, before taking up the story of the Neo-Pentecostal awakening of the last two decades or so, I shall look at glossolalia in the context of the early movement. How do the early Pentecostals themselves regard speaking in tongues, and why is the phenomenon so cardinal for all their groups?

1. By H. P. Van Dusen, a former president of Union Theological Seminary, New York in *Christian Century* (17 Aug. 1955) and 'The Third Force in Christendom' in *Life* (6 June 1968).
2. See Horton Davies, 'Pentecostalism: Threat or Promise' in *E.T.* lxxvi (6) 1965, 197-9; lxxvii (8) (May 1966), 225.
3. W. J. Hollenweger, *Enthusiastisches Christentum* (Zurich, 1969) xvii; As Bryan Wilson remarks 'it was only with modern Pentecostalism that they were fitted into the regular pattern of church life', *Religious Sects* (World University Lib. 1970), 67.
4. S. Durasoff, *Bright Wind of the Spirit: Pentecostalism Today* (Hodder and Stoughton, 1972), 13.
5. For the Apostolic Church it is Jesus as the Ascended Christ.
6. C. Brumback, *Suddenly from Heaven* (Springfield Missouri, 1961), 138.
7. G. F. Atter, *The Third Force* 3rd edit. (Peterborough Ont.: The College Press, 1970), 3, cf. B. Wilson, 'A Study of Some Contemporary Groups in Great Britain with special reference to a Midland City' (Univ. of London Ph.D. thesis 1955), 37 'It is the distinctive and distinguishing doctrine of the pentecostal denominations'.
8. J. T. Nichol, *The Pentecostals* (Logos, 1966), 17.
9. World Pentecostal Conference 1952, 11 cited by Nils Bloch-Hoell, *The Pentecostal Movement* (Oslo, London: Allen & Unwin, 1964), 222 n.60.
10. Acts 2: 38 and 19: 1-7.
11. Acts 2: 4, 10, 44-46 and 19: 6.
12. Bloch-Hoell op. cit. 129.
13. An entry for 8 March 1750 in the diary of Thomas Walsh, one of Wesley's best known preachers, reads: 'This morning the Lord gave me a language I knew not of, raising my soul to Him in wondrous manner'.
14. See Steve Durasoff, *Bright Wind of the Spirit: Pentecostalism Today* (Hodder and Stoughton, 1973), 219. The Molokans, another heterodox sect of the nineteenth century, also acquired glossolalia, see W. J. Samarin, *Tongues*

of Men and Angels, 130, 184. It was the Molokans who were responsible for the conversion of the Shakarian family to charismatic faith.

15. Durasoff, op. cit., 2, 96.

16. e.g. in 1845, 1855, 1875 and 1879 see J. D. Williams, 'The Modern Pentecostal Movement in America: A Brief Sketch of its History and Thought' in *Lexington Theological Quarterly* (1974), 50-59.

17. For the antecedents of modern Pentecostalism see *Enc. Brit.* 11th edit. xxvii; Ira J. Martin, *Glossolalia in the Apostolic Church* (Berea, Kentucky, 1960); C. Braithwaite, *The Beginnings of Quakerism* (London, 1912) 53, 57, 76, 124f., 130 for references to Shakers, Quakers and glossolalic ecstasy; R. A. Knox, *Enthusiasm* (Oxford: Clarendon, 1951); K. Klaude, *The Promise Fulfilled* (Springfield Mo., 1961).

18. For the history of Pentecostalism see J. Nichol, op. cit., D. Gee, *The Pentecostal Movement* (Elim Publishing House) rev. edit. (1949); Nils Bloch-Hoell, op. cit., W. J. Hollenweger, op. cit., now in English translation by R. A. Wilson, *The Pentecostals* (S.C.M. 1972).

19. The first revival setting was a Baptist home at 214 North Bonnie Brae St., on April 9th but by the 19th the meetings were held at the Old Methodist chapel at 312 Azusa St. The room where the revivalists met only accommodated thirty people, the headroom was only ten feet, and the floor was covered with saw-dust.

20. B. R. Wilson, 'The Pentecostal Minister : Role Conflicts and Status contradictions' in *A.J.S.* lxiv (1958-9), 495.

21. Some of these offshoots are the Church of God, Anderson, Indiana; the Pilgrim Holiness Church (later the Wesleyan Church); The Pillar of Fire; and the Church of the Nazarene, see J. D. Williams op. cit.

22. W. W. Menzies, *Anointed to serve: The Story of the Assemblies of God* (Springfield, 1971), 33.

23. H. and E. Goss, *The Winds of God* (N. Y.: Comet, 1958), 128.

24. Bloch-Hoell, op. cit., 12.

25. *E.R.E.* vi 749. Many other names are associated with Holiness Movements, but none deserves to be coupled with that of Smith more so than W. E. Boardman.

26. Nichol, op. cit., 6.

27. ibid., 7.

28. Atter, op. cit., 18.

29. Mario G. Hoover, 'A History of the Origin and Structural Development of the Assemblies of God', unpublished South-West Missouri State College M.A. thesis, (1968) cited by J. R. Gaver, *Pentecostalism* (Award Books, 1971), 69ff.

30. J. D. Williams, op. cit., 52.

31. J. R. Williams, *The Pentecostal Reality* (Logos, 1972), 47n.

32. Bloch-Hoell, op. cit., 36.

33. See Nichol, op. cit., 40; Gee, op. cit., 6.

34. J. J. Morgan, *Dafydd Morgan a Diwygiad* '59 (1906); Henry Hughes, *Hanes Diwygiadau Crefyddol Cymru* (Caernarfon, 1907); T. Roberts, 'Diwygiad '59 a '60 yn Llanbedr a Thalybont, Dyffryn Conwy', in *Y Dysgedydd* 86 (1907), 314-317.

35. *E.R.E.* ibid., one must not forget of course that if the Holiness Movement led to Pentecostalism it also led to the socially aware Student Christian Movement as well as to quietistic movements.

36. *David Thomas : Founder of International Holiness Mission* n.d. 112-3; see also C. G. Williams, 'Teulu'r Gors' in *Y Dysgedydd* (1957), 258-264; 310-312; 341-343; 'Cymru a'r Mudiad Pentecostaidd' in *Y Traethodydd* cxxx (556) (1975), 180-196. Revivalists though they were, the Holiness Movements were against speaking in tongues. Reader Harris's 'Pentecostal Mission' founded in 1888 published a magazine called '*Tongues of Fire*' and an article in it in April 1907 was severely critical of the tongues phenomena. See M. Harper, *As at the Beginning* (Logos, 1965), 37.

37. David Thomas, loc. cit.
38. Gee, op. cit., 6.
39. R. B. Jones, *Rent Heavens : The Revival of 1904, Some of its Hidden Springs and Prominent Results* (London : Stanley Moulton and Co.), 25f.
40. S. B. Shaw, *The Great Revival in Wales* (Toronto, 1905).
41. W. J. Hollenweger, *Enthusiastisches Christentum*, 22; V. Synan, *The Holiness Pentecostal Movement in the United States* (Grand Rapids, Mich., 1971), 97, 119.
42. M. Harper, op. cit., 27-8.
43. Bloch-Hoell, op. cit., 32.
44. J. L. Sherrill, *They Speak with other Tongues*, 43.
45. Bloch-Hoell, op. cit, p.191, n.107.
46. See *Enc. Brit.* 14th. edit, xxii, 283; V. Synan, op cit., 99; *Diary of A. J. Tomlinson* 1901-1923, 1-111 (N.Y. The Church of God, World Headquarters, 1949).
47. Harper, op. cit., 93: C. Brumback, *What Meaneth This?* (Springfield Mo., 1947), 202 quotes from D. A. Hayes, *The Gift of Tongues* (Cincinatti: Jennings and Graham): 'This enabling to speak in what was supposedly an unknown tongue was to many people the most remarkable feature of that remarkable revival'.
48. Synan, op. cit., 119.
49. L. M. Van Eetveldt Vivier, University of Witwatersrand unpublished doctoral thesis on 'Glossolalia' (1960) 117; see also *West Africa. IX* 219 (February 25, 1905), 163.
50. Cited in E. Evans, *The Welsh Revival of 1904* (London: Evangelical Press, 1969), 59.
51. cf. D. Hughes, 'Dechreuad y Diwygiad ym Mhontycymer' in *Y Dysgedydd* 85 (1906), 519 for typical usage of the phrase 'bedydd tân' (baptism of fire): Hughes wrote of a revival meeting: 'Dyma y lle mwyaf ofnadwy y bum ynddo erioed o'r blaen i mi—dyma fy medydd tân: nid anghofiaf byth mo'r lle hwn'. (This was the most aweful place I had ever been in before—this was my baptism of fire, I shall never forget this place).
52. E. Evans, op. cit., 82.
53. E. Evans, op. cit., 195 citing from Evans Roberts and Mrs. Penn-Lewis, *War on the Saints.*
54. D. M. Phillips, *The Great Welsh Revivalist and his work*, 8th edit. (1923), 124f., cf. what may be a much earlier example of what may have bordered on incipient glossolalia in another Welsh revivalist, Hywel Harris. He relates an experience of 18th June 1735 when 'the love of God was shed abroad' in his heart 'by the Holy Ghost', and how he discovered a cry in his 'inmost soul' with which he was totally 'unacquainted before, it was this—*Abba, Father, Abba, Father*' (E. Evans, op cit., 65f.).
55. Brumback, *Suddenly from Heaven*, 58.
56. See B. R. Wilson op. cit., on the decisive role of the charismatic leader in the establishing of Pentecostal and other sects.
57. Bloch-Hoell, op. cit., 180.
58. F. J. Ewart, *The Phenomenon of Pentecost* (St. Louis Mo., 1947), 73.
59. In fact, the new doctrines effected a split of these Mennonites, but their leader, Solomon Eby, chose to adopt the new movement and became a pillar of the Kitchener Assembly.
60. 'Pentecostal Churches in Canada' in *World Pentecost* 2 (1971), 14-16.
61. Gee, op. cit., 4f. It should be pointed out that complete sanctification in the Holiness Movement is to be interpreted in a religious rather than a moral sense. It admits of moral progress and, yet, at the same time, claims a direct and immediate breaking of the power of sin! (See *E.R.E.* vi 749).
62. Brumback, op. cit., 101ff.
63. Brumback, op. cit., 102.
64. A group which published a magazine of the same name under the editorship of E. J. Bell.

65. See Brumback, op. cit., 158.
66. ibid., 157.
67. ibid., 163.
68. M. Harper, *The Twentieth Century Pentecostal Revival* (Logos, 1971 edit.), 38. Similar criticisms were made by Al White, leader of the 'Pillar of Fire', a Holiness Church in Los Angeles, who described tongues as 'this satanic gibberish' and referred to Pentecostal services as 'the climax of demon worship'. The movement has never been without its critics, but none as scurrilous in his rejection as, the eminent Congregationalist, Dr. G. Campbell Morgan, who called it 'the last vomit of Satan', Synan op. cit., 144.
69. Synan, op.cit., 114 and T. B. Barratt, *When the Fire Fell* (Oslo, 1927), 99-126. Barratt is said to have been instrumental in the beginning of Pentecostalism in Sweden, Norway, Denmark, Germany, France and England.
70. Harper, op. cit., 37.
71. Organised by the Reverend Frank Squire who also established an International Bible Training Institute at Burgess Hill, Sussex.
72. D. Gee., op. cit., 128.
73. B. Wilson, thesis, 31.
74. See 'Mining to Ministry' in *The Apostolic Herald* 12 (Nov. 1935), 3.
75. *The Apostolic Church: its Principles amnd Practices*, Apostolic Publications (1961), 11.
76. In the whole of Canada there are only nine churches and these must not be confused with the Apostolic Church of Pentecost founded in 1921 by Frank Small of Winnipeg and amalgamated with the Evangelical Churches of Pentecost of Saskatchewan in 1953, see Atter, op.cit., 102f.
77. T. N. Turnbull, *Brothers in Arms* (Puritan Press, 1963).
78. ibid., 90
79. *The Apostolic Church* etc., 93.
80. ibid., 95.
81. W. J. Hollenweger, *The Pentecostals* E. Tr. R. A. Wilson (1972).
82. Harper, op.cit., 54.
83. Durasoff op. cit., ch.vii; on religion in the Soviet Union see R. H. Marshall Jr. (ed.), *Aspects of Religion in the Soviet Union*, 1917-1967 (Chicago: Univeristy of Chicago Press, 1970); M. Bourdeaux, *Religious Ferment in Russia: Protestant Opposition to Soviet Religious Policy* (London, 1968).
84. Durasoff, op.cit., 104ff.
85. M. Harper, *As at the Beginning*, 44f.
86. *What is the Pentecostal Movement?* a booklet published by the British Pentecostal Fellowship, n.d. 10f.

CHAPTER IV

GLOSSOLALIA IN CLASSIC PENTECOSTALISM

In a proper study of religious experience and practice, it is important to pay due regard to the way in which those who claim the experience and engage in the practice, themselves, explain the nature of their participation. This, of course, is not to say that their understanding is authentic and incontrovertible, but to recognize that it is an essential component of the total phenomenon. The significance of the phenomenon for them is related to the religious milieu in which it occurs and to isolate the phenomenon from the cultural and conceptual context, which accompanies it, is to devitalise the phenomenon itself. In the Pentecostal practice of speaking with tongues at least three inter-related factors must be borne in mind: the impact of the accepted theological beliefs; the expectations these generate within the believing community and the force of both upon and within the experience of the subject.

In this chapter, I shall attempt to present the Pentecostal view of speaking in tongues. As one who looks at this phenomenon from the outside, I shall have to rely upon statements made by acknowledged representative opinion from within the movement. The main member groups of the British Pentecostal Fellowship in the British Isles are the Assemblies of God, the Elim Pentecostal Church, the Apostolic Church and The United Apostolic Faith Church. While, as we have seen, these groups differ on questions of church government, and, in the case of the Apostolics, on the question of the designation of specific persons as prophets and apostles in the charismatic ministry; otherwise, there is a remarkable degree of agreement on fundamental evangelical doctrines. They all claim reliance upon Biblical authority and regard the Scriptures as the infallible 'Word of the Lord' and the touchstone of all revealed truth. The Apostolics come in for some criticism from the others precisely because the others fear the danger of elevating the word of a modern prophet or the declaration of a 'modern apostle' above the Word of the Lord contained in Scripture. However, in their understanding of the nature and function of 'speaking with tongues', there is practical unanimity. It would therefore be tedious and unnecessarily repetitive to present the tenets of each separately. What is attempted is a general account which hopefully would meet with the general approval of most in the Pentecostal Fellowship. Neo-Pentecostalism, which emerged in the sixties, is given separate treatment in a following chapter.

Pentecostalism, with its emphasis on subjective experience rather than on the objective sanctity of institutions, shows a distaste for ritualism, and it has also, in the main, been anti-intellectualist. It is claimed that the teachings and practices of the primitive church are restored in Pentecostalism. The very term Pentecostal, so revered by member groups of the Fellowship, underlines the movement's claim for the scriptural basis of their teaching. The events recorded in Acts 2 are taken quite literally as the fulfilment of the prophecy of Joel 2: 12-19 and also of 'the promise of the Father' that Jesus would baptize His followers with the Holy Ghost (Mat. 3:11). The Day of Pentecost inaugurated a new 'dispensation', a favourite chronological term of reference in Pentecostal terminology. They see time divided into the dispensation of Law, the new dispensation of Grace inaugurated at the Day of Pentecost, and the third dispensation to be inaugurated at the Second Coming of Christ. The charismatic features of present day Pentecostalism, they maintain, are continuous with those which became manifest in Apostolic times and the promise of the Father, fulfilled on the Day of Pentecost, has been continually repeated in the twentieth century. The two distinctive gifts of the Holy Spirit in the present dispensation are Utterance in Tongues and the Interpretation of Tongues, neither having been manifested in the New Testament manner in the Old Testament.[1] The member of the Pentecostal community is expected to seek the visitation of the Holy Ghost, which in turn is deemed to be authenticated by the very same sign given to the Apostles namely speaking in Tongues.

Pentecostal writers offer various reasons to account for the marked paucity of glossolalic manifestation in the Christian Church from the second to the twentieth century. Donald Gee, for instance, attributes this lack to unbelief and the lukewarmness of the church.[2] The North American Pentecostal, Brumback, gives the sinfulness of God's people as the reason,[3] while Ralph M. Riggs says it is due to a lack of belief in the promises of God. He also advances the opinion that 'probably one reason why there has apparently been an excessive manifestation and exercise of the gift of Tongues during recent years is the *abnormal* spiritual condition of a church that has drifted tremendously from New Testament standards, and in nothing more than its denial of the supernatural'[4]. He argues that tongues had been needed once

73

again as a sign even in the church, and then, as always happens, there is the inevitable emphasis placed upon a neglected truth, or experience, when it is first restored. Can anyone really believe that tongues virtually disappeared for some eighteen hundred years due to the ungodly condition of the church and then reappeared when that ungodliness attained a certain degree of abnormality? This attempt to account for the resurgence of glossolalia is stranger than the phenomenon itself! I think Gee provides us with a better clue when he discovers that contemporary interest focuses more on experience than belief.[5] This generation, while it abhors sham in religion, is nevertheless attracted by the religious dimension *per se*. Again, the lively fervour of Pentecostal meetings where tongues occur has an obvious appeal to many who would testify that 'a church throbbing with the fullness of Pentecostal blessing is always a convincing church'.[6]

Pentecostals regard tongues as a normal feature in the New Testament and one of the nine gifts of the Spirit. Yet some of their apologists, on occasion, will admit that it is one of the least of the gifts and some will even maintain that tongues occupy a very small proportion of place and time in their public devotions.[7] At the same time, they insist that speaking with tongues is the initial scriptural sign of the baptism of the Holy Ghost, and for most, it would seem, it is the only sign. Little wonder, therefore, that outsiders consider that undue prominence is given to glossolalia in Pentecostal circles. H. Horton presents a three-fold classification of the nine Spiritual Gifts, in a manner typical of Pentecostal writers and the official statements in the handbooks of the various groups.[8] The first group are the Gifts of Revelation comprising 'A Word of Wisdom'; 'A Word of Knowledge' and 'Discerning of Spirits'. The second group are the Gifts of Power, namely 'Faith', 'The Working of Miracles' and 'Gifts of Healing' while the third group are the Gifts of Inspiration, also referred to as Vocal Gifts. These are 'Prophecy', 'Diverse Kinds of Tongues' and 'Interpretation of Tongues'.

Horton's exposition of these gifts exemplifies characteristic Pentecostal thinking and manner of exegesis. All nine gifts, it is emphasized, are supernatural and not to be confused with the product of human insight or endeavour. They are not the fruit of human intellect nor the amplification of natural persipicacity but supernaturally bestowed. All the gifts are interrelated. 'A Word of Knowledge' is disclosure of facts 'as known to the divine mind' and is a gift which may impart knowledge of men's thoughts, or lost objects and things hidden from human senses. Usually, but not invariably, it concerns the present more than the future. It is knowledge miraculously imparted and is distinct from knowledge gleaned from the study of Scripture or through exegesis. In this gift the light of God is focused upon man's physical and spiritual situation, disclosing what he otherwise would not know, such as revealing the cause of sickness or demon possession. A passage, which it is claimed illustrates the difference between 'A Word of Wisdom' and 'A Word of Knowledge', is Jeremiah 28. 'So far as Jeremiah was concerned, his knowledge of Hananiah's perfidy was a Word of Knowledge, while his prophecy of Hananiah's end was a Word of Wisdom. Both miracles.'[9] The attempt to sustain a distinction of meaning is by no means convincing and often appears strained, and, at times, confusing. The restricting of knowledge to revelation of past happenings or present events, and widsom to events in the future, is somewhat arbitrary and the citing of ostensibly supporting evidence from scripture ignores the whole of modern research into the nature of revelation and its media. What is significant is the constant reiteration of the claim regarding the supernatural source of these gifts. Discerning of Spirits is similarly entirely supernatural and its operation is to reveal the kind of Spirit, be it divine or satanic, that its activating a person. It is, therefore, to be absolutely distinguished from sagacious discernment and psychological insight. Pentecostals, like the New Testament writers, believe in the existence of evil spirits and possession and they are wary of what they regard as counterfeit satanic gifts which can work mighty miracles. Spiritism (or what is more popularly known as spiritualism) is attributed to foul spirits, simulating the spirits of the departed, for the spirits of the just are resting in the presence of Jesus till He comes, while the spirits of the wicked dead are in Hades, fearfully looking for judgement.

As in the case of the first group of gifts, it is insisted, with equal vigour, that the gifts in the other two groups are similarly of supernatural origin. At all times, there is appeal to Scriptural authority and exposition is intensely literalist throughout. It is the third group which is of immediate interest, namely, the 'Gifts of Inspiration', or, as they are also called, the 'Vocal Gifts', namely prophecy, tongues and the interpretation of tongues. In the Pentecostal view of tongues the vocal gifts are not only interrelated to the other groups but show an even greater degree of interdependence within the group itself. For instance, one avenue of prophecy is the interpretation of tongues. Let us consider then how Pentecostals explain the nature and significance of tongues.

First and foremost, as already stated, they are regarded as a sign, that is, the initial outward evidence of the inward baptism of the Spirit. This baptism is of cardinal importance in their doctrines. They do not deny the presence of the Holy Spirit in the believer before his baptism but argue that he does not receive the Spirit as 'a Person who fills his life completely' until the time of the Baptism in the Holy Ghost.[10] Some Pentecostals regard tongues as the necessary manifestation of this baptism and categorically maintain that where there are no tongues, there is no supernatural baptism. Horton, for example, states 'It is inconceivable that a supernatural experience like the baptism should exist without a distinctive super-natural evidence. Tongues is that necessary evidence.'[11] It has been maintained that everyone should speak in tongues at the moment of baptism in the Spirit even though every such person will not be able to speak in tongues afterwards,[12] but, while this is the most representative opinion of Pentecostals, some outstanding leaders have adopted a less rigorous attitude. For instance, T. B. Barratt, 'The Apostle of Europe', and L. Pethrus, the Stockholm Pentecostal leader, both allowed the possibility of Baptism in the Spirit without glossolalia.[13] Similarly, the Elim founder, George Jeffreys, modified an earlier position to allow that tongues as a sign are not always indispensable proof of Baptism in the Spirit, and this position became the accepted view of most in the Elim Church.[14] Possibly it may also represent the views of an increasing number of Pentecostals outside the Elim Church as well. J. E. Stiles Jr. writing in *Christianity Today*[15] has already discerned this trend: 'There is a growing minority among Full Gospel people who do not believe that tongues is the "only" or "necessary" evidence of the initial receiving of the Holy Spirit'. On the other hand, Donald Gee made the official Pentecostal position concerning baptism with the Spirit quite explicit: '. . . the Pentecostal Movement affirms a baptism in the Holy Spirit accompanied as at the beginning with a scriptural initial evidence of speaking with other tongues as the Spirit gives utterance (Acts ii: 4; x: 46; xi: 15; xix: 6). Even if a very few nominally Pentecostal Groups avoid dogmatising on the question of tongues as the initial evidence, the whole Movement is unanimous in affirming that the baptism in the Holy Spirit is marked by an immediate supernatural manifestation to the senses (Acts viii: 15-16).'[16] The official Year Book of the Assemblies of God speaks in the same vein when it makes clear the doctrine of that body, Article 7 declares:

We believe in the baptism in the Holy Spirit, the initial evidence of which is the speaking with other tongues as the Spirit gives utterance (Acts 2:4; 10: 44-46; 11: 14-16; 19: 6; Isa. 8: 18).

In my opinion, it is quite incongruous to infer that the Isaiah passage has a bearing upon charismatic conditions in the Christian Church in general, or upon speaking in tongues in particular, but this is typical of the way in which the Scriptures are employed in fundamentalist groups.[17] Another interesting feature of this declaration is that the utterance in tongues is firmly attributed to the Spirit. No doubt some Pentecostals think of glossolalia as the Spirit taking over and manipulating the vocal organs. Yet Donald Gee, perhaps the most influential writer from within the Assemblies movement, is more subtle in his interpretation. It is a fallacy he thinks to regard the Holy Spirit as actually doing the talking and he argues for the part played by human participation.[18] I shall return to the question when dealing with the view of inspiration generally held by Pentecostals.

Meanwhile, some note must be taken of the distinction claimed by Pentecostals concerning tongues as a 'sign' and tongues as a 'gift'. Very briefly, the sign is the utterance which is indicative of Baptism in the Spirit: 'this audible expression is the sign that those who thus speak have been baptised with the Holy Spirit'.[19] Article 8 of the 'Statement of Fundamental Truths' of the Assemblies of God reads: 'The Baptism of believers in the Holy Ghost is witnessed by the initial physical sign of speaking with other tongues, as the Spirit of God gives them utterance (Acts 2: 4). The speaking in tongues in this instance is the same as the gift of tongues (1 Cor. 12: 4-10, 28), but different in purpose and use.'[20] Subsequent utterances in tongues by the same individual are said to be the gift in operation. The distinction seems hardly necessary and does not appear to have been made in the early stages of the movement,[21] but it is a reminder that not all are able to speak with tongues after the initial experience. Those who possess the gift, however, will use it to 'edify' the church. As well as a sign and a gift, tongues are a means of worship, both privately and in the congregation, and their function as a means of worship is indicated by the expression 'praying in the Spirit' (1 Cor. 12: 15).

Believers who are not given the gift of tongues but who have experienced baptism in the spirit are said to be given one or more of the other supernatural gifts but the gift of tongues is the most usual gift among baptised believers. Gee makes the further point that the sign is spontaneous (Acts 10: 44-46) whereas the gift is subject to control (1 Cor. 14: 28). 'The initial evidence of baptism in the

Holy Ghost was given to very many people simultaneously (120 on the Day of Pentecost, Acts 1: 15 and 2: 4; a room full of people, Acts 10: 24 and a group of at least twelve, Acts 19: 7) whereas the use of the Gift is limited on one occasion to two or at the most three (1 Cor. 14: 27).'[22] As noted previously, while much is now made of this distinction, there is no discrimination made by Pentecostals between the various expressions for tongues in the New Testament namely 'new tongues' (Mark 16: 17), 'other tongues' (Acts 2: 4) and 'strange tongues' (1 Cor. 14:2, 13).

Now what precisely are tongues? Are they gibberish or real languages? There is no doubt at all for Pentecostals, that genuine tongues are languages unknown and unlearned by the speaker and for the most part not understood by the hearers either. Unauthentic and fraudulent instances would, in their view, be merely ecstatic gibberish.[23] On occasion authentic tongues may be intelligible to a listener for it is claimed that 'God can still cause tongues that we speak as unknown tongues to be heard as modern languages, understood by any foreigner that may wander into our believers' meetings'.[24] Pentecostals do not use such jargon as glossolalia and xenoglossia. For them tongues can be unintelligible or intelligible as God wills. In the light of that source, the distinction between glossolalia and xenoglossia becomes superfluous. However, in practice, tongues are mostly not intelligible, and their object of address is God and not men, yet, on occasion, as on the Day of Pentecost, hearers may identify a language known to them. The utterance in such cases has become xenoglossic but as mentioned Pentecostals do not employ these technical terms. For them, the utterance, whether it be a few syllables or more, is a language miraculously given. Sometimes, it may be understood by someone present but, more often than not, it is entirely unintelligible. Believers may on occasion sing in tongues and this is recognized by Pentecostals as singing in the spirit (1 Cor. 12: 8). This, too, it is claimed, is produced quite independently of the understanding: 'It is handing over the task of praising from the realm of mind to that of spirit. It is rising from understood words and rhythms to mystic words and rhythms learned only in the school of heaven. It is marrying mystic meanings and mystic cadences in a glorious rhapsody of adoring worship. The spirit's faculty of words and music soars infinitely beyond the compass of the mere understanding.'[25] A person who witnessed a group 'singing in the Spirit' at Rochester, N.Y. in 1907 described it in these words: 'One of our workers who had no knowledge of music and no natural voice for song, was given a like gift so that she sang as clear as a bird and sweet as an angel with a range and compass past belief. At times several sang together in perfect harmony. A dozen voices would be swelling into a grand oratorio, then sinking into the softest whispers with all the thrills and variations of a practised choir, not one of them knowing the melody until it burst from their lips.'[26]   Atter mentions a similar manifestation at a convention in Wales, when some one thousand 'sang in the spirit'.[27] The same writer alludes to a purported instance of xenoglossic song in Montreal, Canada in 1921: 'A woman who had recently received the baptism of the Holy Spirit was praying in her own home in an apartment building. She began to sing in other tongues. A Jew from a neighbouring apartment heard her. He asked her when she had learned such perfect Hebrew. She had been singing the song of deliverance in that tongue . . .'[28]

Apparently the phenomenon of singing in the Spirit was not unknown among the early Mormons and it is by no means unfamiliar still among Pentecostals of the Southern States and, indeed, elsewhere. The effect on the listener when large numbers sing in harmony in 'unknown tongues', quite unrehearsed, can be, in fact, most impressive and one can appreciate why Horton claims that 'In singing with the spirit not only the words are supernatural, but the melodies and harmonies also.'[29]   It seems to me to exercise a strange attractiveness and possesses a quality of disturbing beauty which reminds one of the effect produced by Tibetan lamas singing in concert (as in the film *Requiem for a Faith*). Through long training and practice each lama is able to produce three different notes simultaneously, and this has a remarkable effect upon the listener when a number chant together. Of course, there are differences. Pentecostal singing in the spirit is not structured and is not the result of training and practice, although frequent participation may increase fluency. Furthermore, the harmony in the case of singing in the spirit is the outcome of several voices blending and there is no hint of the vocal dexterity of the lamas, where each one produces his own harmony, so to speak. However, both can evoke a sense of fascination and mystery which one is tempted to describe as an awareness of the numinous.

Pentecostals insist that tongues do not arise from man's understanding and that they are unrelated to his linguistic ability or intellect.[30]   Has man then any part at all in glossolalic utterance, and, if he does, what is it? Pentecostal opinion is divided, as becomes evident when the views of two writers like Horton and Gee are compared. Donald Gee says that in the early church when the phenomenon first manifested itself it seems to have been 'an almost spontaneous expression of otherwise unutterable ecstasy. Acts

10: 44' but 'at a maturer period of personal experience the gift apparently came under the control of the one who possessed it (1 Cor. 14: 28)'.[31] This would suggest a willingness to recognize a human as well as divine participation in this 'supernatural' phenomenon. Pentecostal teaching, following Scriptural precedent, expects control over the utterance in the interest of order at meetings, but while the worshippers can excercise control upon whether to speak or desist from speaking with tongues, they have no part in determining the sounds uttered. Horton, like many others, thinks in terms of the Spirit taking over. He writes 'It is supernatural utterance by the Holy Spirit in languages never learned by the speaker—not understood by the mind of the speaker—nearly always not understood by the hearer. It has nothing whatever to do with linguistic ability, nor with the mind nor intellect of man. It is a manifestation of the Mind of the Spirit of God employing human speech organs.'[32] Is the glossolalist completely passive then in his experience? According to Horton, the intellect is quiescent but the will, spirit and speech organs are active. Even so there seems to be little participation by the person himself for 'both words and music arise spontaneously to the tongue and the larynx from the mind and heart and the emotion of the Holy Spirit'. Gee, it seems, is more ready to assume greater participation by the human agent, and in his view, as previously stated, it is misleading to talk of the Holy Spirit as the speaker.[33] According to him, in the inspired condition the understanding is temporarily suspended under the rush of spiritual feeling and, in that sense, the Holy Spirit is the inspirer of the utterance which comes, however, 'through human lips and from the depths of the human spirit'.[34] If it is not a case of the Holy Spirit taking over the human vocal organs to speak, and if the understanding is suspended, then the source may well be, says Gee, 'the depths of the human spirit'.[35] He does not develop the inferences, but many Pentecostals dissent from this view, as Horton does, and ascribe to the Holy Spirit a more direct causal role. Gee, in my estimate, is the more perceptive and shows a greater awareness of the implications of an anatomy of inspiration. Yet, although he traces the activity of inspiration to the depths of the human spirit, I am sure he would have been appalled at even the slightest hint of equating the unconscious with God, or with the Holy Spirit. That is, he would not wish to identify the source of inspiration and its channel of operation. The distinction between source and channel, in my view, can be sustained, while at the same time insisting that inspirational influences, however they are rationalised and conceptualised later, can operate in areas beyond normal consciousness structures. The area of operation may, for instance, be indicated metaphorically in spatial terms such as higher-consciousness or the sub-conscious. Even Horton speaks of God revealing 'to heaven sensitized human *spirit* some gleam of divine thought and illumination', but the dominant thought in his account of inspiration is of an outside influence working directly upon what he calls the human spirit, rather than the welling up of the unconscious within man. An either-or view like his would make us choose between God and the unconscious, seeing the one, in exclusive terms, precluding the other. My own feeling is that this need not be the case and that there is both immediate and ultimate causation where inspiration is concerned. There are much wider implications for this question, for inter-faith dialogue for instance. Christians, especially those in the Pentecostal sectors insist upon a power from *without* entering the worshipper. The Indian Tradition, and modern sects deriving from it in the West, tend to speak in terms of realizing the power and resource *within*. Since, for the Pentecostal, the power from *without* has to be realised *within* and for the mystical 'Indian' sects the power that is realised within oneself is not thought of as restricted and confined to the individual, it could be argued that the differences are semantic and doctrinal only rather than experiential. This is too large a question to develop here, but I hope there will be an opportunity to consider it again elsewhere.

In the Pentecostal exposition of the glossolalic state the will is considered active while the mind is passive and by-passed. To give Gee due credit, however, he at any rate acknowledges that the condition of inspiration can and does vary, in degree, as between one individual and another, and even in the history of the same individual.[36] It would be considered presumptuous by Pentecostals to offer an analysis of the process of inspiration in the glossolalic state, and they are generally content to describe it as the action of the Holy Spirit. Yet the human factor forces its attention upon the more discerning, especially in connection with the 'Interpretation of Tongues', even though this activity is considered to be as charismatic, supernatural and miraculous as glossolalia. Even Horton seems to concede a role for the human factors in this case, while, at the same time, insisting that he is not compromising on the question of the divine authorship of interpretation. He writes: 'The temperament, natural gifts and training, as well, of course as the nationality, of the possessor of the Gift will influence the statement but the Gift is not for that reason the less supernatural.'[37]

As to the function of tongues, Pentecostals have emphasized their value for both private and collective worship, but none perhaps has excelled the rhapsodical praise in Horton's description: 'Speaking with Tongues gladdens the heart of God and man. Blessed fountain of ineffable coherence, of inexpressible eloquence! This heavenly Gift will loose the spirit's tongue and burst upon the speechless heart with utterance transcending sage's imagining or angel rhapsodies.'[38] What more can be said?

As means of worship, tongues can be exercised both in private devotions as well as in believers' meetings, and, in both settings, they are said to be means of magnifying God (Acts 10: 46). They take over so to speak when intelligible utterance seems inadequate to the task. It is maintained that in tongues one does not pray with the understanding but *with* the Spirit and this is distinguished from praying *in* the spirit. The latter is taken to mean praying with the understanding.[39] Praying in tongues, on the other hand, 'is an exercise more potent in its own mysterious realm than the mightiest praying with the understanding'.[40] and it is held that St. Paul's reference to the spirit making intercession for us with groanings that cannot be uttered is to be understood in the context of glossolalia.

We are told that tongues edify the speaker only (1 Cor. 14: 4) and, that, in his spirit not his mind. One can understand this view on account of the unintelligibility of tongues, but when tongues are interpreted in the congregation they acquire intelligibility and then they are said to edify the church. It is not clear whether the tongues uttered edify 'the spirit' of the congregation even before their interpretation, as in the case of the individual tongues speaker. What most Pentecostal writers imply is that the interpreted tongues edify the mind of the congregation. Apparently the edification of the church neccessarily involves the understanding, and, therefore, the term edify must mean two different things when used of private devotion and of utterance subsequently interpreted in the congregation. Horton explains it in this way: 'As the hidden meaning of the message in tongues is made manifest through the helping gift of interpretation of tongues the whole of the church that hears it is edified. How? you say. By the simple means of informing the general mind of that which has already served as an edification of the individual spirit.'[41] It would seem then that collective edification has to involve intelligibility while private edification does not. Pentecostals have not adequately examined this distinction nor have they advanced any satisfactory explanation for the roundabout way of informing the general mind through interpretation. Why cannot the same edification be achieved through normal discourse in the first place? Why is it necessary to 'translate' the stirrings of the individual spirit into terms which appeal to the understanding of the group. Edification of the mind of the group could be attained, surely, in a more direct way, while in theory, following Pentecostal reasoning, edification of the spirit of the group could be attained by all the members speaking with tongues!

When such problems are raised, Pentecostals argue that theirs is not to reason why. In company with a host of religious sects, especially those in the Eastern mystical tradition, they would argue that when it comes to the spiritual realm intellectual categories and human logic are transcended. The Pentecostal, however, will appeal to the authority of Scripture and reiterate the Pentecostal teaching that the three gifts of Tongues, Interpretation and Prophecy are interrelated for the edification of the company of believers. Following the exhortations of the Apostle Paul, Pentecostals seek to regulate the number of tongues-speakers in the assembly and to discourage it absolutely where there is no interpreter. They argue for a balance in both kinds of speaking in tongues, private and congregational, for undue indulgence in tongues without interpretation would leave the spirit overcharged and the mind barren! In a meeting only two or at the most three should utter in tongues and no more than three messages given in tongues should be interpreted. The injunction 'Let one interpret' (1 Cor. 14: 27) is understood to signify that one individual message must receive not more than one interpretation, not that there should only be one interpreter in the congregation or for a single meeting. In practice, however, especially in some modern Pentecostal congregations, interpretation is expected from one individual and very often he will be the pastor, but, on the other hand, some Pentecostals resent this restriction upon their charismatic powers.

As stated, the ability to interpret is understood to be equally charismatic with the gift of tongues, but it involves more responsibility. It can be directed to a person or persons in the congregation or to the whole congregation as a body. More often than not, the person who has the gift of interpretation is one who also speaks in tongues freely, and it may happen that he interprets his own utterance. When tongues are interpreted, the interpretation may be longer or shorter than the utterance, as the case may be, so that it would be quite misleading to think of the interpretation as a translation in the normal sense, although it is said that on occasions it can be just that, a claim which would be hard to substantiate, in any case, when the original utterance is unintelligible. Very early in the Pentecostal movement, claims of xenoglossia were more frequent and interpretation deemed less necessary.[42]   Soon, however, there was an increased sense of need for interpretation within the Movement. As early as 1908, Barratt issued a statement on interpretation saying that it takes four different ways:

    A. A comprehensive interpretation rather than a word by word translation.

    B. An outline of the glossolalic message.

    C. An interpretation given little by little and sentence by sentence.

    D. A word by word interpretation.[43]

The Pentecostal speaks of interpretation conveying the burden of the Lord as it pressed in upon the spirit of the speaker.   It is stressed that interpretation is not an operation of the mind of the interpreter but of the 'mind of the Spirit of God', so that the interpretation is claimed to be just as much a miracle as the utterance in tongues which is being interpreted.   Pentecostals also stress their awareness of the difference between their own human thoughts and what they claim to be the Spirit-authenticated words and aver that in the act of interpretation the speaker is 'inspired' to utter. Thus Aimee Semple McPherson recalls an experience : 'The next morning where a message in tongues was given through the brother, I yielded to the Spirit, who seemed literally to lift me to my feet and spoke to me in English the interpretation of the message which had been given in tongues.   I was amazed to find how easy it was.'[44]

The contents of the interpretations are usually of a general nature comprising warnings and exhortations to the congregation, such as encouragement to pursue the spiritual path and avoid the doom which will befall the godless.   When a person interprets his own utterance it could be said that, apart from the significance his message has for the community, the interpreter is also making clear to his own understanding what has already been an edification of his spirit in tongues.   It is the message for the group, of course, which has the greater significance.   Prophetic messages can be delivered in charismatic circles by normal speech usage or by interpretation of 'prophetic' glossalic utterance.

In view of the ambiguities in the relevant scriptural support, it is not surprising that there is an ambivalence in the Pentecostal understanding of the use of tongues in relation to unbelievers.   Gee, for instance, insists that there is no instance in Scripture of the use of tongues in preaching to unbelievers[45] and we are reminded that Peter's preaching on the Day of Pentecost was in Aramaic.   Horton, on the other hand, states enigmatically that tongues were originally intended in a secondary way as a sign to unbelievers.[46] What he seems to have in mind are those instances where claims are made that the speaker actually utters an unlearned language identified by listeners, that is, when he engages in xenoglossy or what some prefer to call xenolalia. At the beginning of this century many Pentecostals went to the mission field in the firm conviction that their gift of tongues would enable them to speak to and be understood by foreigners. Later Pentecostal leaders admitted that those who based their missionary call upon a supposed gift of xenoglossy had presumed too much. Bloch-Hoell has suggested that, as far as we know, the first missionary activity of the Pentecostal Movement was a consequence of the xenolalia theory.[47]

Claims of miraculous xenoglossia are not restricted to modern Pentecostal missionary enterprise. For instance, they have been made in the past within the Roman Catholic tradition, particularly in the history of missions. The most well-known example perhaps is connected with the name of Francis Xavier. What seems to have occurred in his case, however, was that, when first confronted with a congregation whose language he did not know, he would preach in a jargon composed of several languages. With his remarkable linguistic ability, he mastered several new tongues in a comparatively short time but there is no evidence to justify the assertion of his early biographers that he had a miraculous power to speak unlearned tongues. J. Görres attributes such a gift to one Joan of the Cross (15th cent.) and relates how she could communicate to her audience in various languages what she had received from above. This was accomplished when she was in what appears to be an altered state of consciousness (wenn sie ecstatisch wurde). One day, after having been introduced to two Muslim servants who could by no means be persuaded to accept the Christian faith, she fell into a trance (Kam sie in die Ecstase) talking to them in Arabic. In response the two of them at last urgently wished to be baptized, whereupon, later on, Joan still in the same ecstatic state (in gleichem zustande) taught them the (Christian) doctrines in their own language.[48]

Due to lack of data, such examples from the past cannot be pressed as substantiation for the validity of claims of xenoglossy. The same can be said of cases from the early 'classic' Pentecostalism of this century for the reports indicate an uncritical acceptance of the language miracle. This readiness to claim xenoglossy, without attempting even to ascertain in any proper manner the languages purported to be involved, is illustrated in this statement by no less a leader than

T. B. Barratt: 'at least eight languages I spoke that night. How could I know that they were different languages? The positions of my mouth, I felt, were different. The Power took my jawbone and my tongue and expelled the languages, clearly and distinctly, while nothing in myself held back the Power. Once I felt a pain in my throat, then I believe it was Welsh I spoke, a language I know of. Another time there were nasal sounds, probably French. Italian I definitely believe I spoke.'[49]

Why were the early Pentecostals so ready to call attention to the occurrence of xenoglossy in their services? One of the reasons no doubt was the one which I think had appealed likewise to St. Luke. It heightened the sense of the miraculous action of the Holy Spirit. Furthermore, it was regarded quite literally as a means of verbal communication with foreigners. Both aspects cohere in Horton's exposition of its function:

> Now if an unbeliever, a foreigner—say a Spaniard—strayed unrecognized into a believer's meeting today (1 Cor. xiv: 23, 24), God could of course cause some saint to speak in a tongue and further cause the tongue to be Spanish, so that the Spaniard, arrested by the miracle, would say: 'How hear I this man in my own tongue, wherein I was born'?[50]

This explanation may have satisfied a good many on the theoretical level but it does not dispel the anomalous situation which existed in relation to convincing the 'foreign unbeliever', for in practice the exercise of tongues, (and that would therefore include xenoglossy), was not encouraged in the main meetings, which all and sundry could attend, but were generally restricted to after-meetings, where only the faithful gathered. There was so, to speak, a commendable reluctance to parade the gifts before unbelievers, and Pentecostals came to recognize that St. Paul laid greater emphasis upon prophecy as a means of convicting unbelievers. But what do Pentecostals understand by prophecy?

Here there is a distinct cleavage between the Apostolic church and the other main wings of the Pentecostal movement in the British Isles. The Apostolics think of prophecy in association with the office of a prophet. For them the office of prophet is one of the five ascension gifts of Christ to the Church, the others being apostle, evangelist, pastor and teacher.[51] The prophet, like the apostle, is ordained to the office and one of his functions, along with that of apostles, evangelists, pastors, teachers, elders and deacons, is church government. The other Pentecostals think of prophecy as a gift rather than a function of an assigned office. According to the Pentecostal, Horton, it is wrong for one in the act of prophesying to speak in the first person, or in the manner of the introductory announcements of Biblical prophets: 'Thus saith the Lord' or 'The Lord hath spoken', for while prophecy is divine it does not set aside human elements. In fact, his readiness to acknowledge the human element in prophecy is much more explicit than it is in his treatment of tongues, discussed earlier. But all Pentecostals have not heeded this warning and there are many examples, particularly from the Apostolic church, where the utterances of the prophet are given in the first person singular. Apostolics will not admit to the fallibility of the prophet when he is in good standing with God. If, however, the spuriousness of a message becomes apparent, it is explained as a falling away in faith or in spiritual sensitivity on the part of the prophet. The office and its function, as such, are by no means questioned. Horton, in criticism of the Apostolic position, maintains that they place the word of the prophet, alongside, and in addition to, the Word of God, whereas, at all times, it is the latter that should be the final and only criterion of the reliability and authenticity of the prophetic declaration.[52] He seems to suggest that in the Apostolic position there is a covert threat to the supreme authority of Scripture, but the Apostolics quite clearly would not contemplate such a departure. They are quite adamant that the words of the prophet must be judged in the light of the Word of God. Ireson, writing as an Apostolic, imposes both a moral condition on true prophecy and a Scriptural test: (a) The prophet's life must be holy and (b) his words must be tested by Scripture.[53] When a prophecy is predictive the Deuteronomic test of fulfilment (Deut. 18) becomes the criterion of authenticity. In fact, Ireson admits the fallibility of a person with the gift of prophecy and he concedes that he is liable to deceive or to be deceived, so once again the claim to possess charismatic gifts has to be tempered with due allowance for the imperfections of the human agency. The argument between Pentecostals and Apostolics is really one of scriptural interpretation, the latter presuming an office of Prophet as a governmental function in the church. Horton, representing the contrary view of the main Pentecostal bodies, declares that 'there is not a shred more *Scripture* authority for "set" prophets than there is for "set" speakers in other tongues (1 Cor. xii, 28)'.[54] This controversy is of no major consequence with respect to its effect upon the role of tongues. They remain a central feature in both Apostolic and non-Apostolic Pentecostal traditions. Bloch-Hoell states that prophecy is close to glossolalia, but is distinguishable by the fact that it is spoken in a language previously known by the speaker.[55] This may be the usual pattern for prophetic utterance but not invariably so. Speakers in tongues claim that a prophetic message may come through their glossolalia i.e. in a language unknown to them and unlearned. Such 'prophetic' glossolalic utterances, from a subjective viewpoint, we are told, are qualitatively different from the usual kind of utterance by the speaker. The feeling of compulsion seems to be much stronger in the case of glossolalic prophetic utterance than in 'ordinary' glossolalia. Thus we have a situation where prophecy may come through a speaker's normal every day language, or a language known to him, or through an unintelligible glossolalic utterance, which is then interpreted to make the three parts of the prophetic message complete—reception and utterance (a), interpretation (b), and acceptance by the gathered community (c).

While the spontaneous nature of the glossolalic experience is upheld by Pentecostals, nevertheless they speak of conditions which encourage the experience. Above all, the regenerated believer must seek baptism in the Holy Ghost, and, where the conditions have been fulfilled, it is inconceivable to most of them that God would withhold the blessing. This simplistic logic has led to poignant heart-searching on the part of unsuccessful aspirants, who, in the face of continuing disappointment, either redouble their effort to seek in earnest and sincere expectation, or become disillusioned and sometimes bitter. It is also not uncommon for a kind of spiritual discrimination to develop within the Pentecostal community as between the 'haves' and the 'have nots' in terms of charismatic gifts in spite of exhortations to exercise charity.

The conditions incumbent upon the seeker are threefold. An aspirant must *believe* the promise, he must desire it and he must yield to the Spirit.[56] It is emphasized that the *Holy Spirit* is neither an 'object' nor merely an experience but *a Person* and receiving the Spirit is the entry of a Holy Person into one's life. While this event is not dependent upon any intrinsic merit or degree of sanctification on the part of the recipient, it does involve a desire to reciprocate. The Spirit's desire to fill the believer must be met with a willingness 'to be made holy' thereby.

This yielding is not in fact primarily thought of as a readiness to submit to divine imperatives in moral actions, but a willingness to allow emotional upsurge free outlet in unchequered utterance at the visitation of the Holy Spirit. 'We must allow him to have His way as to the manner in which we receive His fulness. If I find spiritual and physical surgings as I seek the Lord, I must not hold back for fear of what may happen or of what others may think.'[57]

Yet it would be quite wrong to think that Pentecostals have concern only for emotional outlet and are completely indifferent to moral challenge for they see the baptism of the Holy Spirit in terms of the beginning of a new life which involves both spititual and moral advance.

The American Pentecostal R. M. Riggs sets out four conditions which prelude the baptism in the Spirit:

1. We must first be saved.
2. We must obey—that is, we must be perfectly surrendered to God.
3. We must ask.
4. We must believe. [58]

Thus the Pentecostals set conditions which do not seem to obtain in the New Testament paradigms. If certain passages are understood in a literalistic Pentecostal way, one could say, for instance, that in the case of Cornelius the bestowal of the Spirit happened simultaneously with the coming of faith (Acts 10: 44-46); the Samaritans were endowed by the Spirit not at their own request but that of the Apostles (Acts 8: 4-24) and similarly no request is made by the Ephesians (Acts 19: 1-17).

Since faith is seen as a precondition of the gift of Tongues, and, since it is held that the gift can become dormant through the lack of faith [59], there is a danger within Pentecostalism of equating the ability to speak with Tongues with the presence of faith, and, conversely, its absence with the absence or lack of faith—a distressing situation for seekers who have not attained their goal.

What of the effects of glossolalia? Here one could expect a variety of claims as varied as the persons who make statements concerning their experience. Some speak of entering realms 'that are worshipful, unspeakable, which could never be plumbed by the mind or spoken by the mouth'. [60] Horton refers to the rest and refreshing which speaking with tongues brings, and regards this as fulfilment of the promise in Isa. 28: 11, 12: 'With stammering lips and another tongue will he speak to his people, to whom he said, "This is the rest wherewith ye may cause the weary to rest; and this is the refreshing", yet they would not hear.' [61] Here is another illustration of the arbitrary manner in which texts are handled by Pentecostals. At its worst, modern scholarship is ignored completely and anti-intellectualism is evident. Horton asks rhetorically, 'Does it not plainly mean that in speaking with tongues God has designed a means whereby weary minds may cease from the fatiguing tasks of finding mental modes of expression in their devotions and cast their burden on the tireless spirit? In other tongues the spirit joyously accepts the task the mind has tired of through physical weariness and mental inability. This is the rest and this is refreshing.'[62] This is peculiar exposition, indeed, and hardly likely to convince any but literalists. On the other hand, there are many claims of the tranquillity and repose that tongues bring to the inner spirit, and their validity can be accepted without recourse to ridiculous exposition as in the example quoted. An outside observer of the stature of H.P. van Dusen, in fact, is convinced of the tranquillizing effect of the experience. Writing of a Pentecostal meeting in the Caribbean, he says, 'It seemed to me that it was a kind of spiritual therapy . . . an emotional release of an ultimately healthy kind. It left people better off: released and relaxed.'[63] Yet while some find tongues restful, others find them exhilarating and a kind of spiritual intoxication.

Since, in this chapter, what has been under consideration is the testimony of Pentecostals themselves no attempt has been made to discuss at length hostile and critical views of outsiders, nor to examine these testimonies in the light of modern theories. This will be attempted later. In subjective appraisals by Pentecostals themselves reference to joy are frequent but so also are references to paroxysms of agonised groans and cries which it is said are peculiar to experiences accompanying tongues.[64] There are references to a sense of being lost to surroundings, which would seem to support the view that glossolalia is produced in a state of dissociation. Contrariwise, others claim that their mind is quite clear when they speak with tongues.[65] Most feel strengthened in will and empowered to witness and serve with greater boldness and efficacy. There is, also, we are told, an enrichening of worship 'in the secret place as well as in the congregation of the saints'.[66]

The physical symptoms associated with the glossolalic experience by Pentecostals include weeping, jumping and laughter.[67] The latter is a well recognized feature and is considered indicative of the joy of the Holy Spirit. It does not, however, appear to be restricted to the experience of speaking with tongues and can occur independently, but is of course qualitatively quite different to ordinary mirth.

Pentecostals are aware of the dangers of excesses and are concerned to prevent the abuse of the practice of tongues. They can be abused by over-indulgence in public meetings, or, conversely, by suppressing and despising inspired utterances (1 Thes. 3: 19-21). For this reason it is emphasised that the speakers are always subject to the government of the assembly, for, according to Gee, the Lord 'will make known His mind and will through the offices of

His own appointment'.[68]   At the same time the carnal ordinances of men seeking to control the things of the Spirit is to be eschewed.[69] Gee does not show how the 'authentic' is actually to be distinguished from the 'spurious' except to appeal to what he calls 'sanctified common sense'.

To conclude this chapter, it can be stated that, in spite of some perplexing differences in the way they are explained, there is all in all a unity of emphasis on tongues among Pentecostals. They are regarded as a normal, and even a necessary, accompaniment of the action of the Holy Spirit. Believers claim that Pentecostalism's real contribution to the Church of Christ lies in this emphasis on Baptism in the Spirit and the Gifts of the Spirit and its task as bringing the fullness of the Gospel to the community of the saved.

1. D. Gee, *Concerning Spiritual Gifts* (Springfield Missouri, n.d.), 62.
2. ibid., 13, 10.
3. C. Brumback, *What Meaneth This?* (Springfield Missouri, 1947), 276, 280.
4. R. M. Riggs, *The Spirit Himself*, (Springfield Missouri, 1949), 98.
5. Gee, op. cit., 107.
6. Gee, ibid.
7. H. Horton, *What is the Good of Speaking with Tongues?* (Assemblies of God Publishing House, n.d.),4.
8. H. Horton, *The Gifts of the Spirit* (Assemblies of God Publishing House, 18th edit. 1966), 33ff., cf. the similar classification in C. C. Ireson, *The Nine Gifts of the Holy Ghost* (Tenets of the Apostolic Church) (1957).
9. Horton, op. cit., 84.
10. A. A. Hoekema, *Holy Spirit Baptism* (Grand Rapids: W. B. Eardmans, 1972).
11. H. Horton, *What is the Good of Speaking with Tongues?*, 8
12. J. D. Williams, 'The Modern Pentecostal Movement in America' in *Lexington Theological Quarterly*, 57.
13. See the 'non-Pentecostal' writer N. Bloch-Hoell, *The Pentecostal Movement*, 131.
14. Bloch-Hoell, ibid.
15. 8th November 1963, 17.
16. *World Pentecostal Conference* (1952), 73.
17. My study has brought home to me the need for an examination of the use of Scriptures in various Christian groups, and, indeed, on a wider scale, in various religions. With respect to Christian usage, I would say, that while the 'liberal' approach has perhaps neglected the contemporaneity of Scriptural revelation, resting content with attempts to establish the original meaning through critical methods, the fundamentalists have neglected the analytical problems involved in the study of the 'infallible' Bible (many of which are identical with actual problems in the study of other bodies of literature). On occasion, they insist upon a literalist interpretation, while on others, through what they sometimes call 'spriritualising the text', they are anything but literalist. What is termed 'spiritualising' is, in fact, very often an eisegetical exercise, reading for instance into the Old Testament the doctrines of a later Christian sect. Susanne Langer in a discussion of cultural conditioning contends that 'In every age exegesis has conformed to the thought form of the time' (Susanne Langer, *Philosophy in a New Key* (New York: Mentor, 1948), 15-16). This contention could be applied to scriptural interpretation in more senses than one.

Not only are there fashions in interpretation, but there are also acceptable metaphors and thought forms within individual sects, so that interpretation can become a creature which feeds on itself. On this question of approaches to Scriptures, I am grateful to Dr. Harold Coward of the University of Calgary, for points raised in discussion and for a copy of his paper 'Structures of Consciousness in Language and Revelation'. See also below chap. ix.n.34.

18. Gee, op cit., 58.
19. V. Wellings, *The Baptism of the Holy Spirit with signs following* (Tenets of the Apostolic Church No.5) (1954), 10.
20. ibid.
21. Bloch-Hoell, op. cit., 142.
22. Gee, op. cit., 142.
23. Gee, op. cit., 57, 61, 62, 96, and, on the American scene, Brumback, *What Meaneth This?*, 112 n.1
24. Horton, op. cit., 25.
25. Horton, op. cit., 21-22.
26. S. Frodsham, *With Signs Following* (Springfield Mo., 1941), 72.
27. G. F. Atter, *Rivers of Blessing* (Toronto, 1960), 33.
28. ibid.
29. Horton, *The Gifts of the Spirit*, 24; See, however, what is said below in chapter nine concerning the mysticism of sound, and what is said in Islamic hadiths concerning the heavenly melody heard by the Prophet.
30. Horton, ibid., 150.
31. Gee, op. cit., 57.
32. Horton, loc. cit.
33. Gee, op. cit., 58
34. ibid.
35. ibid.
36. Gee, op. cit., 102.
37. Horton, op. cit., 171.
38. Horton, op. cit., 152-3.
39. Horton, op. cit., 155.
40. Horton, op. cit., 156.
41. Horton, *What is the Good of Speaking with Tongues?*, 19.
42. In the Azusa St. revival, a person speaking in tongues was said to have spoken Russian, and the following claims were also made: French was spoken by a woman whose only language was English; Hebrew was spoken by a lady who had no previous knowledge of it, and several 'tongues' were identified as African dialects. See S. H. Frodsham, *With Signs Following* (1946), 35ff. On further early and later claims of xenoglossy see J. D. Williams, op. cit.
43. Bloch-Hoell, op. cit., 145.
44. ibid.
45. Gee, op. cit., 56f.
46. Horton, op. cit., 191.
47. Bloch-Hoell, op. cit., 87
48. J. Görres, *Die Christliche Mystik* (Regensburg: Wren 1837), 194.
49. Bloch-Hoell, op. cit., 143f.
50. Horton, op. cit.
51. Apostolic Tracts: *The Ascenscion Gifts.*
52. Horton, op. cit., 180ff.
53. Ireson, op. cit., 20ff.
54. Horton, *The Gifts of the Spirit*, 181.
55. Bloch-Hoell, op. cit., 147.
56. *How to be filled with the Spirit* 10-11, booklet published by the British Pentecostal Fellowship.
57. ibid., 12.
58. Riggs, op. cit.

59. Ireson, op. cit., 29.
60. Ireson, op. cit., 24.
61. Horton, *What is the good of Speaking with Tongues?*, 23.
62. ibid.
63. J. L. Sherrill, *They Speak with other Tongues* (Hodder & Stoughton, 1964), 26f.
64. A. J. Tomlinson, *Diary* 1, 73-4.
65. J. T. Nichol, *The Pentecostals* (Logos, 1971), 37.
66. Tract, Personal Testimonies : *I received the Holy Spirit*, 5.
67. ibid., 11-12; 18.
68. Gee, op. cit., 87.
69. Gee, ibid.

93

CHAPTER V

NEO-PENTECOSTALISM AND GLOSSOLALIA

The resurgence of Pentecostalism in the last two decades or so, manifest in independent groups as well as within traditional churches, is one of the most, if not *the* most, remarkable phenomenon in the Christian world at the present time. Like the emergence of the Classic Pentecostal Movement[1] at the beginning of the century, what has now come to be known as the Neo-Pentecostalism[2] of the fifties, sixties and seventies has no one great founder and yet its story, like that of the earlier Movement, cannot be told without reference to leaders and personalities. Neo-Pentecostalism first appeared between 1955 and 1956 within Protestant circles, while the emergence of Catholic Neo-Pentecostalism[3] is traced to a group of Catholic laymen who met at Duquesne University in Pittsburgh in 1966, whence it spread in 1967 to a congress at the University of Notre-Dame, Indiana, U.S.A.[4] What will be attempted in this chapter is an estimate of the contribution of some personalities to the growth of Neo-Pentecostalism, a brief account of Catholic Pentecostals, followed by a summary of some of the features characterising glossolalia in this renewal of charismatic experience.

There is, at least, one most significant difference between the new and the older movement. Whereas in the main, by the coldness, the indifference, and, on occasion, even the physical persecution they suffered at the hands of traditional churches, the Pentecostals of the early part of the century felt obliged to form their own sects which soon became denominations, while Neo-Pentecostals, on the whole, have remained within the main line traditions.[5] In many instances Neo-Pentecostals claim to have re-discovered the significance of their particular liturgy and are not embarrassed by the credal assertions of the churches which nurtured them. In the case of independent groups of glossolalists, members may come from several denominations or they may have no previous religious alliegiance. These groups may meet in private houses or on university campuses, and there is very little, if any, organisation.

At the beginning of the century 'Classical Pentecostalism' was disparagingly called 'The Tongues Movement' while the Neo-Pentecostal resurgence of the sixties is frequently referred to, even by non-Pentecostals, as the Charismatic Movement or the Charismatic Revival[6]. The traditional churches are still wary, sometimes perplexed, and, in some instances, divided by this new phenomenon. They mostly reserve judgement while expressing a great deal of interest. Yet, it can be said that contemporary leaders of the Christian Church have, on the whole, taken a more positive view of both Pentecostalism and Neo-Pentecostalism, and their attitude, generally speaking, has been much more appreciative than that of their counterparts at the beginning of the century. Bishop Newbigin referred to it as a 'third stream of Christian tradition'.[7] Similarly H. P. van Dusen spoke of a 'third mighty arm of Christian outreach',[8] and of 'The Third Force in Christendom'.[9] To be precise, van Dusen was thinking not only of Pentecostals but also of groups often disdainfully referred to as 'fringe sects'. But, of the twenty million representing the 'third force', he singles out the 8.5 million Pentecostals as the largest single group.[10]

This fairly positive acceptance of the charismatic upsurge by so many leaders of authority is beginning to have its impact on individual churches, synods, and even the World Council of Churches. A document entitled 'Spirit, Order and Organization' approved by The Faith and Order Commission of the World Council of Churches in August, 1971 states:

> The emergence and growth of Independent Churches in Africa, of Pentecostal Churches and of Pentecostalism within the established Churches could point to some deficiency of traditional Roman Catholicism and Protestantism. Theology and practice of these Churches has to a large extent neglected the Holy Spirit, except for some standard affirmations about his continuing presence . . . The doctrine of the Holy Spirit and even more the sensitivity to his active presence in the Church and the world were and still are underdeveloped in the western tradition of Christianity.[11]

John A. Mackay, another eminent ecumenical leader, has expressed approval of both Pentecostalism and Neo-Pentecostalism. He writes:

> Pentecostalism represents the rediscovery of the Holy Spirit as a reality in the life of the Church and in the lives of Christians. Despite all the aberrations that may be attached to it in certain places, Neo-Pentecostalism is a rebirth of primitive First-Century Christianity. Protestants who glory in belonging to

95

Classical or Radical Christianity will look down their noses at Pentecostal Christianity only at their peril. For this is a phenomenon of God's spring-time.[12]

The same writer in the light of post-Vatican II developments made what may well be a prophetic statement:

> In a time of revolutionary change—when all institutional structures are crumbling in the secular and religious order, when the churches of historical Protestantism are becoming increasingly bureaucratized, when more and more church-members are meeting in an unecclesiastical underworld, when the Roman Catholic Church is developing evangelical concern and a deepening sense of what it means to be Christian, when the charismatic movement is growing across all boundaries —might it not happen that unless our Protestant churches rediscover dimensions in thought and life they are losing or disdaining, the Christian future may lie with a reformed Catholicism and a matured Pentecostalism?[13]

Writing of the scene in North America, Robert Rice, a Presbyterian minister and missionary to Korea, stated in 1963: ' . . . no denomination of any consequence in Protestantism today has remained unaffected by this new awakening which began imperceptibly more than a decade ago. It has broken out in the most unexpected and unrelated places: giving new dynamic to high Episcopolians in northern inner-city parishes, and evangelistic drive to Southern Baptists of the deep South. Dozens of college, university and theological seminary campuses from east to west coast, have seen their share of this new charismatic breakthrough.'[14] This article goes on to give examples of healing and the transformation of lethargic and indifferent Christians into active agents of the Holy Spirit. A more recent estimate of the numbers involved in the charismatic renewal in the United States reports 'at least 11% of the membership of Episcopalians, Baptists and Presbyterians and untold numbers of Lutherans and Roman Catholics'.[15] Prof. J. Rodman Williams adds this comment[16]: 'In the Presbyterian church alone the number of ministers in the "Charismatic Communion of Presbyterian Ministers" has grown from 54 in November, 1966 to 268 in May, 1971.[17] The overall rise of Pentecostalism is so rapid that only the word "upsurge" seems appropriate.'

In Neo-Pentecostal circles the atmosphere is not so exuberant and uncontrolled as in some of the early meetings of the classical

96

Pentecostal movement. Glossolalia is practised both privately and in congregation, but without evidence of excessive abandon. In fact, those who experience it, very often speak of subdued emotion and refer to the normality of the occasion. The case of an architect in Wimpole Street in London on 27th August, 1962, illustrates the normalcy which attends it. He writes of his initial experience of glossolalia in his bath: 'I was speaking as easily as though I were speaking English. Though the language was unintelligible to me, it was definitely a language. The rather strange thing about this which I had not expected was that this was quite unemotional, except for the controlled joy and the edification spoken of by Paul. My mind was perfectly clear and I was listening with great interest and noticing recurring phrases. Although I could not at that moment speak a word of English, I nevertheless was giving praise to Jesus with my conscious mind, I was also thinking quite practically while the flow continued inexorably.'[18] While he claims the flow to be inexorable, nevertheless, he was able to interrupt it and to desist from continuing although he felt he 'could have continued all night'.

Another difference is that in Neo-Pentecostal circles far more participants are drawn from the professional and middle classes than was the case with the earlier Pentecostal Movement. John L. Sherrill provides confirmation of this view in an interesting list of occupations of people associated with Neo-Pentecostalism.[19] The anti-ritualism and the anti-intellectualism of the early Pentecostalism are also in abeyance, but in both early and Neo-Pentecostalism speakers have a strong awareness of need and an orientation of expectation.

Classical Pentecostalism appealed to Scriptural Authority as the final touchstone to vouchsafe the authority of doctrine or pronouncement, but while in the process of routinisation from the early years of the revival to the inevitable structuring and organizing of groups and denominations, its dynamic power at all time was derived from the inner experience of Pentecostals. Neither doctrine, theology nor church order, in their view, could replace the *experience* of the Holy Spirit. J. Rodman Williams has expressed this emphasis very neatly:

> Pentecostals tend to be quite wary of talking about a 'theology' or 'doctrine' of the Holy Spirit. It is not that they are fundamentally anti-theological but that they fear the elevating of theology or doctrine to the first place. With the traditional definition of theology as 'faith seeking understanding' the

97

Pentecostals would largely agree; however, they would want to be sure that the faith was not merely formal or intellectual (surely not merely a *depositum fidei* to be accepted), and that it be profoundly experiential. Pentecostals are basically people who have had a certain experience; so they find little use for theology or doctrine that does not recognize and, even more, participate in it. They are convinced that the shape and content of their experience, which they believe to be of the Holy Spirit, is essential to the life and thought of the whole church.[20]

This comment on the priority of the experience holds true also of Neo-Pentecostals and, perhaps, even more so, since, in their case, there appears to be a greater flexibility in theological and doctrinal matters, necessarily so, since Neo-Pentecostals continue in churches of quite different traditions. While the major Protestant churches, and similarly the Roman Catholic Church, paid little heed to Classic Pentecostalism, regarding it as a fanatical fringe element of the Christian Church, and, indeed, in some cases, spurning it as satanic, this is no longer the case, as the many references to the 'Third Force' have shown. Again, while Classic Pentecostalism was cradled-in the atmosphere of the Wesleyan Methodist revivalist tradition and the Holiness Movements, the charismatic revival of Neo-Pentecostalism occurred in the historic Protestant churches from the fifties to the sixties of this century and around 1967 began to manifest itself also within Catholicism.

The growth of Neo-Pentecostalism in the last twenty years is not the result of massive campaigns and conventions but rather of the spreading of influence and expectation through personal contact. As indicated earlier, this history cannot be written without writing of individuals and their convictions, experience and dedication. All that will be attempted here is to mention the work of some of these personalities in the United States where Neo-Pentecostalism first emerged, followed by a very brief account of the charismatic revival in the Roman Catholic Church. Finally, the chapter will conclude with some observations on the nature of glossolalia in this new upsurge of Pentecostalism.

Key-personalities

When the full history of Neo-Pentecostalism comes to be written, much will need to be said about key personalities such as David du Plessis, Demos Shakarian, John L. Sherrill and David Bennett. These cannot be described precisely as leaders of the movement, nevertheless, they, and others like them, have made a significant contribution to the new upsurge of Pentecostalism and the growing acceptance of glossolalia. My reference to their contribution is brief, but the bibliographical guidance will direct the reader to fuller accounts of their work and experiences.

David du Plessis was brought up in South Africa in a Pentecostal home and he himself became a Pentecostal minister. In 1908, two Americans, who had experienced the revival in Azusa St., Los Angeles, arrived in Johannesburg to conduct a mission. It was in this way that du Plessis's father was won over to Pentecostalism, and the son followed in his father's footsteps. At the age of thirty-seven, he was General Secretary of the Apostolic Faith Mission of South Africa. A prophetic vision in 1936 granted to Smith Wigglesworth, a well known Pentecostal, was taken to indicate that David du Plessis was to play an even greater role not only in South Africa, but on a world-wide scale. At that time, there was no reason to believe that this was even a remote possibility and du Plessis shared the prevailing attitude of other Pentecostal ministers to what they considered to be the shiftiness, luke-warmness and, indeed, the blindness of their colleagues in traditional ministries. By 1949 du Plessis had become secretary-general of the World Conference of Pentecostal Fellowships. By this time he was much-travelled but this had not meliorated his censoriousness of non-Pentecostals. He claims that a change came about as the result of his experiences subsequent to a car accident in Tennessee in that same year. Whether this was the cause or not, from that time forward, he became much more interested in what he called liberal churchmen and kinder in his thoughts towards them. He also found his attitude changing to the World Council of Churches which he had hitherto regarded with typical Pentecostal suspicion.[21]

Gradually he was drawn into ecumenical circles and in 1954 he accepted the invitation extended him by Dr. Visser't Hooft, then secretary of the World Council of Churches, to attend the Second Assembly at Evanston. Two years later he addressed a meeting of ecumenical leaders and described his experience thus: 'That morning something happened to me. After a few introductory words I suddenly felt a warm glow come over me. I knew this was the Holy Spirit taking over. But what was He doing to me? Instead of the harsh spirit of criticism and condemnation in my heart, I now felt such love and compassion for those ecclesiastical leaders that I would rather have died for them than pass sentence upon them.'[22]

From that time he became much sought after internationally as a speaker, although some of his erstwhile Pentecostal colleagues had serious misgivings about his new role. He continued to emphasize the primacy of experience and to encourage glossolalia as evidence of Baptism in the Holy Spirit, but he also revelled in dialogue, particularly on campuses and in meetings with the faculty of the most prestigious universities in the United States and elsewhere. In fact, he sustained an incredible number of contacts with 'Spirit-filled' people of all denominations. Reluctant Pentecostals have had to sit up and take notice particularly when du Plessis maintained, that while there is a great outpouring of Pentecost today among the 'liberal' and 'ecclesiastical' sections of Christendom, there is none at all among the 'Fundamentalists'.[23] He has been criticised for his ecumenical activities and the emotionalism of his meetings, but no criticism has halted his enthusiasm and he has gained the confidence of very many in Protestant and Catholic circles, and must be one of the major figures in the resurgence of Pentecostalism.

No account of Neo-Pentecostalism would be complete without reference to The Full Gospel Business Men's Fellowship International and this, in turn, involves the story of an immigrant Armenian family—the Shakarians who originally came from the town of Kara Kala in Armenia.[24] In 1855 a peasant Russian boy had predicted disaster for the Christians in Armenia if they would not heed the warnings of the prophecies and emigrate. This illiterate boy drew maps and charts which indicated America as the country to which they should escape. The same peasant renewed his prophecies forty-five years later and as a result many of his friends and neighbours left for America in 1900 taking with them the written prophecies.[25] In 1905, the Shakarians followed the earlier emigrants, while those who remained ridiculed the whole exercise. There had already been several local revivals in many parts of the Balkans and Russia where the Charismatic features of Pentecostalism, including glossolalia, had been prominent. It was mainly the Pentecostals who took the prophecies of doom seriously and all the Pentecostal families had left Armenia before the devastation of their country by the Turks in the first World War, when three million Armenians were killed, including the inhabitants of Kara Kala.

By accident, Demos Shakarian came across the Azusa St. meetings in Los Angeles and immediately recognized the Pentecostal nature of the services. Thus it was, as Harper says,[26] two streams converged. Isaac Shakarian, the son, became an extremely successful business man, but Demos, the grandson, named after the grandfather, did not seem able to reconcile God and Mammon so adeptly. When he was hit by financial disaster he then saw his life-work to be in the service of God and he began to sponsor revival meetings. He became obsessed with the idea of a Pentecostal businessmen's group and found encouragement from the revivalist Oral Roberts to develop his plans. As a result the Full Gospel Business Men's Fellowship International[27] was founded in 1953 under the presidency of Demos Shakarian, who remains in that office still. The Group has been a powerful force in Neo-Pentecostalism supporting the publication of its monthly magazine *Voice* which has a circulation of over a quarter of a million. The movement is now world-wide with chapters increasing, especially in Europe, and Harper attributes its phenomenal success to the fact that is is a lay movement 'free from the shackles of ecclesiastical sanctions'.[28] It is not, of course, meant to compete with the churches and many church leaders participate in it.[29] It has one serious disqualification which would prevent it ever becoming a church—it is restricted to men only, in accordance with the vision claimed to have been received by its founder. The orthodox critic could no doubt raise other questions particularly concerning its simplistic conceptions of faith and its too ready notion of the success of the godly, both in wordly as well as in spiritual terms, but there is no disputing the fact that it is a prominent vehicle of charismatic renewal, and, through its meetings, many hard nosed business men have come to experience speaking in tongues and other 'Gifts of the Spirit'.

Another key figure on the Renewal scene is Dennis J. Bennett, formerly rector of the episcopal church of St. Mark's, Van Nuys, California. A divinity graduate of the University of Chicago and a highly respected priest with a record of sixteen years of 'successful' ministry behind him, in 1960 he felt obliged to resign from St. Mark's when his new-found Pentecostal experience of speaking in tongues threatened to divide the congregation. He was convinced, however, that he should remain within the episcopal church, and accepted an invitation to St. Luke's Seattle, a church which, at that time, was on the brink of extinction. The story of the remarkable transformation of that church is a moving one[30] and it soon became a vibrant centre of charismatic revival. Bennett was also much in demand elsewhere and he travelled extensively both in the United States and abroad to Pentecostal and non-Pentecostal groups. One of these journeys brought Bennett to England, where he met with members of the 'Fountain Trust', a group of ministers and laymen who had come together to give responsible leadership to the Charismatic Renewal. Bennett came at the invitation of Michel Harper, the executive secretary of the Trust, who had previously given up parish work to take on this new task. In Britain, Bennett conducted seminars at Magdalen College, Cambridge, and preached at Great St. Mary's, the University Church of Cambridge, Southwark Cathedral and Westminster Chapel. He addressed four of the major theological colleges of the Church of England and also talked to several groups of clergy in London and the provinces. Of this trip he says: 'Although my main ministry on this trip was teaching, many received the Holy Spirit, and some were delivered from sickness . . .'[31]

In Bennett's autobiographical account one cannot fail to observe an increasing capitulation of the intellect to 'the spirit' on his part, and he does not adequately discuss the resolving of the tensions he obviously felt, particularly when he first came to Pentecostalism, between his dedication to truth as a trained theologian and his new understanding of the Bible. It is often the case with those who claim Pentecostal experiences, that, while their account of their experience is convincing enough, when they offer an interpretation of it, backed by scriptural exegesis, they irritate and annoy because of their literalism. This is a pity, because the genuineness of their experience does not depend upon the validity of their explanation, but one would expect a divinity graduate to strive to do justice to both.

Such a task could well be performed by members of the Fountain Trust in Britain. This was established as a charitable Trust in 1964 with its prime aim the renewal of the spiritual life of the Christian Church.[32] The Trust declares its aims in these words:

'It seeks to enable Christians to receive the power of the Holy Spirit and the full benefits of the charismatic renewal while at the same time safeguarding these blessings from dangers such as fanaticism, division and doctrinal error.'[33] This is, indeed, a formidable but welcome endeavour.

While the Trust convenes conferences it does not organise groups of its own but works through existing channels, particularly sympathetic churches and house groups, mainly in Britain but also abroad. It publishes its own magazine *Renewal* (edited by Michael Harper), and has set up a Library for Charismatic study at 23 Spencer Road, East Moseley, Surrey. Such a centre will be a boon for the growing number of people, especially students of the Charismatic movement, who know of the vast literature on this subject but find it exasperatingly difficult to track down much of it in scattered denominational magazines.

Testimonies in *Renewal* witness to the impact made by news of revival in espiscopal churches in the U.S.A. on members of the Anglican community in Britain. This was strengthened by visits from people such as D. J. Bennett, and Jean Stone a member of his church of St. Mark's Van Nuys,[34] and since that time the renewal has advanced significantly, contributing not only to the life of the churches but to movements such as the New Life Foundation 'a social and evangelical ministry to the drug scene'.[35]

Catholic Pentecostals

While Pentecostalism gained momentum within Lutheranism and among Episcopalians, it also began to attract Roman Catholics. One estimate of the number of Catholic Pentecostals sets it as high as one million in 1970.[36] This may have been too high and no statistical evidence is provided. That the increase has been substantial is, however, well founded. The renewal is now so strong that Michael Harper felt justified to raise some challenging issues.[37] He urges Charismatic Catholics to make their voice heard on matters such as inter-communion, the population problem and contraception, and above all Vatican politics. Social concern and involvement in the community certainly should stem from every Christian commitment but Harper's criticism could be directed equally to classic Pentecostalism, which has had seven decades of consolation, but has never been in the vanguard of social involvement due to its theology of partition of the wordly and the spiritual.

Catholic Pentecostalism is a most interesting development, for in the eyes of the early Pentecostals, Rome was the manifestation of Anti-Christ. As yet the Charismatic Renewal is too contemporary for a proper assessment, but in the coming years it will be fascinating to see how, on the one hand, the Roman Catholic Church accommodates the charismatic surge, and even more so, how the established Pentecostals react to the new life within Catholicism. Many important issues will become the focus of dialogue, but while as yet, these have been on the whole successfully avoided, there are nevertheless signs of challenging enquiry. Thus Michael Harper in an editorial with the provocative heading 'Too respectable too quickly?'[38] asks the Roman Pentecostals: 'Is there anything which the Holy Spirit has shown you which is at variance with the infallibility of the Pope?' Many Catholic Pentecostals have in fact testified to a new appreciation of the liturgy of their church and a profounder experience of the sacraments. Catholic theologians have encouraged them to work out their worship and theology in harmony and not in conflict with their traditional faith. It remains to be seen whether this is possible. But, in Harper's view, 'the present indications are that Roman Catholics within the movement are not changing their doctrines, only re-emphasising some and relegating others to the sidelines'.[39] He wonders whether support would still be forthcoming from the church hierarchy if things were otherwise. I shall return to this question, but, first of all, a brief account of the emergence of the Catholic Renewal is called for.

Whereas there had been sporadic and isolated instances of the Pentecostal experience for a decade previously, the beginning of what later became a unified Pentecostal movement within the Catholic church occurred at Duquesne University in 1966. From there it spread to the University of Notre Dame and to the Newman Centre at the University of Michigan. From these and other independent beginnings it spread throughout North America and to Europe, Africa, Latin America, Australia and New Zealand.[40]

What is of significant interest is that the initial impetus for renewal came about through non-Catholic agency. At Duquesne University the outbreak of Pentecostalism occurred through the intermediary of David Wilkerson's book, *The Cross and the Switchblade*[41], a book which has subsequently sold in millions. Wilkerson, an Assemblies of God minister, took on the task of evangelising among the youthful gangs of New York City in 1958, and the 'Teen Challenge' movement resulted from his efforts. In other centres such as Boston, Rochester, St. Louis and Cincinnati, Catholics first encountered the charismatic revival through the F.G.B.M.F.I., and, while the revival began as a lay movement, it spread rapidly and some clergy were caught up in it.

The story of the outbreak of Pentecostalism in Catholicism is told by Kevin and Dorothy Ranagham in *Catholic Pentecostals*[42] and since it is an account written from within the charismatic revival it has added interest. The first stirrings occurred in Pittsburgh, Pensylvania in the fall of 1966 when several Catholic laymen on the staff of Duquesne University came together 'to consider prayerfully' the need for renewal in the Church. Already during the National Cursillo Convention, in August, 1966, they had been introduced to John Sherrill's account of David Wilkerson's experience in *The Cross and the Switchblade*. They studied the book after their convention and came to the conclusion that what it said of the work of the Holy Spirit was, indeed, a very traditional and very Catholic doctrine. Yet there was a newness and freshness in the presentation deriving from a sense of the immediacy of the power, so that the book absorbed their attention for a further two months, checking it with Biblical sources and church doctrines. They began to seek groups with first hand experience of the power of the Spirit, being well aware that they would possibly encounter anti-Catholic scruples. In their quest they were pleasantly surprised to discover the quiet and dignified manner in which members of the groups spoke in tongues, and also the general wholesomeness of the theological views expressed. The exposition of scripture was somewhat strange, however, and reminded them of the observations and the highly allegorical manner of the Church Fathers.   It was at such a group meeting in the home of Miss Florence Dodge, a Presbyterian, on 13th January, 1967, that the first instance of glossolalia occurred amongst the Catholic seekers.   Ralph Keifer reports his initial experience in his straight-forward manner: 'I prayed in tongues rather quickly.   It was not a particulaly soaring or spectacular thing at all.   I felt a certain peace—and at least a little prayerful—and truthfully, rather curious as to where all this would lead.'[43]   Later, Keifer 'laid hands' on others who similarly claimed to have received the baptism in the Holy Spirit.   The four Catholics from Pittsburgh who had received the 'Pentecostal' experience by February, 1967 insisted that it presented no intellectual and no theological problem:

> Further it was in no way considered a sacrament of the Church, much less a replacement for the sacraments.   On the contrary, everyone experienced a greater desire for participation in the sac-ramental life of the Church than before.   'Baptism in the Holy Spirit' is not something replacing baptism and confirmation. Rather it may be seen as an adult reaffirmation and renewal of these sacraments, an opening of ourselves to all their sacramental graces . . .
> . . . Nothing was contradictory to the teaching of the Church, on the other hand, the results of 'Baptism in the Holy Spirit' seemed to be greatly desired by all Christians, establishing as they do a closer union with Christ.[44]

From the staff the awakening reached students at Duquesne. What came to be known as the Duquesne 'week-end' is now claimed as one of the most remarkable incidents in the story of the Pente-costal movement.   Many students had hours of 'near physical experience of the Lord'.   'Some praised God in new languages, others quietly wept for joy, others prayed and sang.'[45]
The news from Duquesne reached the campus of Notre Dame University.   Meetings were held with no manifest charisma, but nevertheless a newness of faith was experienced.   These led to united meetings of Roman Catholic intellectuals steeped in the liturgical tradition of the Church and evangelicals from a theological

fundamentalist background. Such a meeting on 13th March, 1967 at the home of the president of the local chapter of the F.G.B. M.F.I. led to many of the Catholics receiving 'that night the gift of praising God in strange languages'.[46] In close-by Michigan State University, the spark from Pittsburgh had already been lit. The Michigan and Notre Dame groups came together and the movement then spread rapidly to other University centres. It survived and overcame adverse and misinformed press publicity and, in the summer of 1967, the Notre Dame Group received encouraging reports from all over the country indicating that their experience was not altogether new to Catholics. According to the Ranaghans, indeed, individuals had previously received the experience, but it seemed they were the first to do so in a group.[47] Within a year it was claimed that there were at least 5,000 Catholic Pentecostals in the United States and several hundred in Canada. While these were mostly young people, there were also some groups of middle aged Catholics. A weekend ecumenical conference on Charismatic Renewal was held at the Bergamo Retreat Centre in Dayton, Ohio to consider the questions posed by Pentecostalism within Catholicism. The Ranaghans quote a report on the conference from *Time* 14th June, 1968: 'This month an ecumenical assembly of 20 churchmen met at Roman Catholic Dayton University in Ohio to discuss the movement . . . Surprisingly, even some Roman Catholic participants at the Dayton conference were cautiously optimistic about the prospect of incorporating glossolalia and healing into the spirituality of their church. Biblical scholar Barnabas Mary Ahern, a *peritus* (expert) at the Second Vatican Council, argued that glossolalia should be "running at the very heart of the Church" since "the life of the Church is the life of the Spirit!" '[48] In less than three years the estimated number of Catholic Pentecostals had risen to 30,000 in the States, 2,000 in Canada and about 200 in England.[49] Some idea of the growth of Catholic Pentecostalism can be obtained by reference to the number of people attending the National Conferences on Charismatic Renewal in the Catholic Church. In the first conference held in April, 1967, 45 attended but more and more attended each subsequent conference.[50] At the seventh conference in 1973 there were 20,000 from 25 nations and in 1974 the number attending reached 30,000.[51] In 1974 the American Catholic charismatic monthly, *New Covenant*, had a circulation of around 40,000, and an estimated 600,000 people involved in the Renewal. In 1973 the first International Leaders' Conference was held in Grottaferrata a suburb of Rome. Thirty-four countries were represented but it emerged that there were 90 countries in which Catholic charismatic groups had appeared. Pope Paul VI personally received thirteen of these leaders.[52]

It is too early to grasp the tremendous significance of this upsurge of 'Pentecostalism' within Catholicism. Yet perhaps it should not be all that surprising, for, both the evangelical fundamentalist previously associated with Pentecostalism, and the tradition-honouring Catholic, acknowledge the value of Authority in the church, even though the nature of the authority differs in classical Pentecostalism and Catholicism. What is interesting so far is the apparent integration of sacramental liturgy and the power of charismatic experience in the testimonies of the 'pioneer' Catholics who make their witness in the volume by K. and D. Ranaghan.

Some see this Pentecostal effervescence within Catholicism as the answer to the call to prayer by Pope John XXIII:

> Renew in our own days your wonders as of a New Pentecost: and grant that Holy Church . . . may extend the Kingdom of the divine Saviour, a Kingdom of truth, justice, love and peace.[53]

This prayer was recited daily by millions of Catholics until the closing of Vatican II on 8th December 1965.[54] Within fifteen months of the end of Vatican II the Charismatic Renewal had been born in the Roman Catholic Church.

Such was the phenomenal spread of the renewal that an investigation was ordered by the American Bishops and the commission released a rather cautious but not a discouraging report on 4th November 1969. The text of the report released by Bishop Alexandra Zaleski reads:

REPORT OF THE EPISCOPAL COMMISSION STUDYING CATHOLIC PENTECOSTALISM TO THE AMERICAN BISHOPS, NOVEMBER, 1969.

Beginning in 1967, the so-called Pentecostal Movement has spread among our Catholic faithful. It has attracted especially college students. This report will restrict itself to the phenomenon among Catholics. It does not intend to treat classic Pentecostalism as it appears in certain Protestant ecclesial communities. In the Catholic Church the reaction to this movement seems to be one of caution and somewhat unhappy. Judgements are often based on superficial knowledge. It seems to be too soon to draw definitive conclusions regarding the phenomenon and more scholarly research is needed. For one reason or another, the understanding of this movement is coloured by emotionalism. For this there is some historical justification and we live with a suspicion of unusual religious experience. We are also face to face with socially somewhat unacceptable norms of religious behaviour. It should be kept in mind that this phenomenon is not a movement in the full sense of the word. It has no national structure and each individual prayer meeting may differ from another.

Many would prefer to speak of it as a charismatic renewal. In calling it a Pentecostal Movement, we must be careful to disassociate it from classic Pentecostalism as it appears in Protestant denominations, such as the Assemblies of God, the United Pentecostal Church, and others. The Pentecostal Movement in the Catholic Church is not the acceptance of the ideology or practices of any denomination, but likes to consider itself a renewal in the spirit of the first Pentecost. It would be an error to suppose that the emotional, demonstrative style of prayer characteristic of the Protestant denominations has been adopted by Catholic Pentecostals. The Catholic prayer groups tend to be quiet and somewhat reserved. It is true that in some cases it has attracted emotionally unstable people. Those who came with such a disposition usually do not continue. Participants in these prayer meetings can also exclude them. In this they are not always successful.

It must be admitted that theologically the movement has legitimate reasons for existence. It has a strong biblical basis. It would be difficult to inhibit the working of the Spirit which manifested itself so abundantly in the early Church. The Participants in the Catholic Pentecostal Movement claim that they receive certain charismatic gifts. Admittedly there have been abuses but the cure is not a denial of their existence but their proper use. We still need further research on the matter of charismatic gifts. Certainly the Vatican Council presumes that the Spirit is active continuously in the Church. Perhaps our most prudent way to judge the validity of the claims of the Pentecostal Movement is to observe the effects on those who participate in the prayer meetings. There are many indications that this participation leads to a better understanding of the role the Christian plays in the Church. Many have experienced progress in their spiritual life. They are attracted to the reading of the Scriptures and a deeper understanding of their faith. They seem to grow in their attachment to certain established devotional patterns such as devotion to the Real Presence and the Rosary.

It is the conclusion of the Committee on Doctrine that the movement should at this point not be inhibited but allowed to develop. Certain cautions, however, must be expressed. Proper supervision can be effectively exercised only if the Bishops keep in mind their pastoral responsibility to oversee and guide this movement in the Church. We must be on our guard that they avoid the mistakes of classic Pentecostalism. It must be recognized that in our culture there is a tendency to substitute religious experience for religious doctrine. In practice we recommend that Bishops involve prudent priests to be associated with this movement. Such involvement and guidance would be welcome by the Catholic Pentecostals.[55]

One can perhaps detect a similar note of concern if not unease in a statement of Pope Paul VI to International Leaders of the Charismatic Renewal (10th October 1973) :

The spiritual lives of the faithful, therefore, come under the active pastoral responsibility of each bishop in his own diocese. It is particularly opportune to recall this in the presence of these ferments of renewal which arouse so many hopes.

Even in the best experiences of renewal, moreover, weeds may be found among the good seed. So a work of discernment is indispensable; it devolves upon those who are in charge of the church, 'to whose special competence it belongs, not indeed to extinguish the Spirit, but to test all things and hold fast to that which is good' (cf. 1 Th. 5: 12 and 19-21) (Lumen Gentium, 12). In this way the common good of the Church, to which the gifts of the Spirit are ordained (cf. 1 Cor. 12: 7), makes progress.[56]

The mood of the American Bishops moved from one of caution to one of basic approval in 1974 although they continued to be aware of several of the dangers involved. While the Catholic Renewal shares many, if not all, the features of Neo-Pentecostalism there is an obvious effort to retain the Catholic identity. Even at Charismatic Conferences the various denominations have held their separate services.[57] Most Catholics would like to think that the Renewal can be seen as a truly Roman Catholic movement and not just an infiltration of Pentecostalism into the church.[58]

In fact, Pentecostalism within Catholicism has not been uniform

and stereotyped and there appear to be diverse patterns. Fr. Massyngberde Ford selects two types:
(a) a structured type or facet modelled on Ann Arbor, Michigan and South Bend, Indiana and
(b) the less structured groups which are found in Southern California, New Mexico, Louisiana, Canada and 'overseas'.

The first group follow seminars which are 'religiously indifferent' i.e. they do not include the Roman Catholic doctrine of sacramental theology, neither do they normally involve priests. They seem to form their own community or covenant group. They encourage speaking with tongues but do not seem to emphasize social concern or social action. In the case of the less structured group, however, the Church is the community and it is both clerically and sacramentally orientated. 'Some celebrate the Eucharist after their meetings or on days of recollection, and confessions are available for the sacrament or confession . . . These groups have wholly integrated the modern sacramental teaching and practice of the church in a most effective way. For them the church is their community and their covenant renewal is found in the Sacraments of Baptism and the Eucharist.'[59] This type employs the liturgy, rosary, silences, the Jesus prayer[60] and seems to have a greater concern for social involvement. Sandidge is probably right to sense that this division is somewhat exaggerated for it is too early yet for stereotypes to become so consolidated.[61]

As we have seen the official response in the Catholic Church has been Gamaliel-like so far in its caution but some individuals have been more outspoken than others. Cardinal Leon Joseph Suenens, for instance, is explicitly in favour of the charismatic renewal even though he is not quite as enthusiastic concerning the place of 'tongues' within it. Nevertheless, he believes they are God-given. He writes : '. . . what's being spoken about and experienced in the charismatic renewal as baptism in the spirit, is what we're looking for'.[62] While he welcomes the renewal he does not understand 'Baptism in the Spirit' in the same way as Pentecostals. For him as for most Catholics it is not a new endowment but a revitalization of the sacramental graces confessed at water baptism.[63] He expresses his dissatisfaction with mere structural changes in the institution and calls for a new sensitivity to the Holy Spirit. 'Tongues' are recognized as 'something God gives, that has a value', and he apparently accepts the validity of claims of xenoglossia for he finds in the recognition of actual languages 'a glimpse of mission'. He stresses the complementarity of the renewal and the institution

110

finding in the former an important contribution to ecumenicity.

The big theological question, not only for Catholics but for all branches of the Christian Church involved in this movement, is how can faithfulness to tradition and sensitivity to the promptings of the renewal be reconciled? Neo-Pentecostalism, speaking generally, so far at any rate, claims to be easily accommodated within a number of different Christian traditions. D. J. Bennett, for instance, writes of an Episcopalian Group meeting: 'The people who attended are the same people who take part in and rejoice in the highly structured and formal services of their Church at public worship on Sunday, and would be the first to object to any modifications of it.'[64] The Lutherans, and other traditions, similarly, encourage respect for the traditional forms of worship of their church. A group of Carmelite Sisters who experienced speaking in tongues made similar discoveries to other Neo-Pentecostal groups. They found a greater harmony and unity among them, a greater freedom of expression in prayer, more openness to one another, and a new discovery of what worship is. The Psalms came alive for them and they found a willingness to take the gospel literally.[65] It has even been claimed that Catholic charismatics generally become more faithful to their church's teaching and spiritual tradition than other Neo-Pentecostals to their respective traditions,[66] but there is as yet insufficient material on which to base any sweeping generalisation of this nature. Harper wonders how long this accommodation of the old by the new and vice-versa can survive.[67] Whatever the eventual outcome, it cannot be denied that as far as the present scene is concerned, there is a rediscovery of doctrines on charismatic gifts within the traditional churches, and the resultant enrichening of tradition. Consequently, the 'New Penetration' is as apt a description as any of the renewal.[68]

A conference held at the University of Surrey, Guildford in July, 1971, was a significant milestone in the history of the new charismatic movement in Britain. 700 Christians from over twenty countries and several different denominations came together to explore 'The Fellowship of the Holy Spirit'. The conference was sponsored by Michael Harper of the Fountain Trust and the speakers, drawn from several religious traditions, included Methodist Leslie Davison, Roman Catholic Kevin Ranaghan, Pentecostal Ralph Wilkinson, Presbyterian Rodman Williams and Anglican David Watson. Also present was David du Plessis, described by James Dunn in his report on the Conference[69] as 'the senior statesman in neo-Pentecostal circles', and as one who 'has done more to commend the message of the Holy Spirit baptism and gifts in more parts of the world than any other man'. Asked about the significance of the Guildford conference du Plessis replied: 'I believe the conference is the demonstration of what Holy Spirit ecumenism is ... The Holy Spirit is creating ecumenicity without organisation, bringing about a unity which organisation so far has failed to achieve.'

One of the intriguing innovations at Guildford was a Roman Catholic 'Charismatic Mass' conducted every morning on the campus. Here, new forms of worship, including singing in tongues, were integrated with traditional liturgical forms.[70] James Dunn in his interrogation of Kevin Ranaghan, elicits some replies which give a clear and succinct Catholic view of the charismatic renewal and particularly the role of glossolalia.

As in Suenen's view, mentioned above, baptism in the Spirit is not seen as *receiving* the Spirit but as a *renewal* or a *release* of the Spirit objectively given in the sacrament of initiation. This seems a departure from the 'Pentecostal' view of baptism in the Spirit as an experience subsequent to, and distinct from, conversion. And yet the difference of description may bear little relevance to the actuality of the situation. Whether one speaks of renewal or initial reception the resultant experience appears to be of the same kind. In both, there is an awareness of a new fullness of power, whether it be a release of what was already present *in posse*, or a new realisation theologically conceived by Pentecostals as a new invasion of the Spirit. According to Ranaghan, when a Catholic prays for baptism in the Spirit, what he asks for is that 'an individual's baptismal initiation be existentially renewed and actualized'.[71]

In reply to Dunn's reference to F. D. Brunner's charge[72] that Pentecostalism encourages Christians to look for something more than Christ, Ranaghan argues that, in Catholic Pentecostalism, what is sought and practised is 'the gradual deepening of the spiritual life' and, to a further question concerning the importance of glossolalia, he pleads for the normalcy of the experience for all Christians. He does not see glossolalia as baptism in the Holy Spirit but as a consequence of it.[73] He would not deny that one can be filled by the Spirit *without* the tangible evidence of tongues, but, in practice, 'from a powerful and expectant confrontation with the Spirit of the Lord the gift of tongues emerges again and again if not as an "evidence" certainly as a "consequence" in the lives of many Christians'. This position is less rigid and schematized than the classic Pentecostal standpoint, a topic to which I shall return.

Another aspect of the Dunn-Ranaghan dialogue will also be

pertinent to later discussion. When asked whether he thought of glossolalia as a language, Ranaghan replied:

> It may be a language. It may be on the other hand some sort of deep psychic release that expresses itself in something similar to a language. I've personally been involved in about 12 instances where the languages have in fact been recognized. Yet I've heard other things and wondered whether that could possibly be a language—some sort of ecstatic rumbling or gurgling or something like that.[74]

This response shows that within Catholic Pentecostal circles, as among other Neo-Pentecostals and 'classic' Pentecostalism, glossolalia can take many forms varying in degrees of articulateness. The incidence of the experience in such theologically disparate groups also strongly suggests that the experience, although it may be coloured and affected by the beliefs held by a group, as I believe it is, is not dependent upon an identical interpretation of Scriptures. For instance, the relation of the Spirit to baptism, is as previously noted, a familiar controversial issue but glossolalia seems to transcend doctrinal differences.

The Catholic Renewal has its severe critics as well as its defenders. The main targets for criticism are the excessive influence of leaders, the dangers of pragmatic use of 'prophecy' and a Protestant charismatic fundamentalist interpretation of the Bible. On the other hand, attitudes to the mother church have by no means been uniformly congenial, for there are Catholic charismatics, who have severely criticized the church that nurtured them, because they feel the Holy Spirit cannot work in Catholicism. According to Sandidge, Flemish Underground Catholic charismatics 'were unhappy with the power invested in the Pope and the many "historical contradictions" in Catholicism'. They reject the authority of the Pope, the bishops and the priests, the systems of confession, and what they called 'magical power of the priest'.[75] The impact of Pentecostalism, then, could become a threat of schism in Catholic circles for there are already those who can no longer consider themselves, theologically speaking, Catholics and those on the other hand who find their previous beliefs and practices more meaningful.

But how have Classic Pentecostals reacted to the Catholic Renewal? It is not so long ago that Pentecostals referred to Rome as the Beast of the Apocalypse and Catholics harassed Pentecostals. Now Pentecostals seem to rival some of the Catholic bishops in their caution.[76] Some are downright suspicious, as this statement illustrates:

'If, for example, the Belgian Cardinal Suenens says nice things about the gifts of the Spirit and their operation in the Church, then I want to know for myself what his attitude toward the Word of God is in order to know what value his sayings have. If it is obvious that he subordinates the Word of God to his theology and that he, being a child of his time, is an enthusiastic participant in the dialogue between the world religions, then the charismatic renewal which he advocates, cannot stand the test.'[77]

This writer illustrates the exclusivism of conservative Pentecostalism with his preclusion of the possibility of participating in both inter-faith dialogue and charismatic renewal. His statement raises a whole host of theological problems for any who are not content with an exclusivist position.

Classic Pentecostals, in fact, have been wary not only of Catholic charismatics but also of Neo-Pentecostals generally. All the more reason, therefore, to welcome the change of tone which appears in the minutes of the Pentecostal European Conference held in Norway 7-13th July, 1975. The general conclusion of that conference was that 'God was indeed at work in these other communities, that Pentecostals must remain open and withhold judgement for now upon the Renewal'.[78] In the previous year The Assemblies of God, U.S.A. had taken a similar positive stance. The Rev. T. F. Zimmerman, General Superintendent, had issued this statement concerning the New Pentecostalism on 30th December, 1974:

'We should not be subject to our traditions nor hold spiritual pride. Neither should we allow exclusiveness to characterize our role in today's world. However, proven guidelines and Bible doctrines should not be abandoned.'[79]

In Britain likewise one detects a mellowing of mood on the part of some Classic Pentecostal leaders. Thus Pastor Percy S. Brewster, revered minister of the City Temple, Cardiff writes:

Between the established Pentecostal movements and the new outpouring of the Holy Spirit upon the traditional churches there has developed a grave gap. The Pentecostal movements have for many years been in isolation and it would seem the time has now come when we have got to emerge from our prejudices that have built up over the years and extend our hand of friendship and fellowship to all who are saved and baptized in the Holy Spirit.[80]

In these statements one clearly detects a greater readiness to acknowledge divine activity in systems other than that of the speaker.

114

At the same time, here, as in Catholicism, there is also equally clearly, a reluctance to compromise and the theological challenge of Charismatic Renewal remains to be faced honestly and with courage on both sides. It is a challenge not only for Catholics and Pentecostals but also for Anglicans and Non-conformists, and most of all, perhaps, for the evangelical wings of these churches which, to say the least, appear to be discomfited by the charismatic upsurge. In a recent article Dr. Ken Walters, Professor of Applied Mathematics at the Univeristy College of Wales, Aberystwyth, bemoans the antagonistic attitude of the Evangelical Movement of Wales to the charismatic renewal.[81] According to Professor Walters, Welsh evangelicalism has in the past been almost entirely Non-conformist but now there is an upsurge of evangelicism among Anglicans. He believes, however, that the Welsh-medium churches, predominantly Non-conformist, have a greater openness to the renewal than their English-medium counterparts. I would hesitate to share this view but what is irrefutable in his estimate of the situation is the statement that Wales has been virtually untouched by the charismatic renewal. However, even since he wrote those words, conferences have been held in Aberystwyth itself in 1977 and 1978, and it is too early to assess their impact as yet.

Glossolalia in Neo-Pentecostalism

What remains to be done in this chapter is to summarize very briefly some of the most prominent features associated with glossolalia in the Neo-Pentecostal witness. A contrast has been made between the emotional excesses of the 'classic' type of Pentecostalism and the more orderly and quiet conduct of the neo-glossolalists. While this distinction generally holds, neverthless one ought to bear in mind that the Neo-Pentecostals do not despise the emotional. Indeed it seems to be very important for them, but overt behaviour is not an infalliable indicator of an inner emotional state. There is more freedom and feeling of comradeship in Neo-Pentecosal group meetings than in the average traditional service, but one could not describe their environment of worship as abnormal. Many who experience glossolalia in such groups speak of tranquillity and normalcy and deny any untoward ecstatic behaviour.[82] One can, indeed, contrast these descriptions with reports of the fervour of earlier Pentecostal meetings, such as, for instance, the one conducted by W. J. Seymour in a Los Angeles home before the opening of the Azusa St. Mission, when the floor gave way under the stamping of feet of the worshippers![83] The Neo-Pentecostals may be more

subdued but still the physical impact of the experience can sometimes manifest itself in many features shared with the earlier Pentecostals. Reading the testimonies of Neo-Pentecostals, both Catholics and others, who have experienced speaking in tongues, one
could compile a long list of the physical and psychical concomitants
of the experience. Here are some of those which seem to occur
quite frequently and which could easily be paralleled by phenomena
from the earlier literature of Pentecostalism:

Sweating,[84]

crying and weeping,[85]

rapid beating of heart,[86]

shaking,[87]

a sensation of a powerful force, like 'a massive jolt of electricity',[88]

hearing sounds like rushing wind,[89]

laughter,[90]

raising of hands,[91]

a sense of bodily warmth,[92]

In one case glossolalia was preceded by an act of exorcism when
the smell of burning sulphur was experienced.[93]

The effect on participants in Neo-Pentecostalism is often reminiscent
of the claims made by the earlier type of Pentecostal, and likewise
by present day members of 'classic' Pentecostal churches:

Claims of peace, joy and refreshment are frequent;[94]

lethargy becomes activity;[95]

timidity becomes boldness of witness;[96]

the desire to read the Scriptures is increased;[97]

a sense of fulfilment;[98]

a stabilizing and integrating effect;[99]

increased fellowship.[100]

Like the earlier Pentecostals, the present day glossolalists also
experience singing in tongues,[101] sometimes they speak in tongues
individually,[102] sometimes collectively.[103] There is also a similarity
in that, in the main, the onset of glossolalia is halting and only a few
words or syllables can be uttered at the initial experience.[104] In
some instances, however, there may be fluency from the beginning.[105]
It is most unusual for an interpretation to be forthcoming for an
initial glossolalic utterance and in Neo-Pentecostalism it seems it is
still more unusual for the same person to utter and to interpret, as
in the experience of A. L. Dunance.[106] It is also not customary for
very young children to speak in tongues, but Bennett[107] recounts
the case of a six year old. The question of infant participation has
on occasion bothered the earlier Pentecostal churches too, and it
may not be so unusual.

116

There is an interesting mention in the Ranaghans' *Catholic Pentecostals* of a 'written tongue' but insufficient details are given to determine whether by this phenomenon is meant automatic writing. Claims of xenoglossia are also made in Neo-Pentecostal circles as they had been in the classical pattern.[108]

As in the case of the early Pentecostals, likewise in Neo-Pentecostalism, utterance in tongues normally only comes about where there is expectation and an act of volition to receive the Spirit. There are instances where it seems to come involuntarily but even there one can usually detect some psychological preparation for it. Neo-Pentecostals, like their forerunners, say there is no compulsion to speak. Thus Bennett writes of his experience:

> There was nothing compulsive about it. I was allowing these words to come to my lips and was speaking them out of my own volition, without in any way being forced to do it. I wasn't 'carried away' in any sense of the word, but was fully in possession of my wits and my will power.[109]

This too, as we saw was Harper's experience[110] and both statements confirm the self-awareness of the glossolalic.

While speaking is an act of volition, the content of the utterance is quite independent of the speaker so it is claimed. As one of my students expressed it in recalling his glossolalic experience : 'My mind no longer connected with my mouth.' The same student, who belonged to a Neo-Pentecostal group in Canada, gives an interesting account of his first experience of prophesying in tongues. Here in fact, unlike his usual gossolalic experience, there was a sense of compulsion, and it proved irresistible. He tried to resist the urge to utter in deference to the 'prophets' who were acknowledged as such in the group and he was also afraid to break in on one of the others. His description is most graphic:

> I felt as if someone had attached a hose to my foot and was pumping up water, which was slowly but surely filling me up —reaching my waist, my chest, my shoulders, and my mouth. I had absolutely no control over my vocal chords. I couldn't even stop the prophecy if I wanted to, because I had lost control of opening and closing my mouth. Just before I spoke my jaw began to quiver and shake slightly. I knew then that I would not be able to prevent the prophecy, so I stopped all resistance and submitted to the Spirit thankfully.

117

Thus it will be seen that the glossolalic event, although it has a discernible pattern of physical and psychical impact, is not so stereotyped as to be without variation. Incidentally the prophecy mentioned above was given in a slow and deliberate voice, whereas the subject's glossolalia was normally uttered rapidly.

In two areas, as previously noted, the Neo-Pentecostal activity differs from the 'classic' pattern. In the latter, on the whole, although Boddy and others tried to work from within their own church, the movement felt impelled to break new ground and sever its connection with the traditional churches. In the new awakening there is no urge nor apparently, as yet, in the vast majority of instances, a need to break away, for there seems to be in most cases no diminution on the part of Neo-Pentecostals in their participation in traditional institutional church life.[111] There is also a greater awareness and involvement in human concerns, such as war and peace, race relations and poverty, although very much more could be done in this direction, but at least the sensitivity is there and the dichotomy of 'church' and 'world' is not so drastic as in the case of early Pentecostalism.[112]

I have already noted that present day Neo-Pentecostals are drawn from all strata of society and particularly from the intellectual and professional classes. It cannot be said therefore that they are economically deprived. There would seem to be a stronger case for theorising in terms of psychological inadequacy. This question will be raised later in dealing with modern evaluation but it will be convenient at this point to identify some testimonies to inadequacies or maladjustment prior to the glossolalia experience which the latter is claimed to have resolved. These are taken from the testimonies in the F.G.B.M.F.I. series *The Acts of the Holy Spirit among the Episcopalians/Presbyterians/Baptists/Methodists Today*.[113] Many are testimonies from clergymen or ministers, who previously experienced frustation in their church work.[114] Other cases are linked with the after-effects of involvement in wars, including World War II, the Korean War or the Vietnam War.[115] Such involvement seems to have induced remorse, perlexity, or left a physical affliction.[116] Alcoholism was a source of concern for some,[117] others speak of an inner discontent;[118] disillusionment with affluence;[119] emotional stress or emotional 'scars'.[120] In one case surviving an air crash led to a more serious attitude to religion;[121] other testimonies speak of failure in career;[122] an agonising bereavement;[123] domestic tensions;[124] illness in family.[125] In each case the experience of discovery of the Spirit led to a victory where previously there had been failure, frustration and disillusionment.

Whether the witnesses suffered more inadequacies than could be expected in a random sample cannot be determined here, and much more research needs to be done in this area. The question will be raised again in dealing with modern evaluations of glossolalia, but it does seem that there could be a correlation between a sense of failure, and the desire for 'tongues'.

As to the function of glossolalia, which will also be discussed more fully presently, it can be mentioned now, in the light of my brief survey of Pentecostalism, that Pentecostals new and old, Catholic and non-Catholic, find in their glossolalia a means of praising God with a deeper sense of devotion and a greater closeness to the divine object than previously experienced. They claim new dimensions in their devotional life and a sense of contact with the unseen power of the Spirit which enables them to transcend their failings and incompetence. Where the verbal flow of everyday language is inadequate and ceases they believe the tongues of the spirit take them beyond the reaches of the intellect into the presence of the Holy Spirit. This, for them, sufficiently answers the question of purpose: 'Why Speak in Tongues?' Most of them would agree with the reasons given by a representative of 'classic' Pentecostalism, Harold Horton of the Assemblies of God in 'What is the Good of Speaking with Tongues?'[126] Among them are:

> that God might speak supernaturally to men;
> that men may speak to God supernaturally;
> to magnify God; to edify ourselves;
> that (with interpretation) the church may be edified;
> that our spirits might pray—as distinct from our understanding;
> that we might sing with the spirit;
> that with the help of interpretation of tongues our understanding might be informed of the mysteries our spirit rehearses in prayer in other tongues;
> that our intellects might rest in adoration;
> that believers may profit.

Most Neo-Pentecostals, like their earlier 'classic' counterparts, see their ability to speak in tongues as God-given and so as miraculous. This belief has a strong uplifting power and gives the speaker a confident assurance that he has been accepted by God. Yet Cardinal Suenens does not see 'tongues' in this light and he describes them as a form of non-discursive prayer—a preconceptual expression of a spontaneous prayer which is within the reach of everybody.[127]

119

Miracle? Peculiar but not supranormal? What has modern research to say? Glossolalia has attracted the attention of behavioural scientists and it is to the topic of glossolalia and the researchers that I now turn in the next three chapters.

1. This expression is now generally adopted for the groups which separated from the historic churches in the early part of this century and developed their own denominational structure.
2. The term refers to a movement which stresses the Holy Spirit's ministry since the late 1950's and cuts across denominational contours. In the U.S. alone it is estimated that over forty denominations are involved (Watson E. Mills, 'Reassessing Glossolalia' in *Christian Century* lxxxviii : 41 (14 Oct. 1970) citing a survey by S. C. Plog.).
3. I regard the Catholic phenomenon as part of the wider Neo-Pentecostal movement despite the disclaimers of some Catholic writers. They prefer to speak of Renewal since they want to separate the Catholic phenomenon from Pentecostalism with its Protestant associations. The term 'Charismatic Movement' is likewise rejected by some Catholics who argue that what is important is the total renewal of the Church, not the charisma, J. L. Sandidge, 'The Origin and Development of the Charismatic Movement in Belgium' unpublished thesis for the degree of Master in Moral and Religious Sciences, Katholieke Univ. Te Leuven, (1976).
4. J. Massyngberde Ford, 'Neo-Pentecostalism within the Roman Catholic Communion' in *Dialog* 13 (1974), 45-50; K and. D. Ranaghan, *Catholic Pentecostals* (1969), 6.
5. See John L. Sherrill, *They Speak with other Tongues*. (London: Hodder and Stoughton, 1965) 46ff.
6. e.g. R. Rice, 'Charismatic Revival' in *Christian Life* xxv (Nov. 1963), 30-32—J. Rodman Williams, 'The Upsurge of Pentecostalism' in *Reformed World* 31 (8) 1971, 339-348.
7. *The Household of God* (1953), 95.
8. *Christian Century* (17 August, 1955).
9. *Life* magazine Vol. 50 (9 June, 1958) cf. John A. Hardon, *The Protestant Churches of America*. (Garden City, N.Y.: Image Books, 1969), 23-24 who also speaks of a 'Third Force'.
10. A table is appended to van Dusen's article giving the relative numerical strength of the U.S. Third Force Groups in 1958.

Churches of Christ	1,700,000
Assemblies of God	482,352
Church of God in Christ	360,428
Seventh-day Adventists	283,140
Church of the Nazarene	281,646
Jehovah's Witnesses	226,797
Church of God (Cleveland, Tenn.)	147,929
Church of God (Anderson, Ind.)	127,395
United Pentecostal Church	125,000
International Church of the Foursquare Gospel	110,568
Pentecostal Church of God in America	103,500
Christian and Missionary Alliance	83,778
Apostolic Overcoming Holy Church of God	75,000
The Church of God	70,911
Independent Fundamental Church of America	65,000
Pentecostal Assemblies of the World	60,000
The Pentecostal Holiness Church	47,323

11. *Faith and Order Louvain* 1971 (Geneva, World Council of Churches 1971), 131-132 cited by J. Rodman Williams, *The Pentecostal Reality* (Plainfield N.J., 1972), 19.
12. J. A. Mackay, *Ecumenics: the Science of the Church Universal* (Englewood Cliffs: N. J. Prentice Hall, 1964), 198 quoted by J. Rodman Williams, 'The Upsurge of Pentecostalism' in *Reformed World* 31 (8) (1971), 342.
13. J. A. MacKay, *Christian Reality and Appearance* (Richmond Va: John Knox Press, 1969), 88-89, quoted by J. Rodman Williams op. cit., 343.
14. ibid., 30.
15. *Christianity Today*, January. 1971, 27.
16. op. cit., 339.
17. His source is 'Newsletter of the Charismatic Communion of Presbyterian Ministers', edit. Rev. George C. (Brick) Bradford, 428 N.W. 34th St., Oklahoma City, Oklahoma 73118, No. 13 (May 1971) Part A, 3.
18. M. Harper, *As at the Beginning* (Plainfield, N. J. Logos, 1965), 82; apart from the 'normality' of the occasion, this case also illustrates the control exercised by the Speaker and his self-awareness.
19. *They Speak with Other Tongues*, 67:
'My research had indicated that in the early days the Pentecostal movement tended to draw most heavily on semi-educated or unskilled people. Now, just glancing over a part of my correspondence file I noted this interesting breakdown of occupations:

mathematician	F.B.I. Agent	attorney
psychiatrist	registered nurse	porter
doctor	Automobile Agency	State Department
police captain	owner	official
dentist	psychologist	oil magnate
real estate agent	Hollywood photo-	Jewish rabbi
housewife	grapher	restauranteur
minister	actor	surveyor
dairyman	airplane manufac-	biologist
tool and dye man-	turer's wife	professor
facturer	I.C.B.M. engineer	headmaster
salesman'		

20. J. Rodman Williams, *The Pentecostal Reality*, 59f., cf. L. Christenson, *Speaking in Tongues*, 40 'There is a sound theology for the baptism with the Holy Spirit. But the baptism with the Holy Spirit is not a theology to be discussed and analysed. It is an experience one enters into'. This emphasis upon the experiential dimension is not the monopoly of any one faith. The claim is often made by Oriental religions that one has to experience the Reality which they point to and that all theologising misses the mark. What makes one experience more authentic than another? Is there a a way of deciding? These are important questions in the Dialogue of Faiths, but our first task is to give as true an account as possible of the various faiths where experience is made supreme. It is more difficult, of course, than the examination of creedal assertions, and some would say an impossible task, since the inner experience remains elusive.
21. D. J. du Plessis saw the promise of a rapprochement between the traditional churches and the Pentecostal movement as the fulfilment of Smith Wigglesworth's prophecy. Since 1966 several important meetings have been held between representatives of the World Council of Churches and the Pentecostal Movement and some Pentecostal Groups such as the Brazilian Igreja Evangelica Pentecostal 'Brasil para Cristo', and the Pentecostal Eglise de Jesus Christ sur la terre par le prophete Simon Kimbangu from the Congo, have been accepted into the World Council of Churches. Nevertheless, it still remains true that most Pentecostals are uncomfortable concerning the growing ties with the W.C.C. One writer insists that the W.C.C. is not based on scriptural foundations;

has a false understanding of the church; is following a path which brings it increasingly close to Rome; is a political association and sets too high a value on itself. (See Hollenweger op. cit., 444f. where he quotes from an unpublished article by Ludwig Eisenlöffel). Hollenweger in his chapter on Ecclesiology reviews the response of the W.C.C. to such criticisms.

22. M. Harper, *As at the Beginning*, 57.
23. *Elim Evangel* 43/51-52 (25: 12: 1962), 824: Hollenweger op. cit., 200.
24. See T. R. Nickel, *The Shakarian Story* (Full Gospel Business Men's Fellowship International, 836 S. Figueroa St., Los Angeles, 1964).
25. See a photographic reproduction of some of the writing and drawings of the eleven year old Russian boy, made in Armenia in 1855, in T. R. Nickel, op. cit., 8.
26. Harper, op. cit., 72.
27. Referred to from now on under the abbreviation, F.G.B.M.F.I.
28. Harper, op. cit., 74.
29. The F.G.B.M.F.I. has published a series of books giving the testimonies of clergy, ministers and laity among Presbyterians, Baptist, Episcopal, Lutheran Church of Christ and Catholic.
30. See D. J. Bennet, *Nine o'clock in the morning* (Logos—Fountain Trust, 1970).
31. ibid., 137 f.
32. Pamphlet 'The Fountain Trust: What it is and What it does' (Fountain Trust, 3A High Street, Esher, Surrey).
33. ibid. See, however, preface above.
34. See M. Harper, *As at the Beginning*, 77ff. T. J. Marzetti in *Renewal* 51 (June/July, 1974), 12ff.
35. Marzetti, ibid.
36. Father Robert Arrowsmith, 'Every Catholic Should be a Catholic Pentecostal' in *Testimony* ix (i) (1970), 4.
37. Editorial in *Renewal* June /July, 1974.
38. ibid.
39. ibid.
40. E. D. O'Connor, *Pentecost in the Catholic Church*, (Watchung N. J.: Charisma Books, (1971), 22.
41. New York: Pyramid Books, (1962).
42. K. and D. Ranaghan, *Catholic Pentecostals* (New York: Paulist Press Deus Books, 1969).
43. Ranaghan, 16.
44. ibid., 20.
45. ibid., 22.
46. ibid., 42.
47. ibid., 46.
48. ibid., 51.
49. *B.W.* 30 July 1971.
50. H. Jansen, E. Hoover and G. Leggett edit. *Live in the Spirit: Council on Spiritual Life Digest*. (Springfield, Mo. Gospel Publishing House, 1972), 204.
51. See also E. E. Plowman, 'Catholic Pentecostals: Something New' *Christianity Today* xviii, 22 (5 July, 1974), 47-48.
52. Paul de Celles, 'Reflections on the 1973 Conference' *New Covenant* iii. 2 (August, 1973), 24-25, cited by Sandidge op. cit., 37.
53. A fuller version of the prayer from *The Documents of Vatican* II, general editor W. Abbott, 709 par. 3 and 4 is given in a booklet entitled *An introduction to the Catholic Charismatic Renewal* published by Charismatic Renewal Services Notre Dame Indiana. It reads: 'Renew Your wonders in our time, as though for a new Pentecost, and grant that the Holy Church, preserving unanimous and continuous prayer, together with Mary, the mother of Jesus, and also under the guidance of St. Peter, may increase the regin of the Divine Saviour, the reign of truth and justice, the reign of love and peace.' L. J. Suenens, 'De Heilige Heest' Pentecost

Letter 88 quoted by Sandidge op. cit., 29: 'Ten years have already gone by since the beginning of Vatican II — a retrospective view confirms our opinion that the Council acted in a prophetic way without realizing it, by expressing its faith in the community, a preparation for the charismatic renewal which nowadays grows steadily before our eyes on the five continents.'

54. Germain Marc'hadour 'The Holy Spirit over the New World' in *The Clergy Review* lix, 4 (April, 1974), 247-48.
55. D. E. Rosage, *Retreats and the Catholic Charismatic Renewal* (Watchung, N. J. : Charisma Books, 1971), 25ff.
56. *An Introduction to the Catholic Charismatic Renewal*, 21.
57. cf. M. A. Jahr, 'A Turning Point, the 1974 Notre Dame Conference' *New Covenant* iv 2 (August 1974), 4-7.
58. R. L. Attaliah edit. *Let the Earth Hear His Voice* (Minneapolis World Wide Publications, 1975), 877; Sandidge op. cit., 39.
59. M. Ford, 'Neo-Pentecostalism within the Roman Catholic Communion' in *Dialog* 13 (1974), 45-50.
60. 'Lord Jesus Christ, Son of God, have mercy upon me' see F. L. Cross, edit. *The Oxford Dictionary of the Christian Church* (London: Black and Son, 1975), 738.
61. Sandidge op. cit., 43.
62. 'A Cardinal looks at Charismatic Renewal' in *Dunamis Digest* vii (Glad Tidings Literature Service, Nagarampalein, India n.d.) 12-18.
63. L. J. Suenens, *A New Pentecost?* (New York: The Seabury Press, 1974), 81-88. Others regard 'baptism with the spirit' as'experiencing the effect of confirmation' and some speak of something new in a person's relationship to God, see S. B. Clark, *Baptized in the Spirit* (Charisma Books 1971) *passim*; and J. R. Williams, op. cit., 26n.
64. D. J. Bennett, 'Speaking in Tongues' in *Living Church* (1 Jan. 1961), 12.
65. Sandidge, op. cit., 79.
66. e.g. Ruben Quenon, 'Des Charismas selon, 1 Corinthians xii et de leur manifestation au sein de quelques mouvements pneumatiques actuels' (Licentiate thesis, Faculté Theologique Protestante du Bruxelles (1970)), cited by Sandidge, op. cit., 122.
67. Editorial in *Renewal* (June/July, 1974).
68. F. Farrell, 'Outburst of Tongues: The New Penetration' in *Christianity Today* (13 Sept. 1963).
69. *B.W.*, 16 July, 1971.
70. James Dunn, *B.W.*, 23 July 1971.
71. *B.W.*, 30 July 1971.
72. *A Theology of the Holy Spirit*, (Hodder and Stoughton, 1971).
73. Ranaghan, op. cit., 220.
74. *B.W.*, loc. cit.
75. Sandidge, op. cit., 94.
76. e.g. 'Les Catholiques charismatiques; l'heure du choix' in *Experiences* iv: 16. (1974) 4-9.
77. J. J. Frinsel) 'Wat denkt u van de charismatische Beweging?' *De Oogst* No. 464 (September, 1974), 12, quoted by Sandidge, op. cit., 128.
78. Sandidge, op. cit., 129.
79. Sandidge, op. cit. 140.
80. *World Pentecost* No. 2 (1973), 9.
81. 'Wales and the Charismatic Renewal' in *Renewal* (1976), 13-15.
82. See Bennett, op. cit., Ranaghan op. cit. D. J. Bennett, *Nine o'Clock in the Morning* (Plainfield, N. J. : 1970), 59; J. R. Bell in *The Acts of the Holy Spirit among the Episcopalians Today* (F.G.B.M.F.I., 1971), 73.
83. J. Sherrill, *They Speak with other Tongues*, 40.
84. Ranaghan op. cit., 102.
85. Ranaghan op. cit., 100; H. Newlin in *The Acts of the Holy Spirit among Episcopalians Today*, (F.G.B.M.F.I. 1971).

86. Ranaghan op. cit., 30.
87. Sherrill op. cit., 127.
88. Sherrill ibid.; W. G. Pulkingham in *The Acts of the Holy Spirit among Episcopalians Today* (1971), 63.
89. D. Carpenter in *The Acts of the Holy Spirit among Presbyterians Today*, 52.
90. Ranaghan op cit., 31; Sherrill op. cit., 128; G. Stockwell in *The Acts of the Holy Spirit among Episcopalians Today*, 30.
91. *The Acts of the Holy Spirit among Episcopalians Today*, 26ff.
92. Ranaghan op. cit., 91.
93. Ranaghan op. cit., 63.
94. cf. Ranaghan op. cit., 95; R. C. Frost, *Aglow with the Spirit* (Plainfield N.J., 1970), 59f.; Sherill op. cit., 128; Ranaghan op. cit., 95.
95. R. Rice 'Charismatic Revival' in *Christian Life* xxv (November, 1963), 30.
96. Ranaghan op. cit., 87, 70.
97. Ranaghan op. cit., 64, 98, 102.
98. Ranaghan op. cit., 98.
99. Bennet *Nine o'clock etc.*, 161.
100. Bennet ibid., 36.
101. Ranaghan op. cit., 53.
102. Frost, op. cit., 113.
103. Bennett op. cit., 181.
104. Frost op. cit., 69; Bennet, op. cit., 20; J. Rushing in *The Acts of the Holy Spirit among Presbyterians Today*, 48.
105. e.g. J. Rodman Williams, in *The Acts of the Holy Spirit among Presbyterians Today*, 11, 'a torrent'!
106. *The Acts of the Holy Spirit among Episcopalians Today*, 23.
107. op. cit., 57.
108. Bennett, op. cit., 107f.; C. Hotchkin in *The Acts of the Holy Spirit among Episcopalians Today*, 67.
109. Bennett, op. cit., 20.
110. Harper op. cit., 82.
111. Ranaghan op. cit., 20, 55, 87, 92; Bennet op. cit., 59.
112. Ranaghan op. cit., 52; G. Stockhowe, in *The Acts of the Holy Spirit among Episcopalians Today*, 31.
113. To avoid tediousness of reference these books will be referred to in the remaining notes as *E* (Episcopalians); *P* (Presbyterians); *B* (Baptists) and *M* (Methodists).
114. *P*. 42; *E*. 39; *P*. 59.
115. *E*. 7; *B*. 19.
116. *B*. 22; 35.
117. *P*. 38.
118. *E*. 45.
119. *E*. 50.
120. *P*. 18.
121. *M*. 22.
122. *M*. 26.
123. *B*. 49.
124. *P*. 49.
125. *P*. 46.
126. Assemblies of God Publishing House, London.
127. Suenens, *A New Pentecost*, 101.

CHAPTER VI

GLOSSOLALIA IN RECENT RESEARCH (I)

The Glossolalist—his personality and condition

The volume of research into the nature of glossolalia in the behavioural sciences during the last twenty years or so has not been unimpressive, particularly in the United States. On the other hand, relatively speaking, little has been achieved by way of correlating the results of various kinds of investigations such as psychological, socio-anthropological researches and the very important contribution of sociolinguistics. An area where even less has been accomplished is the exploration of parallel phenomena in religious and non-religious contexts. While there is obvious need to extend the scope of investigations, attention must also be given to the manner in which they are conducted. Prior to the current charismatic movement, comment was mostly adverse.[1] Even recent studies cannot entirely escape the charge of bias on the part of non-glossolalist observers, particularly churchmen, who may be embarrassed by the upsurge of glossolalia in main line denominations,[2] but bias is by no means restricted to religious writing.[3] One must also be wary of observations made in extraordinary highly charged situations, such as comments made during a trial in England, when a bizarre murder was said to be related to exorcist incidents. The association led some to dismiss the whole charismatic movement, and to call upon church authorities to condemn exorcism, glossolalia and everything else they linked in their mind with Spirit-centric religion.

Research has centred mainly on four topics, namely (i) the personality of the glossolalist, (ii) the glossolalic condition, (iii) the function of glossolalia and (iv) the form of glossolalic utterance. The first two have occupied the attention of pyschological investigations since the early part of the present century, while the function of glossolalia has been examined from both the point of view of psychological and socio-anthropological interest. It is only quite recently that the form of glossolalic utterance has been analytically examined by some sociolinguists. Each one of these topics of interest will now be looked at very briefly, indicating some of the more significant research undertaken in each respective area.

(i)   *The personality of the glossolalist*

Psychological theories of the early part of this century tended to relate the phenomenon of glossolalia with pathological conditions and to classify it as psychotic.[4] The three most often quoted sources are Lombard,[5] Mosiman[6] and Cutten,[7] and all three regarded glossolalia as a regressive pathological experience. Their formal classifications of glossolalia into types show basic similarities. Lombard's fourfold categorisation is: (1) mumbling, groaning, incomprehensible sounds (*phonations frustes*), (2) fabricated sounds, but with well articulated word fragments, repeated and recognizable, often alliterative, sometimes grouped in a sentence (pseudo-language), (3) a mixture of foreign and native phonemes and words in regular linguistic patterns (verbal fascination) and (4) speaking in a foreign language. Mosiman's scheme is almost identical, namely : (1) inarticulate sounds, (2) articulated sounds which simulate words (pseudo-language), (3) fabricated or coined words, and (4) speech with foreign words included. These classifications of the verbal component in glossolalia have been widely used as the basis of more recent typologies,[8] but not without challenge. A. R. Tippett[9], for instance, complains that these classifications were structured to deal with Euro-American cases, and mostly Christian Pentecostal. He finds a more adequate typology in May's categories,[10] which recognized the cross-cultural diversity of communication reported as vocalisation under possession. My own feeling is that, while this extension into the field of parallel phenomena is to be welcomed, much caution is necessary due to the lack of data in that area hitherto.[11] I shall return to this later.

Psychological theories of the early part of this century related the phenomenon of glossolalia with pathological conditions and classified glossolalics as emotionally unstable. Later writers accepted this estimate without scrutiny. Cutten's work, for instance, has been repeatedly cited as authoritative and it has proved extremely palatable to critics of the so-called 'Tongues Movement'. Cutten's views are well known. He thought that glossolalia was linked to schizophrenia and hysteria and he declared speakers with tongues to be non-verbal individuals of low mental capacity, intellectually undeveloped. This estimate has often been repeated by later writers. Among these T. E. Clark, for instance, is most specific and argues that persons given to glossolalia 'are nearly always the ignorant, in whom the lower brain centres and spinal ganglia are relatively strong and the rational and volitional powers, residing in the higher centres of the cortex are relatively weak'.[12]

In considering bold statements of this kind it is important to question the randomness of the samples studied. Cutten, for instance, had based his assumptions upon studies made of psychotic patients in mental institutions and generalised from these nontypical samples. This criticism would hold true of most other early empirical studies which arrived at similar conclusions.[13] The bulk of early investigation did not examine glossolalia in the context of normal church group situations, and, therefore, inevitably perhaps, glossolalia was classified as an abnormal psychic automatism.[14] Even more recent clinical psychiatric studies link glossolalia with psychopathologic conflicts.[15] But each time the correlation of glossolalia and personality conflicts is advanced one has to look closely at the source of the evidence. It is hardly surprising, for instance, to find that glossolalics examined in a suicide prevention clinic turn out to be pre-schizophrenic or to have manifested a psychotic disposition.[16]

Others have looked for additional correlations. A. Boisen compared the behaviour of some of his psychiatric patients and members of a Holy Rollers church.[17] He lists the outward physical manifestations hailed by the Rollers as indicating the Spirit's presence. While they regard 'speaking with tongues' as evidence of baptism by the Holy Spirit, other physical expressions are also held to witness to the moving power of the Spirit among them. They include dancing, jumping, jerking, thrusting up the hands, falling on the floor and even passing into unconsciousness.

Boisen is not convinced by the excesses of such exuberant demonstrations, and he regards the assumption that the divine manifests itself in the unusual as a hazardous assumption. In mental patients, particularly, the danger of attributing an idea which darts into the mind to supernatural sources has obvious dangers. It is similarly presumptuous for glossolalic groups to claim that an idea carries authority merely because of the way in which it comes. He is also critical of the groups' restriction of sphere of interest. They are, he says, indifferent to social involvement while their universe is 'only a little larger than the private world in which the psychotic lives'. On the other hand Boisen's evaluation was not purely negative. For instance, he recognized the therapeutic value of the glossolalic experience, referring to the fact that it can impart hope and courage to many in the face of difficulties and help in the struggle with the 'sense of guilt'. In the main, he regards it as a constructive experience not only for normal individuals, but somewhat surprisingly, to say the least, even in the case of the mentally disturbed as well. In fact, a more recent comparative study of West Indian schizophrenics and a non-psychotic group of immigrants shows that the mentally disturbed cannot maintain sufficient control of autistic and regressive behaviour to fit into the prescribed ritual patterns of the revivalist sects.[18] Most Pentecostals would maintain that glossolalia in the case of such persons could be distinguished from that of those 'genuinely' receiving the Holy Spirit but this assertion would need to be tested against a wide range of investigations. Samarin, for instance, is dubious as to the ability of the glossolalist to distinguish between, what is to him, real glossolalia from the spurious, purely on auditory perception.[19] The Pentecostals of course would counter with the argument that their discernment is not dependent upon audition but on a gift of the Spirit (1 Cor. 12: 10).

It may be true that persons of a certain type are perhaps attracted to the kind of religion where tongues are practised,[20] but a linear correlation between the one and the other has not been satisfactorily established. The hypothesis has been advanced that Pentecostalism attracted uncertain, threatened, inadequately organised persons who felt the need for strengthened interpersonal relationships.[21] Another theory suggests that the success of glossolalia in contemporary Western culture is due to the increase of anxiety syndromes characterizing Western man.[22] No doubt, one can find the uncertain and the anxious among glossolalists, and, no doubt 'tongues' tell us something about the speaker. But is it not equally true that such persons could be found in any religious group since in a religious person one finds an awareness of inadequacy, and, where there is an enlightened conscience as well, there will be a heightened sensitivity to the threats and strains presented by modern civilization. This is a far cry, however, from classifying all glossolalics as psychopathological. Glossolalics belong to a variety of psychological types, and, over against those theories which categorise all of them in terms of emotional and sociological maladjustments, we must place accounts which present an entirely different picture. For instance, Felicitas Goodman found that none of her twenty-nine informants appeared psychotic.[23] Stronger rejection of a nexus with psychopathology is found in a review of M. T. Kelsey's *Tongue Speaking* by Ian Stevenson of the Department of Neurology and Psychiatry, University of Virginia. He writes:

> I believe Mr. Kelsey makes a very good case for dismissing the suggestion of many uninformed critics of glossolalia who identify tongue speaking with mental disorders such as schizophrenia or hysteria. That the experience is 'abnormal' all would admit, but this is not to say it is psychopathological.

The available evidence strongly suggests that glossolalia has no adverse effects on the recipient and is not a symptom of any 'deeper' malady. On the contrary, if we take a Jamesian view of this religious experience and judge it by its fruits, we are bound to acknowledge that the experience itself is constructive or is associated with other changes in the subjects which are constructive. For the subjects generally seem to conduct themselves afterwards in a more loving way and to feel better than they did before the experience.[24]

The question of effect and function will be discussed in the next chapter: my main concern here is to challenge the correlation of personality disposition and tongues speaking. Glossolalics are no more abnormal than other religious groups and this view would find support in a good number of recent investigations in widely separated areas.[25] Much water has run under the bridge since Cutten's explanation of glossolalia in terms of hysteria, schizophrenia and pathological states. These psychological terms themselves are poorly understood still, and it is surprising therefore that the early association of pathological states and glossolalia dies hard and has by no means disappeared from modern theories.[26] On the other hand, it has also been recognized that glossolalia is not necessarily a product of the neurotic mind but may indeed represent the creative, the positive aspect of the unconscious, the source of our artistic creativity.[27]

Pattison calls upon us to consider glossolalia in the light of the socio-cultural context and his conclusions are worth bearing in mind. He maintains that glossolalia can be produced experimentally, as a by-product of psychotic disorganization, as a mechanism of expression of neurotic conflict, or as a normal expectation and behaviour of a normal population.[28] He made observations among lower and lower-middle class persons in both urban and rural areas as well as middle-class and upper-class glossolalists. While many of the cases from the lower class demonstrated behaviour which he classified as frankly dissociative or hysterical episodes of a clinically neurotic nature, the upper and middle classes generally demonstrated no psychopathology. However, he rejects a simplistic association of psychopathology and social class, and concludes that 'the phenomenon of glossolalia *per se* cannot be interpreted necessarily as either deviant or pathological for its meaning is determined and must be interpreted in terms of the socio-cultural context'. This is true and I would add that the conceptual associations within the socio-cultural context are a most important factor.[29] Expressions of basic drives are determined by what is considered proper in a specific culture at a given time[30] and the cultural milieu determines personality needs to a considerable degree. To isolate the verbal part, therefore, from the rest is to ignore most of the cultural conditioning factors. It would be tantamount to saying that, since it is only the utterance which is analysable, the meaning of hymn singing can be as well studied at a rugby international stadium as in a local prayer meeting, or, to offer another analogy, that a mantra 'frozen' on a paper cracker motto is the same mantra as that uttered by the devotee The importance of cultural expectation will be noted again in chapter nine below.

On the question of the personality of the glossolalists, Pattison finds that neither of 'the two most careful and sophisticated studies yet conducted',[31] indicates a correlation with psychopathology nor supports the frequent charge of abnormality levelled against Pentecostals in general or glossolalists in particular.[32] The trend in recent assessment is typified in this statement, cited by Pattison, based on the work of Gerlach and his colleagues in Minnesota:

> Most Pentecostals appear to be normally successful members of their families and communities . . . family relationships are more harmonious than normal in our society when all family members have had the full Pentecostal experience . . . most Pentecostals, though they are different in some behaviours are not 'sick' . . . they function effectively and cope adequately.[33]

On the question of predisposition, these same writers concede that some groups or churches attract more 'troubled' individuals than others and suggest that some groups in more depressed areas attract more deprived persons or more aged, lonely persons. They also say it is possible that some churches stimulate, in some personality types, behaviour which is maladaptive. What is significant in recent studies is an increasing readiness to find differences within Pentecostal groups, thus replacing the practice of grouping them all in one general category. One recent study considers personality differences between high and low dogmatism groups of Pentecostal believers within a highly homogeneous group drawn from three Pentecostal churches in a north western city in the U.S.A. This particular investigation led to the conclusion that non-dogmatic Pentecostal believers appear as well adjusted and interpersonally skilful as do people in general.[34] It seems to me that 'low-dogmatism' is itself an interesting development in Pentecostalism and some would say it can only occur where Pentecostalism has been watered down beyond recognition.

Of the studies which compare the personality characteristics of glossolalics and non-glossolalics[35] the one most often cited is an unpublished thesis by L. M. van Eetvelt Vivier which applies recognized psychological tests to glossolalists.[36] Certain weaknesses in the introductory part should not be allowed to detract from the importance of the empirical sections. For instance, in the early section Vivier's somewhat literalist use of Scripture hardly generates confidence in his interpretation of a phenomenon which seems to be both Biblical and contemporary. He assumes glossolalia in Biblical contexts as well as in ancient non-Biblical contexts where the evidence is simply lacking and he appears sometimes to equate glossolalia with any ecstatic manifestation. For example he writes:

Glossolalia appears among the first Christians but is not confined to Christianity. It occurs (a) under differing circumstances, e.g. Ledad and Medad in Israel; at Byblos among the frenzied youth in Wen Amon's story, among the painted youths of the Syrian Goddess, (b) independent of background e.g. in the Baal Prophets (1 Kings 18: 16-46); the Greek poets ('Plato Ion' 533-534); the Cumean Sybil ('The Aenead' Virgil 6) and the Gergesene Demoniac (Lk. 8: 26-37), (c) among different peoples, e.g. Moses (Num. 11: 7); Miriam (Num. 12: 1, 2); in Israel (Isaiah 28: 10-13), and the Pythoness of Delphi in Greece, (d) in various ages, e.g. the sons of the prophets (1 Sam. 10: 1-13; 19: 18-24 etc.).

It is highly regrettable that all these are lumped together as instances of glossolalia since the evidence is not forthcoming, and, in any case the topic of ecstaticism in the ancient world deserves a fuller and much more scientific treatment than Vivier provides. It would be equally wrong, however, to ignore Vivier's important contribution for this reason, since on the empirical side in the field of his own expertise he has made a much more thorough investigation. His aim was fourfold:

1. To try and determine whether the dissociative phenomenon of glossolalia is due to (a) the impact of a religious dynamism in all its power or (b) a basic inherent weakness in the individual, and, therefore, a sign of psychopathology on a scale hitherto unknown.

2. To establish whether there are any personality differences between frequent and non-frequent glossolalics and between glossolalics and non-glossolalics.

3. To establish whether there are any dynamic factors that may account for the occurrence of glossolalia and possibly suggest mechanisms underlying the process of glossolalia.

4. To see if it is logically conceivable that glossolalia in the Biblical sense of a manifestation of the Gift of the Holy Spirit is possible in modern times.

He conducted his practical investigation through chosen psychological tests and questionnaires on twenty-four subjects who practised glossolalia. This group he referred to as the 'Test Group'. A 'Control Group A' consisted of twenty subjects who believed in glossolalia but did not practise it, and a third group, referred to as 'Control Group B' comprised twenty religious subjects who were doctrinally opposed to glossolalia. Those who have discussed Vivier's work have not always made it clear that the Test Group and Control Groups were not independent of one another.[37] Vivier himself does not conceal the fact that 'fifteen of the twenty-four glossolalics were originally members of the non-Pentecostal Church which provided subjects for the non-tongue-speaking control group. Also, eleven of the members of the control group of pre-tongue-speakers were originally members of the non-Pentecostal church.' This study, then, could have looked at the cause and effect of transitions from a community that precludes glossolalia to another that sanctions it. If Vivier does not explore this aspect, nevertheless he has stimulated others to pursue enquiries along these lines, and, in my view, his contribution represents an important stage in the history of psychological research in glossolalia, and so I now offer a brief account of his method and results.

Vivier's test material included:

(1) a bibliographical questionnaire which contained questions relating to pre-neurotic developmental signs.

(2) a questionnaire relating to the tested person's religious background and religious development,

(3) the Willoughby Scale Questionnaire 'to render an overall picture of the general level of neuroticism of the different groups', and

(4) the Sixteen Personality Factor Test of Cattell, 'to give an insight into personality factors which might pertain to glossolalia'.

Vivier's general conclusions may be summarised as follows:

(a) The bibliographical questionnaire: approximately 50 per cent of the glossolalics tend to show a history of psychiatric and psychopathologic adjustment problems. He mentions alcohol, epilepsy, nervous breakdowns and admission to mental hospitals in connection with the test group. This would suggest that such people would turn to religion as a form of adjustment, and would be 'attracted to a form of religion in which the group situation is the keynote with acceptance and active participation'. On the other hand, Vivier is at pains to remind us that 50 per cent had no problems, and he can confidently maintain that glossolalia 'occurs in completely normal people who take their religion seriously'. Another assessor, however, might justifiably feel that the high incidence of problematic cases in the Test Group cannot be so easily dismissed.

(b) The Willoughby Questionnaire: The glossolalic and pre-glossolalic groups scored higher on the neuroticism test than did the control group opposed to glossolalia. Speculating concerning the psychotherapeutic function of glossolalia, Vivier suggests it may contribute to an emotion of well being.

(c) The Rosenzweig Picture Frustration Test: While the factor of repression seems to be related to glossolalia, Vivier finds it to be a method of adjustment rather than repression in the pathological sense of increase of tension. The glossolalist, he says, evades aggression in an attempt to gloss over frustration and with this goes self-effacement: 'It can be said that there must be self-effacement for glossolalia to occur or possibly that the practice of glossolalia leads to self-effacement'. He adds that this self-denigration is seen as leading to higher spiritual progress.

(d) Suggestibility: Interestingly enough Control Group B (opposed to glossolalia) rated a higher degree of suggestibility than the glossolalics in the Test Group.

(e) The Cattell Personality Test: Vivier's glossolalics showed no inherent tendency to dissociate. There is also a difference between those who engage in glossolalia only infrequently and those who practise it frequently. The former show an above normal emotional integrative capacity, while the latter show a poor emotional integrative capacity and appear to require some form of catharsis.

(f) The Thematic Apperception Test: The glossolalics reflect a poorer tolerance threshold and 'a tendency to cling to objects in the environment for emotional support'.[38]

Vivier states that the results suggest poor verbalisation of emotional content on the part of glossolalics generally, and he poses the question: 'Could it be that glossolalics "break down" in their normal speech when under strong emotional idealisation and that the control groups are unable to experience glossolalia because of a more rigid intellectual verbalisation of emotional ideas?' He is right in saying that a great deal depends on the intensity of the emotional impact but even those with a marked facility in conceptualising emotions would experience a verbal inadequacy if the emotional impact was strong enough. We all know that it is the experiences which move us deeply that leave us feeling 'at a loss for words'. But this kind of experience can be shared by the most articulate as well as the least articulate.

Vivier believes that, while what he calls intuitive and mystical thought is not a prerequisite for glossolalia, those who practise it tend significantly to develop this trait. In this, too, he may be right, but I have reservations concerning another of his major conclusions. He maintains that glossolalics as a group have had a poor beginning in life, psychologically speaking. They have suffered problems of adjustments in infancy and later adulthood, and experience inner conflicts and emotional problems. This may be true of some glossolalics but one cannot speak generally in this way of glossolalics as a group. Where there has been maladjustment, glossolalic groups provide the therapy of an environment of sensitiveness and service. Vivier is no doubt right in this but one can also speak of a therapeutic value even where there had been no unusual degree of inadequacy experienced previously. Vivier is by no means alone in relating a sense of deficiency and glossolalic compensatory release. J. P. Kildahl, for instance, in his study of Neo-Pentecostalism, discovers a connection between a preoccupation with internal psychological factors and predisposition to glossolalia. His research found 'that glossolalics tended to be submissive, suggestible and dependent on authority figures'.[39]

My own view is that glossolalics belong to a variety of psychological types and before one advances a theory that they are unduly neurotic or sufferers from psychological deficiencies one must look hard at the kind of evidence where 'interviewer expectation' is marked as this can exercise a subtle control on results as well as method. I experience the same unease with some psychological theories as I did with earlier views which related glossolalia to social status, educational backgrounds and economic conditions.

The variety of social classes and professions represented in Neo-Pentecostal circles[40] undermines the earlier views and, as Virginia H. Hine has stated, evidence of glossolalia as a result of variations in the socialization process merely clears the ground for more questions.[41] The same applies to the tie with psychological conditions. Even if this could be established, it would not constitute a total explanation of the phenomenon of glossolalia.[42] I have no doubt that psychological factors are involved, very much so, but as in the case of a term like ecstasy, the expression psychological ranges over a wide spectrum of conditions and more than one of these may be associated with glossolalia.

Glossolalia has been correlated with a preceding anxiety crisis and seen therefore as tension release mechanism. Dr. Paul Qualben found that eighty-five per cent of tongue-speakers interviewed 'had experienced a clearly defined anxiety crisis preceding their speaking in tongues'.[43] On the other hand a recent analysis of replies from one hundred and twenty respondents in Australia returns only twenty-five per cent of glossolalics in the category of those who had a prior anxiety crisis.[44] This proportion would not seem excessively high. It might be equalled in a random group, and there is no conclusive evidence that potential glossolalics are more anxiety dominated than the average. Glossolalics it would appear represent a wide variety of psychological types and conditions.

This brings me to what is perhaps *the* centre of the controversy concerning the glossolalic condition, namely, whether glossolalia is produced in an altered state of consciousness or not.

(ii) *The glossolalic condition*

Is glossolalia produced in a normal state of consciousness, or is it manifest only when the subject experiences some kind of trance? This question, of course, leads to several others which cannot be dealt with within the purview of this brief account. It would be well to bear in mind two considerations, firstly, that the pattern of glossolalia need not be rigidly uniform, and secondly, where there is evidence of dissociation, that certain changes of consciousness can be beneficial.[45] An altered state of consciousness may produce a qualitative alteration in the overall pattern of mental functioning. Memory in some cases may be heightened[46] and other abilities enhanced.[47] This needs to be said on account of the more general tendency to link dissociation with what I would term the baser non-creative kind of ecstasy, and to refer to it invariably in derogatory terms.

That glossolalia became associated in people's minds with frenzied behaviour is not surprising since older Pentecostal groups made full use of rhythmic clapping, dancing and singing. The action of rhythm on the mind has been recognized, not least in trance-induction ceremonies and in techniques associated with mystical groups. Rodney Needham raised the problem 'why is noise that is produced by striking or shaking so widely used in order to communicate with the other world?'[48] He was intrigued by co-occurrence of drumming and shamanistic contact with spirits, a connection which is encountered again and again in ethnographical literature. In reply, W. C. Sturtevant, in a letter in the same journal[49], states that the answer already exists in the anthropological literature. He in turn is referring to a paper by Andrew Neher[50] which he summarises as follows:

Rhythmical drumming of a particular sort produces striking abnormal psychological states (comparable to those produced by some drugs) which once encountered, should repeatedly become associated with religious behaviour, These effects include hallucinations (visual, kinaesthetic, cutaneous, perhhaps auditory, and doubtfully gustatory and olfactory): fatigue, confusion, fear, disgust, anger and pleasure; distortion of time perception; and sometimes even epileptic seizures and psychopathology.

Not only rhythm, but the repetition of the divine name is another agent in inducing a new state of mind. This aspect will be discussed later in the contexts also of other religious cultures. At this point, I would simply like to include one or two references by way of illustration. G. Scholem's account of Merkebah mysticism shows how rhythm and repetitive adjurations of God induce in those who are praying a state of mind 'bordering on ecstasy'.[51] The recurrence of the key word of the numinous is an important part of the technique and this has parallels elsewhere of course. Thus, M. Gilsenan[52], notes the dominant role of the word in the rhythmic *dhikr* of the *Hamidiya Shadhiliya*, the word, in this case, united the chanter with the source signified by the word. Gilsenan writes of the *dhikr*:

When the most essential of the Names is chanted, *Hu* (He), indistinguishable from that other source and symbol of power and life which delivers it, the breath, men can experience for a rare moment the unity of the beyond and the within.[53]

That there is an increasing recognition of the effect of rhythm, sound and percussion, on the human mind is relevant to our consideration of the glossolalic condition, particularly in fervent older Pentecostal groups.[54] In Neo-Pentecostal circles, however, it might be argued that conditions are very different and to look to altered states of consciousness as in some measure accounting for glossolalia to be misleading. Here the setting is usually one of tranquillity and repose, in collective, as well as in private, use of glossolalia, and most glossolalics exercise control most of the time over whether to utter or not. Some say the utterance need not be audible but can take place inwardly in the mind alone, and others claim to be able to engage in glossolalia and do some other task at the same time, such as, for instance, driving a car. Kelsey for example writes:

> I now find that I use this phenomenon almost entirely within my mind, that is to say that I hardly ever speak in tongues, but 'think' the activity in the same way that I am now thinking in English as I type this information.[55]

For Kelsey, obviously, loss of consciousness or the state of trance is not a necessary part of the experience.

Sufficient has been said to show that any statement concerning the glossolalic condition needs to be subject to many qualifications, for glossolalia can be accompanied by various kinds of emotional experience, ranging from the tranquil and relaxed to the intense and fervent. Cases occur where apparently there is no change from the normal state of mind and others where the subject seems to be in trance. But what precisely is meant by an altered state of consciousness? This is a question which is esentially relevant to any consideration of the glossolalic condition.

Arnold M. Ludwig finds that what he calls 'possession states' take on the flavour of the predominant culture values, beliefs and expectations.[56] He claims that each of the revivalistic religious cults has its own unique features which characterise possession by the Holy Spirit but common denominators cut across group differences to enable us to think of altered states of consciousness as somewhat related phenomena. He defines altered states of consciousness as:

> any mental states induced by various physiological, psychological or pharmacological manoeuvres or agents, which can be recognized subjectively by the individual himself (or by an

137

objective observer of the individual) as representing a sufficient deviation in subjective experience or psychological functioning from certain general norms for that individual during alert, waking consciousness.

How is this deviation recognized? It may be 'represented by a greater preoccupation than usual with internal sensations or mental processes, changes in the formal characteristics of thought, and impairment of reality testing to various degrees'. Altered states of consciousness, says Ludwig, may be produced by agents 'which interfere with the normal inflow of sensory or proprioceptive stimuli, the normal outflow of motor impulses, the normal "emotional tone", or the normal flow and organization of cognitive processes'. He claims that common factors associated with changes in consciousness enable us to speak of related phenomena. These are alterations in thinking and the predominance of archaic modes of thought, disturbed time sense, diminution of conscious control or inhibitions, change in emotional expression, a propensity to experience a profound sense of depersonalization, perceptual distortions, giving increased significance to subjective experiences, sense of the ineffable, feelings of rejuvenation, and hypersuggestibility. Of course, all these features need not concur in any single experience and change in consciousness *per se* is no indicator of the kind of expression which accompanies it. Ludwig, for instance, considers the functions of altered states of consciousness in terms of two categories: (a) maladaptive expressions which serve no constructive purpose and in which the psychological regression will prove to be atavistic and injurious to the individual and society, and (b) adaptive expressions which enable the individual to acquire new knowledge or experience, to express psychic tensions without danger to himself or others and to function more adequately in society. Such expressions are 'in the service of the ego' and enable man to transcend the bounds of logic and formality, or express repressed needs and desires in a socially sanctioned and constructive way. This reference to function was necessary at this point because Ludwig regards glossolalia as an example of an adaptive altered state. The whole question of function is taken up more fully in the next section, but some observations must be allowed at this point in the light of Ludwig's treatment.

How then does glossolalia 'serve the ego'? Ludwig's answer is that it is an avenue to a new experience, and that, in revival groups, the individual transcends the boundary of self, merging with the group 'thus acquiring the benefits which come from a greater social cohesiveness, as in other non-religious groups' settings. This is a positive aspect of glossolalia, reminiscent of Vivier's point about the therapeutic value of the new environment but it is not claimed that glossolalia is unique in this function nor that an altered state of consciousness is a prerequisite of a similar effect. The new orientation, therefore, does not necessarily indicate a condition of dissociation to prompt it.

Nor does glossolalia always manifest adaptive qualities. Glossolalia often occurs in conditions attributed to possession by malign spirits. In these cases the trance-like nature of the condition is more pronounced. In both maladaptive and adaptive conditions the explanatory system to which the behaviour is linked will influence the behaviour expected.[57] One would for instance expect a disturbance of the 'speech profile'[58] in a condition which involves a changed state of consciousness and deemed to require exorcism, but in the case of positive adaptive glossolalia it would be difficult very often for an observer to detect any outward sign of an inward change of consciousness. Clinical tests indicate that, unlike gross trance states, glossolalia is not linked with detectable physiological changes such as galvanic skin responses or EEG tracings.[59]

What may be termed the physiology of glossolalia is in fact the area studied by Gary Palmer.[60] The central theme of his study is that trance is a physiological event, with physiological causes and effects. It is argued that dissociative behaviour is characteristic in spirit possession, religious ecstasy, some forms of psychosis, the psychedelic drug experience and various other trances, and that dissociation can be in the form of reaction to mental stress. Glossolalia is regarded as an example of a trance state and an attempt is made to examine the arousal level and brain wave pattern in subjects who experience glossolalia, the arousal indicators being skin conductance and heart rate. A number of subjects were interviewed for their subjective accounts of their experiences, and many referred to a feeling of repose and relaxation. It is known that in Yoga meditation, for instance, the rise of electrical resistance of the skin is an indicator of a relaxed mood, another is the lowering of breathing rate.[61] In Minnesota a patient examined by a doctor in 1965 began to 'pray in the Spirit', while on the examination table, and it was noticed that the heart rate of the patient dropped several beats per minute. The investigating team regarded this as favouring the claims of people who speak of the tranquillizing effect of this experience. They sought, however, a further method to test the idea that glossolalic experience is relaxing and beneficial to the patient's heart and general well being. A portable skin conductance meter was employed to indicate activation level and electro-encephalograms to discover any unusual electrical activity in the brain, 'not as something pathological, but perhaps as something out of the ordinary'.[62] A third string of enquiry compared the latter with the electrical pattern of a subject in hypnosis. All three together, it was hoped, would provide a partial answer to those who hold the glossolalic event to be a trance experience. Electrocardio-grams were taken as a by-product of the exercise in taking electro-encephalograms.

The study engages in a technical account of electrodermal phenomena with constant citation of recent work in psycho-physiol-ogical research and related studies. A galvanometer was used for the measurement of skin conductance, and readings made on ten subjects in a total of four meetings at the homes of the subjects, the recording sessions lasting about an hour and a half. A second group examined was a prayer group comprising ten females and two males. In the second group glossolalia, which Palmer sub-sumes under the more inclusive expression 'praying in the spirit', was much more fervent. In the first group, it was almost inaudible, but in the second group 'the praying, both in the Spirit and in English, was at least as loud as normal speech. At times the sub-jects would laugh in their excitement and joy.' The tests covered periods of active glossolalia, relaxation, silent prayer and normal conversation, and the aim was to see whether glossolalia differed significantly from the other periods. During the session, group 1 showed no significance difference in skin conductance. Using this test of relaxation the investigation, contrary to expectation, showed that glossolalia seemed to be slightly less relaxing than silent prayer. Of course, the presence of the experimenter may have affected the results. The data from group 2 on skin conductance levels indicate that glossolalia is no more relaxing than ordinary silent prayer and voluntary relaxation.

Electroencephalography 'monitors electric potential changes between two poles on the cortex (bipolar) or between one pole on the cortex and some distant area of the body (unipolar). In this technique alpha waves are measured, the dominant EEG (electro-encephalogram) rhythm in the adult human with eyes closed being "the alpha rhythm of 8 to 12 waves per second and about 50 micro-notes in amplitude".' When the subject is awake and relaxed the alpha activity is at its peak. It diminishes and may even dis-appear when the subject becomes more than usually alert or drowsy. Thus, the frequency on alpha activity has been used as an indicator of the level of consciousness. The experiments conducted in the

University of Minnesota hospitals only recorded EEGs of the subjects in normal wakeful condition, and then during periods of 'praying in the Spirit', silent prayer and normal conversation. The glossolalic sessions were periods of five to fifteen minutes, but it is not clear from the report whether the subjects examined were speaking in tongues for the whole period, intermittently, or for only part of it. The results were inconclusive and various subjects responded in different ways, one, for instance, showing an increase of alpha frequency, and another, a slowing of alpha activity in glossolalia.

The third line of investigation involved taking ECGs (electrocardiograms). Previous research[63], as one would expect, had indicated an accelerated heart rate for conditions of 'inspiration' and 'excitement' but it also showed a slowing of the rate for conditions of fear or grief. Deceleration is characteristic also 'where visual attention or empathic listening to the environment "is required" and cardiac acceleration "where the subject must concentrate on internal symbolic manipulations or is exposed to noxious stimuli"'. Palmer finds that 'a slight cardioacceleration may accompany silent prayer and glossolalia' and this suggests to him 'cortical activation', since, if earlier work is valid, the heart rate increases when consciousness is applied to internal symbolic manipulation, rather than to perception of the external environment. The results of these tests, to my mind, provide no basis for firm conclusions since there are so many other factors, including physiological causes which have to be taken into account.

In the trance state of dissociation, there is a loss of generalised reality-orientation.[64] Some would argue that there is no evidence that this is the case with the glossolalic condition. That is a question to be returned to again. Meanwhile, to continue with Palmer's views which assume that glossolalia involves some degree of dissociation: it is not always clear whether glossolalia is the product of the state or the cause of it. If dissociation is related to a physiological state of general disorganisation of the brain, then, it is argued that trance induction procedures will consist of techniques which can cause such a disorganisation of the conjunctive and sensory system of the brain. The induction techniques mentioned include rhythm which has the same effect as monotony on the mind and can lead to fixation of attention, fasting, suspension of breath, such as happens sometimes in the course of singing, or indeed glossolalia where there can be long intervals between breathings. Such suspension can lead to an inordinate concentration of carbon dioxide in the lungs and blood and this in turn may lower the efficiency of the brain as a reducing valve and induce entry into consciousness of experiences and visions. Dancing is another form of behaviour which can be trance inducing and exercise a dual function. 'It may help maintain and accentuate the perception of the rhythm as does singing, and it may tend to increase the CO_2 content of the lungs, particularly if there is intermittent singing.'

All these, of course, namely rhythm, song and dance may promote emotional excitement which in itself reduces the range of sensory perception while strengthening the central or dominant response. If that response be glossolalia, then it could be facilitated by the excitement. This may well be true in numerous instances but, as stated previously, excitement is not a necessary inductor for glossolalia, nor is it for certain forms of trance where on the contrary relaxation serves as part of the induction, as for example in Yoga. Glossolalia, similarly, can be associated with more passively induced states. It can occur in a relaxed atmosphere or in conditions of excitation, but irrespective of the presence or absence of excitement it seems to be in most cases a 'learned' behaviour appropriate to the situation. But where there is increased excitement this mobilises a greater amount of energy. In Palmer's view, if the individual has ruminated about what he would like to do, this has actually become learned behaviour. In other words, what transpires in a condition of dissorientation is not unrelated to what has been reflected upon in conscious thought.

Palmer regarded the glossolalic state of subjects in group 2 of the physiological study to be more passive than group 1, but, in his view, there is no hard and fast line between the active and passive categories. Other passive states would be hypnosis and Yoga and in these as in the glossolalic 'passive' state fixation of attention is more paramount than in the more active states. Relaxation and arrest of anxiety are also reported as after-effects.

The subjects of group 2 reported that clear consciousness was retained. Their EEG records were indistinguishable from the spontaneous waking record. Palmer then takes up the question whether such an experience as theirs can be considered to be dissociative. He explains what dissociation means: ' "Dissociation" is a construct applied to a certain set of behaviours. From some of these behaviours the inference is made that the mind is undergoing a loss in the generalised reality—orientation.[65] From some other of these behaviours we infer that a small portion is functioning in relative isolation from the structured frame of reference and the external environment. There are different levels in each of these two processes.' This definition of dissociation, of course, is so wide that it can accommodate most of our waking moments! As I am writing these words, I may be excluding or dampening many sensory impressions such as the barking of the dog on a distant hill, or the sound of a car passing by, or the chiming of the grandfather clock. A high degree of concentration means that a portion of the mind functions in isolation, and this, in Palmer's understanding of the term, could be described as a state of dissociation. It seems to me, however, that a person may be absorbed in an aspect or aspects of his waking generalised reality-orientation without ceasing to be aware of, or in close communication with, the rest of it at all times. As Shor says, it is when this close communication is lost that the resultant state of mind may be designated as trance but even in the deepest trance or deepest sleep the generalised reality-orientation does not fade away completely.[66] 'Only in the foetus can one conceive of an ideally pure trance state.'[67] Some of Palmer's subjects claimed to be able to drive a car while they were praying in the Spirit. I suppose most of us experience moments of 'temporary inattention' and some may know of what is more serious, the so-called 'highway hypnosis', which is a fatigue and monotony state occasioning a disruption of generalised reality-orientation.[68] There would seem to me to be degrees of dissociation and this can vary in the same individual at different times. In the case of glossolalists, occasionally the general environment may seem to be blocked out entirely, on other occasions the speaker may well be aware of all around him. Studies have tended to show that 'trance experiences' become fewer and lighter as the individual grows older, suggesting an increasing inability with age to let go of the generalised reality-orientation. Trance states explained as 'spirit possession' are usually associated with the teenage group and sometimes even with children. Age therefore may be an important factor for investigation.

Another area of interest is the effect produced by the experience. This indeed can be indicative of the nature of the experience. For instance, amnesia is a feature of trance and Palmer suggests that 'it may be that the memory process is dependent upon the continual association of present with past experience, an association which probably does not take place while the individual is in a state of trance'.[69] All these features and others need further field investigation and so far the case for identifying glossolalia as a trance state is by no means closed, and physiological 'translations' are not conclusive. What is forced upon us is the recognition that since the explanatory system to which it is linked will necessarily influence the behaviour exhibited,[70] any appraisal must pay due regard to the socio-cultural context as well as factors relating to the individual.

To conclude this section on the glossolalic condition, I would like to refer very briefly to the opposing views of Felicitas D. Goodman and W. Samarin. They bring into sharp focus the question whether glossolalia is a state of trance. Goodman conducted her field work among the Apostolicos (an offshoot of the Pentecostals) in Mexico City, in the Yucatan with Maya Indians and in Hammond, Indiana.[71] In these different cultural settings, Goodman found an agreement of 'the phonological and suprasegmental features' of the recorded glossolalic utterances. This led her to conclude that speech behaviour is modified in a 'trance like state'. Glossolalia is regarded as an artefact of what she calls an 'hyperaroused mental state'. In fact, Goodman makes a stronger assertion: 'glossolalia is *always* associated with an altered mental state'.[72] Glossolalia for her includes 'interpretation' as well as speaking with tongues since the speaker who interprets remains in light trance and his speech still bears 'some of the earmarks of true glossolalia'. These are described as follows: 'The throat muscles continue to appear rather tense, the phrases are strongly rhythmical and tend to be of approximately equal length. In addition, grammar and coherence of thought are often neglected'.[73] One should interject here that interpretation can be, on the other hand, very coherent and sometimes grandiloquent in style. It differs from glossolalia by nature of its intelligibility, as glossolalia 'for the most part' is totally unintelligible.

Goodman compared individual utterances and examined identifiable units within the utterances and claimed to have discovered a significant cross-cultural agreement in the manner in which the glossolalist speaks. There is 'a threshold of onset, a brief rising gradient of intensity, a peak, and a final, often precipitous decay'. The glossolalist speaks in this way 'because his speech behaviour is modified by the way the body acts in the particular mental state, often termed trance, in which he places himself'. Her position is clear, and, as stated, she describes glossolalic utterance as an artefact of a hyperaroused mental state or the surface structure of the altered state of consciousness.

In an interesting comparison of male and female characteristics Goodman finds that women go into glossolalia more easily than men but their utterance is not as loud. In the case of men, she found 'an impressive concomitant kinetic behaviour such as lifting arms, shaking the head, a twitching in the face' while among the women 'the only observed consistent accompanying behaviour was crying'.[74] In at least one case, however, Goodman discovered that the line of demarcation 'between the conscious state and dissociation appears so indistinct, so obliterated, that crossing it becomes an adventitious occurrence'.[75] It could be argued that to concede one exception is to concede all, but that would be somewhat cavalier and over-assertive.

J. R. Jaquith rejected the assumption that glossolalia is performed while in some other-than-normal psychological state,[76] and W. J. Samarin has come out even more strongly against the position that glossolalia is an artefact of an altered state of consciousness. Trance, he says, is rare in the experience of Christian glossolalists.[77] Concerning glossolalia, he makes the point that it is understood only when one enters the Pentecostal's world and sees it from the latter's point of view, and in this he is of course perfectly correct. That point of view, however, is different from Samarin's! According to Pentecostals, even the practised speaker, although he can most times turn his speaking off or on at will, has no choice in determining the content of his utterance. For Samarin, on the other hand, there is nothing mysterious about glossolalic verbalisation at all and he states that the tongues speaker is 'most often a sophisticated user of speech, selecting this and that variable with commendable delicacy'.[78] Samarin's linguistic analysis will be considered below under 'The Form of Glossolalia', but it would be inappropriate not to mention now certain observations relevant to our discussion of the glossolalist condition. He holds that while the metaphysical language used by tongue speakers to describe their experience might seem to indicate loss of control or consciousness, this in itself does not point to altered states. Furthermore, in his finding, subjective reports speak of a perfectly normal state of consciousness[79] and glossolalist writers confirm that they are not deprived of their powers of thinking or conscious action.[80]

In his book *Tongues of Men and Angels*, perhaps more clearly than in his previous articles, Samarin does not deny that there can be some degree of dissociation in some instances, but he insists still that the state *per se* is not the cause of glossolalia. He writes: '. . . we would argue that the acquisition of charismatic or Pentecostal glossolalia is *sometimes* associated with *some* degree of altered state of consciousness, that this *occasionally* involves motor activity that is involuntary or, rarely, a complete loss of consciousness, and that in any case subsequent use of glossolalia (that is, after the initial experience) is *most often independent* of dissociative phenomena'.[81] He believes that anyone can practise glossolalia but this does not answer the question why some do and others do not or why many who seek this manifestation fail to acquire it.

With Goodman and Samarin, then, we have two opposed views,

strongly argued in each case. Much more field work is necessary before the problem can be resolved. My own view, based on reading and some non-technical observation, is that there can be much variety in the condition ranging from a trance state to what seemingly appears to be a perfectly normal state of consciousness. Even in the latter, however, there would be a focusing of attention on the act of glossolalia, with the resultant diverting of attention from generalised-reality orientation and immediate concerns. Whether this is low key dissociation or not may be arguable. What I would claim, and here probably I would part from Samarin, is that in the glossolalic act the unconscious levels of personality have a more ready access to speech functions than is normally the case, not only in obvious states of dissociation but even where there appears to be very little trace of an altered state of consciousness. It has been argued, for instance by Shor,[82] that 'when the generalized reality-orientation fades that various mental contents excluded before can now flow more fully into phenomenal awareness'. Thus what he calls primary-process modes of thought can flow more easily into awareness. In the case of glossolalia, I would suggest that primary sound patterns, formed in an individual's unconscious function, surface in glossolalic utterance. Once spoken, they make it easier for a repetition of the performance on the next occasion and, in this way, a 'glossa' or particular tongue is born.

In concluding this section, it can be said that much more needs to be done empirically by empathetic observers before authoritative statements can be made. If little headway seems to have been made in this subject during the first half of the century, recently new avenues are beginning to be explored. One of these is the question of function and another the form of glossolalia and these will now be discussed.

1. Not all as uncharitable as those of O. L. Haavik, 'Pentecostalism or the Tongues Movement' in *Lutheran Herald* (23, 30, Oct. 1934), 935-937; 959-963. Conybeare in the *Encyc. Brit.* 11th edit. is typical of many critics. He compares glossolalia with oracular possessions among both savages and the cultured ancients and refers to 'morbid and abnormal trance utterances in Christian revivals in every age.' M. T. Kelsey (op. cit., 144) says this is to confuse the experience itself with the atmosphere which has sometimes been known to surround it.
2. See the warning given by V. H. Hine, 'Pentecostal Glossolalia: Toward a Functional Interpretation. in *J.S.S.R.* 8 (1970), 217f. and the references given there.
3. Many earlier psychological studies assume the abnormality of glossolalics, with this, cf. W. J. Samarin, *Tongues of Men and Angels*, 175n for his comment on W. La Barre's interpretation of the condition of snake handlers. La Barre describes the condition as psychopathic. (W. La Barre, *They Shall Take up Serpents: Psychology of the Southern Snake-handling Cult* (Minnesota, 1962). For further useful comments by Samarin see ibid., 215n, and on prejudice, 229.

4. e.g., see A. Mackie, *The gift of Tongues: a study in pathological aspects of Christianity* (1921).
5. E. Lombard, *De la Glossolalie chez les Premiers Chrétiens et des Phénomenes Similaires* (Lausanne: Bridel, 1910).
6. E. Mosiman, *Das zungenreden geschichtlich und psychologisch untersucht* (Tubingen: Mohr, 1911).
7. G. B. Cutten, *Speaking with Tongues: historically and psychologically considered* (New Haven: Yale, 1927).
8. See P. Damboriena, *Tongues as of Fire: Pentecostalism in Contemporary Christianity* (Washington, 1969).
9. ' "Glossolalia" as Spirit Possession: A Taxonomy for Cross Cultural Observation and Description', a paper read to the American Academy of Religion in Los Angeles, Sept. 1972.
10. L. Carlyle May, 'A survey of glossolalia and related phenomena in non-Christian religions' in *American Anthropologist* 58 (1956), 75-96.
11. The question of parallel phenomena will be discussed later. It is sufficient to refer at this point to Samarin's salutary note in *Tongues of Men and Angels*, 131n. 3. He reminds us that May's survey depends on library sources and that the observers concerned used the term 'glossolalia' for a wide variety of local phenomena: 'All that May has documented, therefore, is that some kind of anomalous vocalizations occur in some religious behavior in different parts of the world.' Such anomalous vocalizing may no doubt be of much interest to the anthropologist, phenomenologist and others, but one has to plead for caution until more information is available concerning the actual nature of the vocalization and the setting in which it occurs. Samarin's criticism could be applied similarly to an aritcle by George J. Jennings, 'An Ethnological Study of Glossolalia' in *J.A.S.A* 20 (1968), 5-16.
12. T. Elmer Clark, *The Small Sects in America* revised edit. (New York, 1949), 97. Similar associations of glossolalia and psychopathologic conflicts have been made by H. K. Schelderup, 'Psychologische Analyse eines Falles von Zungenreden' in *Zeitsch. fur. Psychol.* 122 (1931), 1-12 and Jean Bobon, 'Les Pseudo-Glossolalies Ludiques et Magniques' in *J. Belge de Neurol. et de Psychiat.* 47 (1947), 327-395.
13. See E. M. Pattison, 'Behavioral Science Research and the nature of glossolalia' in J.A.S.A. 20 (1968), 75.
14. e. g. A. Le Baron, 'A case of psychic automation, including "speaking with tongues",' in *Proceedings of the Society for Psychical Research* xii (1896-97), and further T. Flournoy, *From India to the Planet Mars: a study of a case of Somnambulism with Glossolalia* trans. by D. B. Vermilye of *Des Indes à la Planète Mars: Etude sur un Cas de Somnambulisme avec Glossolalie* (Geneva, 1900); Oskar Pfister, *Die psychologische Enträtselung der religiösen Glossolalie und der automatischen Kryptographie* (Sonderabdruck aus dem *Jahrbuch für Psychoanalytische und psychopathologischen Forschungen*, Band 11, Leipzig and Vienna, 1912).
15. E. M. Pattison and R. L. Casey, 'Glossolalia: A contemporary Mystical Experience' in *International Psychiatry Clinics* 5 (1969), 138 mention reports by Maeder, Schjelderup and Jean Bobon. See also the preceding note 12.
16. K. Thomas, 'Speaking in Tongues' unpublished paper, Berlin Suicide Centre (1965) cited by E. M. Pattison in *J.A.S.A.*, op. cit., 76.
17. A. Boisen, 'Economic Distress and Religious Experience: A Study of the Holy Rollers' in *Psychiatry* 2 (1939), 185-194, and 'Religion and Hard Times: A Study of the Holy Rollers' in *Social Action* v (1939) 8-35.
18. A. Kiev, 'Beliefs and Delusions among West Indian Immigrants To London' in *British Journal of Psychiatry* 109 (1963), 362.
19. See Samarin, op. cit., 76.
20. Samarin, *Psychology Today* (Aug. 1972), 79.

21. W. W. Wood, *Culture and Personality Aspects of the Pentecostal Holiness Religion* (Paris: Mouton, 1965). See also J. T. Richardson, 'Psychological Interpretation of Glossolalia: A re-examination of Research' in *J.S.S.R.* xii (2), 199-207.
22. Jennings, op. cit.
23. F. Goodman, *Speaking in Tongues: A Cross-cultural Study of Glossolalia* (Chicago, 1972).
24. *J.A.S.P.R.* 60 (1966), 301.
25. See A. Alland, 'Possession in a revivalist Negro Church' in *J.S.S.R.*, 1:2 (1961); V. H. Hine, 'Pentecostal glossolalia: toward a functional interpretation' in *J.S.S.R.* 8 (1969), 212-226; V. Garrison, 'Marginal religion and psychosocial deviancy: a controlled comparison of Puerto Rican Pentecostals and Catholics' in Irving I. Zanetsky and Mark P. Leone eds. *Pragmatic religions: contemporary religious movements in America* (Princeton) cited by Goodman, ibid.; A. Lovekin and H. N. Malony, 'Religious Glossolalia' in *J.S.S.R.* xvi (4) (Dec. 1977), 383 and cited there N. L. Gerrard and L. B. Gerrard, *Scrabble Creek Folk: Mental Health Part 11*, see also *Trans-Action* (May, 1968).
26. Pattison and Casey in *Int. Psych.* loc. cit. on E. Bourguigon and L. Pettay, 'Spirit Possession, Trance and Cross-cultural Research' unpublished paper, Ohio State Univ. (1966).
27. This point is made by A. W. Sadler 'Glossolalia and possession: an appeal to the Episcopal Study Commission' *J.S.S.R.* 4 (1964), 84-90.
28. E. M. Pattison in *J.A.S.A.* 20 (1968) and *International Psychiatry* loc. cit.
29. cf. the comments of Erika Bourguigon on the influence of the explanatory system on Trance Behaviour in R. Prince edit. *Trance and Possession States* Proceedings of Second Annual Conference R. M. Buck Memorial Society 4-6 March, 1966, Montreal.
30. cf. P. H. van der Walde, 'Trance States and Ego Psychology in R. Prince, ibid.
31. S. C. Plog, 'Preliminary analysis of group questionnaires on glossolalia' unpublished data, Univ. of California, Los Angeles (1966) and L. P. Gerlach and V. H. Hine, 'The charismatic revival: Process of recruitment, conversion and behavioral change in a modern religious movement,' unpublished papers Univ. of Minnesota (1966) ,neither of which indicates a correlation with psychopathology nor supports the frequent charge of abnormality levelled against Pentecostals in general or glossolalists in particular.
32. See e.g. D. W. Burdick, *Tongues: to speak or not to speak* (Chicago, 1969), 75, who writes, 'There is reason to believe that present day glossolalia is an abnormal psychological occurrence.'
33. The observation is made on the basis of many population samples, L. P. Gerlach and V. H. Hine, op. cit. quoted by Pattison in *J.A.S.A.* 20, 76; see also Gerlach and Hine, *J.S.S.R.* 6 (1967), 23-37.
34. Susan E. Gilmore, 'Personality differences between High and Low dogmatism groups of Pentecostal Believers' in *J.S.S.R.* 8 (1968), 161-4.
35. e.g. those of Wood, Vivier and Kildahl.
36. A thesis for the degree of Doctor of Medicine (Psychiatry) at the University of Witwatersrand, Johannesburg (1960), for a summary see L. M. Vivier, 'The Glossolalic and his Personality' in *Beiträge zur Ekstase* edit. Th. Spoerri, *Bibl-psychiat. neurol.* No. 134 (Karger, Basel/New York, 1968), 153-175.
37. Richardson, op. cit., 203.
38. Vivier, Thesis, 382.
39. See Richardson op. cit., 201; J. P. Kildahl, *The Psychology of Speaking in Tongues* (N.Y. Harper and Row, 1972), 58.
40. cf. M. T. Kelsey, *Tongues Speaking, An Experiment in Spiritual Experience* (N.Y.: Doubleday, 1964).
41. 'Pentecostal Glossolalia: Toward a Functional Interpretation' in *J.S.S.R.* 8 (1969), 221.

42. Richardson, op. cit., 205n.
43. Cited by J. P. Kildahl, *The Psychology of Speaking in Tongues* (Hodder and Stoughton, 1972), 57.
44. G. Stanley et alia, 'Some, Characteristics of Charismatic Experience: Glossolalia in Australia' in *J.S.S.R.* 17 (3) (1978), 269-278.
45. cf. A. H. Maslow, 'Eupsychia—The Good Society' in *Journal of Humanistic Psychology*, (1961).
46. See M. T. Kelsey, op. cit., 198 on Jung.
47. In certain mystical states there can be a change in perception which Evelyn Underhill has called 'clarity of vision, a heightening of physical perception', E. Underhill, *Mysticsm* (1955), 235.
48. Rodney Needham 'Percussion and Transition.' in *Man* n.s. vol. 2 (1967), 606-13.
49. *Man* n.s. vol. 2 (1968), 133f.
50. 'A physiological explanation of unusual behaviour in ceremonies involving drums' in *Hum. Biol.* 34 (1962), 151-60.
51. G. Scholem, *Major Trends in Jewish Mysticism* (Jerusalem, 1941), 59.
52. M. Gilsenan, *Saint and Sufi in Modern Egypt* (Oxford, 1973).
53. ibid., 187. For a view of the significance of repetition in a wider context see S. J. Tambiah, 'The Magical Power of Words' in *Man* Vol. 3 No. 2 (June, 1968), 175-208.
54. On the effect of percussion see A. T. Boisen, 'Religion and Hard Times, A Study of the Holy Rollers' in *Social Action* Vol. 5 (March, 1939), 8-35.
55. Kelsey, op. cit., 149.
56. Arnold M. Ludwig, 'Altered States of consciousness' in *Arch. Gen. Psychiat.* (1966), 225-234.
57. For a parallel, see the discussion of shamanism by E. Bournguignon in R. Prince edit. *Trance and Possession States.*
58. See, Th. Spoerri, edit. 'Ekstatische Rede und Glossolalie' in *Beitragen zur Ekstatse. Bible. psychiat. neurol.* 134 (Basel, 1967).
59. E. M. Pattison, 'Behavioral Science research and the nature of glossolia' in *J.A.S.A.*, 20 (1968).
60. G. Palmer, 'Trance and Dissociation: A Cross-cultural study in Psychophysiology' (Univ. of Minnesota M.Sc. unpublished thesis, 1966); 'Trance' a paper presented at the annual meeting of the Central States Anthropological Society, Chicago, April 1967.
61. Palmer, thesis, 15ff. with reference to the work of Bochi and Wenger (1959)
62. ibid., 72.
63. ibid., 87.
64. A phrase used by R. E. Shor 'Hypnosis and the Concept of the Generalised Reality-Orientation' in *American Journal of Psychotherapy*, Vol. 13, (58) (1959), 582-602.
65. ibid., 591.
66. ibid., 595.
67. ibid., 600.
68. ibid., 588.
69. Palmer, op. cit., 101.
70. E. Bourguignon, op. cit., 12.
71. F. D. Goodman, *Speaking in Tongues: A Cross-cultural Study of Glossolalia* (Chicago, 1972).
72. ibid., xx.
73. ibid., 4.
74. ibid., 10.
75. ibid., 77.
76. J. R. Jaquith, 'Toward a Typology of Formal Communicative Behavior in Glossolia' in *Anthropological Linguistics* ix (8), (1967), 1.
77. 'Variation and Variables in Religious Glossolalia' paper given at the 69th Annual Meeting of the American Anthropological Association, San Diego, Calif. 22 Nov., 1970.
78. ibid.

79. W. J. Samarin, *Tongues of Men and Angels: The Religious Language of Pentecostalism* (London: Collier-Macmillan, 1972), 32.

80. cf. R. Gasson, *The Challenging Counterfeit* (Plainfield NJ., 1966), 44.

81. Samarin, op. cit., 33.

82. Shor, op. cit., 597ff.

CHAPTER VII

GLOSSOLALIA IN RECENT RESEARCH (II)

The Function of Glossolalia

As we have seen, theorists have attempted to explain glossolalia in terms of abnormal pathological states, social disorganisation, economic deprivation and cultural conditioning. Each approach, and all of them together, merely clear the ground for more questions concerning root causes. Another line of enquiry is what may be called a functional interpretation. While this may ask a different set of questions, nevertheless, it operates in some of the same areas of investigation as the enquiries already discussed. In other words, the functional approach does not necessarily preclude psychological or sociological interest. It seeks to establish the effect, if any, glossolalia has upon the subject, whether cognitively or in attitudinal and behavioural terms. Highly relevant in this area of enquiry are the psychological analyses of conversion phenomena undertaken by Sargant,[1] Frank,[2] Maslow,[3] Wood,[4] Hine's socio-cultural interpretation in terms of movement dynamics,[5] and a brief article by Lovekin and Malony which considers the degree to which the experience of glossolalia integrates the personality.[6]

I should like, first of all, to consider the view that glossolalia functions as abreactive release. For Sargant, it is a form of regressive abreactive behaviour when the brain, being in what may be described as a state of cortical inhibition, can produce new patterns of speech. He compares the abreactive release induced in neurotic patients by the use of drugs altering cerebral function with accounts in Wesley's Journal of the Revivalist's preaching to groups. The technique of the latter is described thus:

> In a quiet but devastating way he would first bring home to such groups the dire consequences of the life they were leading and the perils of eternal damnation. Somebody in the audience would start to shout and groan, many would feel stricken with acute terror, people fainted and convulsed on the floor, and soon a whole group might become involved one person apparently starting off the others. Acute pain round the heart

and many other psychosomatic manifestations seen were carefully and accurately recorded in his diary by this somewhat unorthodox Fellow of Lincoln College, Oxford.[7]

Sargant suggests that the conversion experience induced a sudden change in mental outlook similar to what he had seen in the abreactive treatment of war neuroses. His thesis being that nervous excitement, which may be precipitated whether by psychological, biochemical or electrical stimulus, can bring about cortical inhibition of varying degree and a state where old habits may be dislodged and replaced by new ones. This is to posit a state of dissociation on the part of the subject, the degree being dependent upon 'the constitutional stability and type of nervous system subjected to these stresses'.

He provides some concrete examples from the religious scene. One was a religious group in Durham, North Carolina where poisonous snakes were being used in an abreactive and cathartic form of service. A build up of excitement by singing, rhythmic clapping of hands led to the handing round of the snakes to those about to 'break'. Effective use was made of periods of increased suggestibility to bring about acceptance of new attitudes and beliefs. He found the same tremendous group pressure accompanied by increasing stimulation and excitement at revival meetings at Cincinatti, Ohio. Here the evangelists and their workers exerted pressure on those likely to attain the experience of sanctification. Sargant compares this inducement to the encouragement given to converts in other sects to 'talk incoherently' as part of the release mechanism. One noteworthy impression which he formed was that the psychological shock methods in the religious circles got at some who would be quite untouched by his own clinical abreactive treatments. He also draws a parallel between the break up of previous mental and emotional patterns in revivalist settings and the effect produced by electro-shock therapy. He is thinking of the physiological state of the brain which can bring about behavioural and attitudinal changes of a permanent order. That is to say, cognitive restructuring is understood to be occasioned by a temporary interruption of normal brain functioning. Whether this degree of physiological breakdown occurs in glossolalic experiences is questionable, although as Hine suggests[8], there may be physiological correlates of lesser intensity. While Sargant's thesis might hold good, not only for conversion experiences, but also for many glossolalic experiences in revivalist settings with their build up of excitement, inducing states of high suggestibility, it does not account for glossolalia and the attitudinal changes claimed for it in more relaxed situations such as is often the case in Neo-Pentecostal groups. Excitement, though often present, is not a *sine qua non* of glossolalia, nor of trance states for that matter.

Like Sargant, Frank also finds that revivalist experiences can effect attitudinal and behavioural changes of a permanent nature and may be compared with the processes of psychotherapy. These changes stem from a reorganization of the subject's world view. What is significant is that both these investigators claim that it is not necessary to refer to pre-disposing personality characteristics to explain participation. The common denominator in psychotherapeutic processes and revivalist experiences is not, according to this view, a psychological state but a physiological one which can be induced in any normal individual. If that is so, then, one need not look to theories of pathological abnormality nor to theories of sociological maladjustment to explain participation. In fact, a pathological condition is more likely to cause immunity to suggestion. Normality on the other hand is no deterrent to involvement in religious conversion and glossolalia. Resistance to suggestion can be maintained by a condition of emotional detachment, such as pathological immunity to suggestion, or by a stronger commitment to some other belief system or way of life that is obsessive.[9]

There is no reason to demur at the findings of Wood and Maslow that intense religious experience is correlated to cognitive changes and mental reorientation. In Maslow's view, peak religious experiences may produce, as well as a type of cognition different from normal states, differences also in visual and auditory perception and Hine thinks that such perceptions are similar to those reported by Pentecostals during their glossolalic experiences. While this may well be the case, I would contend equally that the belief system forming the conceptual setting in which the experience occurs is of decided importance. A permanent attitudinal change can hardly be effected unless the experience relates to a conceptual system regarded as authoritative. For this reason there is a difference in function between glossolalia artificially produced as a pseudo-language for playful purpose and one which originates with all seriousness in the milieu of committed body. One may analyse glossolalia in terms of psychological, sociological and linguistic factors, but unless one takes into account that the act is, in itself, one of commitment to or confirmation of beliefs and attitudes and one of identification with the group one is missing out an important, if not the most salient ingredient, in the glossolalia of Pentecostal groups.

Outwardly, to the observer, there may be little if anything to distinguish the pseudo from the authentic, but the experienced Pentecostal would claim the ability to detect the spurious. There is the interesting experiment reported by W. Cohn of a Pentecostal minister who when confronted with simulated glossolalia described it as 'true glossolalia', but nevertheless held that it came from sources other than God.[10] In fact, the source of this particular sample of glossolalia was the researcher Cohn and his actor assistants. He was putting to the test a theory that perhaps glossolalia 'quite aside from any religious significance exerts an attraction upon an identifiable psychological type' a theory which as we have seen is far from convincing. In Cohn's experiment, 'tongues' were produced in simulation of what the collaborators had heard in Pentecostal groups and this was done to the accompaniment of West Indian drumming. A film was made of one of the sessions and it was this which was later shown to the Pentecostal minister. W. J. Samarin also viewed this film but his comment was that 'only one person uttered anything resembling glossolalia'.[11]

Though Cohn's original thesis was not substantiated, be advances another in the light of his experiment, namely that 'an acceptance of the religious doctrine is not necessary for glossolalia'. This could be so if one meant by glossolalia simply the lexical component. No doubt parallels for glossolalia as aberrant speech can be found in many communities, ancient and modern, particularly where spirit possession and prophesying prevails. My argument is that to isolate the lexical part will not disclose the meaningfulness of glossolalia as a spiritual exercise. The utterance has its roots in experience and that in turn is not uninfluenced by the conceptual system of the culture in which it occurs. The whole glossolalic event must, therefore, be taken into consideration and not simply the verbal form, for there is a mutual interrelatedness of experience, belief and utterance. The experience is authenticated and given meaning by the belief system in which it occurs, and the belief system is endorsed and given power by the experience. Maybe the success of Pentecostalism is due in no small measure to this emphasis on both belief and experience, and the glossolalic event is a focal point where the interplay is fully active and recognized. In this cultural framework they are interdependent, and, where they are divorced, those instances of glossolalia would be declared spurious by the committed. What is intriguing and challenging in our day is that Christian glossolalia is now related to an ever widening conceptual framework which includes both Catholic and Protestant Christian cultures. This poses a challenge to theologians on either

154

side, for this new penetration needs to be taken fully into account in any attempt at theological evaluation of glossolalia.

What has just been said about interrelatedness might seem to find support in an article by J. Laffal.[12] He stresses the importance of the link between language and experience within the individual but he goes on to identify that link in psychological terms, employing Freudian ideas about vocalization as an energy discharge even in the conscious state.[13] Language, he argues, has a dual function, since it is not only an instrument of communication and social union but also serves a discharge function. In certain conditions, psychosis for instance, the discharge function may, as it were, overwhelm the channels of expression and the subject produces utterances which have no intelligible reference for the ordinary observer. Laffal presents glossolalia as 'perhaps the clearest example of the discharge function of language' and he maintains that we may assume that glossolalic utterances 'in which recognizability and specificity of reference have been lost serve the purpose of discharging the psychic energy associated with wishes and conflicts'. In his earlier work, the same writer regards glossolalia as providing verbal form to a conflicted wish 'while at the same time hiding the wish by stripping the verbalization of meaning'.[14] Samarin's criticism is that Laffal's samples of glossolalia are the utterances of a schizophrenic patient,[15] and the motivation in such a case could be very different from what motivates most religious glossolalists. There is a difference, also, in the speech form, since the language of the schizophrenic is obviously determined by his primal tongue, while, in glossolalia, any dependence on the grammar of the original tongue, if it can be established at all, is certainly veiled.

To return to the theory that glossolalia functions as energy discharge, it is held that the speaker derives the benefit of discharge while avoiding the guilt of despair which could be generated by specific identification of his conflicts. Furthermore, since, in the speaker's own estimate, his words are not his own but 'divinely given', he would not of course relate energy release to his own conflicts and needs. Lapsley and Simpson similarly understand glossolalia to be a regression in the service of the ego, providing a unique kind of release for disturbed persons who have internalised their emotional conflicts.[16] While this 'Freudian' interpretation in terms of an outlet for hidden repressed conflicts and energy discharge may be true, there seems to be no way to determine if this is so. When the language of utterance is unintelligible, the inner processes of the experience cannot be said to have been raised to the level of consciousness and without identification of these conflicts one can rely only on the descriptive but subjective accounts of glossolalics themselves as to the therapeutic effects of the experience. It is by no means proven that glossolalics have suppressed disturbing experiences which find an outlet of release in meaningless speech.

E. M. Pattison, however, speaks of a discharge of affect through thought as well as utterance.[17] One may well ask how thought can be in any way associated with what is linguistic nonsense. Here Pattison refers, *inter alia*, to the early work of Oskar Pfister, the Swiss psychoanalyst.[18] Pfister's method was to encourage free association on the part of a glossolalist and behind each neologism he found thoughts for the most part infantile—representing repressed painful experience. What appeared as nonsense to the observer had considerable meaning for the individual glossolalist.[19]

Pattison speaks of two categories of glossolalia, namely, playful and serious. The former includes what Spoerri describes as 'Kuntsprachen', or 'art speech', namely, 'devices to express a feeling or mood which cannot be expressed by common vocabulary words'.[20] Playful glossolalia is produced volitionally and is a consciously manufactured pseudo-language. It can be used to relieve boredom or to reduce anxiety, but the person who employs it in this way would most probably be unaware of such motives, just as, in serious glossolalia, the primary motive is not the reducing of tension. Pattison is of the opinion that serious glossolalia can also be produced volitionally and with intention. This is so, but as previously stated, there is no conscious structuring of content in this case. Pattison refers to subjects creating new words for their glossolalic vocabulary. This I am sure would neither be condoned nor practised among serious glossolalists such as Pentecostals, nor would they experience 'aesthetic delight' in their own vocalisation, though they might comment upon the beauty of the speech of others. I am not convinced by a thesis advanced by Castaldo and Holzman that there is intense focus of attention by the glossolalist on his own voice.[21]

Another distinction used by Pattison is that of inner and external speech and he regards glossolalia as a borderline phenomenon between the two.[22] Inner speech is 'fragmented, underdeveloped and incomplete so that, if externalized, it would be extremely difficult to understand'.[23] Germane to the present discussion is that inner speech may subserve emotional needs, since the 'thought' brought into awareness in this way may be strongly affect-laden. Among other functions, it is the vehicle by which memory traces laden with emotion can be carried. It can exercise these functions without making the utterances audible; on the other hand, external speech need not be in each instance a manifestation of thought.

While I can accept that the feeling tone of thoughts in inner speech may be encoded in external glossolalia utterance, I would not make the process such a deliberate one as Pattison does. He writes:

> Glossolalia initially utilizes the mediative or task orientation of an individual's inner speech. When the glossolalic phrases which have been heard and stored in memory are brought into awareness, they are practised over and over again in inner speech until an acceptable form of glossolalia is mastered. With its mastery, the inner speech is reproduced externally and the spontaneous glossolalic utterance may be heard for the first time. With repeated use of his 'tongue' his speech becomes more and more automatic, no longer requiring the use of the inner speech mechanism. The verbal part of the inner speech mechanism is used only in the initial state of glossolalia and later in the habitual stage when affect and mood states arise which call for creation of more expressive words. When new words are not being made and the automatic utterances are spoken as in the serious category, the individual may simultaneously engage in inner speech mechanism with a number of thoughts and feeling states *while* speaking in tongues. It is an impression that the feeling tone of these thoughts in inner speech is encoded onto the automatic speech utterances.[24]

Whatever the case is in 'playful glossolalia', I cannot accept that glossolalic phrases are practised in inner speech in serious glossolalia. What I find no difficulty in accepting is that glossolalia becomes a vehicle for conveying 'meaning' through the intonational features superimposed on the external speech, for intonation can convey moods of anger, joy, sadness etc. This being so, as Pattison avers, the serious category may also serve to aid in the reduction of tension. One might add that this could be done even more effectively than in the case of playful glossolalia. The 'meaning' conveyed however remains vague and unspecified and should perhaps more properly be described as a communication of mood or feeling. This of course is not the conscious aim of the glossolalist nor is he concerned with glossolalia as a discharge of energy and a reducer of tensions. Yet it may perform all these functions without revealing the content of tensions to others, nor for that matter, to the subject himself.

While it may well be the case that glossolalia often provides a release mechanism for inner tensions and conflicts, these need not be other than the kind of pressures borne by most, but it is by no means proven that there is a correlation between inner conflict and

157

glossolalia. Glossolalia does not illumine the nature of the tensions and conflicts, for, however intense they may be, they remain at the unconscious level. This has not deterred attempts at identification, for instance, in terms of regression to infantilism or some form of narcissism.[25] Pattison's view is that while in some glossolalists the regressive state is pathological, in most it is not, but rather a regression in the service of the ego, while in yet other cases there is little if any regression of associated ego functions. Lapsley and Simpson consider the inner conflict of the glossolalist in the light of what they regard as the apparently universal concern of both Pentecostalism and neo-Pentecostalism with the activity of satanic power. They see this conflict as being due, genetically, 'to an unconscious attachment to parental figures characterized by strong feelings of both love and hate'. The individual is unable to express either of them directly and tension is produced. Glossolalia is then 'viewed' as an indirect, though powerful expression of primitive love toward the parent and the demonology a projection of the hate and fear in that childhood relationship.[26]

Others have seen the regressive function of glossolalia as a means of 'restoring infantile megalomania'[27] or even 'a reverberation of very early days in the history of the race'.[28] As previously stated it is hard to come by concrete evidence to support these 'Freudian' speculations of 'unconscious contents kept away from the conscious by the expenditure of psychic force'.[29] What cannot be gainsaid are the subjective claims of reduced tension by participants though the nature of the tensions remain elusive, and so the assessor is left to surmise.

Another aspect of glossolalia is what has been called its unifying function. Glossolalic experience may strengthen an individual's acceptance of the normative attitudes of his group. In this way he integrates with the community, conforms to its norms of behaviour and attitudes, and in that way may resolve some conflicts in his own personality through the expulsive power of the force generated by the community's code of expectation. Virginia Hine, for instance, found that in the case of subjects observed by her while the majority had always accepted the Bible as authoritative the experience of glossolalia almost invariably led to acceptance of a 'fundamentalist' position even, or indeed, especially, in the case of those with a liberal gackground. As a result of their experience the latter were much readier to accept the authority of Scriptures than most.[30] American Catholic Bishops have come across a similar tendency among Catholic glossolalists in the contemporary charismatic renewal. A report of a committee of the National Conference of Catholic Bishops, while basically approving of the charismatic renewal, stressed that it must have a strong bond with the total life of the church, and specifically warned that the renewal must avoid the dangers of 'elitism' and 'biblical fundamentalism'.[31]

Hine advances a functional interpretation of glossolalia in terms of what is called movement dynamics. A sample of two hundred and thirty-one glossolalists were classified as

(a)   frequent tongue speakers who spoke in tongues daily, or more than once a week, and

(b)   those who spoke with tongues less frequently.

It was found that while second generation Pentecostals belonged to group (b), most of those in group (a) had a 'liberal' rather than 'conservative' or 'fundamentalist' background. If this sample was a true indicator then the most frequent glossolalists 'were those who had been least socialized to accept the practice'.[32] Erstwhile 'liberals' tended to become fundamentalist as a result of the experience, but there were other changes in attitudes and social behaviour. Very properly so, these were not traced to the mere verbal act of glossolalia but to 'the experiential complex of which the linguistic behaviour is one component'. The experience may strengthen a believer's confidence in the authority of the group and in the authenticity of its basic beliefs, and the total environment may effect attitudinal and behavoural changes such as an increased capacity for love towards others, inner calm and joy, and greater social fellowship with new friends. Investigations of a wider range of types of Pentecostal groups confirmed this reorientation even among well-educated, socially successful and well-adjusted personality types. Frequent tongue speakers in non-Pentecostal churches, as well as members of Pentecostal sects and independent groups showed a significant tendency to meet in group activities. Gerlach and Hine regard this as an involvement indicator, since, in their view, glossolalia is significantly related to commitment to Pentecostalism as a movement. The commitment is analysed in this way:

'The two components of commitment which we have been able to identify in Pentecostalism, Black Power, and other movements are: first, an experience through which an individual's image of himself is altered and some degree of cognitive reorganization in the direction of movement ideology takes place; and second, the performance of an objectively observable act. This must be what we have called a "bridge-burning" act which sets the individual apart from the larger society to some degree, identifies him with the group in which he experienced it, and commits him to certain changes in attitudinal or behavioural patterns.'[33]

159

As might be expected when society frowns upon what it regards as the abnormal behaviour of some Pentecostal groups, this has had the effect of binding the members of the group more closely together and of setting them apart from others. Glossolalia itself constitutes a bridge-burning act for American Pentecostals in a society which tends to frown upon any display of emotion in the religious arena. In other cultural settings there will be functional alternatives for the bridge-burning act. For instance, Hine finds that, in rural areas of Mexico or Latin America, merely walking into an Evangelico church constitutes a bridge-burning act and in Haiti a ritual burning of Voodoo objects reinforces commitment to Pentecostalism and signalises separation from the larger community, with its attendant risk. In this country in revivalist contexts, the discarding of pipes and tobacco pouches by the newly converted has served a similar purpose. Glossolalia functions as the 'language' of the group, and may be compared to the function of the special language adopted in bodies like the Melanesian cargo cults.[34] In each case the 'language' exercises a demarcating function to separate members from other groups and a unifying function within the group as in glossolalic circles.

In Pentecostal groups the non-glossolalist may not be denied full acceptance into the fellowship but to speak with tongues is an expression of a person's commitment to the beliefs, way of life and value of the group and one might add that it inevitably has certain elitist overtones. It can also be an open declaration of a person's abandonment of previous groups and of his identification with the new. Hine's conclusion merits full quotation:

> Cross-cultural studies of religious behaviour support the assumption accepted by most anthropologists that the capacity for ecstatic experiences and trance, or other associated behaviour is panhuman. Only the interpretation of it, the technique designed to facilitate or inhibit it, and the form it takes, differ cross-culturally. When such states and behaviours are valued in society (as they are in many non-Western societies), this capacity can be systematically encouraged in some or all of its members. When they are devalued, they can be culturally inhibited, and appear only as deviant behaviour. If such 'deviant behaviour' functions to set practitioners apart from the larger society through specific and desired personal changes, these extra-ordinary experiences may be institutionalized to make what David Aberle would call 'religious virtuosi of the ordinary worshippers'.[35]

Through a functional approach to the phenomenon, we have come to assess glossolalia as a non-pathological linguistic behaviour, which functions in the context of the Pentecostal movement as one component in the generation of commitment. As such, it operates in social change, facilitating the spread of the Pentecostal movement, affecting nearly every denomination within organized Christianity, and in personal change, providing powerful motivation for attitudinal and behavioural changes in the direction of group ideas.[36]

This is a positive estimate on the basis of careful study, and as such to be welcomed. Hine has not raised the question of theological evaluation, but whoever undertakes such a task would do well to heed the work of behavioural scientists. Theologians in the past have tended to neglect such investigation on the plea that they were reductionist and indeed irrelevant. Some of it may justify the charge of reductionism from a theological viewpoint but irrelevant it is not. The whole question of theological evaluation demands separate treatment but some aspects can be noted here. Pentecostals offer explanations of psychical experiences which would be precluded by the very nature of their 'world-view', by many, if not most, present-day Christians in main-line traditions. For instance, where there is no subscription to literalist belief in spirits, there will be greater readiness to explain glossolalia entirely in socio-psychological terms. The fact is that Western Christendom on the whole has moved away from the milieu of New Testament thinking with its ready acceptance of notions of possession and inspiration, and this, no doubt, has had severe impact upon the nature and form of Christian worship. This is why H. P. van Dusen could say: 'Peter and Barnabas and Paul might find themselves more at home in a Holiness service or at a Pentecostal revival than in the formalized and sophisticated worship of other churches, Catholic or Protestant.'[37] While the pre-scientific views represented in the New Testament cannot be honestly thrust upon the present generation, and while it is also admitted that even within the New Testament itself there are signs of development and creative interpretation[38] nevertheless the committed Christian has to insist upon the status of the belief in the Holy Spirit and His work. In other words, belief in disembodied spirits is not of the *esse* of traditional Christian faith but belief in the work of the Holy Spirit is. It may well be that the success of the modern charismatic movement may be due to its fostering of emotional and psychological conditions conducive to the same kind of genuine experience as in primitive

Christianity, conceptually related, in both instances, to the work of the Holy Spirit. The glossolalic regards himself as possessor of truth, a status confirmed for him by his glossolalic experience. The experience brings about therefore a new confidence and buoyancy. Is this claim justified?

Richardson called for a study which would look at potential tongue-speakers before and after their participation in glossolalia.[39] He complained that previous research had ignored a time series design. Even an extensive study, involving eight hundred subjects, such as Plog's[40] relied upon retrospection when it came to accounts of pre-glossolalic attitudes. Lovekin and Malony similarly complain at the dearth of what they call longitudinal studies, that is, studies which assess personality before and after glossolalic experience.[41] Since studies have been mostly restricted to post-glossolalic conditions[42], there has been no conclusive evidence 'regarding what, if any, personality changes occur as a function of becoming glossolalic'.[43]

Lovekin and Malony attempt to fill the gap by assessing personality change over a period of time among a group of persons who became glossolalists during what were known as 'Life of the Spirit Seminars' in 1972.[44] What they sought to discover was whether glossolalia was integrative to the personality. Others had established that non-pathological mystical experiences could be integrative resulting in a change of life style and better life-adaptation[45] but this study looked specifically at glossolalia. If the latter had an integrative function, then they would expect among other things (in their own jargon!):

> a significant increase in the Salience of Religion defined as reported rating regarding the importance of religion;
> a significant increase in the Salience of Religion defined as a self report of hours per week spent in church activities; a significant increase in Ego Strength
> a significant decrease in Anxiety Trait... Anxiety State, Depression, Hostility, Problems and 'Extrinsic Orientation' to Religion.

Tests (such as the Multiple Affect Adjective Check List and various scales) were administered at the beginning of the seminars, then, one week after participants had experienced 'the Baptism of the Holy Spirit', and three months later. From the fifty-one persons attending the Seminars, twelve, who became fully glossolalic for the first time, are designated the 'New Tongues Group', while

162

thirteen, who had been glossolalics before attending the Seminars, were called the 'Old Tongues Group'. Jung had considered the experience of glossolalia to be a positive preparation for the integration of personality, [46] but these tests offered no support as far as the initial experience of speaking in tongues was concerned. In only one case was there an enhancement of personality integration. However, the New Tongues Group at first testing showed a significant minimisation of State Anxiety only to lose this effect at the later follow-up test, while the Non-Tongues Group showed less State Anxiety at both periods. The New Tongues Group showed no marked evidence of fulfilling the other test expectations such as less depression, hostility etc. The researchers found little evidence to support the views that glossolalia can resolve neurosis or re-establish the ego, views which had been proposed *inter alia* by Kelsey[47] and Lapsley and Simpson. [48]

What did emerge however was that the Seminars themselves had an integrating effect. Of course, attitudinal changes brought about by group support and group expectation can be achieved similarly by non-religious groups, but they are surely strengthened where there is believed to be divine sanction and approbation for the group and its activity. Glossolalia is considered to be an expression of divine acceptance and it cannot therefore, be as negative in integrative significance as these results would lead us to believe. Even the Non-Tongues Group would regard the glossolalic manifestations as authenticating the Seminars although they themselves had not spoken in tongues. In other words, what the participants themselves believe and what the researchers say actually happens need not necessarily coincide. The participants would attribute attitudinal change to the glossolalic act within the group, while the researchers assign it to group support only. Many more cross-cultural investigations are called for before statements can be made with confidence and furthermore the value of the tests themselves needs to be carefully assessed.

Meanwhile, the subjective testimonies of participants must be given due weight. Glossolalia can be seen as a symbol of a break with the past and identification with the new community. It confirms the individual in his new association but it also serves to nurture the group and the movement. At the same time, one must note a falling away in the use of glossolalia in some older groups. [49] It is to be expected that the incidence of glossolalia will, of course, vary from group to group and a variety of reasons can be given for any inactivity. Traditional Pentecostals will speak of 'backsliding' or increasing worldliness on the part of glossolalists. It is interesting to find that in response to Samarin's question 'Does a failure to speak in tongues for a long time indicate a bad relationship with God? Why?' Categorical answers in an affirmative tended to come from older Pentecostals. Most respondents, however, gave a negative reply. Out of eighty-five, fifty-six said 'no' or 'not necessarily', and Samarin finds in the contrast with representative replies from the older tradition with its penchant for either/or categories, 'further evidence for the evolution toward personalism and pluralism in modern western religion'.[50] He dissents from the usual Pentecostal view that inactivity leads to inability to manifest glossolalia, since 'a skill as easy as this one cannot really be "lost"'. He can take this view because he isolates the vocal component in the glossolalia event and his observation is similar to saying that an ability to utter prophetic oracles cannot be lost as long as the power of speech is retained.

In its unifying function, glossolalia is a symbol of identification with the group not simply because of its unusualness or status as the 'language' of the new group but, above all, by virtue of its deemed supernatural source. For Pentecostals, it is of supernatural origin, and its occurrence a sacred occasion. They would say that even to call it 'a linguistic symbol of the sacred'[51] is not enough, unless one insists that the symbol in this case participates in what it symbolises. In practice, those who experience glossolalia prefer not to call it a symbol at all. Observers, however, see it as a symbol of the bridge-burning kind, and in its unifying function, as one of identification with the new group. The speaker with tongues could in fact be persuaded to regard it as a symbol in a different sense. He conceives of glossolalia as an act which demands total submission to allow God to 'take over'. That God can manipulate his tongue could become symbolic for him of what is far more significant, namely, that God can use the whole person for His divine purpose. It would then symbolise submission to God, and, conversely, a rejection of what is wordly when it represents a self-assertive stance over against the authority of society. The functions of glossolalia may vary considerably from one group to the next, and, in many instances, it is considered the high water mark of spirituality in a meeting. It has also become in many instances a badge of elitism within the group. In most charismatic groups, in the initial stages, before the development of organizational structures, anyone can practice glossolalia in public, but, with routinisation, speaking with tongues becomes more and more associated with the role of the leader and control over general glossolalic activity increases.

In the early days of Pentecostalism, a kind of inverted pride developed. Leaders expressed anti-intellectual sentiments and openly boasted of their lack of educational training and qualifications. Just as Muslims have emphasized the illiteracy of the Prophet in order to maximise the miracle of the Qur'ān, so Pentecostal leaders paraded their lack of formal education to draw attention to their charismatic powers. Glossolalia gave them stature and authority in the sight of the group and also in their own eyes. Calley provides an illustration of this association of glossolalia and authority among a group of West Indian immigrant Pentecostals in London.[52] When a member challenged the authority of the leader, the latter responded by speaking in tongues. Not to be outdone, the church member came back with his own glossolalic answer and for a while both of them were 'speaking to each other' in tongues! Leaders have had occasion to rebuke the ambitious in their midst when they saw the danger of a 'wordly' attitude eroding the 'spiritual' even in the very exercise of spiritual activity. Even so, there is no doubt that the possession of the gift of tongues added to a person's stature in the eyes of his companions and might even evoke envy. There seem to be recognized grades within the group, not of course in any regimented sense nor in a manner resembling the offices assigned in the Apostolic Church, but in terms of respect and honour. Thus a person who interprets tongues will be deemed to be higher in the spiritual hierarchy than the one who only speaks. Prophecy would rate a higher status still and an ambitious member seeking the leadership of the group would seek these 'higher' gifts. This may be much too cynical a view, however, and I must confess that in my experience of Pentecostals and charismatics generally, the thought of seeking gifts for the sake of authority and power would be abhorrent and the person who harboured such ambition would be as despicable in their sight as Simon the Sorcerer who believed that the power of healing could be acquired by purchase (Acts 8:20).

For Pentecostals, any status which may be associated with glossolalia is not one of merit, innate ability, social position or any other consideration, but is wholly of divine conferment. One of the results of this thinking is that women glossolalists have not been denied a prominent role in an institution that is traditionally dominated by men. Samarin's comment on this is that 'even in non-Christian societies, religions of enthusiasm provide women with more involvement and more status than they traditionally had'.[53]

Samarin, however, rejects the notion of glossolalia as a divine gift. It is, he declares, neither supernatural as the Pentecostal believes, nor abnormal, as the man-in-the-street believes. It is for him a normal, if anomalous, exercise. While he denies its divine source, he nevertheless does justice to its function as a symbol, since he is aware that it indicates for believers that the participant is 'involved in something—at a given moment in time or as part of a pattern of life—that transcends the ordinary'.[54]   The glossolalists, he says, knows in some fashion or other that tongues represent the presence of God.   'Glossolalia *says* "God is here" (Just as a Gothic cathedral says, "Behold, God is Majestic".).'

To sum up, then, on the question of function, psychologically considered, glossolalia may be a release mechanism leading to a reorientation which could be of a permanent order.   It is an energy discharge which can have therapeutic value as a reducer of tension and resolver of inner conflict.   Viewed sociologically, it can be seen as one component in the act of commitment to a new group, and a bridge-burning declaration in severing connection with the former, wider community.   It becomes the badge or 'language' of the new group and also a 'linguistic symbol of the sacred', provided, as stated, that by a symbol, in this instance, we mean that which participates in what it signifies namely the presence of the Holy Spirit.[55]

Possession of this 'gift' can pose problems in the emergence of ambitions to attain the most highly esteemed status, but, in practice, the spirituality of the groups has curbed excesses in a remarkable way.   Next we need to look at the form of glossolalia and the contribution of linguistics to our understanding, and, after that, at the question of kindred phenomena in other religious cultures.

1. W. Sargant, 'Some Cultural Group Abreactive Techniques and Their Relation to Modern Treatments' in *Proceedings of the Royal Society of Medicine* (section of Psychiatry, Feb. 1949), 367-374; also *Battle for the Mind* (N.Y.: Doubleday, 1957).
2. J. Frank, *Persuasion and Healing: A comparative study of Psychotherapy* (Baltimore: John Hopkins Press, 1961).
3. A. H. Maslow, *Religions, Values and Peak Experiences* (Columbus; Ohio State Univ. Press, 1964).
4. W. W. Wood, *Culture and Personality: Aspects of the Pentecostal Holiness Religion* (Paris: Mouton, 1965).
5. Virginia H. Hine, 'Pentecostal Glossolalia : Toward a Functional Interpretation' in *J.S.S.R.* 8 (1969), 211-226.
6. Adams Lovekin and H. Newton Malony, 'Religious Glossolalia' in *J.S.S.R.* 16 (4) (Dec. 1977), 383-393.
7. Sargant, *Proceedings etc.*, 368.
8. Hine, op. cit., 223.
9. Hine, ibid.
10. W. Cohn, 'Personality, Pentecostalism and Glossolalia: A Research Note on Some Unsuccessful Research' in *The Canadian Review of Sociology, Anthropology*, vol. v (1968), 39.
11. W. J. Samarin, *Tongues of Men and Angels*, 75.
12. J. Laffal, 'Language, Consciousness and experience' in *Psychoanalytic Quarterly* 36 (1967), 61-67.
13. See further J. Laffal, *Pathological and Normal Language* (New York, 1965).

14. Laffal, ibid., 88; cf. W. La Barre's description of glossolalia among southern snake-handlers as 'externalization of characterological conflict', see *They shall take up serpents: Psychology of the southern snake-handling cult* (Minneapolis, 1962).
15. Samarin, op. cit., 35ff.
16. J. N. Lapsley and J. H. Simpson 'Speaking in tongues: Infantile babble or song of the self' in *Pastoral Psychology* (Sept. 1964), 20-21 cited by J. T. Richardson, Psychological Interpretations of Glossolalia: A Re-examination of Research in *J.S.S.R.* 12 (2), 200.
17. E. M. Pattison, 'Behavioral Science Research and the nature of glossolalia' in *J.A.S.A.* 20 (1968), 73-86.
18. O. Pfister, *Die psychologische Entratselung der religiosen Glossolalie und der automatischen Kryptographie (Jahrbuch psychoanaly, psychopath. Forsch.* 111 (1912)).
19. Pattison refers to some more recent work on the association technique in relation to nonsense words, namely I. Iritanti, 'A Study of the expressive values of nonlinguistic sounds and their influence on the articulation of perceived objects', unpublished doctoral dissertation, Clark University, 1962.
20. Pattison, op. cit., 81, T. H. Spoerri, *Sprachphanomene und Psychose* (Basle, 1964).
21. V. Castaldo and P. S. Holzman, 'The effects of hearing one's own voice on sleep mutation' on *J. Nerv. Ment. Dis.* 145 (1967), 2-13.
22. Pattison op. cit., see also E. J. McGuigan, *Thinking : Studies of Convert Language Processes* (New York, 1966).
23. Pattison, op. cit.
24. ibid.
25. John B. Oman in *Pastoral Psychology* 14 (Dec. 1963), 48-51.
26. J. N. Lapsley and J. H. Simpson, 'Speaking in Tongues' in *Pastoral Psychology* 15 (1964), 16-24; 48-55.
27. P. Worsley, *The Trumpet shall Sound* (London, 1957), 247 cited by Samarin op. cit., 41. See also J. B. Oman op. cit., 49. W. E. Oates 'A socio-psychological study of glossolalia' in F. Stagg, E. R. Hinson and W. E. Oates *Glossolalia: Tongue Speaking in Biblical, Historical and Psychological Perspective* (Abingdon Press, 1967), 96.
28. G. B. Cutten, *Speaking with Tongues*, (New Haven: Yale Univ. Press, (1972)), 2.
29. This is how it is admirably expressed by C. T. K. Chari in his Introduction to the new edition of Th. Flournoy, *From India to the Planet Mars* (New York, 1963), xiii.
30. V. H. Hine, op. cit., 221.
31. *New Covenant* iv (8) (Feb. 1975), 26.
32. Hine, op. cit., 222.
33. Hine, op. cit., 224 see also L. P. Gerlach and V. H. Hine, 'Five factors crucial to the growth and spread of a religious movement' in *J.S.S.R.* 6 (1967), 22-39.
34. Samarin, op. cit. chap. xi.
35. The reference is to D. F. Aberle, *The Peyote Religion among the Navaho* Wenner-Gren Foundation for Anthropological Research No. 42, Viking Fund Publ. (New York, 1966).
36. V. H. Hine, 'Pentecostal Glossolalia' in *J.S.S.R.* 8 (1969), 225.
37. *Life* vol. 50 (9th June 1958), 122.
38. See D. Cupitt's letter in *Times*, 2nd June 1975.
39. Richardson, op. cit.
40. S. Plog, 'UCLA conducts research in glossolalia' in *Trinity* 3 (1965), 38-39.
41. A. Lovekin and N. H Malony, op. cit., 16.
42. Those who make direct comparisons of glossolalics and non-glossolalics are Vivier, Wood and Kildhal.
43. Lovekin and Malony, op. cit., 385.

44. These were seminars during a seven week course in the Roman Catholic Church, Albuquerque, New Mexico and the Episcopal Church in Claremont, California in 1972, see S. Clarke, *Team Manual for Life in the Spirit Seminars* 2nd edit. (Notre Dame, Inc.: Charismatic Renewal Series).
45. A. J. Deikman, 'Deautomatization and the mystic experience' in *Psychiatry* 29 (1966), 324; A. M. Ludwig, op. cit.
46. See Kelsey, op. cit., 199.
47. Kelsey, op. cit., 207-208.
48. Lapsley and Simpson, op. cit., 210-211.
49. See Bloch-Hoell, op. cit., 146, 163.
50. Samarin, *Tongues*, 195.
51. ibid., 231.
52. M. J. C. Calley, *God's People : West Indian Pentecostal Sects in England* (O.U.P., 1965), 46, 48, 78, 79 cited by Samarin, op. cit., 218.
53. Samarin, op. cit., 223.
54. ibid.
55. c.f. P. Tillich, *Dynamics of Faith*, 42 where he holds that symbols arise out of the unconscious and have an internal connection with that which they signify: they 'participate in that to which they point'.

Chapter VIII

GLOSSOLALIA IN RECENT RESEARCH (III)

The Form of Glossolalia

Early investigators, like Cutten, Lombard and Mosiman, outlined the *form* of glossolalia. While their general impression is one of incomprehensible sounds, they detected well articulated word fragments as well as characteristics such as repetition and alliteration. Since then there has been very little discussion of the form, *per se*, except perhaps to call attention to some fairly general marks of glossolalia such as open syllables and the avoidance of clusters of consonants. All the more credit, therefore, to socio-linguistic researchers, especially W. J. Samarin, for highlighting the importance of focusing attention upon this aspect. He has laid firm foundations, and invites further research particularly in field work among bilingual communities. While Samarin has concentrated upon linguistic analysis of the verbal component, Goodman pays more attention to features such as intonation and pause, discovering a vocal pattern despite linguistic and cultural differences. These two seminal contributions cannot be ignored in a discussion of the Form of Glossolalia.

Samarin provides a number of glossolalic texts.[1] One represents the glossolalic utterance of a Presbyterian minister in a fairly long passage of one hundred and fifty six phrases arranged in twenty-eight breath groups or 'sentences'. Of these phrases, sixty-five segments of speech constitute permutations on a basic theme of what may be called 'consonantal chiming'.[2] The prevailing consonantal sounds in this case are s, sh, zh, n, d, tr. With variations of vowels the resulting effect verges occasionally on the kind of aesthetic appeal a portion of Welsh 'cynghanedd' might have e.g. sozhándre kéla zhindrá. 'Cynghanedd' is peculiar to Welsh poetry and the rules governing it are precise, explicit and sometimes complicated. These rules, it is said, appear to have been kept secret in earlier centuries until the close corporation of bards disintegrated in the sixteenth century.[3] In spite of the calculated ingenuity of 'cynghanedd', it is not unknown for certain individuals,

169

for whom it is almost second nature, to speak naturally and effort-lessly in this medium. This may also be due partly to the structure of the Welsh language itself since it tends to take that form organically.[4] Of course, although 'cynghanedd' is for the ear and not for the eye, it is more than emotive sound, for the very sound in fact can contribute as a communicative factor to imprint the words, and so the message, upon the mind and memory of the hearer. In considering the uses of speech, one can think of the scientific use in which words symbolise a reference which can be verified in relation to external reality, and one can also refer to the evocative or emotive use in which words simply become signs of emotions or attitudes, their representative power being secondary.[5] While utterance in 'cynghanedd' may be emotive, this, as it were, is a bonus added to its referential function. Glossolalia, therefore, differs radically from it and from any kind of intelligible prose or poetry for it has no such referential function. Yet, in terms of sound and attraction listening to some forms of glossolalic utterance may have a similar pleasing effect upon the ear as 'cynghanedd', while other forms can strike one as monotonous and on occasion even discordant. Much, of course, depends on the rhythm adopted in addition to the consonantal sequence. Samarin elucidates many features associated with glos-solalia such as echoism, alliteration, repetition, paradigmatic permutations, and he sheds many insights on topics which need ventilation such as the relationship of glossolalia and the speaker's primal language, sound/meaning correlations, emotional impact, the aesthetic appeal of glossolalia, and diaglossa, a feature of speak-ing with tongues. A brief comment is now offered on some of these.

Alliteration is a well known feature of glossolalia. In some of the texts by the Presbyterian minister already referred to, t, k, s, y, p, account for 52 per cent of all consonants. This inevitably produces alliteration, but it is also indicative in another sense, according to Samarin, in that the speaker tends to use what is common in English, and he advances this as an example of how the 'creator of extemporaneous pseudolanguage' may maximise what is already most frequent in his native tongue. Alliteration is also featured in a glossolalic text where the speaker uses a similar sequence of sounds each time he produces a breath group. Within the syllable-sequences there is a phonetic resemblance which Samarin calls paradigmatic relationship or a 'disguised' subtle repetition. This feature is found to be present in other texts cited. Thus we have sante, shante, sante, and kante, in one, and in another shandre, zhandre, shantre, yandre. This paradigmatic relationship is strikingly illustrated in the syllables of a glossolalist's 'Russian' glossa, which Samarin arranges to show how a large number of 'words', is produced by effecting consonantal and vowel changes.[6]

I do not consider that these variations on a basic pattern are performed consciously, but this feature is noticeable in most forms of transcribed glossolalia and this seems to suggest that when the mind is set in 'automatic gear', so to speak, it prefers to move in what could be called 'link' fashion where the relationship between one stage and the next is one of smooth gradation in terms of sound change rather than random disparity. The cortical centres controlling speech may be described as being lazy in glossolalia. There is a lack of inventiveness in supplying new sound formations, but, at the same time, an ingenuity in formulating so many variations from the basic material. In consequence, features such as echoism and repetition are common in glossolalic samples. In echoism subsequent material imitates antecedent material, while by repetition is meant the recurrence of segments of speech which occur more often than any random segment one might pick. A small number of sounds and syllables are found to be far more frequent than others in the case of the glossolalic utterances of a typical glossolalic. The effect has to be *heard*, since the visible transcript may reflect the analyst's penchant for a certain order, whereas another would perhaps divide the text differently. Even trained linguists experience difficulty in transcribing glossolalic texts since they find transcription easier when sound and meaning are associated; where there is no such semantic link, transcription can be arbitrary in dividing syllabic sequences into 'words'. As Samarin reminds us, some glossolalists deny that they are speaking words at all.[7]

Much more research needs to be done on the connection between glossolalia and the speaker's natural tongue. Examples from bilingual communities would be particularly useful as would those in areas where cultural diffusion is least. Samarin finds in glossolalia a tendency to maximise what is most frequent in one's own native tongues, but, at the same time, contrariwise, he finds a selectivity at work in that not all the sounds of one's native language are used. In fact, what is truly distinctive in one's native tongue will either be disguised in the glossolalia utterance or be abandoned altogether. The present writer for instance has heard examples from Welsh speaking persons where there was no trace of the Welsh sounds 'ch' and 'll' so prominent in the speaker's normal tongue. This tendency prompts Samarin to suggest a kind of levelling of speech that produces a common denominator of sounds.

Speakers with tongues often claim that they have different

171

'languages' or 'glossas'. According to Samarin the difference may be one of intonation or the introduction of a new sound or cluster of sounds.[8] Yet the sample of a glossolalist's 'Spanish' tongue quoted by Samarin[9] seems to have a different quality to the same speaker's 'Russian' tongue and the Russian features are absent in the 'Spanish' passage.

My own impression is that traces of the speaker's native language can be detected in glossolalia but not in such a recognisable manner, say, as in the non-religious fabrications of the remarkable medium Hélène Smith. Her speech delivered in trance, is designated glossolalia by Flournoy. Strictly speaking it should be termed xenoglossia since the 'language' is translatable with identifiable and constant semantic correspondence between sounds and meanings. Her early 'Martian' language, probably the product of her subconscious, turns out to be 'disguised French'.[10] The question of xenoglossia is given separate treatment below.

In Christian glossolalia, while the native background is not camouflaged beyond recognition, there seems to be little, if any, trace of the idiosyncrasies of dialect. Yet there is, in fact, very little 'borrowing' of sources from languages other than the speaker's native tongue and both factors taken together may be indicative of regression to a person's 'most natural' sounds. Proper names seem to be in an exceptional category since they are often 'borrowed' though they may be given a more exotic form. Forms such as Yezu or Yeshua, for instance, appear in several texts and presumably stand for 'Jesus'.

According to Samarin variation is often correlated with emotion, or indeed, the context of speaking. This is indeed so. Glossolalic speech for instance, may differ according as to whether it is uttered in private or public. Not only is this the case with glossolalic utterance but even in the case of normal language; private conversation may be very different in character from public oration and even more so from liturgical language. That sacred matters demand a special language or a special treatment of the ordinary language is a feature of cultures widely separated in time and locus. In Wales, preachers developed a peculiar sing-song delivery in sermons referred to as the 'hwyl', but by now only traces of it remain. Many preachers adopted one of few well known intonational contours while others improvised their own particular 'tune' or 'melody'. Repetition, stress, alliterative phrases and protraction of vowels played their part with telling effect upon an audience. The preacher would build up the power of his oratory slowly and deliberately to reach a peak of enthusiasm or the most tense moment of pathos and then subside to a more conventional style. With the ebb of intensity comes repose and a sense of pleasant tiredness for both preacher and congregation. The 'hwyl' obviously has aesthetic appeal and compensated the auditory faculty for what was generally the absence of optical attraction in austere chapels. It may also be said to have brought colour to lives where there was a great deal of monotony and much adversity. It did not meet with universal approval even in its heyday and it declined from the early decades of this century. One who was not enamoured of it has described it in these words: 'When the preacher moved into the *Hwyl* it was formal notification that he had become possessed of the living Word, that the *afflatus* had descended upon him; he spoke as if with the gift of tongues, but the tongue was Welsh embellished with the most striking and esoteric words which happened to fit at the moment'.[11] This particular writer says that such impassioned utterance had a terrifying effect upon him as a child, but most adults, I am sure, found it exhilarating. Whatever the response, the 'hwyl' illustrates the power of oratory and the fact that manner of delivery is as important as content. The smooth rhythm and fetching melody evoked emotional responses which a plain down to earth delivery would not perhaps have achieved in those times. It is interesting to note in this connection that some have claimed that the prophetic speech of the ancient Hebrew prophets would most likely be rhythmic.[12] T. Lewis is even more emphatic saying that rhythm is an essential of prophesying. He argued that the presence of alliteration, assonance and even rhyme in Old Testament prophecy cannot be explained away. It was, he claims, natural for the prophet to chant or sing when he wanted his audience to understand that he was uttering an important oracle of Yahweh.[13]

Glossolalia, likewise, can exercise an aesthetic appeal, some forms more so than others, and in modern Pentecostal circles it is not unusual for a pastor or leader to lapse into glossolalia in the middle of an oration. Just as the 'hwyl' represented the peak in worship for some Non-Conformists, so glossolalia became *the* 'language' of spirituality in Pentecostal groups. Although those who practised either might deny this, in each there is an aesthetic quality which can evoke deep emotional response. As in the 'hwyl', in glossolalia also, song is used for the apparent enhancement of religious experience.[14] The tune may be one which is known or one which seems to be improvised on the spot, and occasionally a whole group will sing together in glossolalia. Believers claim such an activity is referred to in the New Testament as 'spiritual songs' (e.g. Col. 3: 16) and 'sing with the spirit' (1 Cor. 14: 14-15). Samarin says 'the singers have no apparent difficulty in fitting the music to the 'words' (or vice-versa) because of the syllabic nature of glossolalia.[15] Lest this should give the impression that it is nothing more than matching sound to a known melody, I should stress that the melody is not known beforehand in collective glossolalic singing, and furthermore, that the resultant harmony may be the actual blending of several melodies.

While glossolalia can lend itself to song, a feature also of several poetic forms, I would be reluctant to describe any glossolalic utterance as poetry. Samarin is surely right in his appraisal of this aspect. He writes:

> If anything like poetry occurs in a glossolalic discourse, it is only in the sense that certain poetic devices are used. There are surely no poetic discourses in the sense of units of speech with a definite internal structure, but the use of meter, alliteration, and even rhyme might give short stretches of speech the appearance of poetry. Of course, if a person were to remember stretches of glossolalia, he could mold them poetically; the task, in fact, would be easier than in natural language, for he would not be constrained by lexicon and grammar.[16]

In view of the recurrence of certain 'words' and 'phrases' in glossolalic samples it would be tempting to speculate concerning a possible correlation of sound and meaning. As I have stated repeatedly, in my view it is the absence of sound-meaning correlations which characterizes glossolalia. Sounds are not semantically related to concepts, hence the denigrating of glossolalia as gibberish. Yet some glossolalists themselves have attempted to assign meanings to certain recurring 'words'. Samarin finds such words more expressive than denotative[17] and I would agree that the denotations are strained and fanciful in the majority of cases. Yet one sometimes has an intuition, nothing more so far, that certain utterances may derive from depths of memory, where the sound once had significant associations. One speaker, for instance, finding *lê lê* occurring frequently at the end of his sentences assumed it must mean 'Praise God' or something similar. If it could be shown that in glossolalia there is a regression to archetypal sound, then this surmise would deserve scrutiny particularly if the glossolalist had a Judeo-Christian background in which Semitic terms and concepts have had a dominating influence, for in the Semitic world the consonant 'l' preceded by a smooth breathing is the oldest name for deity. It became the *Il* of Babylon and the *El* of ancient Israel and is probably not unrelated to the Arabic Ilâh which compounded with the definite article *al* gave Allâh.[18]   But in this particular case I would very much doubt that any such significance is to be ascribed to the utterance and it may have simply been a disguised echo of Hallelujah.

The 'interpretation' of glossolalia is not an exercise in translation, so one should not be surprised to find the same sound 'translated' differently in interpretations.   This feature also weakens the possibility of relating a constant semantic meaning to a particular sound.   This has not prevented translation being advanced on occasion even by glossolalists of long standing.   Samarin refers to the Shakers and how glossolalia provided the 'words' to many of their songs.   A sample is given together with interpretation.   It seems exceedingly artificial and not typical of glossolalia.   Both the glossolalic lines and the interpreted lines rhyme, and 'me' in glossolalia corresponds in sound and meaning to 'me' in interpretation, and there is a similar correspondence in the case of 'I'.   As Samarin says, what this example and other instances of attempts at glossolalic song and poetry illustrate is 'a universal tendency among men to use "non-casual" speech with those parts of experience that have high personal and cultural value'.[19]   Most glossolalists in their waking state can never recall their utterances,[20] but on occasion one 'word' may stand out and be remembered.   Others claim to recognize short connecting words 'like conjunctions and prepositions', but further recall of structure is absent.

One of the most interesting features of glossolalia is what Samarin designates *diaglossa* to indicate certain segmental similarities in glossolalic utterances, sometimes over very widely separated areas. For instance, in North America, a favourite glossolalic 'word' comprises an initial (s) or (sh) then a vowel, followed by (nt) or (nd) and another vowel.   It appeared in a tenth of the responses to Samarin's question 'Do you recall any words from your tongues or from the tongues of other people?'.   It occurs in a Neo-Pentecostal source and even in samples from the snake-handlers of West Virginia. I myself have noticed also in Wales a high frequency of variations on an almost identical consonantal base sh-nd-r.   Thus in the same passage 'shundar', 'shondar', 'shindir' have occurred.   How is this to be accounted for?   It could be the result of emulation, in other words, a learned behaviour when the 'word' is passed on from a leader to a group and from one group to another.   Considerable traffic to and from Europe would account for its presence on both sides of the Atlantic.   Even so, one finds it hard to credit that interaction explains the presence of the same segment in a Puerto Rican meeting in the Bronx, in Seattle, Washington and in a mining village

in Wales.   To attribute this to coincidence is no explanation either.
One possible explanation, among others suggested by Samarin is
that it may be an improvisation on a basic syllable derived from
a word like Sunday or sanctum.   This does not convince, particularly in texts where Welsh is the first language of the speaker and
the word for 'Sunday' would be 'Sul'.   There is a stronger case
for some connection with the word 'sanctum' for the Welsh cognates
similarly derived from Latin is 'sanct', 'sanctaidd' and 'sant'.
There is, however, no solution as yet and one must await the
gathering of more tapes from many different areas to see whether
there are other predominant diaglossas, and what clues there are to
their presence.   I suspect that in glossolalia generally there is a
regression to a phonologically simplified form of speech, and, if that
is so, further examples of diaglossa could prove highly significant.

Felicitas Goodman, it will be recalled, insists that when a person
utters glossolalia he is in a state of dissociation however light it is and
however faint the diagnostic signals.   She can refer to glossolalia
therefore as dissociative vocalization, and to the experienced glossolalist 'slipping into dissociation'.[21]   In her investigations she discovered how congregations urged new members to bring about their
manifestation and describes it as the single most powerful cohesive
factor of the group.   Yet, in spite of every encouragement, many
found it difficult to acquire it.

The transition from language to 'dissociative vocalization' when
it comes may be hardly perceptible or dramatic.   On the other hand,
there may be a period of high-energy vocalization followed by what
Goodman calls a 'stereotypy on a somewhat reduced level'.[22]
The former, she thinks, is predominantly physiology—produced and
the latter model-oriented, the vocal content being in the mould of
the 'guide who led the way into glossolalia'.   Goodman's terminology should be explained.   Stereotypy in this context meant that
the subject keeps saying the same thing and the utterance does not
vary from one occasion to the next.[23]   A pulse is the smallest vocal
unit, usually a consonant + vowel, or rarely a consonant + vowel
and consonant group.   Pulses are united into bars, which are separated from each other by a pause.   Several bars form a phrase . . . . .
An utterance consists of several phrases, an episode of several
utterances.[24]   Goodman discovered a change in the character of a
speaker's utterance over a three-year period.   It is assumed by
glossolalists that experience brings proficiency, fluency and an
increase in the inventory of sounds, but this hypothesis needs to be
tested.[25]   What Goodman's data showed was a considerable decline in the energy content discharged and this was evidenced in a

176

decrease in loudness and in the disappearance of the majority of the high-effort vowels (i, u) with others (a, e) taking their place over a period of time.

Goodman's intriguing thesis is that there is a configuration of patterns for glossolalic utterance in cross-cultural contexts. This, she argues, provides strong support for the dissociation-based character of glossolalia. She stresses the importance of giving attention not only to the vowel-consonant structure, but also to the totality of the utterance. This means that in addition to vocal content, pause and stress must be observed together with the intonational pattern. Intonation, as she points out has been largely ignored on the assumption that is was more or less identical from one language to the next. Recent research discovers that this is not so and suggests 'that every language has a system of basic speech melodies, which is as unique to the language as its set of vowels and consonant phonemes'.[26] Unfortunately transcriptions of glossolalia omit the intonation pattern, and are, therefore, in Goodman's view, seriously incomplete. In her own samples, vocal transcripts are accompanied by a section representing intonation. She says of intonation that it is '*perceived* intonation, represented by such factors as loudness, intensity, pitch, or occasionally "crowding", the occurrence in a bar of several more pulses than before'.[27] In fact, the diagrammatic representation provided for her sample can only indicate pitch and the spectogram illustration, which comes from a tent revival, seems much more informative. It indicates a very high pitched initial stage with a succession of peaks and then a sloping gradual curve indicating a drop in energy level. It is said that before the tenth peak, if there is any articulation, it is inaudible. It may be, according to the investigator, that there is an energy level beyond which articulation no longer occurs.

Goodman introduces an unexpected element, namely, an intelligible utterance in which there are no pulses devoid of semantic content. I should hesitate to refer to this as glossolalia at all. Yet Goodman claims it as such because of the following features : 'It starts off at a relatively high pitch, almost as high as the tent revival utterance. The pulse-frequency rate is considerably elevated, "panting" or "urgent" to use the expessions of some authors who describe glossolalia.'[28] She goes on to say that its stress and intonation pattern is the same as in the figures of her other samples. The same intonation curve is observed in the case of vocalization of a woman said to be possessed by a spirit. Further tapes from the Cuarta Iglesia Mexico City and of individuals from Utzpak, Yucatán, including bilinguals speaking Maya and

Spanish, were analysed for intonation stress and pause. Goodman maintains that the glossolalic utterance exhibits important agreements across seven cultural settings and with the background of four different languages. She summarises her findings and conclusions in this way:

(a) On the phonetic level, every pulse begins with a consonant and there are no initial consonant clusters. Nearly always the pulse is open, i.e. it does not end in a consonant.

(b) Bars are usually of equal duration, especially if the pauses are also considered, as one would do in music.

(c) The accentual system is one of stress with a primary and secondary accent. The primary one falls on the first pulse of each bar, giving the impression of scanning, in a trochaic rhythm. The primary stress is always preceded by a pause.

(d) Phrases are of equal length. Within an utterance unit (i.e. with one peak), the intonation pattern regularly shows an onset in the medium range, a peak, and a sloping gradient leading to an often precipitous decay.[29]

She adds further cross-cultural similarities:

(e) Glossolalia is not productive. Once an audio signal has been internalized, it becomes stereotyped.[30]

(f) The stereotyped utterance mirrors that of the person who guided the glossolalist into the behaviour. There is little variation of sound patterns within the group arising around a particular guide.

(g) The glossolalia utterance changes over time, apparently as a function of the attenuation of the hyperarousal dissociation. This is perceivable in a loss of intensity (loudness, pitch), increase in pattern variation, lengthening of utterance time, and shortening of the episode (sum of utterances given at one time)...

(h) Glossolalia is lexically noncommunicative. The utterer of the glossolalia and his listener do not share a linguistic code ... What it does communicate is, initially, the commitment to the group and, later on, a sharing of its ritual behaviour with all that this involves on the personal and social side.[31]

Goodman contends that this agreement of pattern, despite linguistic and cultural differences, 'can be explained only if we assume

178

that the glossolalia is not simply uttered while in dissociation but is an artifact of the mental state, or rather of its neurophysiological processes'.[32] She explains how this comes about:

'It is thought . . ., for example that in epilepsy the cortex is driven by discharges from subcortical structures. I am proposing that something similar is happening during glossolalia. In some manner, the glossolalist switches off cortical control. Then, with considerable effort, at least initially, he establishes a connection between his speech center and some subcortical structure, which then proceeds to drive the former. Thereupon the vocalization behaviour becomes an audible manifestation of the rhythmical discharges of this subcortical structure, resulting in the described pattern.'[33] That glossolalia is produced when the brain is in a peculiar state of cortical inhibition is a view rejected by Samarin[34] since he finds that speaking with tongues occurs in a number of very normal situations. He categorically disagrees with this view that glossolalia is an event of vocalization uttered while the speaker is in a state of dissociation and most emphatically rejects Goodman's assertion that it is 'an artifact of trance'.[35]

It is somewhat precarious to choose one of these two opposed positions. Goodman's identification of an intonational pattern requires further investigation and more data to substantiate it. Samarin believes it could be nothing more than a style of speaking 'that can be used in any religious discourse'.[36] My own suspicion is that intonation patterns from a wider selection of cases would show many variations from Goodman's 'regular' pattern, much as one finds similarities and differences in examples of 'hwyl'. As to glossolalia being an artifact of trance, it has to be established that there is trance wherever glossolalia occurs, a postulate which Samarin cannot accept.[37] In the case of long experienced glossolalists, who seem to be in perfect control of the time and place to utter, there seems to be little, if any, sign of dissociation, while there are other examples, particularly during the initial experience, when most of the symptoms of trance can be discerned. It depends a great deal, as previously stated, on what we believe constitutes trance. If some divorce of attention from general surroundings and a focusing of concentration upon the object of praise is 'trance', then it is present in varying degrees of intensity in most if not all cases of glossolalic utterance, as in many other acts we normally perform. While there may be some change of consciousness in all forms of serious glossolalia, in many instances the symptomatic features of what is usually understood by trance are not discernible, and, that being the case, one can only surmise concerning the question whether dissociation is a universally required condition of glossolalia. My own view is that, in 'serious' as opposed to 'playful' glossolalia, there is a degree of dissociation which varies in intensity in each instance. One must also allow that there can be a division of attention, or something in the nature of partial dissociation. One part of the glossolalic's consciousness can be aware of his environment while the other is deeply immersed in his glossolalic activity. This view is confirmed by answers received to a question which I posed in a questionnaire, namely, 'When speaking with tongues, are you aware of your surroundings? For example, would you know if someone came to kneel beside you?'

As to the linguistic form of glossolalia, I hardly think many new insights will come by way of analysing stress, duration or even intonation. Much more significant in my view, as previously stated is the possibility of discovering diaglossic terms, and most important of all perhaps, whether xenoglossia occurs at all. Pentecostal writers often refer to examples of xenoglossy. Dr. H. V. Synan, an ordained minister in the Pentecostal Holiness Church in the United States, cites many claims. He mentions how Miss Agnes N. Ozman a student at Charles F. Parham's school at Topeka began 'speaking in the Chinese language' at a watchnight service on December 31, 1900.[38] This was as a result of the laying of hands and, while she spoke, a 'halo seemed to surround her head and face'. Synan adds, 'Following this experience, Ozman was unable to speak in English for three days, and when she tried to communicate by writing, she invariably wrote in Chinese characters. This event is commonly regarded as the beginning of the pentecostal movement in America.' Parham and his students visited Galena, Kansas to conduct meetings and claims were made that the students, Americans all, 'spoke in twenty-one languages, including French, German, Swedish, Bohemian, Chinese, Japanese, Hungarian, Bulgarian, Italian, Spanish and Norwegian'.[39] Parham vouched for the authenticity of the claims insisting that his students had never studied these languages 'and that natives of the countries involved had heard them spoken and had verified their authenticity'.[40] It was claims such as these that inspired the early conviction that this gift was given for the purpose of missionary activity in foreign countries and inevitably led to disillusionment.[41] Chinese seems to have been a favourite tongue among glossolalists in the early part of the century, for over on this side of the Atlantic, it figures again in connection with a visit by T. B. Barratt, the 'Scandinavian' revivalist, to Alexander Boddy's Church in Sunderland in 1907. At his first meeting which lasted into the early hours of the morning, three persons spoke with tongues. Reports of the meeting produced sensational headlines including this one:

'STRANGE REVIVALIST SCENES—VICAR'S CHILD TALKS CHINESE'[42]

Meanwhile, in the United States, Parham had moved his school to Houston in Texas, and there claims were made 'that twenty Chinese dialects were spoken' and that others were 'able to command the classics of Homer, or talk the jargon of the lowest savage of the African jungle'.[43] At Mukbi in India, it was claimed that over a period of three years 1905-1908, illiterate girls at an orphanage spoke and prayed in English, Greek, Hebrew and Sanskrit, all languages which they had never learnt.[44]

The kind of reports of xenoglossy which one finds in Pentecostal Literature is well illustrated in this reference by Nichol to an incident in revival meetings in 1907 on the campus of a Missionary Training Institute: 'Later Sally Botham, a student, commenced to speak in an unknown tongue that was recognized by two missionaries from the Belgian Congo as Kefonti'.[45] No data or further information supports the bald statement. Horton is a little more informative in his examples:

A Chinese student named Wang, aged seventeen, received the Baptism in the Spirit at Luh Hsi, China, in 1927. Speaking in other tongues he was clearly understood in English, a language not a word of which he knew. His very words are recorded by the missionary who heard him. 'Those that walk with Him in white and are faithful will ascend at His appearing. Behold, He is coming very soon!' Wang knew nothing of the coming of the Lord. Mr. Burton of the Congo was present in Preston as a brother received his baptism and spoke with tongues. The languages he spoke was Kiluba, as familiar to Mr. Burton as English. One of our missionaries, also of the Congo, was present when a young man of his black flock received the Baptism in the Holy Ghost. He was amazed to hear the man speaking in perfect English, repeating Old Testament instances of creation and history. He knew no word of English and nothing of the instances he was recording. The missionary was so astonished at this mighty miracle that he left the hut in search of his wife as witness. When he returned with his wife the man was still speaking in his English 'unknown tongue' but he had changed over to New Testament revelation concerning the imminent coming again of the Lord.[46]

181

These reports are made in good faith but much more information would be required to make them convincing. Claims of xenoglossia are so widespread and comparatively frequent in glossolalic circles that the phenomenon cannot be ignored and obviously deserves more investigation than it has attracted. Most books dealing with the older Pentecostalism, or, indeed, the new charismatic movement cite numerous examples of xenoglossia. Sherrill, for instance, who suggests that the miracle of Pentecost 'was not so much a phenomenon of the lips as of the ears', provides some interesting examples which he is inclined to explain in term of miraculous hearing rather than miraculous speaking. Emphasis on the auditory aspect would, he says, explain many instances in which nonsense syllables are combined with meaning.

One instance given is the one referred to in a letter sent to Sherrill in 1934 concerning a Mr. L. B. Richardson. In this example a Chinese Christian, Brother Ko, claimed he heard Brother Richardson not only speaking in Chinese but about things in China which Brother Ko was familiar with.[47] Another letter from a Mr. W. C. Pickthorn refers to an incident in 1932 in which a Swedish lady, Mrs. Erickson, heard a young boy of twelve pray in Swedish, a language he had never learned. A remarkable example, which challenges the theory that memory provides the explanation, is the case of the person who had been a deaf mute since a disease had destroyed his hearing at the age of two months. He received the Baptism in the Holy Spirit and began to speak in 'A fluent beautiful High German'. While Sherrill suggests that these examples are to be explained perhaps more as auditory miracles than xenoglossia, such an explanation is, according to him less adequate where not one but several people hear the same thing. He then reports the story told by Dr. T. J. McCrossan of Minneapolis of nine Filippino U.S. marines who were amazed to hear an American woman whom they knew give a message in tongues in 'an obscure Filippino dialect' which she could not possibly know.

A similar experience was reported in Indiana, when a group of Italians were amazed to find themselves addressed in perfect Italian by a member of a small Pentecostal congregation, whom they knew, and who had no previous knowledge of Italian. The case of H. B. Goulock in Africa in 1922 is even more astounding. Confronted by aggressive cannibals in Pahn territory he was miraculously enabled to speak their language. Sherrill however realised that his 'evidence' was at second and often third-hand. He, therefore, conducted his own experiment and submitted tapes of glossolalic utterance to a group of six linguists, two being specialists in modern languages, three in ancient languages and one an expert in the study of language structure. No language was identified but the experts succeeded in detecting two spurious examples which had been purposely introduced among the genuine tapes. They were able to identify language patterns on the latter but no known language, and this seems to confirm Goodman's thesis of a regularity of pattern mentioned above.

Pentecostals are undeterred by the inability of experts to identify languages on tapes of glossolalia for they refer to the 2,800 known languages and dialects currently spoken in the world, ancient tongues which have vanished, and unknown tongues of the spiritual spheres. The chances against recognition, they say, is enormous, yet at the same time, their claim that familiar tongues are being recognized remains undiminished except when language experts are present.

M. T. Kelsey likewise gives several instances of xenoglossy, but does not consider the possibility of auditory illusion.[48]   Ian Stevenson, in a review of Kelsey's important book, complains that he does not provide any documentation which would satisfy the canons of psychical research.   He then comments: 'He seems to be unaware of the possibilities of auditory illusions in such cases.   An auditor, thinking he hears some phrases of a foreign language, may convince himself that he has heard much more than he has.   He may deceive himself either by straight imagination or by suggesting to himself that a phrase which sounded somewhat like a phrase in an identified foreign language was actually this phrase which it may not have been at all.'   Stevenson, while he is not convinced by Kelsey's examples, nevertheless safeguards his position when he writes 'I do not say Mr. Kelsey's examples could not be instances of xenoglossy, only that we would need much better evidence to believe this so.   I myself think (from other evidence) that religious glossolalia does not involve (usually) a marked alteration of consciousness and therefore I would be surprised if instances of genuine xenoglossy occurred among these subjects.'[49]

The present writer, exercising the same caution as Stevenson, would not insist absolutely that xenoglossia could never occur, or indeed has never occurred, but would insist that in reviewing any claim, 'natural' explanations should be considered in each case before seeking a supernatural source.   Documentation is invariably meagre and this should place us on our guard against over-confident assertions either way.   Xenoglossia needs no interpreter, while glossolalia does, before it can communicate a message which is intelligible. In the Corinthian church, at any rate, interpretation was necessary, and even more highly honoured than tongues.   This leads me to believe that xenoglossy did not occur at Corinth, and, as I tried to argue in the second chapter, it is unlikely to have occurred at Pentecost either. I am likewise hesitant to accept claims of modern xenoglossy on the basis of second-hand testimony. Auditory illusion is the most likely explanation in most cases. One could for instance imagine a parallel situation arising from listening to Tolkien's fabricated language. A Welsh speaker might be led to believe that the ancient tongue of the Elves was none other than a dialect of his own language when he encounters the familiar plural verbal ending 'ant' in *echant* and *teithant* or, indeed, an identical equivalent to a word in common usage such as *eleni*.[50]

Xenoglossia in Non-Religious Settings

What of the non-religious scene? Any account of xenoglossy must consider the phenomenon in as wide a context as possible. Claims have been made for xenoglossy in trance-states, particularly those of 'spiritualist' mediums. Assuming that some of the reports of xenoglossia may be authentic, what kind of natural causes could possibly account for such a phenomenon? Flournoy's discussion of the remarkable feats of the medium, Héléne Smith, could still provide some useful leads in this connection. I am not suggesting that there is any theological affinity between spiritism and glossolalia, but there may be similarities in the psychological processes involved particularly as far as claims of speaking in known tongues are concerned.

Flournoy employs the term glossolalia in the sense which I would reserve for xenoglossia. According to him, it 'signified the "gifts of tongues" or the ability to speak foreign languages without having consciously acquired them'.[51] It is in this sense that the word 'glossolalia' is applied to Héléne Smith's accomplishments, namely, speaking unlearned languages. In her case, there were at least four categories of automatisms.

(1) Verbo—auditive automatism, hallucinations of hearing accompanying visions in the waking state. In the case of spontaneous visions she would note in pencil, either during the vision or immediately afterwards, the unintelligible sounds which she heard. There were many gaps in the record since she could only recall the first and last phrase of an utterance addressed to her by personages in her vision. In this case she was reproducing what she had heard.

(2) Vocal automatism ('verbo-motor hallucinations of articulation'). The subject was in a state of trance and spoke

184

'with a tremendous volubility'. In this case she would not be reproducing what had been heard, but engaging in what was purported to be an unknown language, notably, at one stage 'Martian'! A Martian personage was deemed to speak through her and this tongue was then translated by another spirit called Esenale. A distinction is observed between 'the relatively clear and brief phrases which are later translated by Esenale, and the rapid and confused gibberish the signification of which can never be obtained, probably because it really has none, but is only a pseudo-language'.[52] What is here called 'pseudo-language' probably corresponds to unintelligible glossolalic utterance whereas the 'translatable' portions correspond to interpretations and these show a high degree of inventiveness.

(3) Verbo-visual automatism, being as the terms signify grapho-glossic rather than glossolalic utterance. Apparitions of exotic characters appeared before the eyes of the subject when she was awake, and just as she reproduced sounds in the case of verbo-auditive automatism, now she reproduces as faithfully as possible the mysterious hieroglyphics which had appeared to her.

(4) Graphic automatism. This category comprised writing traced by Hélène Smith in trance and hailed as the handwriting of three Martian personages, the calligraphy in each case showing distinct differences.

Flournoy's devastating but humorous comment is: 'It is not always easy to represent a language and its pronunciation by means of the typographical characters of another. Happily, the Martian, in spite of its strange appearance and the fifty millions of leagues which separate us from the red planet, is in reality so near neighbour to French that there is scarcely any difficulty in this case.'[53]

The 'Martian' tongue in both written and spoken form is not without relevance for the study of the relationship of glossolalia and a speaker's native tongue. What strikes me immediately on looking at the 'Martian' transcripts is the heavy preponderance of the (i) and (e) and (ê) vowel sounds. These vocalisations require a higher energy output than the (a) sound which is more prominent in glossolalia. The 'i' sound occurs much more often in 'Martian' than in French while French is much richer in diphthongs and nasals. Tone also differs, being higher in 'Martian'. Yet in spite of these differences, 'Martian' is unmistakably French in origin. Flournoy calls our attention to the following features:

185

The phonetic value of the letters is the same; similarly the simple vowels of the Martian alphabet correspond exactly to the five French vowels with corresponding ranges of pronunciation, and 'grammatical' constructions are similar.

This instance of 'xenoglossia' is probably the product of the subconscious activities of the mind, although such an explanation might well be appropriate in other instances in which the subconscious derives its materials from individual experience, and, as far as we know, perhaps from a collective repository of symbol and image. In the case under consideration, the medium herself became aware of the similarity in structure between her native French and her strange Martian tongue, and, according to Flournoy, from that time she exerted herself to complicate her lexicon and rendered her words more and more unrecognizable. This suggests a conscious element deliberately exercising ingenuity, whereas the utterances came while the medium was in trance and states of dissociation. Another possibility is that control was exercised unconsciously. The consistency in matters of terminology suggests a prodigious memory, if the feat was performed consciously, but if this was the product of subconscious activity, then it is even more remarkable. The literary form is also outstanding and is much nearer poetry than prose. Flournoy's observations in this connection are perceptive and provoking. He argues that since everywhere in literary history poetry precedes prose, imagination comes before reason, and the lyric style before the didactic, he can conclude that by its figures and its style, the 'Martian' language (or the French phrases which serve it for a skeleton) brings to us the echo of a past age, the reflex of a primitive state of mind, from which Mlle. Smith later found herself very far removed in her ordinary and normal states of mind. I would suggest that, in the case of Héléne's vocalizations, there is an intermingling of activity flow at the subconscious level, the unintelligible representing a deeper more primitive state than the translatable 'Martian' or 'Hindu' (sic) with their logical constructions. In her trance state, one can expect an indication of a primitive condition not perceptible in more normal behaviour. At the same time, certain abilities are elevated to produce a 'new' language with correspondence of sound and meaning such as one finds in the 'Martian' tongue. In relation to Hélène Smith's experiences, any explanation must be purely speculative of course but a perusal of the transcripts presented by Flournoy leads one to believe that the medium's 'tongues' were not deliberately fabricated pseudo-languages but an amalgam of the interplay of the aroused higher cortical centres and deeper drives in the subconscious. The production of Sanskrit terms in the 'Hindu' cycle of utterances as well as the Arabic writing produced in trance may be instances of cryptomnesia which signify an unusual fortification of memory in an altered state of consciousness. This is a more charitable evaluation than to attribute the Sanskrit words to a likely coincidence on the ground that the proportion of the 'a's' to the other vowels in Sanskrit is almost four to one, so that in uttering three or four syllables one would very likely produce a Sanskrit word. Flournoy is even more sceptical when he declares that 'these fragments of graphic automatisms betray a knowledge of Hindu writing such as a curious mind might be able to acquire by perusing for some moments, the first two or three pages of a Sanskrit grammar'. [54]

The cryptomnesic theory finds support in recent research by I. B. Stevenson. He has divided xenoglossy into two categories, namely, 'recitative' and 'responsive'. [55] By recitative xenoglossy is meant a subconscious remembering of words and phrases of a foreign language. There is no ability to converse in the language and the recalling is done in an altered state of consciousness. It is suggested that the phenomenon can be best understood as cryptomnesia, but in some cases perhaps telepathic communication provides the explanation. In responsive xenoglossy the subject can converse intelligently in a foreign language in which he or she would have no command normally. Stevenson considers responsive glossolaly evidence of a learned skill and recitative xenoglossy evidence only of information somehow acquired by the subject. Stevenson regards the case of Hélène Smith as almost certainly an example of cryptomnesic recitative xenoglossy. [56] In some of the other examples he mentions he thinks there is a reverting to childhood memory. For instance, a young woman of about twenty-five spoke Latin, Greek and Hebrew during a delirium. It transpires that when she was a young child her foster father 'had declaimed in her presence from his favourite books written in these languages'. [57]

While cryptomnesia may be the explanation in many cases of recitative xenoglossy it is hardly the universal or the total explanation. Adherents of faiths in the Indian tradition have a much readier explanation at hand, namely reincarnation and Stevenson himself supplies examples of xenoglossy which he calls 'reincarnation types'. [58] Instances of responsive xenoglossy are rarer than recitative xenoglossy. [59] According to Stevenson, of the many examples of xenoglossy of all kinds which have been reported, only three 'have received anything approaching thorough contemporary recording and investigation'. [60] These are the early report by

Richet who coined the term xenoglossy,[61] the Rosemary records[62] and the 'Jensen communications' investigated by Stevenson himself. The subject of the latter was a thirty-seven year old housewife of Jewish parentage. She was born in Philadelphia and grew up there but her parents had emigated originally from Odessa in Russia. In the course of hypnotic experiments, she began to communicate in Swedish although she had no previous contact with Scandinavian languages. The communications were deemed to come from a character named Jensen Jacoby. Stevenson classifies the communications as an example of responsive xenoglossy for the subject conversed in a sensible manner with investigators. One of these commented upon the accuracy of the pronunciation and the correctness of diction: 'By and large she used the correct articles (attached to the noun in Scandinavian) and correct inflectional endings. Having taught Swedish, I know how difficult it is for an American even to repeat after the teacher the correct endings. She even made the proper elisions, such as "ja" (I) for "jag".'[63]

Another interrogator found that Jensen's speech contained a great deal of Danish and Norwegian and confessed that he had some difficulty in understanding the communication. According to yet a third investigator, a taped session showed that the subject knew at least thirty-seven Scandinavian words but when not manifesting the Jensen personality, even though deeply hypnotized, the medium understood no Swedish whatsoever. Furthermore the subject returned a low score in The Modern Language Aptitude Test devised by Carroll and Sapon, and Stevenson interprets this to mean that it was unlikely that she had acquired her knowledge of Swedish 'casually and effortlessly by normal means'.[64] The subject herself and her family made written statements avowing that there had never been anything more than casual contact with Scandinavians and no opportunity to learn details of Swedish life or the language. Further tests[65] yielded no evidence of conscious or unconscious deception.

Stevenson considers various possible explanations of this responsive xenoglossy, namely, cryptomnesia, sleep learning, telepathic communication—and finds none of these convincing in this particular case. In the end he inclines to the view that this example 'strongly indicates survival of *some part* of human personality'. This is not the full oriental doctrine of reincarnation nor is it a doctrine of the survival of human personality after death. I can only say that this involves us in questions to which there have been no satisfactory answers and ones which have been surrounded by much taboo. Perhaps someday, and sooner than we think, someone will cast more light on this subject and people will be more ready than they have been in the past to think, for example, in terms of a hereditary genetic memory. My own view is, that while a great deal, perhaps most of what is described as recitative and responsive xenoglossy, is probably explained by cryptomnesia on the part of speakers and, indeed, in many instances also by auditory illusion on the part of the listener, nevertheless, the stubborn fact remains, that some cases, like Stevenson's 'Jensen' phenomenon, evade all rational explanation. Until we know more about memory banks and memory inheritance, judgement must be suspended. Neverthless I adhere to the view that, in Pentecostal circles generally in contradistinction to 'spiritualist' trance sessions, what is uttered is glossolalic rather than xenoglossic. Those instances of xenoglossy which are reported have not been satisfactorily examined to enable us to substantiate beyond all doubt that an unlearned foreign tongue has been spoken. Where xenoglossy is claimed, and the claims may be genuine enough, explanations will most probably point to auditory illusion.

As to glossolalia, certain diaglossic traits, it seems to me, may indicate reflexes of primitive structures within the sub-conscious. In this respect, a parallel may be drawn with the effect produced by hallucogenic agents which allows increased retrieval of long-term memory traces.[66] I am not suggesting that glossolalia as a whole, or even any one instance, is produced entirely in this way, for I am also convinced that there is the inter-play of conscious factors, such as memory and sub-conscious emulation, at work also. Even where there is no outward indication of dissociation, I believe there is some loss of reality orientation and a more pronounced activity than usual of the sub-conscious forces, and in the case of xenoglossy, or indeed, xenography, we cannot rule out the possibility that the sub-conscious is somehow not unconnected with a collective memory or is endowed with hereditary recall. We are merely on the fringe of things in this region, but our understanding may be advanced a little if we look at what appears to be related phenomena and this will be the subject of the next chapter.

1. W. J. Samarin, *Tongues of Men and Angels*, 77ff., 25ff.
2. A phrase used by Gerard Manley Hopkins for the alliterative qualities of Welsh 'cynghanedd'.
3. Wyn Griffith, *The Welsh* (Pelican, 1950), 83.
4. ibid., 92.
5. S. J. Tambiah, 'The Magical Power of Words' in *Man* v.3 (1968), 188.
6. Samarin, op.cit., 86.
7. ibid., 82.
8. ibid., 94.
9. ibid., 80.

10. Th. Flournoy, *From India to the Planet Mars* with intro. by C.T.K. Chari, E. Tr. by D. B. Dermilye (N.Y., Harper 1900; University Books, 1963).
11. G. Rees, *A Bundle of Sensations* (London, 1960), 24.
12. T. H. Robinson, *Expositor* 8th series xxi (1921), 229.
13. T. Lewis, *Llenyddiaeth a Diwinyddiaeth y Proffwydi* (1923), 59, 80.
14. Samarin, op. cit., 179.
15. ibid.
16. ibid., 181.
17. ibid., 91.
18. A. Guillaume, *Islam* (Pelican, 1954), 6.
19. Samarin op. cit., 182.
20. F. D. Goodman, *Speaking in Tongues*, 97f. gives an example of memory recall in a dissociative state, but avers that in the waking state the glossolalist may not even remember that he spoke.
21. ibid.
22. ibid., 94.
23. ibid., 97.
24. ibid., 103.
25. Samarin, op. cit., 86f.
26. C. F. Hockett, *A course in Modern Linguistics* (N.Y., Macmillan, 1958), 34.
27. Goodman, op. cit., 104.
28. ibid., 110.
29. ibid., 121 f.
30. Also noted by E. M. Pattison, 'Behavioral science research on the nature of glossolalia' in *J.A.S.A.* xx. (1968), 80 and Th. Spoerri, 'Ekstatische Rede und Glossolalie' op. cit., 150.
31. Goodman, op. cit., 123.
32. ibid., 123f.
33. ibid., 124.
34. Samarin, op. cit., 26.
35. F. Goodman, 'Phonetic analysis of glossolalia in four cultural settings' in *J.S.S.R.* viii (1969), 238.
36. Samarin, op. cit., 34.
37. ibid.
38. H. V. Synan, *The Holiness-Pentecostal Movement in the United States* (Grand Rapids, Michigan 1971), 101.
39. ibid.
40. ibid., 102.
41. ibid., 111 for the case of A. G. Can who went to India and later China.
42. M. Harper, *As at the Beginning* (Logos, 1965), 38.
43. Synan, op. cit., 104, *The Houston Chronicle*. 13 August 1905.
44. Synan, op. cit., 115, *The Chicago Daily News*, 14 Jan. 1908, and Harper, op. cit., 33.
45. J. T. Nichol, op. cit., 39.
46. H. Horton, *The Gifts of the Spirit*, (Assemblies of God Publishing House, 1966), 163-64.
47. J. L. Sherrill, *They Speak with other Tongues* (Hodder and Stoughton, 1964), 102.
48. M. T. Kelsey, *Tongue Speaking: An Experiment in Spiritual Experience* (New York, 1964).
49. I. Stevenson. review of M. T. Kelsey Tongue Speaking in J.A.S.P.R. lx (1966), 302.
50. J. R. R. Tolkien, *The Lord of the Rings* (Unwin Paperbacks 1966), 322, 398.
51. T. Flournoy, op. cit., 3rd edit., 11.
52. ibid., 154ff.
53. ibid.
54. ibid., 333.
55. I Stevenson. *Xenoglossy: A Review and Report of a Case* (The University of Virginia Press, 1974).

56. ibid., 3.
57. S. T. Coleridge, *Biographia Literaria* (N.Y.: Macmillan, 1926), 70f. See also a similar example in H. Freebron, 'Temporary reminiscences of a long-forgotten language during delirium' in *J.S.P.R.* x (1902), 279-83 and *The Lancet*, 14 June (1902) 1685-86.
58. Stevenson, op. cit., 5, 14ff.; see also G. Delanne, *Documents pour servir a' l'etude de la re'incarnation* (Paris, 1924).
59. For examples see E. Bozzano, *Polyglot Mediumship*, E. Tr. I Emerson (London: Rider, 1932); F. Podmore, *Modern Spiritualism* i-ii (London: Methuen, 1902); F. van Eden, 'Account of sittings with Mrs. Thompson' in *Proceedings S.P.R.* xvii (1901-3), 75-115.
60. Stevenson, op. cit., 86.
61. C. Richet, 'Xénoglossie: L'ecriture automatique en langues étrangères' in *Proceedings S.P.R.* xix (1905-07), 162-194.
62. See F. H. Wood, *This Egyptian Miracle or The restoration of the lost speech of ancient Egypt by supernormal means* (London: The Psychic Book Club, 1939); F. H. Wood, *After Thirty Centuries* (London: Rider, 1935); A. J. H. Hulme and F. H. Wood, *Ancient Egypt Speaks* (London: Psychic Book Club, 1937).
63. Stevenson, op. cit. 37f.
64. ibid., 50; on aptitude tests see further J.B. Carroll and S. M. Sapon, *Modern Language Apitude Test Manual* (New York: The Psychological Corporation 1955).
65. e.g. the Minnesota Multiphasic Personality Inventory test (see W. G. Dahlstrom, *A Minnesota Personality Inventory Handbook* (rev. edit. Minneapolis, 1972); a polygraph lie-detector test, not too reliable (!) (see S. Abrams and D. Gibbons, 'The validity of the polygraph with hypnotically induced repression and guilt' in *American Journal of Psychiatry* cxxvi (1970), 143-46.
66. cf. M. Jarvik, 'Drugs, Hallucinations and Memory' in W. Keup, ed. *Origin and Mechanism of Hallucinations* (New York, 1970).

Chapter ix

GLOSSOLALIA AND KINDRED PHENOMENA

The Mysticism of Sound

In this chapter, an attempt is made to indicate some areas in diverse cultural fields where phenomena occur which seem to have features in common with glossolalia. One soon realizes how little there is in the field of cross-cultural investigation, and, if this exploratory effort will prompt others to undertake the thoroughgoing research it deserves, it will not have been in vain.

Writers who have entered this field almost invariably refer to an article by L. C. May[1], but useful though it is, particularly for its references, it must be seen as a beginning only. Since there has been a dearth of material by way of cross-cultural evaluation, the tendency has been to overestimate what little is available.[2] Informed comparative studies of glossolalia and kindred phenomena could lay the foundation for a proper treatise on the mysticism of sound. This will not be attempted here, but I hope that what is offered will encourage others to proceed in that direction.

Areas which could attract the student of glossolalia by virtue of seemingly parallel manifestations are the behaviour of spirit mediumships, particularly as found, say, in various forms of shamanism or in cargo cults and the employment of sound and chant in Kabbalistic, Sufi and mantric circles. As we have seen, in the previous chapter, in discussing the form of glossolalia, claims of xenoglossy in trance states need also to be considered, while in a more exhaustive treatment manifestations such as glossographia and automatic painting would not be beyond the purview of investigation. In this chapter I shall restrict myself to certain forms of verbal behaviour which seem to have one or more features in common with glossolalia.

Shamanism and Spirit Mediumship

It is obvious that many external features associated with glossolaalia, particularly as manifested in classical Pentecostal revivalism, are by no means restricted to such groups. I am not, of course, suggesting that similarity of external behaviour indicates a common inner state or an identical experience. For instance, chanting, the rhythmic clapping of hands and the use of percussion instruments are familiar features in diverse religious settings. These activities by themselves, therefore, do not attract my attention, but when these occur in conjunction with unusual speech behaviour, then this alliance calls for scrutiny. In shamanism, spirit possession also manifests itself in acts of prophesying, and this in turn validates the shaman's standing in his society. This is why shamanism appears to be a fruitful area for investigation. Not least among the shaman's several capabilities is his peculiar linguistic ability and he may evoke the spirits in 'secret language'. For instance, in the Zar cult of Ethiopia, the shaman speaks in 'zar language'. There is a distinction, however, between this kind of secret speech and glossolalia. While there can be an element of learning in the latter nevertheless, where it occurs, it is in unconscious emulation of others, or at most, at the initial stage, a deliberate effort to produce sounds at the behest of a leader or instructor. Subsequent efforts are invariably spontaneous. The secret language of shamans, on the other hand, can be a learned language passed on as esoteric inheritance in the shamanistic succession.[3] Eliade reports that the existence of such a specific secret language has been verified among the Lapps, the Ostyak, the Chukchee, the Yakut and the Tungus.[4] On the other hand, according to Eliade, while the shaman's secret language is learned from a teacher, it can also be acquired by the shaman's own efforts, that is, directly from 'the spirits'. If this category signifies what is spontaneously generated utterance then the resemblance to glossolalia would be closer, for glossolalic utterance also tends to become a 'tongue' i.e. a recognizable pattern of utterance and a glossolalist can in fact develop several different 'tongues'.

The fact is that shamanism offers very many different kinds of manifestations and Eliade maintains that 'animal language' is only a variant of 'spirit language'.[5] In many of the reported examples of spirit possession, when the shaman is deemed to become the mouthpiece of a spirit, his language changes and it is then that his utterances are regarded as the words of the spirit working through him. In such instances, the 'language' could be said to be unlearned by him, that is, it is that kind of speech which is not the result of a teacher's instruction and it is also unintelligible to the audience. The shaman himself would be oblivious to what he utters. Bagoras provides an example when he describes how when the Ke'let spirit enters the shaman's body the shaman utters a series of new sounds, supposed to be peculiar to the Ke'let.[6] He shakes his head violently, producing with his lips a peculiar chattering noise, almost like a man who is shivering with cold. The vocal emissions in this particular case remind one of the efforts of some glossolalists in the early stages of their glossolalia when all they can produce is a repetition of a sound or syllable. In the instance in question, the shaman's voice changes and he gives vent to such exclamations as 'O to, to, to, to,' or 'I pi, pi, pi, pi,' in what one could say is not unlike some cases of incipient glossolalia. These utterances are understood by both shaman and audience as characterizing the voice of the Ke'let. When the spirits speak in unintelligible language, it is not unknown for the shaman to call for a spirit interpreter, which makes the parallel with glossolalic practice even closer.[7] Like the glossolalist, the shaman in the 'inspired' state has no knowledge of what he utters, and likewise he cannot recall it when the state of possession has passed.[8] It is the bystanders who memorise the shaman's utterance when he is the mouthpiece of the spirit.

In fact, it is a common feature of the speech of divine beings that it is an 'unknown language' to ordinary mortals, and, also, beyond recall by the one who utters it. A good example is provided by the medicine man (*hala*) of the Semang who sings to invoke the *cenoi*, a group of celestial beings referred to as nephews of the gods. After a while, the voices of the *cenoi* themselves are heard. They speak in a language unknown to the *hala* and he professes not to be able to recall the actual utterance.[9] The medicine man is said to be controlled by the *cenoi*.[10] It would seem, however, that the *hala* is not at the mercy of the *cenoi* as is the case with the Batak medium in relation to the spirit of the departed person (*begu*) who speaks through him.[11]

I would not wish to suggest that there is a uniformity of pattern in all shamanistic dealings with the spirit world. Far from it: in fact, this is not the case even where the same individual is concerned. The shaman may experience for instance both what I described earlier as transportation ecstasy and the kind of spirit possession described here. What I am suggesting is that similar psychological factors may come into play in the shaman's utterance of unknown and unlearned 'language' as in the case of the glossolalist, insisting at the same time that the totality of the experience will differ qualitatively in each case, due to the difference in conceptual conditioning which each brings to the experience thereby affecting the latter. As I have already stated, to identify the psychological channel by which the phenomenon is manifested is not to preclude a transcendent source.

As in shamanism, so in the case of spirit possession generally, there are features which recall aspects encountered in the study of glossolalia. What is more pronounced than in glossolalia is the liberal sprinkling of foreign words in the 'inspired' speech of spirit possessed mediums. In Shango spirit possession in Trinidad 'the power' may talk in a mixture of Patois, English and nonsense syllables,[12] but such a phenomenon is not restricted in terms of time or culture. Apparently this mixing of foreign words and meaningless words had been a feature of ancient Egyptian necromancy,[13] while on the contemporary scene the utterances of Bantu prophets provide a good example of the combining of known and unintelligible elements. G. M. Sundkler describes the fusion of earlier pre-Christian elements and Christian elements in an emergent Bantu syncretism.[14] He finds speaking in tongues to be a feature of both the pre-Christian form and the syncretic form. He states that in Zulu Zionist ideology the fundamental concept is *U Moya*, the Holy Spirit. *U Moya* may visit a person even before his baptism but it comes with mighty power mainly when the recipient first joins the Zionists. This visitation is thought to indicate a stage that the believer passes through. All kinds of abilities are attributed to *U Moya* such as the power to locate lost objects[15] or the power to heal the sick.[16] The way in which *U Moya* is conceived is arrestingly concrete for it is held that, as in the case of possession by the ancestral spirit, *U Moya* likewise is always felt in the shoulders! However, diviners who claim to have experienced both say that the actual feeling is different! In Zionist talk Spirit and Angel (*ingelosi*) are often used indiscriminately, but Sundkler thinks they are distinguished in that *U Moya* is a general state of being divinely possessed whereas *ingelosi* and the Voice are channels by which *U Moya* reveals itself and makes its will known.

He gives two examples of 'this language of the angels' the like of which could be heard at any service of Zionist or Full Gospel type:

1. De de de de de de de de ....
     Hlo hlo hlo hlo hlo hlo ....
     Blood river sign. Blood river sign. Blood river sign. Amen.
2. Z z z z z z z z z z z z z z z z z z z z z z z
     Hhayi hhayi hhayi hhayi
     Sorry Jesu Sorry Jesu Sorry Jesu
     Spy spy spy spy spy, Naughty boy naughty boy
     Hhayi hhayi hhayi,—Hallelujah, Hallelujah. Amen.

According to Sundkler, the combination of English terms and meaningless vocalisation seems to have been a feature of pre-Christian glossolalia likewise. He makes the interesting observation that, in his view, when a Zulu prophet follows his Corinthian colleague, he does so because it is an old heathen pattern, for various forms of native speaking with tongues has been known since time immemorial among the Zulus.[17]   One cannot resist suggesting that a sustained piece of glossolalic utterance has a different quality of impact from the inane parrot-like exclamations in the above illustrations but without denying a social function to either.   In each case the utterance may derive from deeply rooted emotional structures in the human organism but the degree of phatic communion in less hybrid forms of glossolalia is, I would suggest, much more pronounced.

Similar admixture of senseless utterance and snatches of pigeon English occurs in the 'tongues' of Congo cults.   Bia, an agent of the spirit Kekesi (a friend of Jesu Kerisu) in the village of Manau invented polyglot lyrics and several English words found their way into the strange speech of Kekesi.[18]   In his account of the Manau movement, Worsley refers to a school conducted by Bia, and, while he mentions speaking in tongues, he does not elaborate.   The movement is associated with the Taro sect which has incorporated many 'Christian' elements in its practices and 'tongues' represents one of these elements.[19]   In Papuan cults, other practices were parodied, including the Holy Communion service.   Extraordinary powers were attributed to their leaders in emulation of powers associated with Biblical figures.   These include the ability to raise the dead and to speak with tongues.   In the examples given of the latter, one comes across such unexpected verbicide as 'we wantum kackai (food)' or 'he all right' interspersed among unintelligible expressions.

Among the Arabs the *kahin* represents an interesting instance of spirit mediumship.   True there are cases where the *kahin* is inspired by the great gods, for instance the *Kahina* Sarifat al-Shair inspired by 'the Lord of all the peoples',[20] but in most cases the *kahin* obtained his supernatural knowledge from a spirit or demon. The shaitan speaks with the *kahin's* tongue, and the fact that we hear nothing of ecstatic behaviour in connection with him may be simply due to our lack of data.[21]   The *kahin* usually speaks rhymed prose and the content is mostly coherent and intelligible.   However, on occasion, the utterance is unintelligible and in such instances and in this respect at least it resembles glossolalia.

Sufism

Unintelligibility is not the only feature of glossolalic utterance, for repetition is another well known feature of the phenomenon.   In this respect one might compare the *dhikr* of some Sufi orders and the enthusiasm of some Christian glossolalia groups, for, in the latter, one can come across repeated murmurings of the name Jesus, and, in the former, the repetition of the syllable 'Hu', which represents the Greatest Name of God, or, more precisely, the *h* at the end of the word Allah. In the so-called 'sawing dhikr', practised primarily among Central Asian and Turkish orders, the repetition has developed into a rhythmic expulsion of breath which produces sounds indeed reminiscent of a cross-cut saw.[22] It has a telling effect when listened to even from a taped version. In glossolalic groups, however, repetition is not a structured group action,[23] and, even in group glossolalic singing, there is a greater element of spontaneity. It is readily seen of course that there is much stereotyping and repetitiveness in glossolalia too, but these are psycholinguistic features rather than structural ones.[24] There are differences in theological motivation also. In Sufi circles the chanting of the divine name is deemed able to effect the unity of the devotee and his God. The Sufis also indulged in cabbalistic speculations and developed a secret language out of the letters of the Arabic alphabet 'in order to hide their thoughts from the common people'.[25] In glossolalia, on the other hand, the divine name is not repeated in order deliberately to induce an experience but it is seen rather as an expression of exultation in the authentication of an experience. It is his ability to speak in tongues that assures the speaker that he is accepted by the deity and this, I would suggest, is the dominant aspect of the event though it may remain unexpressed. It is this sense of acceptance that, in turn, builds up further surges of emotional pressure which gain release in repetitive utterance. In the case of the Sufi, on the other hand, while the furious exclamation of the syllable 'hu' indicates the feeling of the *numinosum*, as Otto perceived,[26] such repetitions occur in a more structured effort to attain that unity with the Divine which transcends all relational distinctions. To recall Gilsenan's description once more: 'When the most essential of the Names is chanted Hu (He), indistinguishable from that other source and symbol of power and life which delivers it, the breath, men can experience for a rare moment the unity of the beyond and the within.'[27]

I do not wish to engage in a lengthy discussion at this point of the question whether there is a radical difference between the mystical experience of realising the beyond within and the experience of being filled by the Holy Ghost, thought of as entering from without, yet a brief word may not be amiss. The conceptual associations are, of course, different and in Christian glossolalia the subject even when overwhelmed by the spiritual presence retains a con-

197

sciousness of being overwhelmed. In mystical states of union, however, whether in Sufism or in Vedantism, unity transcends ordinary modes of consciousness, all thought and predication. In advancing to this unity utterance tends to trail off towards the silence of the ineffable, and this can happen through stages along the way which are deliberately structured. At the risk of over-simplifying a complex matter, I would suggest that the mystical idiom which stresses the reality 'within' tends to belong to monistic circles, while the idiom which speaks of power and reality entering from without usually belongs to theistic contexts.

As already stated, in Islamic mysticism a secret language developed out of interpretations of the letters of the Arabic alphabet. A single verse might be linked with thousands of meanings. This could be reduced to a shorter verbal catalyst, until a single word, or even one letter, could evoke a host of associations. In the *dhikr*, repetitions of the word Allāh, or the first part of the shahada, *lā ilāh illā Allāh*, or the formulae *Ismu'z Ẓat* (Name of the Divine Essence) or *Hu El-Haiy*, accompanied by rhythmic movements, could induce a state of dissociation. In most verbal techniques employed by mystics, the uttered points beyond itself to a meaning, or rather an experience, not contained by it and the uttered tends to be whittled down to a rhythmic reiteration of one sound. It is the silence beyond the sound which attracts, just as in visual contemplation of mantric syllables in Tibetan mysticism, the adept visualises the syllable withdrawing into itself in a tiny little dot in the letter before vanishing completely. [28]

The association of sound and revelatory experience is found in traditions concerning Muhammad. Several ḥadiths relating to the experience of the Prophet indicate his inner awareness of a mysterious language which had an intense effect upon the recipient. [29] When he received revelations he heard sounds similar to the ringing of bells. The Qur'ān does not mention this but it is held that the mysterious letters which introduce some of the surâs [30] can form fourteen vocal units which when chanted in proper sequence produce various tunes like the ringing of bells. In their written form the letters (ALM — ALMS — ALMR — ALR — KHYᶜS — ṬH — ṬSM — ṬS — YS — Ṣ — ḤM — HMᶜSQ — Q — N) do not possess the living quality which the Prophet heard. As B. F. Skinner has so aptly expressed it, to study words on a page is not to study the living utterance, for the printed page is a record left by verbal behaviour. [31] It is claimed that, as heard by the Prophet, the vocal units would pulsate with rhythmic beat and form an integral part of a tune which gathered together the totality of the Qur'ān. The

198

gift to understand this mysterious language was vouchsafed only to Muhammad and to those other prophets, who, likewise, had heard the bell-sound as they received the heavenly books which had preceded the Qur'ān. Since the days of the Prophet, it is said, no ordinary mortal has been able to interpret the meaning of these mysterious letters.

The obvious distinction between the impact of hearing the words of revelation and reading the written record must not be overlooked. It may serve to remind us that in mystic practice the style and force of a rendition can themselves convey a mood. There can be what Malinowski calls 'phatic communion'[32], where the vehicle of speech may serve to express in a cathartic rather than a communicative sense, feelings or states of mind which the adept cannot otherwise express. The function of 'language' is not restricted to conveying meaning for it can be used to express a relationship also, or to create ties of union.

Spontaneous Utterance

Turning once more to glossolalia, in my view, it is the style and manner of rendition that saves it from the tediousness which could attend stereotype and repetition. Intonation, pitch, volume, forcefulness, all contribute to the character of the utterance. These, in turn, externalise an inner condition which in some measure they disclose. Glossolalists themselves attach less significance to the manner of speaking than to the spontaneity of its generation. They insist that, while normally they can exercise control over the act of uttering in tongues, the actual content of the utterance is unstructured and spontaneous. Neither glossolalia nor its interpretation is regarded as the product of reasoning, or reflection, but as evidence of the prompting of the Holy Spirit. It is the uninhibited out-pouring of charismatically generated utterance. To characterise what is spontaneous as divinely inspired is by no means uncommon, where inspiration is understood in terms of the spirit imparting revelation. In early Mormonism, for instance, an unpremeditated utterance was highly regarded, and references to glossolalia in this sect may in fact have in mind words or sounds emitted without reflection in response to group expectation of some word from the Lord. An elder wrote of such 'instant' delivery in this way: 'the members instead of waiting for a suitable word to come to their memories utter the first sound their tongues can articulate no matter what it is'.[33] In some non-conformist circles one can still sometimes encounter prejudice against set liturgy and the prepared prayer since these are deemed to thwart the freedom of the Holy Spirit. What is not spontaneous is thought less likely to be divinely inspired. Similarly, with regard to the sermon there are those who regard as 'inspired' only what originates spontaneously during the delivery in contrast to what may have been diligently prepared. In those parts of it which are, so to speak, spontaneously generated the sermon is thought to take on some sacramental quality not necessarily present in the whole of it, and by virtue of which the words of the preacher became vehicles of the Divine Word itself. It is then that the preacher is thought to become the mouthpiece of the Holy Spirit.[34] What needs to be said in the face of such confidence is that spontaneity is not *ipso facto* a guarantee of the divine afflatus nor does the perspiration of preparation preclude the inspired state. The 'inspired' utterance, in whatever religious tradition it occurs, has that quality of pointing beyond itself, and this may be the product of reflection as well as sudden impulsion. In the history of religion, however, the latter seems to have been attended with more convincing power for the listener, by virtue of its dramatic quality.

Another good example of the correlation of inspiration and the sudden unpremeditated utterance is found in Kabbalistic mysticism with its high regard for what may be paradoxically described as 'induced spontaneity'. As Werblowsky has said, the assumption is that whatever 'falls' suddenly into consciousness is of supernatural origin.[35] He provides this example: 'Again we wandered on the 15th day of Shebat, my master and myself alone, and the words of *Torah* were shining in us and the words were *spoken of themselves*.'[36] Werblowsky adds the comment that this brings the experience very close to the phenomenon of automatic speech known as 'maggidism'[37]. He does not, however, use automatic 'in the sense of completely autonomous compulsory or obsessional activation of the organs of speech'. He describes the experience rather as the suspension of conscious control over the speech organs so that the stream of ideas from a flow of uncontrolled thinking could immediately translate itself into speech. This both resembles and differs from glossolalia. It resembles glossolalia since here, also, in most cases, there is a deliberate yielding of the speech organs. The glossolalist can usually resist or desist, except in cases where the experience overwhelms him and he has to utter. Normally, however, it is a case of suspending control. Where the experiences differ is that, conceptually, glossolalia is a non-starter, that is, the sounds emitted have no semantic value, but they may well transmit mood and feeling. The *maggid* experience, on the other hand, seems to be nearer that prophetic condition where a particular word related to a chance sight evokes another by homophonic association and the second becomes the core of the prophetic oracle.[38]   In the case of the prophetic oracle a degree of reflection may be involved in the association evoked by the similarity of sound between the trigger word and the oracle word.   Each also bears a rational meaning.

Before I leave the question of the high evaluation of spontaneity, I should emphasize that this feature is not restricted to the religious scene.   The unpremeditated 'word' and idea are often given an authoritative status in states associated with creative inspiration.[39] A solution to a problem which had for years seemed insoluble may come suddenly in a flash.   Poets sometimes speak of the sudden flow of a line or two or even a whole stanza into their minds churned by emotion.   One of the most interesting examples of sudden eruption, and one which parallels the way in which a 'word' can surface from the glossolalic depths in an unaccountable way, is provided by Lewis Carroll:

> I was walking on a hill-side, alone, one bright summer day, when suddenly there came into my head one line of verse—one solitary line—'For the Snark *was* a Boojum you see'.[40]

As Marghanita Laski comments, Carroll knew that this was nonsense, but he also knew it was valuable.[41]   And so he wrote it down and within a couple of years it became the last line of a poem which 'pieced itself together'.

Mantras and the Mysticism of Sound

If we now turn to another area, namely mantras, we find, in some cases at least, the use of utterances which are unintelligible and seem to have no rational content.   Carmen Blacker maintains that, in fact, rational observation will not yield the meaning of mantras, and she describes a mantra as 'a sound which conveys nothing to the rational mind, but whose whole intention is to resound on a deeper level, awakening echoes which ordinary language is too superficial to reach'.   Mantras, in her view, are to be regarded 'as sonorous forms of the divinity, as icons composed of sounds'.[42] It would seem to me that mantras can be approached at different levels.   One can as an outsider even reflect in a rational manner upon their symbolic significance as explained by the pundits. Again, the uttered sounds can occasion a meaning, at first hidden, to burst forth, while at a deeper level still, the initiate, we are told, can relate experientially to the repetition of sounds, and, depending upon his progress, the symbolical will recede before the deepening of intuition and experience.[43]

201

Experience, it is said, is a prerequisite of the proper understanding of mantras, that is, they can only have meaning for participating initiates. The rational significance referred to is not the 'meaning'— this has to be intuitively discerned, and, according to L. A. Govinda, it is only possible for one who has gone through a particular kind of experience connected with the mantras.[44] A mantra may appear absurd and pointless to the uninitiated, but for the initiate it may be expressive of deity and that in a more direct and immediate sense than merely by virtue of the sacred associations with which it has been invested by tradition. It is maintained that a single syllable or a specific word repeated over and over with complete concentration of thought can be expressive of the divine essence. Indeed, mantras are 'the very speech of the gods'. This speech is not to be identified with the physical sound for the real sound of the mantra (*śabda*) is a spiritual one. Mantras are manifestation of *śabda*. By themselves they are bereft of power, yet they are means for concentrating existent forces. In this respect, they are like devotional formulae such as Namo - o-mi - to - fu in Buddhism or the Jesus prayer in the orthodox Church, and like them also, the mantra can be the means of transcending the cognitive and establishing communion with the divine.[45] It seems to me one must think in terms of three levels with regard to mantras. There is the actual utterance which could be described as an ordinary utterance by the outsider, and there is the unuttered to which it is said to point. In between is the symbolic function of the mantra which can bring the participant an experience of the unuttered. In Indian liturgies, mantric syllables are the 'seed' of divinity, and they are thought to present in phonic symbolism the correlation between the various planes of existence. They are deemed to reflect the play of cosmic forces.[46] This would account for the magical efficacy with which the repetition of the mantra is endowed as say in the ritual o *vajrayāna*.[47] However, to repeat them mechanically without understanding their secret power is said to be useless. Thus it is the mantra *plus* its ideational associations and experiential thrust that constitutes the agency of power. This faintly echoes what was said concerning glossolalia earlier namely that the mere mechanical rendition of a piece of glossolalia by a second party outside the circle of believers is a different event altogether from the occasion when it was first uttered. In the case of glossolalia the associated beliefs must be taken into account in the totality of the event. There is, of course, an obvious difference between the mantric chants and glossolalia in that the latter is not 'taught'. If there may be in some cases an element of learning, this never over-rides the charismatic quality and the spontaneity and innovation which goes with it. What is common in mantra and glossolalia is the belief in the special quality of the sound uttered. Christian glossolalists generally believe that their tongues, being of divine origin, are of a sacred nature and some glossolalists believe that the Holy Spirit actually speaks with their tongue particularly when the glossolalia constitutes a prophecy. In the prophetic condition they regard themselves as the agency for divine communication to others in the fellowship, while normally, on other occasions, glossolalia is seen as an expression of the adoration of God in a manner ordinary words could not accomplish. In each case, however, the glossolalist regards his 'tongues' as a power of speech charismatically endowed although there may be an element of 'induced spontaneity' in the initial manifestation of his glossolalia. As stated, the mantric user, on the other hand, has learned his particular mantra from another in a more formally structured manner, but nevertheless he distinguishes between the outer form and the 'inner' sound of the utterance. It is the latter which he claims to be of divine character. Glossolalists usually do not make such a distinction between outer form and inner essence.

Another point of resemblance between glossolalia utterance, mantras, and the 'inspired' speech of spirit possession, is the admixture of intelligible and unintelligible utterance. True, the occurrence is minimal in glossolalia where unintelligibility is the rule. In mantras, on the other hand, most of the words bear a surface meaning, which is intelligible, as well as a deeper meaning, which is experiential and non-communicative. In practice, the situation can, of course, vary. In Tantric forms of worship, for instance, apparently unmeaning monosyllabic sounds occupy a prominent place in mantras;[48] in Sinhalese mantras, depending upon the occasion, Sanskrit expressions, Pali words and classical Sinhalese literary forms are employed, while in exorcist rites a polyglot mixture of ancient and modern languages is used.[49] On the efficacy of mantras in exorcism, Tambiah says that their literal intelligibility to humans is not the critical factor in understanding their logic. They have power by virtue of secrecy and they can influence the actions of demons. In fact these mantric utterances are referred to as 'demon language'.[50] They are of considerable interest, therefore, to the observer of cross-cultural phenomenon. He will be led to compare this function with 'spirit' language in shamanism and with the notion that glossolalia is the special language of the angels. 'Power' is also associated with all three kinds of sacred language. It is well known that glossolalia has been used alongside intelligible prayers, in acts of faith-healing because of the power ascribed to its agenay.

Man, it seems, experiences a need for a special language to converse with the powers of the unseen. Tibetan Tantrism calls its secret language for converse with the divine, 'the tongue of the dākinī' and Indian Tantric schools refer to their 'twilight language'. The reluctance with which religious bodies in the major religions turn to the vernacular from canonical languages is familiar, even when the classical canonical language is not understood by the congregation. But canonical languages, such as Pali, Sanskrit, Latin, Hebrew, Arabic etc., are not in the same category as secret esoteric languages, although they may be endowed with a sacred quality and a creative power in their respective traditions. It can be argued, justifiably so, that truths expressed in certain languages can evoke a deeper response for some persons than the same truths expressed less adequately (for them) in other languages. It would be interesting to speculate in this connection why certain words in Christian liturgy, such as 'Amen' and 'Hallelujah', have been retained in their original forms, unless virtue was deemed to be inherent in the sound, or could it be simply that people liked the sound and tradition did the rest. (Once again we note that language is more than a means of cognitive communication.) But when there is no knowledge of the language employed, it is only a small step before the frontier of verbal magic is crossed. When that occurs one may find examples of what Malinowski described in dealing with magical language, namely, the belief that the repetitive statement of certain words can produce the reality stated.[51] The danger of degeneration into magic is ever present in all forms of religious expression. In this respect the parable of the wheat and the tares is most apt, for, at certain stages of their growth, they can be indistinguishable and this seems true of forms of magic and certain forms of religion likewise. Just as on the Christian scene glossolalia has been used in some cases almost as a charm, so in some Hindu and Buddhist contexts the very repetition of the mantra may be thought to release creative power. In the logic of glossolalia and mantra the line of demarcation can be very thin between faith and magic. Mantras can degenerate to become meaningless gibberish,[52] in which case their use becomes merely superstition. Govinda observes that what once streamed forth from religious ecstasy and inspiration in lively fashion later turned to 'dogma' and that this, in turn, without the corrective of experience turned into superstition.[53]

One perhaps may be allowed the speculation that some forms of mantras may have originated from glossolalic utterance. As in glossolalic expression, the utterance of the sacred mantra sound is both release from 'an overwhelming psychic pressure' (to borrow Govinda's phrase) and a spontaneous expression of the inner experience. It was when this fell victim to the speculations and analyses of those who disregarded the experience that mantras came to be regarded as magic spells. Many utilitarian mantras are, in fact, so used. It would be well therefore to stress once more that in glossolalia and mantra-exercise the totality of the event must be kept in mind, for with glossolalia, at any rate, it is the associated beliefs of the community shared by the participant that provide the experience of the numinous with a faith content, mediated and conveyed though the sense of the numinous may be through unintelligible utterance. In the case of the glossolalist, I would suggest once more that the value of glossolalia, whatever psychological processes are involved, is that it provides assurance of acceptance for the speaker by his circle, and, by implication, affirmation of the beliefs which are held in common.

One would not expect Mantras to perform the same function, since religions in the Indian tradition are more individualistic in appeal, and in the main seek an experience of the transcendent beyond all thought and predication. So it would seem that the 'belief association' in the case of mantras is not an integral part of the experiential event. To test this assertion, however, it would be helpful to look at what is the best known of Mantras, namely, OM MANI PADME HUM, and consider how its symbolism is explained by an authority of stature like Govinda. According to him the rhythm of poetry (*Rgveda*) and the melody of music (*Sāmaveda*) find their synthesis and their solution 'in the one profound and all-embracing vibration of the sacred sound of OM'.[54] He calls it the seed-syllable (*bija-mantra*) of the universe,[55] and says that when freed from metaphysical speculation it became a medium of concentration and a means of inner unification. In the *Māṇḍukya Upaniṣad* each sound value in the sacred syllable (written also AUM) is given its symbolic interpretation. Thus 'A' represents the waking consciousness, 'U' the inner world of dreams and 'M' the dreamless state of deep sleep. Beyond these states is the highest consciousness of all, *turiya*, and this all-encompassing consciousness is represented by a combination of that one syllable AUM and the silence in which the final 'M' subsides. Govinda says that 'had this sacred syllable been identified with any conceptual meaning, had it entirely yielded to any particular ideal, without retaining that irrational and intangible quality of its kernel, it would never have been able to symbolize that super-conscious state of mind, in which all individual aspirations find their synthesis and their realization'.[56]

We are told that what makes it a mantra and something other than a mere vehicle of communication is the irrational, but real, element in it which produces spiritual vibration. This spiritual vibration is not to be confused with physical sound,[57] and the efficacy of the mantra does not seem to depend upon correctness of enunciation since the Great Mantra takes many forms in diverse languages and dialects. Granting all this, and allowing that the mantra is not to be identified with a specific conceptual meaning, nevertheless, I maintain that the mental and psychic associations are already present for the reciter and cannot be ignored. Govinda himself says that the power and effect of the mantra depend on the spiritual attitude, the knowledge and the responsiveness of the individual. The real power of the mantra is somehow related to the mind of the mantra wielder, for Govinda insists that the mantra itself has no power of its own as claimed say for a magical formula or spell. It is my view that the uttering of the mantra, as in glossolalic utterance, must then be seen in its totality involving the speaker, and his attitude, as well as the utterance itself. Whatever spiritual quality or power is evoked would not be accomplished without the mental and psychic associations which the adept brought with him to the chanting of the mantra, even though there may not be a constant or identifiable semantic referent for the mantra and although the experience attained transcends all such associations. I am, however, talking as an outsider and Govinda re-emphasizes that the mantra has power and meaning only for the initiated.

Govinda employs a useful analogy to illustrate the function of mantras: 'They do not possess any power of their own; they are only the means for concentrating already existing forces—just as a magnifying glass, though it does not contain any heat of its own, is able to concentrate the rays of the sun and to transform their mild warmth into incandescent heat.'[58] They may not possess any power of their own and yet some claim a mysterious correspondence between the mantra and the deeper reaches of the psyche. While the physical sound is not the spiritual śabda there is somehow a link between certain physical sounds and movements in consciousness. Blofeld stresses the function of the mantra as the arouser of deep intuitive experiences of the mystery it symbolises and holds that it can be understood only in the light of this experience. Here, of course, he talks of the 'great mantras' and not the more utilitarian types. He says that 'they are not arbitrarily invented groups of syllables, but intimately connected both with the energy invoked

206

and with their counterparts in the depth consciousness of the adept'.[59]

Some help for the understanding of mantras may come from studying the linguistic phenomena associated with dreaming. The latter could, perhaps, support the idea that there may be echoes of phonetic structures in the unconscious. Some would say that the real dream is purely visual while the spoken words in dreams would derive from the 'super-ego'. This is the view of Otto Isakower[60] who says that while a dreamer is still waking up it often happens that a word or short sentence reaches him for which he feels 'an inexplicable respect, although they are very often a quite unintelligible jargon'.[61] Whether they derive from the 'super-ego' or the unconscious they are not controlled verbalisations, and it seems to me that they originate in a way not unlike the manner of glossolalic speech. Blofeld refers to a Shingon mantra which is effective in allaying fear and hysteria, and it is intriguing to find in this particular mantra the expression SENDARI particularly since the consonantal base SNDR is, as we have seen, a frequently recurring diaglossa in glossolalic samples, over a wide area.

Blofeld's reference to counterparts in the depth consciousness of the adept indicates what may be then a common source for the original mantra form and primary forms of glossolalic utterance. In the case of the latter, I would suggest that certain 'primal' sounds are released, admixed though they are with verbal fragments drawn from the speaker's linguistic repertoire and combined with them in peculiar fashion. Much more needs to be done, however, by way of collecting samples from widely dispersed areas before any statement can be made with true confidence. It is my contention also that a comparative study of the logic and operation of both mantra and glossolalia will help in a better understanding of each of them. For instance, it is not unknown in glossolalic circles for a charismatic person, merely by touching another, to cause that individual to emit a torrent of glossolalia, although that person had no previous experience of the phenomenon, while in similar fashion in some Hindu circles some gurus are said to have the power to give the *Shaktipāt Dikshā* which effects the awakening of the *Kundalini*, a mysterious reservoir of pent-up force which is defined as 'the coiled up, the sleeping Divine power in all beings'.[62] The *Kundalini shakti* can produce psycho-physical effects not unlike what has been witnessed in extreme forms of revivalism such as violent shaking, laughing or crying, elation or depression. The subject may start performing yoga *āsanas* automatically, fall into a trance, dance, receive auditions and visions etc. The effect may vary from person to person but what is of particular interest to this study is the claim that some have chanted mantras in this state although they had no previous knowledge of Sanskrit. The *Kundalini* works in an individual according to his temperament and state of development. It can open up before him other higher worlds and enable him, so we are told, to hear the sound of the divine melody,[63] an experience which, as we have seen, Muhammad also shares although he would never have heard of the Kundalini!

Of course in these studies, one must be alert to the danger of taking subjective impression to be objective fact, or equating experience with the interpretation of it. An individual's interpretation of his own experience is not necessarily nearer the mark than that of the impartial evaluator. The subjective interpretation will be highly coloured where certain expectations are high. This can lead to obvious misunderstandings and the outsider's confidence in mantras or glossolalia as acceptable religious phenomena severely shaken to say at least. For example, Blofeld relates the delightful story of a Tibetan who had great confidence in an Indian guru. When he called upon the Indian guru at an inauspicious moment he was dismissed with a sweeping gesture and a shout 'Go away'.[64] The Tibetan who had but little knowledge of Sanskrit, mistook the shout for a powerful mantra and the gesture as a mudra. This, perhaps, could be matched by the story of the person who ventured to speak in his native Welsh tongue in a revivalist meeting whereupon it was immediately translated by the charismatic 'interpreter'! Such tales add fuel to the fire of those who would dismiss mantras as useless and glossolalia as gibberish without further examination, but this would be as unjust as it would be to accept without question the miracles attributed to the use of mantras and the healing attained through glossolalic prayer.

While I plead for more comparative work this is not to say that I subscribe to the view that what we are dealing with in the mysticism of sound is always basically identical. The psychological processes may be similar when forces from the depth of the personality are released and the psycho-physical effects may be similar. Both glossolalist and mantra wielder may for instance talk of experiencing a realm of consciousness beautiful and serene, yet there are differences. The Christian glossolalist does not transcend the subject-object awareness while the mantra wielder, according to Blofeld, arrives at a state of keen awareness and inconceivable purity devoid of object. The adept's assumptions concerning the nature of reality and man's relationship to it must have a qualitative effect upon his experience.[65] It is, therefore, a major assumption on the part of Blofeld when he can make such a confident statement as this, namely, that 'it would be absurd to suppose that those great mystics of the past who spoke of inspiration by the Holy Spirit, of the Christ Within and of union with the Godhead were talking of something fundamentally different from the path and goal of Buddhist mysticism'.[66]

The question of the fundamental identity of all mystical experience is far too wide a field to be entered into here but it needs to be said that in the past the mysticism of sound has been neglected and studies in this area have an important contribution to make to the examination of mysticism generally, and of glossolalia too.

1. L. C. May 'A Survey of Glossolalia and Related Phenomena in Non-Christian Religion' in *The American Anthropologist*, 58(1956), 75-96.
2. See for example, J. R. Jaquith, *Anthrop. Lingusitics* (1967), ix (8) 2.
3. S. D. Messing, 'Group Therapy and Social Status in the Zar Cult of Ethiopia' in *Magic, Witchcraft and Curing* edit., J. Middleton, (1976), 288f.
4. M. Eliade, *Shamanism: Archaic Techniques of Ecstasy* E. Tr. W. Trask (Princeton, 1964), 96.
5. ibid., 93.
6. W. Bagoras, 'Shamanistic Performance in Inner Room' in *Reader in Comparative Religion* edit. W. A. Lessa and E. Z. Vogt. (2nd edit. 1965), 456.
7. Bagoras, ibid., 458.
8. J. Lindblom, *Prophecy in Ancient Israel* (1962), 7.
9. Eliade, op. cit., 337, P. Schebesta, *Les Pygmées* (1940), 153ff.
10. Ivor H. N. Evans, *Studies in Religion, Folk-Lore and Custom in British North Borneo and the Malay Peninsula*, 160.
11. Eliade, op. cit., 346.
12. Walter and Frances Mischel, 'Psychological Aspects of Spirit Possession' in *Amer. Anthrop.* 60 (1958), 250.
13. A. Erman, *Life in Ancient Egypt* (London, 1894), 352-355.
14. G. M. Sundkler, *Bantu Prophets in South Africa* (O.U.P. 1961).
15. cf. the power of the Hebrew seer (*Roeh*), 1 Sam. 9: 20.
16. cf. again the power mediated through the prophet 2 Kings 4:32ff.
17. Sundkler, op. cit., 249.
18. See P. Worsley, *The Trumpet shall sound: A study of Cargo Cults in Melanesia* (Schocken, 1968).
19. Worsely, ibid., 68ff.
20. See A. Lods, *Israel from its beginnings to the Middle of the Eighth Century* E. Tr. by S. H. Hooke (1932), 443.
21. J. Pedersen, *Israel: its Life and Culture* i-ii E. Tr. (1926), 134; 158ff.
22. A Schimmel, *Mystical Dimensions of Islam* (University of Carolina, 1975), 411.
23. See M. Gilsenan, *Saint and Sufi in Modern Egypt* (1973), 158, n. 3.
24. See H. A. Osser, P. F. Ostwald, B. MacWhinney and R. L. Casey, 'Glossolalic speech from a psycholinguistic perspective' in *Journal of Pyscholinguistic Research*, Vol. 2 (1) (1973), 9-19.
25. Schimmel, op. cit.
26. See Lindblom, op. cit., 9.
27. Gilsenan, op. cit., 177.
28. See J. Blofeld, *Mantras* (1977), 88.
29. Abū al-Maʿālī Ṣadr al-Dīn al-Qawnawī, *al-Tafsīr al-Sufī li-al-Qurʾān*, edit. by ʿAbd al-Qādir Aḥmad aʿta (Cairo, 1969), 16. I am indebted to Mrs. Yvonne Haddad for calling my attention to this work and for much useful information concerning Islamic mysticism.

30. 2, 3, 7, 10, 11, 12, 13, 14, 15, 19, 20, 27, 28, 29, 30, 31, 32, 36, 38, 42, 43, 44, 45, 46.
31. B. F. Skinner, *Verbal Behaviour* (New York, 1957).
32. See also Samarin's use of the term in *Tongues of Men and Angels*, 165, 176.
33. S. Hawthornthwaite, *Mr. Hawthornthwaite's adventures among the Mormons as an elder during the last eight years* (Manchester, 1857), 91.
34. Such views are usually allied to a certain approach to Scriptures, namely, one in which the Scriputres have the status of divine revelation as distinct from mere 'human literature'. Of course, such a view of a body of script-ures is not peculiar to the Christian faith, and interesting comparisons can be made between some Hindu approaches to the Vedas and some Christian attitudes to the Bible. In Christian contexts, there are those who, while they recognize the contribution of Higher Criticism and Biblical scholarship, nevertheless complain of a neglect of the poetic and intuitive impact of Scripture. They respect the need to engage in critical problems but call for an appreciation of the direct, dynamic revelation of Scripture. One who has addressed himself to this question is Harold G. Coward, and in his paper entitled 'Structures of Consciousness in Language and Revelation', he relates the viewpoint of the fifth century scholar Bhartrhari to the Western Jewish and Christian traditions. In his *Vākypadīya* Bhartrhari looks at the question 'How is language, especially the language of revel-ation, received and understood by man?' Coward thinks in terms of patterns of consciousness and argues that the rational and empirical have dominated in biblical scholarship, and so attention has focused on 'human things—by whom a passage was written, at what date, under what social and political circumstance and in what linguistic form'. He, therefore, calls for an openness to 'meditative-intuitive study in which the hearer allows himself to be caught up into "the poetic experience of the words"'. But surely this kind of approach need not be restricted to Scriptures, but can be applied similarly to other forms of literature. Furthermore, there is the danger of over-emphasizing the 'poetic' appreciation in the search for a direct contemporary revelation when that is done irrespective of analysis concerning the assumptions, back-ground and intention associated with the original writing. It may even come close to magic in its naivety. I am not, of course, suggesting that Dr. Coward is in any such danger, but a less erudite exegete could unwittingly indulge in eisegesis while avowing that what he has done is to allow the Scriptures to speak for themselves. With the uninformed, it might encourage confidence in a practice which is still by no means uncommon, namely, opening the Bible at random to discover in the passage upon which the eye happens to alight the needful living message for an individual or group in a particular situation. Dr. Coward's concern is to redress the balance and he would certainly not wish to abandon the fruits nor the methods of biblical scholarship, and in this I would agree with him. It is a matter of balanced approach and Harold Coward's call is a salutary one.
35. R. Werblowsky, 'Mystical and Magical Contemplation: the Kabbalists in Sixteenth Century Safed' in *History of Religions* i (1) (1961), 17.
36. Werblowsky, ibid., 19.
37. The Hebrew term *maggid* bears two meanings. It can indicate (a) a popular preacher, who is often an itinerant preacher, and (b) an angel or heavenly spirit, which communicates teachings in a special way. This spirit can speak words from a person's mouth. See *Encyclopaedia Judaica* (1971) *maggid* q.v.
38. e.g. Amos sees summer fruit *Kais* and from this comes the message of the end *Kēs* (Am. 8; 1-2); Jeremiah's blossoming almond tree, harbinger of spring and poetically called 'awake' (*shākēdh*), provides the unbidden message *shōkēdh*, I am wakeful (*shōkēdh*) over My Word to fulfil it (Jer. 1: 11, 12); cf. the predictions generated by chance sights in Bedouin augury (A. Guillaume, *Prophecy and Divination* (1938)).

39. See M. Laski, Ecstasy (London: The Cresset Press, 1961); R. E. M. Harding, *The Anatomy of Inspiration*, 3rd edit. (Cambridge, 1940).
40. Harding, op. cit., 63; Laski, op. cit., 346.
41. Laski, ibid.
42. Carmen Blacker in J. Bowman edit. *Comparative Religion*, (Leiden: Brill, 1972), 89.
43. cf. the tendency in the ancient Mystery Religions with respect to a movement through symbolism to mysticism, see S. Angus, *The Mystery Religions and Christianity* (N.Y., 1966), 102.
44. L. A. Govinda, *Foundations of Tibetan Mysticism* (London, 1969), 38.
45. See Blofeld, op. cit., 22.
46. G. Tucci, *The Theory and Practice of the Mandala* E. Tr. A. H. Brodrick (N. Y.: Samuel Weiser, 1973), 61.
47. See W. de Bary, edit., *Sources of Indian Tradition* i (Columbia 1957), 185ff and 260ff.
48. Chintaharan Chakravarti, *Tantras: Studies on their religion and literature* (Calcutta, 1972).
49. See S. J. Tambiah, 'The Magical Powers of Words' in *Man* vol. 3 (1968), 176.
50. Tambiah, ibid., 178.
51. B. Malinwoski, *Coral Gardens and their Magic* (Bloomington: Indiana Univ. Press, 1935), 238; cf. Tambiah op. cit., 186.
52. A. Waddell, *The Buddhism of Tibet or Lamaism* (London, 1895) dismissed mantras as gibberish on the grounds that they had neither grammatical structure nor logical meaning.
53. Govinda, op. cit., 70.
54. Govinda, op. cit., 22.
55. cf. the expression 'root-sounds' used in Mithraism for formulas which give birth to certain divine power (Blofeld op. cit., 84).
56. Govinda, op. cit., 25.
57. cf. what was said above in connection with the distinction between the mysterious letters in the Qur'an and the auditory experience of the Prophet.
58. Govinda, ibid.
59. Blofeld, op. cit., 61.
60. O. Isakower, 'On the Exceptional Position of the Auditory Sphere' *Int. J. Psa* 20 (1939), 340-348; see also C. Fisher, 'Spoken words in Dreams: A critique of the views of Otto Isakower in *The Psychoanalytic Quarterly* 45 (1976), (1) 100-109; O. Isakower, 'Spoken Words in Dreams. A Preliminary Communication' in *The Psychoanalytic Quarterly* 23 (1954), 1-16; F. Bandry, 'Remarks on Spoken Words in the Dream' in *The Psychoanalytic Quarterly* 43 (1974), 581-605.
61. *Int. J. Psa.* loc. cit., 348.
62. J. C. Oman, *The Mystics Ascetics and Saints of India* (Delhi Oriental Publishers, 1973), 180.
63. It is interesting to find that the Islamic hadiths speak of a divine sound as the sound of a bell for this is an analogy Hindus also employ for the divine melody. Perhaps, no modern sect has paid so much attention to light and sound as the Radhasoamis, 'Yogis of sound'. See A. Caycedo, *India of Yogis*, (Delhi: National Publishing House, 1966) According to this sect, the Universe owes its being to the sound current, and their goal is the union of the soul with the Transcendent Melody (Shabd). The yogis before they go into samadhi can hear some special sound which they feel as the sound of a big bell or a big conch (Caycedo, ibid., 114).
64. Blofeld, op. cit., 96.
65. cf. the case of dreams. Erika Bourguignon makes the important point that cultural dogma 'influence not only the *reporting* of dreams and other pseudo-perceptions, including secondary elaborations, but also, as far as we can tell, the subjective experience of these states'. *American Anthropologist* 56 (1954), 262-268.

66. Blofeld, op. cit., 58. It should be explained that his confidence becomes intelligible when it is known that for him Buddhas and Bodhisattvas are recognized as being simultaneously emanations of all-embracing mind, and, in a sense, creations of one's own mind. Theism is seen as being in error by externalising deity. For further comment on the question whether the inner spiritual experiences are identical in Hindu, Buddhist and Christian mysticism, see C. G. Williams, 'Selflessness in the Patttern of Salvation' in *Religious Studies* 7 (1971), 153-167.

Chapter x

COMMENT AND APPRAISAL

Inadequate though our data is concerning glossolalia at present, appraisal is necessary. In many quarters there is a growing interest in the manifold features of the charismatic renewal, and, not least, in speaking in tongues. Explanations are sought by many who are inwardly torn between attraction towards this phenomenon and disquiet concerning it. Appraisals will inevitably be made, and, all too often, by the uninformed. Much more field work needs to be done before an adequate evaluation of the many aspects of glossolalia can be offered, but meanwhile every little step forward through proper study deserves encouragement.

In this present work, I have looked briefly at the Biblical evidence for 'Tongues' and concluded that, while pointers to various degrees of enthusiasm are not infrequent in the Hebrew Scriptures, there is no concrete evidence of glossolalia. As for the New Testament, the view favoured was that the relevant material in both Lucan and Pauline sources have to do with a basically identical phenomenon. Furthermore, it was assumed that the Biblical phenomenon, in turn, is to be identified with tongues speaking in early Pentecostalism in this century, and, likewise, in contemporary charismatic Neo-Pentecostalism. This is, of course, a major assumption to make but it is one which is universal among Christian glossolalists. In accepting this identity, this is not to say that one must also subscribe to the theology of the glossolalists nor accept their interpretations of the primary source and significance of their experience.

I have urged the value of a multidisciplinary approach to the study of glossolalia, but this does not mean that I regard the phenomenon to be easily classified with other, seemingly kindred, phenomena of unusual verbal behaviour. I have insisted throughout this study that, while there may be several common features, the total context must be taken into account in each case, and this is where the difficulty lies in our present state of knowledge. It may be possible in certain states, producing unusual verbal behaviour, to discern similarities in hyperarousal and dissociation, a common physiological basis, perhaps, and strikingly similar behavioural patterns, but the inner quality of the experience can only be surmised by the observer.

It is reasonable to assume that cognitive factors can and do affect the tone of the experience. Glossolalists claim that their experience awaken and deepen their sensitivity to the spiritual dimension. Similar claims have been made for techniques of meditation, and indeed, the use of hallucogenic stimuli. If the spiritual dimension is left vaguely undefined, there could be a low level denominator which is common, but Christian glossolalists engage in their activity within a cognitive—creedal context, and it is my contention that this has a qualitative effect upon the experience involved in the event. It is in such distinctiveness that the special significance of religious glossolalia must be sought, but this is precisely what is beyond the outer limits of investigations so far.

In evaluations so far, there is a tendency to polarise the options, that is, to think in terms of either-or categories. For example controversy has often focused on a question such as whether glossolalia needs a theological explanation, that is whether it is to be explained in terms of a transcendent origin, or can be explained purely in terms of psychological and physiological causation. Another example is the question already mentioned, namely, whether Christian glossolalia is wholly different from kindred phenomena in non-Christian settings or completely identical, but, while the man-in-the-street has shown an interest in this particular question, unfortunately specialists in comparative religion have sadly neglected this topic. My plea has been a simple one, namely, for more evidence of effort to collate the various investigations of historians, linguists, psychologists, theologians etc. and for a growing awareness and recognition of work achieved in more than one area of specialization. This is, in any modern study, a tall order, and some would say an impossible demand, but nevertheless the effort must be made. At any rate, the inadequacy of the unilateral approach will then be recognized and it will be more easily allowed that one method does not necessarily preclude another. For instance, even the theological assertion concerning the divine origin of glossolalia need not preclude recognition of the psychological processes involved. To insist upon the distinctiveness of religious glossolalia need not necessarily mean a disavowal of common features with other so-called inspirational states described by anthropologist or comparativist while to advance sociological considerations for the resurgence of tongues is not to deny the value of comparisons with mystical techniques elsewhere. This final chapter does not attempt a theological appraisal, but it is hoped that some of the comments offered will be useful for those who will essay that task.

Why the upsurge in the present century? As noted in preceding chapters, apart from sporadic incidence, there has been little speaking with tongues in the history of the Christian church from Apostolic times to this.   The early Church Fathers give scant attention to it, and, from the time of Origen in the third century, they did not seem to recognize that tongues speaking had ever been a common practice.[1]   Even in the Eastern Church, where the environment seemed conducive to the exercise of individual enthusiasm, glossolalia never assumed the significant role that it has among its practitioners today.[2]   Since the Reformation, glossolalia has appeared sporadically in Europe, sometimes among oppressed minority groups, and on the American scene e.g. in Mormonism, but more especially in frontier revivals.   This infrequency clearly supports the view that glossolalia has not been an essential factor in the diffusion and maintenence of Christianity.[3]   At the same time it makes the probe for causes of the modern upsurge more intriguing.   In previous chapters I tried to show how many investigators have sought explanations along psychological lines and how some are still inclined to see a correlation between personality abnormalcy and tongue speaking.   If that correlation could be incontrovertibly established, then it would raise serious questions concerning our present age, since, never before, has glossolalia been practised on such a large and widespread scale.   Those who argue that there is greater incidence of mental disturbance in this age than in any previous era might, understandably, see a link between such a situation and the prevalence of glossolalia, which could then be regarded simply as a means of emotional release.   The initial premise, however, needs to be proved.   Today, there are better means for earlier detection of psychotic problems and a growing readiness to recognize such as ill-health but there is no real ground for linking the two factors of psychotic disturbance and glossolalia.   While there may be deeper unrest and more frustration than in previous ages, personal deficiency and maladjustment are not quite the same as psychological abnormalcy, but, what is more important, glossolalists do not appear to be more disorientated or inadequate than other groups.[4]   Samarin has made quite clear that there is nothing in the psychological make-up of the glossolalist *per se* that predisposes him or her to speak in tongues.[5]   The same conclusion has been reached by investigators of speech behaviour in shamanism namely that this verbalisation cannot be correlated with incipient or latent abnormality.[6]   Abnormalcy may or may not be present among glossolalists as among any other group but it is not a determining factor.   At the same time, and this is not a contradiction of the previous statement, many who have a keen awareness of insufficiency appear

215

to be drawn into glossolalic circles, as indeed it could be said of the populace in general that those who feel inadequate are drawn to the church. Contact with glossolalist groups seems to accentuate the sense of insufficiency and this kind of awareness is encouraged by the group as a prerequisite of the fulfilment, which comes in the glossolalic event, and is, therefore, often dramatic and regarded as all the more satisfying.

The state of dissatisfaction, of course, when exacerbated to a very high degree can lead to instability and emotional ill-health, but this is certainly not the case with the majority of glossolalists. Alfred Metraux's comments on voodism are equally appropriate to glossolalia, when he said that the numbers involved are too large for all of them to be labelled hysterics![7] One can say that a sense of inadequacy underlies all religious quest, but it takes different forms both in the area of awareness and consequently in the means to remedy it. For some, the quality of the inner spiritual life is seen as low and inadequate These will seek, by various means, to heighten the sense of the spiritual, whether, mistakenly, as we might suppose, by chemical means, or by meditative techniques and prayer, or glossolalia. Others will be more keenly aware of inadequacies in the social outreach of their faith commitment and will have little time for, or patience with, what seems to them to be the irrelevant luxury of so-called 'spiritual' indulgences. More work needs to be done on this very question, in fact, to discover whether glossolalic activity actually weakens or strengthens the degree of involvement of the participant in mundane matters. What is surprising in the history of mysticism, generally speaking, is the practicality and undoubted involvement of so many mystics in the affairs of this life, but for mystics it is probably not at all suprising. The same may be true for glossolalists. But is it? The early Pentecostals were prone to regard the present world as the domain of the devil and to withdraw from it as much as possible in the interest of preserving their purity. Yet this does not seem to be the case in the Neo-Pentecostalism where involvement in the larger community is higher on the priority list of the participants.

Jennings suggests that the loss of 'Christian vitality and dynamic qualities of spirituality in a sceptical and secularist environment' may offer a partial reason at least for the notable success of the tongues movement of our time.[8] No doubt, those who have not yielded to nihilism and strive to find some promise of meaning and significance to life, will often be frustrated. Much more fortunate, in a sense, are those who have successfully integrated their lives on a lower plane around obtainable goals responding to those drives in a competitive world which are succoured unceasingly by the pressure of the media, I mean those who have abandoned all hope of a higher significance to existence or who have never been disturbed by such elevated thoughts. For the others, their experience of frustration has produced, in abundance, terms such as anomie, alienation, absurdism and so forth and the more sensitive among them may be overwhelmed by the sheer loneliness of human existence. It has become commonplace to remark that this has been a century of unprecedented rapidity of change. Nevertheless, the trite, more often than not, contains much more than a grain of truth. In this particular case, it is a truth which is way beyond our efforts to adapt to it, and, furthermore, adaptation to change is uneven, with understanding of the ethical implications, for instance, lagging far behind technological advance. In the surge of change, social and personal problems multiply. An arresting illustration of the upheavals caused by rapid change is provided by the oil exporting countries, particularly Saudi Arabia, which has been thrust from a nomadic society into modern urbanisation with breathless haste. The result has been a remarkably high incidence of psychiatric problems. Changes in the Western World are not so dramatic, nor would I suggest that social change is the only factor in increasing dissatisfaction and its syndromes, but future studies may well discover some connection between these conditions and the remarkable resurgence of glossolalia and similarly with the quest for contact with the transcendent as offered in various imported oriental cults.

In a brief but discerning article, Amos N. Wilder[9] bemoans the many confusions which compound the cult of ecstasy today, often leading to the travesty of divine widsom. While he deprecates the pseudo-cults and contrived physiological interference, nevertheless he appreciates the contemporary thirst for transcendent liberation in our society. He describes it as a reassertion of the rights of spontaneity by heirs of a twofold tradition contributing to the stifling of the spirit and the emotions: 'the sway of rationalism and of an inhibiting religious asceticism'. This reassertion has taken many forms, one being the religious dynamism of charismatic groups where glossolalia is practised. Participation in glossolalic activity may indeed represent a reaction to inhibitive forces in society but it is also an agency of solace at a time when the spread of urbanisation has meant a break up of previously smaller close-knit communities and a diminishing neighbourliness. When a person engages in glossolalia in charismatic circles, this means for that person recognition and acceptance by God and the people of God identified as members of the group. This sense of acceptance dispels fear and anxiety

217

and replaces meaninglessness and alienation with significance and confidence—no small reward in a world of uncertainty.

If, as some have argued, economic deprivation may have been one of many contributory factors in forming attitudes predisposed to appreciate the compensatory comfort and assurance provided by revivalism in the early decades of this century, when classical Pentecostalism emerged as a growing force, it could likewise be argued that the alienation which accompanies affluence has been a significant conditioning element in the resurgence of Neo-Pentecostalism in the post-war era. Of course, such speculation will be dismissed as idle conjecture by glossolalists who do not wish to question the divine authorship of their Tongues, and do not look for any other factors besides divine initiative. The moderate among them, however, will be prepared to allow that even divine inspiration can operate through channels of human agency and conditions. They will concede that cultural expectation, training and predisposition can be taken into account. In my view, expectation is certainly an inducing factor since the overwhelming majority of glossolalists have moved in circles where tongue-speaking was known. Very often, they follow friends or parents or peers, and it is extremely rare to come across a glossolalist who had no previous acquaintance with the practice. The power of environment is also seen in the fact that it is by no means unknown for investigators to end up by becoming glossolalists themselves, thereby indicating also the magnetic appeal of conformity within pressure cultures. I contend that those who subscribe to a theological explanation have no cause to dismiss as irrelevant these other partial explanations of contributory factors which determine attitudes and predispositions.

However, the question, which will be pressed upon the investigator, is whether it is of God or man. From church leaders and theologians, especially, an unequivocal answer will be sought, but the fact is that there is a wide cleavage of ecclesiastical opinion. There are those who accept a transcendent source, those who associate glossolalia with demon possession, and those who are content with explanations in terms of what I have termed contributory factors without recourse to appeals to a metaphysical order. Thus, V. R. Edman[10] lists three possibilities: demonic possession, the Holy Spirit and psychological inducement. R. T. Hitt had a similar list of possible causes but quite rightly he does not appear to regard divine manifestation and psychological manifestation as necessarily exclusive for his third category is described as 'a psychological manifestation within the context of divine superintendency'.[11] Glossolalists themselves, of course, regard their activity as an expression of the work of the Holy Spirit. They will admit, however, that there can be spurious counterfeiting of the genuine thing, but this they would attribute to the work of the devil. I tried to show, in describing the beliefs of Pentecostals and Neo-Pentecostals, how most of them regard their initial experience of glossolalia as one which is subsequent to conversion. They regard it as evidence of baptism in the spirit and this has led to much disquiet and dispute within traditional churches which see this as a threat to orthodox doctrine and the status of confirmation. Some commentators have referred to this initial experience of glossolalia as God's 'gift',[12] and many never progress beyond the initial outpouring, but most Pentecostals, while of course they attribute the initial experience to the work of the Holy Spirit, nevertheless restrict the use of the term 'gift' to the continuing exercise of glossolalia.

The testimony of the Reverend Dennis J. Bennett provides an interesting example of how a contemporary glossolalist understands the phenomenon. He describes himself as a one time Liberal Protestant. After seven years as a Congregational Minister he became an Episcopal priest because he was 'looking for definite doctrine and a rationale of worship'.[13] Subsequently, he developed Anglo-Catholic leanings and avers that he had no sympathy with the weird or occult in religion. Nevertheless, when glossolalia was beginning to manifest itself in traditional churches, he could speak of 'these experiences which are opening to some church people' as 'part of the main stream of Catholic and historic Christianity'. Bennett affirms the calmness of the scene in a parish prayer-group of some one hundred people in those early days. The tenor was one of 'quiet joy' and there was 'no overt emotionalism'. Yet there may have been deep religious emotion. Of tongues and their interpretation he declared 'one finds it difficult to deny that this source is God the Holy Spirit'.

Like many other glossolalists, Bennett testifies to the beneficial effects deriving from the prayer-group, specifying for example the stabilizing and overcoming of personal problems, the intensification of interest in church work and a new conviction of the reality of God. The sense of the reality of God has declined in our age, even as secularisation has increased, and so any agency which promises resuscitation of faith will be sure to attract many.

In glossolalic prayer-groups the experience of speaking in tongues is regarded as authenticating the doctrines proclaimed. These have in the past been almost invariably fundamentalist in content and based on an understanding of scriptures which has often been literalist. The result has been that there are several instances of erstwhile Liberal Protestants who have taken on the whole package-deal of utterance, experience and group doctrines in most uncritical fashion. Not infrequently, with the characteristic indignation of the convert to a new position or allegiance, they have been the severest critics of liberal theology and particularly of the attitudes and methods of higher critics. So anxious are they to preserve definiteness of doctrine, that any threat must be challenged.

The investigator needs to bear in mind the interrelatedness of the cognitive and experiential components in the total glossolalic event. I have constantly argued for viewing the event as a whole. I have also recognized the role of the non-rational in religious experience, particularly in inspirational states. Paradoxically, deeply emotional, non-rational activity can stimulate rational creativity of thought and induce a heightening of consciousness. Yet, although the doctrinal component affects the feelings aroused, and they, in turn, may be taken to affirm these same beliefs, the Christian believer is not exempt from the need for strenuous intellectual effort in calmer moments in the process of discernment and discretion. Truth will not suffer at the hands of genuine scholarship, but it may be distorted when it rests on intuitive grounds alone. Non-rational experience, which is authentically spiritual, has nothing to fear from the glare of rational discussion. In fact, it will always exceed the outer limits of the light of reason. The belief component, which attends the experience, is another matter. Doctrines have to be examined as thoroughly as possible, as well as the bases upon which they are held, such as the authority of the church or the inerrancy of Scripture. For instance, a doctrine which presents a seemingly immoral God would obviously need to be challenged, even though it is accepted by a person who claims to have acquired a deepened sense of the reality of God through his glossolalic activity. When the attendant doctrines are challenged, this is not to say that the sincerity of the glossolalist is in question. Interrelated though the inner experience and the objectified doctrines are, and, while the experience may be genuine, it does not necessarily follow that the glossolalist's account of it is the valid one.

What I am saying, therefore, is that, while the event is to be viewed as a whole, paradoxically, the components need to be examined each by the discipline appropriate to it, for instance the emotional aspects psychologically, and the attendant doctrines, theologically. Once again it is a case of both/and rather than either/or, that is, the event invites examination as a whole as well as in terms of its separate aspects. What is exciting in the present situation is that glossolalia occurs in the context of diverse doctrinal backgrounds. This would seem to suggest that what is common can only be a vague sense of the reality of God, hardly distinguishable, if at all, from the sense of the transcendent aroused by artificial means. This is not so. Irrespective of church allegiance *the* common emphasis of glossolalists is the action of the Holy Spirit. They may differ on practically all other theological questions but here there is an unmistakable convergence of conviction. Yet, I have still to come across a reference to a 'liberal' glossolalist, meaning by 'liberal' one who *inter alia* does not disdain critical methods of Biblical Study and does not subscribe to the inerrancy of Scriptures. This gives cause to ask whether there is something in the critical approach which precludes the possibility of speaking in tongues. Does the liberal have to abandon his particular attitude before he can receive the gift? While the mysteries of the Christian faith, as the mystery of existence itself, transcends the limits of the intellect, the condition of inspiration, surely, can hardly involve the vacating of reason. It would be as erroneous to insist on that as it would be to deny the non-rational factors in the religious complex.

At this point, I would like to reconsider some representative appraisals from Reformed, Episcopal and Catholic circles before offering my conclusion. Within the Reformed tradition the emphasis of the Pentecostal stream on the presence and power of the Holy Spirit has been appreciated by a succession of church leaders and theologians.[14] The succession has been traced briefly in an informative article by J. Rodman Williams[15], and in it references are made to Pentecostalism as 'a phenomenon of God's springtime' and a 'rebirth of Christianity'.[16] This scholar refers to Berkhof's work as the first attempt in Reformed theology 'to focus directly upon the Pentecostal witness and to affirm its theological viewpoint as important for the whole church'.[17] Berkhof believes that Pentecostals are right in speaking of a working of the Holy Spirit beyond that which is acknowledged in the major denominations.[18] The work of the Spirit, he says, is not restricted to justification and sanctification, but extends to *charismata* including speaking in tongues and prophesying. This endowment equips a person to become 'an instrument for the ongoing process of the Spirit in the church and in the world'.[19] Charged or 'filled' by the Holy Spirit, the community is enabled to exercise a charismatic ministry with bold and compelling witness. J. R. Williams finds himself in substantial agreement with Berkhof and regards Pentecostalism as a vital renewal of Christianity at its original source. He concludes his article with these remarkable words:

If, finally, it is the case that there is something going on here comparable in importance to the advent of Apostolic Christianity and the Protestant Reformation—and I am coming increasingly to suspect that there is—then we are called upon to delay no longer in giving ourselves to fuller experiential and theological understanding.[20]

Bold words indeed and the claims excessive, but time alone will tell. No Christian will question the need for the guidance and influence of the Holy Spirit, yet many would deny any role to the tongues phenomenon in a true revival. This categorical exclusion of 'tongues' without an attempt to understand their function has led to Berkhof's lament at the 'water-tight partition-wall' between these (Pentecostal and Revivalist) groups and the theology in seminaries and universities.[21]

While J. Rodman Williams is convinced that what Pentecostalism represents is essential for all churches, nevertheless he hastens to add that this does not mean that everything in Pentecostal theology and practice is to be accepted. Indeed, he concedes that there is doubtless much in Pentecostalism 'that is unessential perhaps even misleading'.[22] One can respect the reservations of a theologian who is more than ready to look closely at the claims of charismatics. What is to be deprecated is the disdain encountered in some quarters among church authorities and theologians likewise, which precludes any serious examination, thus justifying Berkhof's lament. Equally unfortunate is the suspicion of academic motives and methods on the part of many glossolalists.

Officialdom and church leaders have in the main generated a negative response towards speaking in tongues. Comment tends to be ultra cautious and inhibiting within the established traditions. Thus early in the history of neo-Pentecostalism the late Bishop Pike and his suffragan, Bishop Millard, expressed concern that a number of clergy and hundreds of the laity in the diocese of California spoke in tongues. They issued a pastoral letter which was read in the churches of the diocese on May 5th 1963. Since their attitude is representative of that of many traditional Christian bodies far beyond the Western Coast of North America, both then and now, it will be of value to consider this early reaction.

The bishops see their responsibility as two-fold (a) to be open to manifestations of the Holy Spirit's revelation and power 'in an incalculable and unpredictable variety of ways' and (b) to maintain the unity, doctrine, discipline and worship of the church. Exercising this responsibility the diocesan council was directed to set up a group to study the phenomenal growth of 'speaking in tongues'. The group comprised a theologian, a New Testament scholar, two psychiatrists, a priest–anthropologist, a priest engaged in research work in parapsychology, two parish priests (one of whom spoke in tongues), and two canons of the cathedral church. The group studied the report of the Chicago diocese commission, published two years previously,[23] a wide selection of literature as well as actual manifestations of the phenomenon. They produced what was claimed then as 'the most thorough objective report on this subject yet to be issued in the Anglican Communion'.[24] The Bishops made full use of this report, supplemented by further consultations and a review of the whole scene. They agree that proponents of the Tongues movement are right to emphasize the need for greater awareness of the activity of the Holy Spirit in the Church, and concede that this activity may express itself in ways other than the normative vehicles of the reading and preaching of the Word, and administering the sacraments. One of these ways could be glossolalia, but they maintain that the dangers encountered by St. Paul in relation to the phenomenon at Corinth had become evident in the diocese, in spite of the patent sincerity and the good intentions of participant priests.[25] The Bishops also seriously question whether the religious categories and practices 'borrowed' from Pentecostal denominations are consistent with the sacramental theology of the Holy Catholic Church. In particular, they see the emphasis upon the crucial character of the experience of 'spirit baptism' as a threat to the church's conviction as to the real action of the Holy Spirit in Baptism, Confirmation and the Eucharist.

Charismatics could have countered with the fearless declarations of no less a theologian than Karl Barth from a publication which appeared in translation in the same year as the Bishops' letter.[26] Barth asserts that 'a presupposed spirit is certainly not the Holy Spirit' and 'a foolish church presupposes his presence and action in its own existence'. It is, he declares, 'only where the Spirit is sighed, cried, and prayed for does he become present and active'.[27] In the Bishops' letter, polity and authority seem to be paramount, and could be regarded as restricting the freedom of the spirit. It queries the validity of presbyters or laymen laying on of hands in connection with glossolalia since this raises questions as to what ministers are authorized to confess the Holy Spirit in sacraments and rites! The letter also directs that 'the clergy shall not speak in tongues as the bishop lays on hands in Confirmation'. One can of course sympathise with the bishops in their dilemma. Here was a phenomenon, which proponents claimed had beneficial effects, such as 'physical cures, personal integration, marital reconciliation, the elimination of alcoholic addiction and greater devotion of (*sic*) the work of Christ in the world'.[28]   At the same time, this same phenomenon had reached a point where it was 'dangerous to the peace and unity of the Church and a threat to sound doctrine and polity'.[29]   They proposed a *modus operandi* which pleased neither proponents nor conventional Episcopalians 'horrified at the very thought of Pentecostal practices among churchmen',[30] namely to restrict speaking with tongues to the private devotional life.   For glossolalists, speaking in tongues can be both a private exercise or a collective, communally inspired art, but the conservative Episcopalians would reject the phenomenon absolutely.   The Bishops' directive urged that there be no services or meetings in churches or in homes or elsewhere 'for which the expression or promotion of this activity is the purpose or of which it is a part'.   Furthermore, the clergy were advised not to lead, or even take part in, such gatherings under whatever auspices and in their preaching not to emphasize this particular gift 'in distinction from the other gifts and fruits of the Holy Spirit'.[31]

The need for such a directive shows the deep inroads which the charismatic thrust and 'tongues' had already made in the diocese. One could understand the anxiety of church leaders for order and discipline, but, even more so, if the new practice dissipated the effort to service and weakened social concern.   This, in fact, is precisely the criticism directed against the 'spirit' movements by A. D. Stewart, another Episcopalian Bishop.[32]   He bewails the fact that energy expended in the tussle among Christians over subjective religious experience could have been more profitably directed to social endeavour.   Like the other bishops, he, too, complains of the tendency for glossolalia to split congregations and speaks in the same vein of the 'misuse' of the term 'baptism' by glossolalists.   While he allows that the glossolalic experience can be helpful for those 'to whom it happens', he thinks nevertheless that there is a danger in the manipulation of those without the experience into maximum exposure to it by speakers with tongues.   This kind of objection could be applied to the whole effort of church mission in its many facets by those outside the church.   Perhaps it should be borne in mind that negative inhibition can be as manipulative as glossolalic enthusiasm, but Stewart is no doubt right when he mentions the disillusionment which can be felt by the unfulfilled seeker.   This can lead to despondency and is psychologically hazardous.

One is left with the impression that the episcopalian leaders mentioned were embarrassed by the threat to the *status quo*. In spite of their acceptance of the validity of the glossolalic event as a spiritual experience, one senses they would have preferred the phenomenon to disappear. The earlier "Preliminary Report of the Episcopalian Commission of the Diocese of California' had even been charged with some confusion, for, while it first of all speaks of 'spirit possession', that is, possession by the Holy Spirit, in connection with the tongues phenomenon, later, for some reason, the phrase 'demonic possession' is used.[33] The ambivalence in the directives and reports only reflects a deep seated division of opinion within the churches themselves, and for this reason the threat to unity may be real enough.

Having referred to Reformed and Episcopalian response, a brief additional word on Roman Catholic appraisal is in order. As mentioned earlier, many proponents within Catholicism do not regard 'tongues' as a threat to the centrality of the Sacraments as some leaders have feared. Furthermore, while Tongues had pre-eminence of emphasis in classical Pentecostalism, neo-Pentecostalim has regarded it with less intensity. Not all who participate in the charismatic renewal possess the 'gift' of tongues. Catholic Pentecostals, it is said, 'deplore the excessive emphasis on glossolalia in discussions of their movement',[34] and they insist it is only one charisma among many. Yet as René Laurentin, a theologian on the staff of the Catholic University of Angers, France, states, despite 'numerous minimizing declarations', glossolalia occupies a prominent place in the charismatic movement.[35] In France for instance it is estimated that eighty per cent of the charismatics there speak in tongues. According to Laurentin, those speaking in tongues likewise seem to be in the majority among charismatics elsewhere except in Canada and 'in some groups that distrust the unusual'.

Laurentin regards glossolalia as a kind of 'sacred language' and thinks it significant that it suddenly sprang up when Latin disappeared from the Roman liturgy. He is not persuaded by claims of xenoglossia and is not prepared to regard glossolalia as a miracle. Yet he believes it has value and his eight fold list of religious functions deserves to be mentioned:

1. Tongues represent a form of spontaneous prayer, and is therefore a factor in overcoming the formalism of the past.
2. It has a musical function as an inspiration for sacred music. Here Laurentin considers the hypothesis that collective glossolalia may have inspired the Gregorian chant in the Eastern Church. Such conjecturing is beyond historical verification, and, similarly G. Rubach's view that glossolalia

in the Eastern Church was the germ of sung liturgical prayer.[36] Nevertheless, Rubach's thesis is certainly attractive and it is his opinion that 'In the almost unearthly harmony of ancient church melodies and in Gregorian chant, we hear an echo from the glossolalic depths'.

3. Glossolalia has a liberating effect, and overcomes the inhibition occasioned by the lack of words in approaching God.

4. It provides a 'sacred' language, comparable to the language of initiates, belonging to a special group.

5. It is a means of escaping the poverty of the new official liturgy in the Roman Catholic Church which has proved unsatisfactory to all sections, right and left. It moves from 'life' to language as 'an exteriorization of the gift of grace in man's heart'.

6. It creates a close bond with God, 'while the gift of interpretation guards against the danger of individualism and esotericism'.

7. Like the gift of tears, it meets the need for an ineffable language that endeavours 'to reach God through a kind of discourse "beyond language"'.

8. It provides a 'new language' (Mark 16.17) and gives expression to the 'new man'.

It appears, then, that within the main sections of traditional churches, Protestant and Catholic alike, glossolalia has taken firm roots, and will demand theological evaluation. Yet I venture to predict that this emphasis upon Tongues will eventually recede in Neo-Pentecostal circles. I find it significant, for instance, that Tom Smail, secretary of the Fountain Trust in the British Isles, in reviewing the twelve years since he was 'baptised in the spirit' wrote these words: 'But what is it that has lasted? The tongues, the prophecy, the gifts, yes indeed, but they do not loom nearly so large now as they did then. Much more the new sense of the presence of the living God that has accompanied us down these years as it never did before . . .'.[37] What has happened on a personal level for a leader of the charismatic movement could well be the pattern for the movement generally.

Meanwhile, opinion within the churches will differ concerning the authenticity of tongues, that is, whether they are divinely inspired. Even glossolalists themselves recognise that some forms of glossolalia are spurious, and so no simple straightforward answer can be expected. I have stressed the importance of regarding the glossolalic event in its totality bearing in mind the interrelation

226

of the parts. At the same time, I have argued that this does not mean neglecting to examine the various aspects of the event. What is not permissible is the reductionism which would restrict evaluation and understanding to one aspect, be it speech, emotion, or indeed theological value. Three main areas call for comment, namely, (a) vocalisation (b) the cultural background and (c) the inner experience.

(a) The utterance is not religious *per se*. What is vocal in glossolalia is semantically meaningless. This, however, does not mean that it is bereft of all power of communication. Language is not the only communicating agency. One may draw a parallel with music which can transcend conceptual limitations and convey a great deal. Music can arouse, create, convey mood through pitch, tone, intensity, and rhythm. These are also features of glossolalia which can express emotions from the glossolalic depths. In musical composition, however, even when language is not involved, cerebration occurs, while glossolalic utterance, in my view, does not involve conscious deliberation and is to be categorised with action such as automatic writing, or painting and other creative acts of 'inspired states'. This whole area of inspirational states needs much more comparative investigation than has been given to it hitherto. Of course, it must be done with circumspection and without subservience to sensationalism. To give but one further instance in addition to those mentioned in the previous chapters, a phenomenon which suggests a parallel is the oracle writing which occurs still in modern Taoism. The writer, in a state of trance, writes figures in sand set before him. Alongside are three interpreters who 'translate' the writing into a verbal message which is sublime in style and noble in content. Yet, again, a distinction must be made between glossolalic utterance and the productions of trance states, for, as we have seen, the degree of dissociation in glossolalia can be almost negligible and in any case the experienced glossolalist is in control in that he can, in most cases, choose whether to speak or not. What he does not seem able to control is the manner of speaking and the actual phonemes employed.

The vocalising, in my view, expresses in a less inhibitive way than normal language, the inner mood of the speaker, and that without cerebration. It can be an expression of hope, joy, awe or any of the emotions which dominate the unconscious and can be aroused in the religious context by the sense of the numinous. Divorced from this inner response, the verbalising is an activity which in itself is neither religious nor irreligious. In its overt form, Christian glossolalia can resemble ecstatic utterance in non-Christian settings. The

227

actual form of the vocalisation has no distinctively religious quality when divorced from the other features of glossolalia. Even the intelligible words of a hymn can be sung in devotional worship, or on a football field, with a totally different significance. A recent television play realistically portrayed the attitude of some young soccer supporters at Wembley who thought the hymn 'Abide with Me' was the peculiar property of a certain football club! If the environment and cultural background is vitally relevant in the case of a hymn which has an intelligible verbal content, they are even more important in the case of glossolalia. The paradox is, that while there is no conceptualisation involved in the actual utterance, the belief system assumed is of immense significance in the preconditioning of the unconscious attitude and the programming of the response. Emulation of peers is, no doubt, also a factor, particularly a revered teacher or leader. At the same time, I suspect that certain recurrent phonemes in widely dispersed examples are of independent origination and may be derived from basic structures of the unconscious. In other words, the verbal utterance, which is a surface activity with roots in unconscious drives, produces similar phonemes in examples drawn from widely separated areas. Many more examples need to be collected before any statement can be made with confidence and before coincidence or emulation can be ruled out as explanations of recurrence.

(b) The cultural scene is of essential significance when considering glossolalia, and this includes the conceptual environment. In Christian circles, the charismatic community shares assumptions and beliefs concerning the nature of the transcendent and its relationship to the world and man. Glossolalia, as we have seen, is regarded as an audible sign of the visitation of the divine and is therefore encouraged within the group. The newcomer is instilled with expectation, and, when he achieves glossolalic utterance, he knows that he is accepted by the group, and, more important, by God. It is this cultural conditioning which gives his glossolalia its particular Christian quality. The proponent will become aware that the utterance can be feigned, that there are instances of spurious counterfeiting, and such will be attributed to demonic possession. He will not accept that glossolalia can be produced by unaided human effort, even when he regards a particular example as spurious. The glossolalist also has confidence in the ability of the group, and particularly the leader, to discern between true and false. In the group, 'tongues' are not regarded as the only manifestation of the Holy Spirit. There are other fruits of the spirit and where they are absent the glossolalic act would be regarded with suspicion. In other words, even within the group, it seems after all, notwithstanding the gift of discernment, that the criterion for testing the authenticity of the glossolalic act is exterior to it. It resides in that cardinal virtue which St. Paul designated 'love' and which I believe must express itself in moral action.

(c) Nevertheless one needs to allow that the glossolalic event may also involve inner effects which elude empirical observation. The quality of the inner experience, in the nature of the case, is subjective and one can only listen with due respect to the accounts of glossolalists themselves concerning it. Yet the observer can compare the accounts provided by various individuals. He is also entitled to relate these to reports and observations of experiences elsewhere which seem to find similar overt expression. This is admittedly a precarious exercise since dissimilar causes and inner conditions can produce outward symptoms and external behaviour which are not dissimilar to each other. The fact that the apostles at Pentecost were charged with drunkenness is a salutary reminder of this simple fact. Furthermore, if the more lasting and worthwhile effects of the glossolalic experience are directed inwardly, the observer has no means to evaluate such claims except, as noted above, by the pragmatic test whether there is a change for the good in general conduct. For instance, glossolalists claim a deepening of the prayer life and a more vital sense of the reality of God as a result of their glossolalia. The observer has no means to deny nor to confirm that this is so. He can only allow that the inner experience is real enough subjective though it has to be. But does this subjective change actually come about through the act of producing strange utterance, and, in some cases, exhibiting unusual behaviour, or from the beliefs held concerning both. The glossolalist regards his mysterious speech as a sign of God's presence and he has seen in others that the sense of God's presence can produce other physical effects besides manipulation of the vocal mechanism. While we can conceptually separate the two things, attendant beliefs and resultant experience, in the glossolalic event they are bound together. The 'expected' physical symptoms can strengthen the beliefs held by glossolalists, and the beliefs, in turn, can have a qualitative effect upon the inner condition. What I am saying is that the belief component in glossolalia is organically related to the inner experience. Outward forms of behaviour may be similar, as, say, between certain glossolalic cases and those drawn from cults where spirit possession is induced, nevertheless, one must allow that beliefs held concerning the character of glossolalia will have a decided effect upon the quality of the inner experience itself.

229

John Bowker in *The Sense of God* is right in saying that the label for an experience does not lie in the experience itself but derives from the conceptual background which provides the particular symbols to any experience.[38] At the same time, he is careful to point out that this does not mean that we are necessarily talking about undifferentiated experience which is then cognitively identified. I favour his suggestion that the conceptual structure itself is experientially affective, but this, in the nature of the case, is beyond demonstration.

In conclusion, then, divorced from the other ingredients of belief and experience, glossolalic speech *per se* would hardly merit serious study and could be viewed as a piece of eccentricity fanned into an 'in-vogue' practice. It could be dismissed as being entirely of human origin. Within a worshipping community, however, where the utterance is seen as an external manifestation of a spiritual experience, it takes on a different significance. By those within the community, it is regarded as coming from God, and the outside observer is in no position to deny that it can be a medium of worship, divinely inspired. Where this claim is made, however, the observer in the light of his comparative studies of parallel phenomena is equally entitled to insist that it is factors other than the meaningless speech itself which authenticate it. These include the validity of the beliefs held and the quality of the inner experience. The latter eludes the observer, dependent upon reported behaviour, and, as for the former, there is no escaping the kind of examinations to which any religious beliefs must be subjected.

It might be objected that the 'interpretation' of tongues in the believing community renders them meaningful, and that the prophetic messages so derived provide irrefutable proof of the divine origin. Unfortunately, the messages which come in this way are almost invariably vague in content, and often cryptic. In ermeneglossia, as in glossolalia proper, there is no easy way to determine the genuineness and validity of the utterance. The present situation is not unlike what it was in ancient Israel in relation to true and false prophecy. Prophecy could be from God, but there was no handy criterion to indicate that this was indeed the case with any particular oracle. It is likewise with glossolalia. Indeed, as with intelligible prayer or formal liturgy, it can be a vehicle of worship, and when that occurs, it is not of man alone. Even when factors come into play which may be illumined by psychological or sociological theory such as unconscious drives or economic conditioning, this is not to say that such channels exclude divine action. For my own part, while I cannot regard glossolalia as essential for all members of the Christian community, nevertheless when it promotes greater love and strengthens moral fibre I cannot dismiss it as the gibberish of eccentrics. I am much more prepared to see in it a channel of divine agency for the refreshing of drooping spirits and the revival of the believing community.

I would suggest that, in spite of the different conceptual backgrounds, the glossolalic condition has certain psychological factors in common with some states of mysticism. While the former occurs within what can be categorised as 'enthusiasm', the latter belongs to the tradition of quietism, yet there are similarities. A. J. Deikman has hypothesized that mystic phenomena were a consequence of what he called de-automatization.[39] By de-automatization he means changes in the psychological structures that 'organize, limit, select and interpret stimuli'.[40] When de-automatization occurs, the shift may be toward 'a perceptual and cognitive organization characterized as "primitive"'. In this state, imagery and thought can be more vivid and animated than usual and in fact is the testimony of many who have come upon a mystical experience unexpectedly. Deikman thinks descriptions of this condition, which he categorises as 'untrained-sensate experience'[41], strongly imply a change in sensory perception, and that this change is in the direction of a more 'primitive' organization.[42] I venture to suggest a parallel in the case of the glossolalic condition with respect to vocalising, particularly in the initial stages. There seems to be a suspension of the usual automatization of sound and meaning in a highly integrated fashion to a de-automatization, where certain upsurges from the unconscious demand vocalisation, sometimes with compelling force comparable to the 'primitive' vividness of imagery and thought in the 'untrained-sensate experience'. It is not beyond conceiving that the sounds so released are not only vocal discharges from the individual's memory, but, in so far as that they may be rooted in the collective memory of a group, they may represent echoes of a numinous chorus from the past. I am not suggesting that every utterance is to be so regarded, no more than every image is equally vivid in 'untrained-sensate' mystical experience, but that some of the eruptions may represent primal numinous sounds.

Does this involve equating the unconscious and God? This, it would seem, is what may happen in the case of mystics, both East and West, who speak in terms of the ground or base of the soul—beyond sensory perception—where Reality is realized. One must distinguish between the source and channel of divine operation and this, I would argue, is more faithfully done by the glossolalist than by the mystic. The former, as in various forms of spirit possession, will think of an invading energy from without whereas the mystic,

231

even within theistic traditions, will often think in paradoxical terms of the divine immanence of the transcendent. For him, to arrive at the depth of his being is to become aware of his ontological unity with God. That condition will be more real for him than the empirical world around him. The outsider will regard this identity of the deep inner self and Reality as a major assumption and will inevitably ask whether the mystic has truly transcended his subjectivism even when he has gone beyond thought, image and perception. Is it not his own psyche that he is still exploring, uncharted though the great void may be?

It is a major assumption to make that in the depth of his being man participates in the divine nature. A major theological rift occurs at this point between those who see the reflection of the *imago Dei* in man's deepest nature and those who insist that corruption is total, reaching the roots of man's being. For the latter, only a transforming act of divine grace from without can effect redemption. Pentecostal glossolalists will almost invariably subscribe to the theology of man's depravity. The contemporary Charismatic movement cuts across church divisions with their respective doctrinal emphases and is almost invariably Calvinist in theology.[43]

As we have seen, Pentecostal glossolalics see glossolalia as an activity subsequent to redemptive conversion, but while the latter can only be effected by God, and man is held to be totally depraved, yet paradoxically, the self is considered able to respond to divine initiative and is not obliterated but sustained in an I-Thou relational dialogue. Glossolalia is a manifestation of the exploration of the relationship between redeemed and Redeemer, activated by the Holy Spirit. This relationship respects the frontier between human and divine, and while there is a sense of oneness with God there are no such utterances as 'I am Truth' or 'I am God'. The glossolalic experience does not transcend the subject-object awareness as in forms of contemplative mysticism[44], and some recent research in Australia reaffirms this 'relational' context of glossolalia.[45]

Irrespective of theological or conceptual considerations, however, there are often strong similarities in overt behaviour attending ecstatic experiences in various forms of mysticism and the glossolalic experience. What could be called 'natural mysticism' where belief in God or the Absolute is not involved, absorption mysticism in both monistic and theistic contexts, and glossolalic conditions, all these, can provide examples of behaviour which resemble each other. To take but one instance from natural mysticism—Imakita Kosen, a Zen master, might well be describing a glossolalist scene when he says of his *satori*:—'In the excess of delight I forgot that my hands

232

were moving in the air and that my feet were dancing'.[46] *Satori* is a state beyond awareness of being and 'outside one self' and, I would suspect, qualitatively different from the inner condition of the glossolalic, yet the outward physical response is not unlike some glossolalist conditions.

As we have seen, one can also discover similarities in techniques to induce the experience sought, whether they are employed in a structured deliberate way or not. Song, dance, repetiton of the divine name, these figure prominently in earlier forms of Pentecostalism and they are frequently employed in mystical exercise also. The preparatory techniques need not always even involve sound. In some glossolalist circles, 'quiet' glossolalia is practised, that is, the glossolalic utterance is not made audible but 'spoken' internally. Of course, silent prayer is common enough in most religions, and, in parallel fashion, the silent recitation of mantras as a means of contemplation in mystical faiths is not infrequent.[47] It is not unreasonable to suggest that similar psychological processes are at work. As J. Bowker has observed, one can find in most, if not all religious traditions mechanisms, whose effect is to abstract the mental processes of an individual from the intrusion of external stimuli, and, indeed, the intervention of the internal environment.[48]

Another area where resemblances can be sought is in the effect upon attitudes encouraged by glossolalic and mystical experiences. There is no uniform pattern, of course, but in the case of some mystics, an inner detachment from the empirical world has not prevented them from giving themselves with greater concentration than previously to the task in hand. This has certainly been the case with Zen Buddhists, for whom the whole world is transformed, and seeing, hearing, speech, motion, become 'different from every day'.[49] In mysticism, generally, however, and particularly the extreme forms, quietism prevails. In those regions beyond good and evil there is no call for moral codes that bind. Mundane distinctions become redundant in the undifferentiated divine. The mystic's world is within him and action or non-action are viewed with equal indifference when a state of complete passivity is reached As for glossolalics, if in Classic Pentecostal glossalic experience the empirical world became devalued, modern glossolalics, in spite of their theology, seem to be more world affirming and more able to accommodate their experience of divine action within and the need for social involvement without. It must be admitted, however, that tensions can and do arise for the individual when the prior claims of piety are challenged by loyalties deemed to be in conflict with the demands of the new relationship.

233

Notwithstanding such similarities, there are conceptual differences which, as I have suggested, have an affective impact. The genre of the glossolalic experience is the prophetic condition considered in truly Hebraic fashion as animation, inspiration, and being filled from without, rather than the mystical condition of absorption in the ultimate, whether arrived at by outreaching for the transcendent or delving introspectively into the depths of being. The contemplative mystic seeks to go beyond all forms to the ultimate, 'to be silent before the void'. To borrow Schuon's terminology, his goal is in the esoteric rather than the exoteric,[50] or as Huston Smith has said of this absolute, categorical, undifferentiated unity, 'anthropologically it precludes final distinction between human and divine, epistemologically between knower and known'.[51] Schuon's esoteric/exoteric distinction turns on psychological types and cuts across the usual vertical divisions between religions. The esoteric belongs to a minority who will realize that they are fragments of the Absolute. While they may respect religious forms such as scriptures, prophets, and incarnations, they realize that they are but forms pointing beyond themselves to a transcendent unity. For the Christian glossolalic, on the other hand, the exoteric form is very real and earnest for it endorses above all the fundamental redemptive relationship which for him is an all absorbing goal to be explored for ever, though realized in its inception in this present world. He experiences the transcendent-immanent, or to use much older terminology, he is an 'enthusiast', that is one in a state of being filled with God. But although filled with the God who may speak through him, the glossolalic normally has not lost his consciousness of himself, as, say, in the case of the *entheos* of Dionysiac mysticism.[52] He is aware of himself as a subject and of the Holy Spirit as the 'Other' within him. There is an inner dialogue of spirit and Spirit as it were (Rom. 8: 16). Admittedly, on occasion the frontier may be crossed where the 'Other' is all. This latter condition can be compared to certain forms of mysticism, but extreme mysticism goes beyond awareness of both subject and object to the stillness of the Great Silence and the formless desert:

> Where is my biding-place? Where there's nor I nor Thou
> Where is my final goal towards which I needs must press?
> Where there is nothing. Whither shall I journey now?
> Still farther on than God—into a wilderness.[53]

There is no way for the external observer to assess the realness of the mystic's reality nor the validity of the glossolalic condition. A

234

Christian observer has to apply the norms of faith he finds within his own tradition. This faith, as I interpret it, emphasizes the relational-dialogue between man and God. Indeed, it expects a moral response from man to the divine initiative of love, and so, in my own case, I would employ a Scriptural pragmatic test, namely to look for 'fruits' even in the world from which the mystic or the glossolalic may feel gloriously separated. If love be the highest virtue, as Christians assert, then since love is life-affirming what is of the highest source must also be life-affirming. The paradox of the religious life of glossolalics is that their experiences, which have varying degrees of the quality of renunciation, have not seemed to diminish their capacity for involvement nor their activity in their service of the community. It may have been true of earlier Pentecostal glossolalics that they despised the 'world' and avoided involvement, but this is far from being true of contemporary glossolalics. They see their activity in terms of reciprocal response to the creative love of God which envelops their neighbour and his world. They know that to love God involves service to neighbour.

Finally, to conclude this all too inadequate study, I venture to suggest that both the glossolalic and his critic need to be open to each other. The critic who rejects all forms of enthusiasm and all claims based on subjective experience would do well to reflect upon the rich diversity of revelatory media. Glossolalia in the Christian context may be seen as a sign of a deeply felt real need for the action of the Spirit and inasmuch as the Spirit creates that sense of need it can indeed be a by-product of divine arousal. As for the glossolalic, if in the past he may have disdained the intellect and regarded all rational enquiry as superfluous, he, too, needs to be reminded that the mind is also a gift from God. In our discourse with the divine, there is an inter-play of the rational and the non-rational and to ignore or over-emphasize either is to arrive at a distorted view of an engagement with the spiritual and our role in the world. What glossolalic and non-glossolalic need above all is the guidance of the Spirit of Truth.

1. Kelsey, op. cit., 39; see also G. Jennings, 'An Ethnological Study of Glossolalia' in *J.A.S.A.* 20 (1968), 7; for surveys of glossolalia in church history see R. L. Carroll, 'Glossolalia: Apostles to the Reformation' and Vessie D. Hargrave, 'Glossolalia Reformation to the Twentieth Century' in W. Horton, edit., *The Glossolalia Phenomenon* (Cleveland, Tennessee: Pathway Press, 1966), 69-94 and 97-139 respectively.
2. Jennings, ibid.
3. ibid.
4. Gerlach, op. cit.
5. W. J. Samarin in *Psychology Today* (Aug. 1972), 79.

6. Jennings, op. cit., 11f.; M. Eliade, trans. W. R. Trask, *Shamanism: Archaic Techniques of Ecstasy* (N.Y. 1964); S. F. Nadel, 'A Study of Shamanism in the Nuba Mountains' in W. A. Lessa and E. Z. Vogt, *Reader in Comparative Religion: An Anthropological Approach* (N.Y. 1965), 464-79.
7. A. Metraux, trans. H. Chateris, *Voodoo in Haiti* (O.U.P. 1959), 135; Jennings, op. cit., 11.
8. Jennings, op. cit., 14.
9. A. N. Wilder, 'Theology and Theopoetic 111: Ecstasy, Imagination and Insight' in *The Christian Century* 91 (1974), 284-288.
10. V. R. Edman, 'Divine or Devilish' in *Christian Herald* (May 1964), 14-17.
11. R. T. Hitt, 'The New Pentecostalism : an Appraisal' in *Eternity* 14 (7), 15.
12. D. G. Bloesch, in *Religion in Life* 35 (1966), 375.
13. D. J. Bennett, 'Speaking in Tongues' in *The Living Church* Jan 1 1961, 12.
14. See L. Newbigin, The Household of God (1953); H. P. van Dusen, in *The Christian Century* (Aug. 17 1955), 'The Third Force in Christendom' in *Life* (June 6 1958); J. A. Mackay, *Ecumenics: the Science of the Church Universal* (1964); *Christian Reality and Appearance* (1969); G. S. Hendry, *The Holy Spirit in Christian Theology* (rev. 1965); H. Berkhof, *The Doctrine of the Holy Spirit* (1964).
15. 'The Upsurge of Pentecostalism: Some Presbyterian/Reformed Comment' in *The Reform World* 31 (8) (Dec. 1971).
16. Mackay, op. cit., 88f.
17. J. R. Williams, op. cit., 345.
18. Berkhof, op. cit., 87.
19. ibid., 89.
20. J. R. Williams, op. cit., 346.
21. Berkhof, op. cit., 85; J R. Williams, op. cit., 347n.
22. J. R. Williams, op. cit., 348n.
23. *Living Church* (1 January 1961).
24. *Living Church* (19 May 1963).
25. *Living Church* (18 November 1962).
26. *Evangelical Theory: An Introduction* (New York: Holt, Rinehart and Winston, 1963.)
27. Barth, ibid., 58.
28. *Living Church* (19 May 1963).
29. ibid., 12.
30. ibid.
31. ibid.
32. See 'A Bishop's Concern' in *Psychology Today* (August 1972), 51.
33. See A. Sadler, 'Glossolalia and Possession: An Appeal to the Episcopal Study Commission' in *J.S.S.R.* 4 (i) (1964), 84-90.
34. 'Speaking in Tongues' in *Sign* (February 1978), 10.
35. René Laurentin, *Catholic Pentecostalism* (Doubleday, 1977).
36. See *Sign*, op. cit., 13.
37. Letter to Ministers. Dec. 1977.
38. J. Bowker, *The Sense of God* (Oxford: Clarendon 1973), 141.
39. A. J. Deikman, 'Implications of Experimentally Induced Contemplative Meditation' in *Journal of Nervous and Mental Disease*, 142 (1966), 101-116.
40. He claims to follow earlier work on deautomatization by Heinz Hartmann, *Ego Psychology and the Problem of Adaptation* (N.Y. 1958) and Merton M. Gill and Margaret Breuman, *Hypnosis and Related States: Psychoanalytic Studies in Regression* (N.Y. 1959) and on psychological structures by D. Rapport and Merton M. Gill 'The Point of view and Assumptions of Metapsychology' in *Internat. J. Psychoanal* 40 (1959), 153-161.
41. A. J. Deikman, 'Deautomatization and the Mystic Experience' in *Psychiatry* 29 (1966), 324-338.
42. ibid. 331.
43. A Church of Scotland report in 1974, however, condemns the Arminianism of classic Pentecostalism! I. Jones, *Tyst* Jan. 11, 1979.

236

44. For a differing view see W. N. Pahnke, in L. Brown ed. *Psychology and Religion* (Harmondsworth; Penguin, 1973).
45. G. Stanley, et alia, 'Some Characteristics of Charismatic Experience: Glossolalia in Australia' in *J.S.S.R.* 17 (3) (1978), 277.
46. H. Dumoulin, *A History of Zen Buddhism* (London: Faber and Faber, 1963), 273.
47. For silent prayer in Yoruba tradition see W. Abimbula, 'Yoruba Traditional Religion' in Yusuf Ibish and Peter Lambourn Wilson eds., *Traditional Modes of Contemplation and Action* (Thames and Hudson, 1977), 183ff. and on silent mantras see Lama L. P. Lhalungpa, 'Interdependence of Contemplation and Action in Tibetan Buddhism' in Ibish and Wilson, ibid, 251ff.
48. J. Bowker, op. cit., 139.
49. Dumoulin, op. cit.
50. Frithjof Schuon, *The Transcendent Unity of Religions* (Harper and Row, 1953).
51. See Ibish and Wilson, op. cit., 89ff.
52. On Dionysiac ecstasy see G. Van der Leeuw, *Religion in Essence and Manifestation* (Allen and Unwin, 1938), 409ff.
53. Angelus Silesius *The Cherubinic Wanderer*, I, 7 quoted by Van der Leeuw, op. cit., 493.

237

JOURNALS, PERIODICALS, NEWSPAPERS*

American Anthropologist
American Journal of Psychotherapy
American Journal of Semitic Languages and Literatures
American Journal of Sociology
American Journal of Theology
Anthropological Linguistics
Anthropos
Apostolic Herald
Archives of General Psychiatry
Archives de Psychologie
Archives de sciences sociales des religions
Bible et vie chrétienne
Bibliotheca psychiatrica et neurologica
Biological Psychiatry
British Journal of Psychiatry
British Weekly
Canadian Journal of Theology
Canadian Review of Sociology and Anthropology
Christian Century
Christian Herald
Christianity Today
Church Quarterly Review
Clergy Review
Comprehensive Psychiatry
Confinia Psychiatrica
Contemporary Review
Current Anthropology
De Oogst
Dialog
Diseases of the Nervous System
Dunamis Digest
Dysgedydd
Ecclesiastical Review
Elim Crusade Witness
Elim Evangel
Elim Foursquare Crusader
Elim Missionary Courier
Elim Missionary Evangel
Eternity
Expositor
Expository Times
Evangelische Theologie
Faith and Thought
Fellowship Monthly
Gregorianum
Hartford Quarterly
Harvard Theological Review
History of Religions
Homiletic Review
Human Biology
International Journal of Psycho-Analysis
International Psychiatry Clinics

Interpretation
Jewish Quarterly Review
Journal of the Acoustical Society of America
Journal of the American Scientific Affilitaion
Journal of the American Society for Psychical Research
Journal of the Ancient Near Eastern Society of Columbia University
Journal Belge de Neurologie et de Psychiatrie
Journal of Biblical Literature
Journal of Humanistic Psychology
Journal of Nervous and Mental Diseases
Journal of Psycholinguistic Research
Journal of the Royal Anthropological Institute
Journal for the Scientific Study of Religion
Journal of Speech and Hearing Disorders
Journal of Theological Studies
Lancet
Language and Speech
Language in Society
Lexington Theological Quarterly
Life
Linguistics
Living Church
L'oratoire
Lutheran Herald
Man
Man, Myth and Magic
Mind
Missionary Review
New Covenant
New Testament Studies
Numen
Pastoral Psychology
Pattern
Pentecostal Evangel
Plain Truth
Practical Anthropology
Princeton Seminary Bulletin
Proceedings of the Royal Society of Medicine
Proceedings of the Society for Psychical Research
Psychiatry
Psychoanalytic Quarterly
Psychology Today
Psychonomic Science
Psychotherapy and Psychosomatics
Redemption Tidings
Reformed World
Religion in Life
Religion: Journal of Religion and Religions
Renewal
Review of Religious Research
Revue de l'histoire des religions
Revue du monde musulmans
Riches of Grace
Science
Science Religieuse/Studies in Religion
Semiotica
Sign
Social Action
Sociological Analysis
Supplements to *Vetus Testamentum*

Testimony
Theological Monthly
Theology
Tōhoku Psychologica
Torch and Trumpet
Traethodydd
Trans-Action
Tyst
Verbum Domini
Vetus Testamentum
View
Voice
Vox Reformata
Zeitschrift für alttestamentliche Wissenschaft
Zeitschrift für Kirchengeschichte
Zeitschrift für Psychologie

*Articles at the beginning of titles have been omitted in most cases

BIBLIOGRAPHY

ABERLE, D. F. *The Peyote Religion among the Navaho*, Wenner-Gun Foundation for Anthropological Research No. 42 (New York: Viking Fund Publ. 1966)

ABRAMS, M. 'Baptism of the Holy Spirit at Mukti', *Missionary Review* 19 (n.s.) (Aug. 1906), 619

ABRAMS, S. S. and GIBBONS, D. 'The validity of the polygraph with hypnotically induced repression and guilt', *American Journal of Psychiatry* 126 (1970) 143-46

Abū al-Maʿālī Ṣadr al-Dīn al-Qawnawī, *al-Tafsīr al-Ṣūfī li-al-Qurʾān*, edit. by ʿAbd al-Qādir Ahmad aʿta (Cairo, 1969).

ALLAND, Alexander 'Possession in a revivalist Negro Church', *J.S.S.R.* 1: 2 (1961)

AMANDRY, Pierre *La Mantique apollinienne à Delphes. Essai sur le fonctionnement de l'Oracle* (Paris, 1950)

ANDREWS, E. 'Tongues, Gift of', *I.D.B.* R-Z, 671

ANDREWS, E. D. *The People Called Shakers* (O.U.P. 1953)

An introduction to the Catholic Charismatic Renewal (booklet published by Charismatic Renewal Services, Notre Dame, Indiana)

ARMITAGE, W. H. G. 'The Moravian Communities in Great Britain', *Church Quarterly Review* 158 (April-June 1957), 141-152

ARNDT, W. F. and GINGRICH, F. W. *A Greek-English Lexicon of the New Testament and Other Early Christian Literature* (Chicago: University of Chicago Press, 1957)

ARROWSMITH, R. 'Every Catholic Should be a Catholic Pentecostal', *Testimony* ix (1) (1970), 4

ATTALIAH, R. L. ed. *Let the Earth Hear His Voice* (*Minneapolis World Wide Publications*, 1975)

ATTER, G. F. *Rivers of Blessing* (Toronto: The Full Gospel Publishing House, 1960)

The Third Force 3rd. ed. (Peterborough, Ont.: College Press, 1970)

BACH, Marcus *The Inner Ecstasy: the Power and the Glory of Speaking in Tongues* (New York: World Publishing Co., 1970)

BAIRD, H. M. *History of the Rise of the Huguenots* i-ii (London: Hodder & Stoughton, 1880);

The Camisard Uprising, American Soc. of Church History, vol. 11 Pt. 1 (New York, Knickerbocker Press, 1890)

BAIRD, W. *The Corinthian Church—A Biblical Approach to Urban Culture* (Abingdon Press, 1964)

BANDRY, F. 'Remarks on Spoken Words in the Dream', *The Psychoanalytic Quarterly* 43 (1974), 581–605

BARRATT, T. B. *When the Fire Fell* (Oslo, 1927)

BARRETT, C. K. *The First Epistle to the Corinthians* (London: Black, 1968);
The Holy Spirit and the Gospel Tradition (New York and London: Macmillan & Co., 1947)

BARTLEMAN, F. edit. J. Walker, *What Really Happened at Azusa St., The true story of the great revival compiled by Frank Bartleman himself from his diary*. (Northridge, Calif.; Voice Christian Publ. Inc., 1962)

BAXTER, R. *Narrative of Facts characterising the Supernatural Manifestations in members of Mr. Irving's Congregation*. (London, 1833)

BEADLE, J. H. *Life in Utah, mysteries and crimes of Mormonism* (Philadelphia Nat. Pub. Co., 1870)

BEARE, F. W. 'Speaking with Tongues: A Critical Survey of the New Testament Evidence', *J.B.L.* 83 (1964), 229–52

BEEL, A. 'Donum linguarum juxta Act. Apost. ii 1–13', *Collationes Brugenes* 35 (1935), 417–20

BELO, Jane *Trance in Bali* (New York: Columbia University Press, 1960)

BENNETT, D. J. *Nine o'clock in the morning* (Logos, Fountain Trust 1970)

BENNETT, W. J. E., ed. *The Church's broken unity—on Presbyterianism and Irvingism* (London: Hayes, n.d.)

BERGOMA, S. 'Speaking with Tongues', *Torch and Trumpet* 14 (10) (Dec. 1964), 2

BERKHOF, H. *The Doctrine of the Holy Spirit* (Richmond, Va.: John Knox Press, 1964)

BERUSTEIN, B. 'Linguistic Codes, hesitation, phenomena and intelligence' *Lang. and Speech* 51 (1962), 31–46

BEVAN, E. *Symbolism and Belief* (London: Collins, 1962)

BEYER, S. *The Cult of Tārā: Magic and Ritual in Tibet* (University of California Press, 1973)

BLEWETT, D. *The Frontiers of Being* (N.Y. 1969)

BLOCH-HOELL, N. *The Pentecostal movement: Its Origin, Development, and Distinctive Character* (Oslo, London: Allen & Unwin, 1964)

BLOFELD, J. *Mantras* (London: Mandala Books, George Allen & Unwin, 1977)

BOBON, Jean 'Les Pseudo-Glossolalies, Ludiques et Magiques' *Journal Belge de Neurologie et de Psychiatrie* 47 (April 1947), 219ff., (June 1947), 327ff.

BODINE, Ann 'The phonological system of a five-year-old mongoloid' Berkeley, Univ. Calif. Summer Workshop on Language, Society and the Child, 1968, unpublished paper.

Bois, Henri *Le Réveil au Pays de Galles* (Toulouse, 1906)

Boisen, A. 'Religion and Hard Times', *Social Action* v (March 1939), 8–35;
'Economic distress and religious experience: A study of the Holy-Rollers', *Psychiatry* 2 (1939) 185–194

Boisen, A. J. *Religion in Crisis and Custom: A Sociological and Psychological Study.* (New York: Harper and Brothers, 1955)

Boring, M. E. 'How we may identify oracles of Christian Prophets in the Synoptic Tradition? Mark 3: 28–29 as a Test Case', *J.B.L.* 91 (4) (1972), 506, 508

Boulton, E. C. W. *George Jeffreys—Ministry of the Miraculous* (Elim Pub. House 1928)

Bourguignon, Erika 'Dreams and dream interpretation in Haiti', *American Anthropologist* 56 (1954), 262–68;
'Divination, transe et possession en Afrique Transsaharienne', A. Caquot and M. Liebovici eds. *La Divination* (Paris: Presses Universitaires de France, 1968);
A cross-cultural study of dissociational states (Columbus: Ohio State University Research Foundation, 1968);
'World distribution and patterns of possession states', Raymond Price, ed., *Trance and possession states* (Montreal: R. M. Bucke Memorial Society, 1968);
'Hallucination and trance: an anthropologist's perspective', Wolfram Keup., ed. *Origin and mechanisms of hallucinations*, (New York, London: Plenum P. 1970);
'Dreams and altered states of consciousness in anthropological research', F.L.K. Hsu ed., 2nd ed. *Psychological anthropology*, (Homewood, Illinois: Dorsey Press, Inc., 1971);
'The Self, the Behavioral Environment, and the Theory of Spirit Possession', in M.E. Spiro ed. *Context and Meaning in Cultural Anthropology* (New York: Free Press, 1965)

Bourguignon, Erika and Pettay, L. 'Spirit Possession, Trance and Cross-cultural research' (Ohio State univ., 1966) unpublished paper

Bouvat, L. 'Les Premiers Mystiques dans la littérature turque,' de Kieuprilizâdé, analyse critique'. *Revue du monde musulman* 43 (Feb. 1921), 236–66.

Bowker, J. *The Sense of God* (Oxford: Clarendon 1973)

Bowman, J. ed. *Comparative Religion* (Leiden: Brill 1972)

Bozzano, E. *Polyglot Mediumship*, E. Tr. I. Ewerson (London: Ricler, 1932)

Braithwaite, C. *The Beginnings of Quakerism* (London: Macmillan, 1912)

BRAY, A. E. *Revolt of the Protestants of the Cevennes* (London: Murray, 1870)

BREWSTER, P. S. *Is lasting Revival Possible ?* (Elim Publ. House, 1939)

BROOKE, J. *Light on the Baptism of the Holy Ghost* (Elim Publ. House, 1937)
Light on Speaking in Tongues (Elim Publ. House, 1935)

BROWN, David 'The Acts of the Apostles, Chapter ii, The Day of Pentecost' *Expositor* i (1875), 392–408

BROWN, L. B. ed. *Psychology and Religion* (Harmondsworth, Penguin Books, 1973)

BROWN, V. G. 'Exciting Prayer Week at Eastern Pentecostal Bible College' *Fellowship Monthly* 15 (Feb. 1970)

BRUCE, F. F. *1 and 2 Corinthians* (Oliphants, New Century Bible, 1971)
Commentary on the Book of Acts (London: Marshall Morgan and Scott, 1954)

BRUMBACK, C. *What Meaneth This ?* (Springfield Missouri, 1947, Assemblies of God Publ. House 1946).
Suddenly . . . from Heaven (Springfield, Mo.: Gospel Publ. House 1961)

BRUNER, F. D. *A Theology of the Holy Spirit: The Pentecostal Experience and the New Testament Witness* (Grand Rapids: Eerdmans, 1970, Hodder and Stoughton)

BRYANT, Ernest & O'CONNELL, Daniel 'A phonemic analysis of nine samples of glossolalic speech', *Psychonomic Science* 22 (1971), 81–83

BUBER, M. *The Prophetic Faith* E. Tr., C. Witton-Davies (New York: Harper and Row, 1960).

BURDICK, D. W. *Tongues: to speak or not to speak* (Chicago: Moody Press, 1969)

BURLING, Robbins *Man's Many Voices* (New York: Holt, Rinehart and Winston, 1970)

BUTLER, A. *Lives of the Saints* 4 Vols. (London 1756–59)

CALLEY, Malcolm J. C. *God's people: West Indian Pentecostal sects in England* (O.U.P. 1965)

CARROLL, J. B. and SAPON, S. M. *Modern Language Aptitude Test Manual* (New York: The Psychological Corporation 1955)

CASTALDO V. and HOLZMAN, P. S. 'The effects of hearing one's own voice on sleep mutation' in *J. Nerv. Ment. Dis.* 145 (1967), 2–13

CAYCEDO, A. *India of Yogis* (Delhi: National Publishing House, 1966)

CHADWICK, Nora K. *Poetry and Prophecy* (Cambridge, 1942) 'Shamanism among the Tartars of Central Asia' *Journal of the Royal Anthropological Institute* lxvi (1936), 75–112

CHAKRAVARTI, Chintahavan *Tantras: Studies on their religion and literature* (Calcutta, 1972)

CHANDLER, R. *Christianity Today* 12 (4) (24. 11. 1967), 39–40

CHARLES, R. H. *The Apocrypha and Pseudepigrapha* (Oxford, 1913)

CHOMSKY, Naomi 'Current issues in linguistic theory', Jerry Fodor and Jerrold J. Kats. eds., *The Structure of Language: Readings in the Philosophy of Languages* (Englewood Cliffs, New Jersey: Prentice-Hall, Inc. 1964)

CHRISTENSON, L. *Speaking in Tongues and its significance for the Church* (Minneapolis: Bethany Fellowship Inc. 1968)

CLARK, Elmer T. *The small sects in America* (New York and Nashville: Abingdon-Cokesbury Press, 1934, rev. 1949)

CLARK, S. *Team Manual for Life in the Spirit Seminars*, 2nd edit. (Notre Dame, Inc.: Charismatic Renewal Series)

CLARK, W. H. *Chemical Ecstasy* (Sheed and Ward, 1969)

CLEMENS, Carl 'The "Speaking with Tongues" of the Early Christians', *E.T.* 10 (1898–9), 344–52

COHN, N. *Pursuit of the Millenium* (Seeker and Warburg, 1957)

COHN, Werner 'A movie of experimentally produced glossololia', *J.S.S.R.*, 7 (1968), 278
'Personality, Pentecostalism and Glossolalia: A Research Note on Some Unsuccessful Research', *The Canadian Review of Sociology, Anthropology* 5 (1968), 39

COME, Arnold C. *Human Spirit and the Holy Spirit* (Philadelphia, Pa.: Westminster Press, 1959)

CONYBEARE, F. C. Tongues, Gift of, or Glossolalia, *Enc. Brit.* 11th edit. 27 (1910), 9–10

CONZELMANN, H. *The Theology of Luke* (New York: Harper & Row, 1960);
Der erste Brief an die Korinther (Göttingen, 1969);
Die Apostelgeschichte (Tubingen, 1963)

COWARD, Harold and PENELHUM, Terence eds. *Mystics and Scholars: The Calgary Conference on Mysticism* 1976. (Waterloo Ontario: Wilfrid Laurier Univ. Pres, 1977)

CROSS, F. L. ed. *The Oxford Dictionary of the Christian Church* (London Black and Son, 1975)

CRYSTAL, D. Review of W. J. Samarin's Tongues of Men and Angels: the religious language of Pentecostalism, *Language in Society*, vol. 3 (1) (April 1974), 126–31.

CUMMING, J. Elder, *Through the Eternal Spirit* (London: Marshall, Morgan & S cott Ltd. 1937)

CURRIE, S. D. ' "Speaking in Tongues": Early evidence outside the New Testament bearing on "glossais lalein" '. *Interpretation* 19 (1965), 274–94

CUTTEN, G. B. *Speaking with tongues: historically and psychologically considered* (New Haven: Yale University Press, 1927)

DAHLSTROM, W. G., WELSH, G. S. and DAHLSTROM, L. E. *A Minnesota Personality Inventory Handbook* rev. edit. (Minneapolis, 1972)

DALTON, R. C. *Tongues like as of fire* (Missouri: The Gospel Publishing House, 1945)

DAMBORIENA, Prudencio *Tongues as of Fire: Pentecostalism in Contemporary Christianity* (Washington and Cleveland: Corpus Books 1969)

DAVENPORT, F. M. *Primitive traits in religious revivals* (London, Macmillan 1905)

David Thomas: Founder of the International Holiness Mission (n.d.; no details of author and publisher)

DAVIES, Horton 'Pentecostalism: Threat or Promise' *E.T.* 76 (6) (March 1965), 197–99; 77 (8) (1966), 225.

DAVIES, J. G. 'Pentecost and Glossolalia' in *J.T.S.* 3 (1952), 228–31

de BARY, W. ed. *Sources of Indian Tradition* i (Columbia 1957)

de CELLES, Paul 'Reflections on the 1973 Conference' *New Covenant* 3 (2) (August, 1973), 24–25

DEIKMAN, A. J. 'Implications of experimentally induced contemplative meditation' *J. Nerv. Ment. Dis.* 142 (1966), 107–16. 'Deautomatization and the mystic experience' *Psychiatry* 29 (1966), 324–338

DELACROIX, M. H. *Etudes d'histoire et de psychologie du mysticisme* (Paris, 1908)

DELLING, G. *Worship in the New Testament* (Philadelphia: Westminster Press, 1962).

DENES, P. and MILTON-WILLIAMS, J. 'Further studies in intonation' *Language and Speech* 5 (1962), 1–14.

d'EPINAY, Christian L. 'Toward a Typology of Latin American Protestantism' *The Review of Religious Research* vol. x (1) (1968) 4–11

DERMENGHEN, *Muhammad and the Islamic Tradition* (N.Y.: Harper & Row 1958)

deROUGEMONT, Jean *Eindrücke über die Erweckung in Wales* (Basel, 1906)

Diary of A. J. Tomlinson, 1901–1923 i-iii (New York: The Church of God World Headquarters, 1949)

DODDS, E. R. *The Greeks and the Irrational*, Sather Classical Lectures xxv (Berkeley and Los Angeles, 1951)

246

DONOVAN, J. 'The Festal Origin of Human Speech', *Mind* 16 (1891) 498–506; 17 (1892) 325–39

DRIVER, G. R. 'The Original Form of the Name Jahweh', *Z.A.W.* NF 5 (1928)

DRIVER, H. E. *Indians of North America* (University of Chicago Press, 1961)

DRUMMOND, A. *Edward Irving and His Circle: Including Some Considerations of the 'Tongues' Movement in the Light of Modern Psychology* (London: James Clark, 1937)

DUNN, James G. *Baptism in the Holy Spirit* (S.C.M. 1970)

du PLESSIS, David J. *The Spirit Bade Me Go* (Dallas: David J. du Plessis, 1961) (obtainable from the author, 3472 Linwood Ave., Oakland, Calif.)

DURASOFF, S. *Bright Wind of the Spirit: Pentecostalism Today* (Hodder & Stoughton 1972)

ECCLES, J. C. ed. *Brain and Conscious Experience* (Berlin: Springer–Verlag, 1966)

EDMAN, V. R. 'Divine or Devilish?' *Christian Herald* 87 (May, 1946), 14–17

EDWARDS, Hubert E. 'The Tongues at Pentecost: A Suggestion', *Theology* 16 (1928), 248–52

ELIADE, Mircea *Le chamanisme et les techniques archaiques de l'extase* (Paris: Payet, 1951); *Shamanism: Archaic Techniques of Ecstasy* E. Tr. W. R. Trask, (Princeton, 1964)

ELLIOTT, Alan J. A. *Chinese Spirit Medium Cults in Singapore* (London, 1955)

ELLIS, E. E. *Paul's use of the Old Testament* (Edinburgh, 1957)

ENTWISTLE, Doris R. *Word-Associations of Young Children* (Baltimore: The John Hopkins Press, 1966)

ERMAN, A. *Life in Ancient Egypt* (London, 1894)

ERVIN-TRIPP, Susan 'Sociolinguistics', Working Paper No. 3 (Berkeley: University of California, Language-Behaviour Research Laboratory, 1967)
'Language development' in Lois and Martin Hoffman (eds.), *Review of Child Development Research*, vol. 2 (Russell Sage Foundation, 1967), 62–63

EVANS-PRITCHARD, E. E. *Theories of primitive religion* (Oxford: Clarendon Press, 1965)

EVANS, E. *The Welsh Revival of 1904* (London: Evangelical Press, 1969)

EVANS, Ivor H. N. *Studies in Religion, Folk-Lore and Custom in British North Borneo and the Malay Peninsula* (Cambridge University Press, 1923)

247

Ewart, F. J. *The Phenomenon of Pentecost* (St. Louis Mo. 1947)

Farrell, F. 'Outburst of Tongues: The New Penetration' *Christianity Today* 7 (Sept. 13, 1963), 3–7

Ferguson, C. *Confusion of Tongues* (N.Y., 1928)

Ferguson, D. A. 'Baby Talk in six languages' in 'The Ethnography of Communication', J. J. Gumperz and D. Hymes eds. *Amer. Anthropologist* 66 (6) Part 2 (1964), 103–14

Festinger, Leon *A theory of cognitive dissonance* (Evanston: Row, Peterson and Co. 1957)

Finch, J. G. 'God-Inspired or Self-Induced ?' *Christian Herald* 87 (May 1964), 12–13, 17–19

Findlay, G. G. *St. Paul's First Epistle to the Corinthians*, in W. R. Nicoll, *The Expositor's Greek Testament* (London: Hodder and Stoughton, 1901)

Fischer, Roland (with Philip A. Marks, Richard M. Hill, and Marsha A. Rockey) 'Personality structure as the main determinant of drug induced (model) psychoses', *Nature* 218 (No. 5138) (1968), 296–98

Fischer, R. 'The perception-hallucination continuum. A re-examination', *Diseases of the Nervous System* 30 (1969), 161–71; 'A biochemistry of behavior ?' *Biological Psychiatry* 1 (1969), 107–9

Fisher, C. 'Spoken Words in Dreams: A critique of the view of Otto Isakower', *Psychoanalytic Quarterly* 45 (1) (1976), 100–109

Fiske, E. B. report in *New York Times* (2 May 1971)

Fitzgerald, D. K. 'Prophetic Speech in Ga Spirit Mediumship' Working Paper 30 (Berkeley: University of California, The Language Behavior Research Laboratory 1970)

Flournoy, Th. *Des Indes a la Planete Mars: Etude Sur un Cas de Somnambulisme avec Glossolalie* (Geneva: Evvimann 1900) E. Tr. D. B. Vermilye, *From India to the Planet Mars* (N. Y.: Harper 1900) new edit. (1963) 'Nouvelles observations sur un cas de somnambulisme avec glossolalie'. Extrait des *Archives de Psychologie*, t. 1 No. 2 (décembre 1901)

Foakes-Jackson, F. J. and Lake Kirsopp, *The Beginnings of Christianity*: The Acts of the Apostles 5 vol (London, Macmillan, 1933)

Ford, J. Massyngberde 'Neo-Pentecostalism within the Roman Catholic Communion' in *Dialog* 13 (1974) 45–50; 'Toward a Theology of "Speaking in Tongues" ' in *Theological Studies* 32 (1) (March 1971), 3–29; *The Pentecost Experience* (New York, 1970); *The Spirit and the Human Person* (Dayton, 1969)

FRANK, J. *Persuasion and Healing*: *A comparative study of Psychotherapy* (Baltimore: John Hopkins Press, 1961)

FRINSEL, J. J. 'Wat denkt u van de charismatische Beweging ?' *De Oogst* 464 (Sept. 1974), 12

FRODSHAM, S. H. *With Signs Following* (Springfield Mo: Gospel Publ. House, rev. edit. 1940)

FRY, D. B. 'Duration and intensity as physical correlates of linguistic stress', *J. of the Acoustical Society of America* 27 (1955), 765–68

FRYER, A. T. 'Psychological Aspects of the Welsh Revival', *P.S.P.R.* 51 vol. 19 (1905), 80–161

Full Gospel Business Men's Fellowship Int'l 836 St. Figueroa, Los Angeles, Calif. 90017 publications:—*Voice*; *Vision*; *View*.

GARDNER, Ernest *Fundamentals of neurology* (Philadelphia & London: W. B. Saunders, 1963)

GARRISON, V. 'Marginal religion and psychosocial deviancy: a controlled comparison of Puerto Rican Pentecostals and Catholics', in I. I. Zaretsky and Mark P. Leone, eds. *Religious Movements in Contemporary America* (Princeton, 1974)

GASSON, R. *The Challenging Counterfeit* (Plainfield N.J., 1966)

GAVER, J. R. *Pentecostalism* (Award Books, 1971)

GAXIOLA, Maclovio L. *Historia de la Iglesia Apostolica de la fe en Cristo Jesus de Mexico* (Mexico, D.F.: Libreria Latinoamericana, 1964)

GEE, Donald *The Pentecostal Movement* (London: Elim Publishing Co. 1941); *Concerning Spiritual Gifts* (Springfield Mo.: Gospel Publishing House, 1947); *The Pentecostal Movement, Including the Story of the War Years 1940–47* (London: Elim Publ. Co. 1949)

GELPI, D. L. *Pentecostalism*: *A Theological Viewpoint* (New York, Toronto, 1941)

GERLACH, L. P. and HINE, Virginia H. 'Five Factors crucial to the Growth and Spread of a Modern Religious Movement' in *J.S.S.R.* 6 (1967), 23–39
'The charismatic revival: Process of recruitment; conversion and behavioral change in a modern religious movement'. University of Minnesota, paper (1966); *People, Power, Change*: *Movements of Social Transformation* (Indianapolis: Bobs-Merrill, 1970)

GERRARD, N. L. and L. B. *Scrabble Creek Folk*: *Mental Health* Part 11, report, Department of Sociology, Morris Harvey College, Charleston, West Virginia, see *Transaction* (May 1968).

249

GIBB, H. A. R. *shath* q.v. *Shorter Enc. of Islam* (1953)

GILMORE, Susan K. 'Personality differences between High and Low dogmatism groups of Pentecostal Believers' *J.S.S.R.* 8 (1968), 161–64

GILSENAN, M. *Saint and Sufi in Modern Egypt* (Oxford Univ. Press, 1973)

GLEN, J. Stanley *Pastoral Problems in First Corinthians* (Westminster Press, 1964)

GLOCK, Charles Y. and STARK, Rodney *Religion and Society in Tension* (Chicago: Rand McNally & Co., 1965)

Glossolalia in *Enc. Brit.* 11th edit. xxvii q.v.

GODET, F. *Commentary on St. Paul's First Epistle to the Corinthians* (Edinburgh, 1898)

GODWIN, Donald W., et al. 'Alcohol and recall: state-dependent effects in man', *Science* 163 (1969), 1358–60.

GOETTMANN, J. 'La Pentecôte premices de la nouvelle création' *Bible et vie chrétienne* 27 (1959), 59–69

GOLDSMITH, H. 'The Psychological Usefulness of Glossolalia to the Believer', *View* 11 (Nov. 2, 1965), 57–8

GONDA, Jan 'The Indian Mantra' *Oriens* 16 (1963), 244–297

GOODMAN, F. D. 'Phonetic Analysis of Glossolalia in Four Cultural Settings' *J.S.S.R.* 8 (1969), 227–39;
'Glossolalia: speaking in tongues in four cultural settings', *Confinia Psychiatrica* 12 (1969), 113–29;
'The acquisition of glossolalia behavior' *Semiotica* 3 (1971), 77–82;
'Glossolalia and single-limb trance: some parallels', *Psychotherapy and Psychosomatics* 19 (1971), 92–103;
Speaking in Tongues: A Cross-Cultural Study of Glossolalia (Chicago, 1972);
'The Apostolics of Yucatan: a case study of a religious movement', Erika Bourguignon, ed. *Religion, altered states of consciousness, and social change* (Columbus: Ohio State U. Press 1972)

GÖRRES, J. J. *Die christliche mystik* (Regensburg: Manz, 1836–42) *La Mystique divine, naturelle, et diabolique* Fr. Tr. C. Sainte-Foi (Paris, 1862)

GOSS, H. and E. *The Winds of God* (New York: Comet Press Books, 1958)

GOVINDA, L. A. *Foundations of Tibetan Mysticism* (London, 1969)

GRABBE, Lester L. 'Glossolalia, The New "Tongues" Movement' in *The Plain Truth* (Oct., 1971), 20–24

GREEN, E. 'Phonological and grammatical aspects of jargon in an aphasic patient: a case study' *Language and Speech* 12 (1969), 103–113

GREENE, D. 'The Gift of Tongues' in *Bibliotheca Sacra* xxii (1865), 99–126

GRIEVE, A. J. 'Charismata' in *E.R.E.* iii q.v.

GRIFFITH, Wyn *The Welsh* (Pelican, 1950)

GROF. S. 'Beyond the Bounds of Psychoanalysis', *Intellectual Digest* 61 (Feb. 1972);
'Varieties of transpersonal experiences: observations from LSD psychotherapy', *J. of Transpersonal Psychology* 1 (1972)

GUILLAUME, A. *Islam* (Pelican, 1954);
Prophecy and Divination (London: Hodder and Stoughton, 1938)

GUNDRY, R. H. 'Ecstatic Utterance (NEB)?' in *J.T.S.* n.s. 17 (1966), 299–307

GUNKEL, H. 'The Secret Experiences of the Prophets', *Expositor* 9th series 1 (1924), 356–66;
Die Wirkungen des heiligen Geistes nach der populären Anschauung der apostolischen Zeit und der Lehre des Apostloes Paulus (Göttingen, 1899)

GUNNISON, J. W. *The Mormons or Latter Day Saints in the Valley of the Great Salt Lake*, (Philadelphia: Lippincott 1860)

HAAVIK, O. L. 'Pentecostalism or the Tongues Movement', *Lutheran Herald* (Oct. 23 and 30, 1934), 935ff

HACKMANN, H. 'Die geistigen Abnormitaten der alttestamentlichen Propheten', *Nieuw Theologisch Tijdschrift* 23 (1934), 23–48

HAENCHEN, E. *Acts of the Apostles* (Oxford, 1971)

HALL, Edward T. *The Silent Language*, (Garden City: Doubleday & Co. Inc. 1959)

HALLOWEL, A. Irving 'Psychological leads for ethnological field workers', D. G. Haring, ed., *Personal Character and Cultural Milieu* (Syracuse: Syracuse University Press, 1959)

HAMMOND, W. A. *Spiritualism and allied causes and conditions of nervous derangement*, (N.Y.: Putnam, 1876)

HANSON, R. P. C. *The Acts of the Apostles* (Oxford, 1967)

HARDING, Rosamond, E. M. *An Anatomy of Inspiration* 3rd edit. (Cambridge, 1940)

HARDON, John A. *The Protestant Churches of America* (Garden City, N.Y.: Image Books, 1969)

HARING, D. G. ed. *Personal Character and Cultural Milieu: A Collection of Readings*, (Syracuse: Syracuse University Press, 1948)

HARMAN, W. 'The New Copernican Revolution', *Journal of Humanistic Psychology*, No. 2 (1969), 129

HARPER, M. *As at the Beginning* (Logos, 1965)

HASKETT, W. J. *Shakerism unmasked* (Pittsfield: Walkeley, 1828)

251

HASTINGS, J. ed. *Dictionary of the Bible* (N.Y.: Scribners, 1909);
The Encyclopaedia of Religion and Ethics (1908–26)

HATHWAY, W. G. *Spiritual Gifts in the Church* (Elim Publ. House, 1933)

HAWTHORNTHWAITE, S. *Mr. Hawthornthwaite's adventures among the Mormons as an elder during eight years* (Manchester, 1857)

HAYES, D. A. *The Gift of tongues*, (N.Y., 1913)

HEATH, R. 'The Little Prophets of the Cevennes', *Contemporary Review* 49 (Jan. 1886), 117

HENKE, F. G. 'Gift of tongues and related phenomena at the present day', *American Journal of Theology*, 13 (April 1909), 193

HENNEY, Jeanetta 'Trance behavior Among the Shakers of St. Vincient'. Ohio State University Cross-Cultural Study of Dissociational States, working paper No. 8 (1967);
'Spirit possession belief and trance behavior in a religious group in St. Vincent, British West Indies'. Unpublished Ph.D. dissertation, 1968, Ohio State University, Columbus, Ohio (1968)

HÉRING, J. *The First Epistle of St. Paul to the Corinthians* (London, 1962)

HESS, Werner, R. *The biology of the mind*, E. Tr. G. von Bonin, (Chicago: University of Chicago Press, 1964)

HINE, Virginia H. 'Pentecostal glossolalia: toward a functional interpretation', *J.S.S.R.* 8 (1969), 211–26
'Bridge burners: Commitment and participation in a religious movement', *Sociological Analysis* 31 (1970), 61–66

HITT, Russel T. 'The New Pentecostalism: An Appraisal', *Eternity* 14 (July, 1963), 10–16

HOCKETT, Charles F. *A course in modern linguistics*, (New York: Macmillan, 1958)

HOCKETT, Charles F. and ASCHER, Robert, 'The Human Revolution' in *Current Antrhopology* 5 (1964), 135–68

HOEKEMA, A. A. *Holy Spirit Baptism*, (Grand Rapids: W. B. Eerdmans, 1972)
What about Tongue-Speaking? (Grand Rapids: W. B. Eerdmans, 1966)

HOENIG, T. 'Medical research on yoga', *Confinia Psychiatrica* 11 (1968), 69–89

HOLLENWEGER, W. J. Handbook of the Pentecostal Movement. Monumental D.Th. thesis in ten volumes, copy deposited at Yale, Chicago and Vancouver;
Pentecost between Black and White (Belfast: Christian Journals Ltd., 1974);

ed. *Die Pfingstkirchen* (Stuttgart: Evangelisches Verlagswerk, 1969);

Enthusiastisches Christentum (Zurich: Zwingli Verlag/Wuppertal: Theologischer Verlag Rolf Brockhaus, 1969);

The Pentecostals E. Tr. R. A. Wilson (S.C.M., 1972)

HÖLSCHER, G. *Die Profeten* (Leipzig: Hinrichs, 1914)

HOMANS, P. ed. *The Dialogue between Theology and Psychology* (Chicago, 1968)

HOOKER, M. R. *The Full Blessing of Pentecost* (Elim Publ. House, 1928)

HOOVER, Mario G. 'A History of the Origin and Structural Development of the Assemblies of God', South West Missouri State College, unpublished M.A. thesis (1968)

HORIKAWA, K., OHWAKI, Y., WATANABE, T., 'Variation of verbal activity through different psychological situations', *Tohoku Psychol.* 15 (1956), 65–90

HORTON, H. *The Gifts of the Spirit* (London: Assemblies of God Publ. House, 1954)
What is the Good of Speaking with Tongues? (Assemblies of God Publ. House n.d.)

HORTON, W. ed. *The Glossolia Phenomenon* (Cleveland, Tennesee: Pathway Press, 1966)

HOUSMAN, A. E. *The Name and Nature of Poetry* (Cambridge, 1933)

HOUSTON, J. Proceedings of the Conference on Altered States of Consciousness in Washington, D.C., 1971, transcribed from the tape broadcast by CBO radio March 19, 1973.

HUGHES, D. 'Dechreuad y Diwygiad ym Mhontycymer', *Y Dysgedydd* 85 (1906), 579

HUGHES, Henry *Hanes Diwygiadau Crefyddol Cymru* (Caernarfon, 1907)

HULME, A. J. H. and WOOD, F. H. *Ancient Egypt Speaks: A Miracle of Tongues* (London: Rider, 1940)

HYMES, Dell H. ed. *Pidginization and Creolization of Language* (Cambridge Univ. Press, 1971)
'The Ethnography of Speaking' in Gladwin, Thomas and W. C. Sturtevant, *Anthropology and Human Behavior* (Washington D.C. Anthropological Society 1962)

IBISH, YUSUF and WILSON, P. L. eds. *Traditional Modes of Contemplation and Action* (Thames and Hudson, 1977)

INGLIS, J. 'Gift of tongues: another view', *Theological Monthly* 5 (1891), 425

IRESON, C. C. *The Nine Gifts of the Holy Ghost* (Tenets of the Apostolic Church, 1957)

IRVING, E. 'On the Gifts of the Holy Ghost', *Collected Works* v (London 1866)

IRWING, O. C. and CHEN, H. P. 'Infant speech, vowel and consonant frequency', *J. Speech and Hearing Dis.* 13 (1948), 123–35

ISAKOWER, O. 'Spoken Words in Dreams. A Preliminary Communication', *The Psychoanalytic Quarterly* 23 (1954), 1–16; 'On the Exceptional Position of the Auditory Sphere' *Int. J. Psa* 20 (1939), 340–48.

JACKSON, F. J. Foakes *The History of the Christian Church from the earliest times to A.D.* 461 sixth edit. (Deighton, Bell & Co. Ltd., 1954)

JACOBI, W. *Die Ekstase der alttestamentlichen Propheten* (München, 1920)

JAHR, M. A. 'A Turning Point, the 1974 Notre Dame Conference' *New Covenant* 4 (2) (August, 1974), 4–7

JAKOBSON, R. and HALLE, M. *Fundamentals of Language* (The Hague Mouton, 1956)

JAKOBSON, R. *Selected Writings* Vol. 4 Slavic Epic Studies. (The Hague: Mouton & Co., 1966); *Child Language, Aphasia and Phonological Universals* (Janua Linguaram, Series Minor, 72) (The Hague: Mouton & Co., 1968)

JANSEN, H., HOOVER, E., GEGGETT, G., eds. *Live in the Spirit: Council on Spiritual Life Digest* (Springfield Mo.: Gospel Publishing House, 1972)

JAQUITH, James R. 'Toward a typology of formal communicative behavior: glossolalia', *Anthropological Linguistics* 9 (8) (1967), 1–8

JEFFREYS, G. *The Miraculous Foursquare Gospel* 2 vols. (Elim Publ. House, 1929)

JOHNSON, A. R. *The Vitality of the Individual in the Thought of Ancient Israel*, 2nd edit. (Cardiff: University of Wales Press, 1964); *The Cultic Prophet in Ancient Israel* 2nd edit. (Cardiff: University of Wales Press, 1962); *The Cultic Prophet and Israel's Psalmody* (Cardiff: University of Wales, 1979)

JONES, Albert C. 'Myfyrdod wedi'r Pentecost: Dawn y Tafodau' *Y Tyst* (29 Mai, 1969), 6–7

JONES, Daniel *An Outline of English Phonetics*, 3rd edit., (Cambridge, 1932)

JONES, J. Ithel *The Holy Spirit and Christian Preaching* (Epworth 1967)

JONES, R. B. *Rent Heavens: The Revival of 1904, Some of its Hidden Springs and Prominent Results* (London, 1931)

254

JOYCE, G. C. *The Inspiration of Prophecy* (Oxford, 1910)

JUNG, C. G. *Collected Works* (London: Routledge and Kegan Paul, 1953—)
1. *Psychiatric Studies* (1957)
5. *Symbols of Transformation* (1956)
7. *Two Essays and Analytical Psychology* (1953)
9. (Part 1) *Archetypes and Collective Unconscious* (1959)
9. (Part 11) *Aion* (1959)
11. *Psychology and Religion: West and East* (1958)
12. *Psychology and Alchemy* (1953);
Memories, Dreams and Reflections (New York: Pantheon Books, 1963);
Psychological Types (London: Routledge and Kegan Paul, 1953)

JURIEU, P. *Lettres pastorales adresses aux fidéles de France* (Rotterdam, 1686–87, E. Tr. 1689)

KAMIYA, T. 'Conscious control of brain waves', *Psychology Today* 50, (1968), 56

KELSEY, Morton T. *Tongue Speaking* (New York: Doubleday, 1968); 'And there appeared to them Tongues of Fire', *Saturday Evening Post* (16 May, 1964)

KENDRICK, Klaude *The Promise Fulfilled: A History of the Modern Pentecostal Movement* (Springfield Mo., 1961)

KENNEDY, J. H. *Early Days of Mormonism* (N.Y. Scribners, 1888)

KEUP, W., ed. *Origin and Mechanism of Hallucinations* (New York, 1970).

KIEV, Ari 'The Study of folk psychiatry', *Magic, faith and healing: studies in primitive psychiatry* (Beverly Hills, Calif.: Glencoe Press, 1964), 3–35
'Psychotherapeutic aspects of Pentecostal sects among West Indian immigrants to England', *British Journal of Sociology* 15, (1964), 129–138

KILDAHL, J. P. *The Psychology of Speaking in Tongues* (New York; Harper and Row, 1972)

KLEITMAN, Nathaniel *Sleep and wakefulness*, rev. ed. (Chicago: University of Chicago Press, 1963)

KNOBEL, A. W. *Der Prophetismus der Hebräer* i (Breslau, 1837)

KNOX, R. A. *Enthusiasm* (O.U.P., 1950)

KNOX, W. L. *The Acts of the Apostles* (Cambridge, 1948)

KOELLA, Werner P. *Sleep* (Springfield, Ill.: Charles C. Thoms, 1967)

KÖPRÜLÜZADÉ, M. F. *Influence du chamanisme turco-mongol sur les ordres mystiques musulmans* (Istanbul, 1929)

KRETSCHMER, G. 'Himmelfahrt und Pfingsten', *Zeitschrift fur Kirchengeschichte* 66 (1954–55), 209 ff.

KULBECK, Gloria G. *What God Hath Wrought, a History of the Pentecostal Assemblies of Canada*, edit., W. E. McAlister and G. R. Upton (Toronto: Pent. Assemblies of Canada, 1958)

LA BARRE, Weston *The ghost dance: the origins of religion* (Garden City, New York: Doubleday, 1970);
'Materials for a history of studies of crisis cults', *Current Anthropology* 12 (1971) 3–45;
They Shall take up serpents: psychology of the Southern Snake-Handling Cult. (Minneapolis: University of Minnesota Press, 1962)

LAFFAL, Julius *Pathological and Normal Language* (N.Y.: Atherton Press, 1965);
'Language, consciousness and experience, *Psychoanalytic Quarterly* 36 (1967), 61–66.

LAMPE, G. W. H. *The Seal of the Spirits. A Study in the doctrine of Baptism and Confirmation in the New Testament and the Fathers.* (London: Longmans. Green & Co., 1951)

LAMSON, D. R. *Two years experience among the Shakers . . . a condensed view of Shakerism as it is.* (Lamson: W. Boyston 1848)

LANGER, Susanne *Philosophy in a New Key* (New York: Mentor, 1948)

LAPSLEY, J. N. and SIMPSON, J. H. 'Speaking in tongues: Infantile babble or song of the self?' *Pastoral Psychology* (Sept. 1964), 16–24 ;
'Speaking in Tongues' in *Princeton Seminary Bulletin* 63 (1965), 3–18 ;
'Speaking in Tongues: Token of Group Acceptance and Divine Approval' in *Pastoral Psychology* (May 1964), 48–55

LASKI, Marghanita *Ecstasy* (London: The Cresset Press, 1961)

LAURENTIN, René 'Speaking in Tongues' *Sign* (Feb. 1978), 10–15

LE BARON, Albert (pseudo.) 'A case of psychic automatism, including speaking with tongues', *P.S.P.R.* 12 (1896–97), 277–97

LENNEBERG, Eric H. *Biological foundations of language.* (New York: John Wiley & Sons, 1967)

LEHISTE, Ilse and PETERSON, G. E., 'Vowel amplitude and phonemic stress in American English', *Journal for the Acoustical Society of America* 31 (1959), 428–35)

LEIDERMAN, P. H. and SHAPIRO, D., eds. *Psychological Approaches to Social Behaviour* (London, 1965)

LESSA, W. A. and VOGT, E. Z., eds. *Reader in comparative religion: on anthropological approach* 2nd edit. (New York: Harper and Row, 1965)

LEUBA, J. H.   *The Psychology of Religious Mysticism*, 2nd edit. (London, 1925)

LÉVI-STRAUSS, Claude   *Totemism*, E. Tr. Rodney Needham (Boston: Beacon Press, 1963)

LEWIS, I. M.   *Ecstatic Religion: An Anthropological Study of Spirit Possession and Shamanism* (Penguin, 1971)

LEWIS, T.   *Llenyddiaeth a Diwinyddiaeth y Proffwydi* (1923)

L'HERMITTE, Jean   *True and False in Possession*, E. Tr. P. J. Hepburne Scott, (N.Y.: Hawthorn, 1963)

LIBET, B.   'Brain stimulation and the threshold of conscious experience', J. C. Eccles, ed., *Brain and conscious*, (Berlin, Heidelberg, New York: Springer Verlag, 1966)

LINDBLOM, J.   *Prophecy in Ancient Israel* (Oxford, 1962)
'Einige Grundfragen der alltestamentlichen Wissenschaft' in *Festschrift für Alfred Bertholet* (Tübingen, 1950)
'Die Religion der Propheten und die Mystik' in *Z.A.W.* NF 42 (1939), 54–74

LINGS, Martin   *A Sufi Saint of the Twentieth Century* (Allen and Unwin 2nd edit., 1971)

LODS, A.   *Israel from its beginnings to the Middle of the Eighth Century*. E. Tr. S. H. Hooke, (Routledge and Kegan Paul, 1932; 1953)

LOMBARD, Émile   'Essais d'une classification des phénomenes de glossolalie', *Archives de psychologie*, tome vii (juillet 1907);
De la glossolalie chez les premiers chrétiens et des phénomenes similaires (Lausanne; Bridel 1910)

LOMMEL, Andreas   *Die Welt der Fruhen Jager: Medizinmanner, Schamanen, Kunstler*, (Munich: Callwey, 1965)

LOVEKIN, A. and MALONY, H. Newton, 'Religious Glossolalia' in *J.S.S.R.* 16 (4) (Dec. 1977), 383–93

LOWIE, Robert H.   'Dreams, idle dreams', *Current Anthropology* 7, (1966), 378–82 (posthumous).

LUCHSINGER, Richard and ARNOLD, G. E. *Voice—Speech—Language. Clinical Communicology: Its physiology and pathology* (Belmont, Calif.: Wandsworth Publishing Co., 1965)

LUDWIG, A. M.   'Altered States of consciousness', *Arch. Gen. Psychiat.* 14 (1966), 225 ff.;
'The trance', *Compr. Psychiat.* 8 (1967) 7ff

LYONNETT, S.   'De glossolalia Pentecostes eiusque significatione' *Verbum Domini* 24 (1944), 65–75

MacDERMOT, V.   *The Cult of the Seer in the Ancient Middle East* (London: Welcome Institute of the History of Medicine, 1971)

MacDONALD, W. G.   *Glossolalia in the New Testament* (Springfield Missouri: Gospel Publ. House, 1964)

MACKAY, J. A. *Ecumenics: the Science of the Church Universal* (Englewood Cliffs, N.J.: Prentice Hall, 1964)
Christian Reality and Appearance (Richmond Va.: John Knox Press, 1969)

MACKIE, A. *The Gift of Tongues: a study in pathological aspects of Christianity* (New York: George Doran and Co., 1921)

MAEDER, Alphonse 'La Langue d'un Aliéné: Analyse d'un Cas de Glossolalie', in *Archives de Psychologie*, March 1910, 208ff.

MALINOWSKI, B. *Coral Gardens and their Magic* (London: Allen and Unwin, 1935)

MALMBERG, Bertil *Structural Linguistics and Human Communication* (Berlin, Heidelberg, New York: Springer-Verlag, 1967)

MANDELBAUM, D. G. 'Transcendental and Pragmatic Aspects of Religion' in *American Anthropologist* 68 (1966), 1174–91

MANN, C. S. 'Pentecost, the Spirit and John', *Theology* 62 (1959), 188–90

MARC'HADOUR, Germain 'The Holy Spirit over the New World', *The Clergy Review* 59 (4) (April 1974), 247–48

MARECHAL, J. *Studies in the Psychology of the Mystics* (Albany, N.Y.: Magi, 1964)

MARION, E. *La Theatr Sacré des Cevennes* (London, 1707)

MARTIN, I. J. *Glossolalia in the Apostolic Church: A Survey of Tongue-Speech* (Berea Ky., 1960) 'Glossolalia in the Apostolic Church' in *J.B.L.* 63 (1944) 123–30

MASLOW, A. H. *Religions, Values and Peak Experiences* (Columbus: Ohio State University Press, 1964)

MASSIGNON, L. *Essai sur les origines du lexique technique de la mystique musulmane* 2nd edit. (Paris, 1954)

MAUCHLINE, J. 'Ecstasy' in *E.T.* 49 (1937), 295–99

MAY, L. Carlyle 'A Survey of Glossolalia and Related Phenomena in Non-Christian Religions' in *American Anthropologist* 58 (1) (Feb. 1956), 75–96

McCASLAND, S. V., GAIRNS, G. E., YU, D. C., *Religions of the World* (N.Y.: Random House, 1969)

McCLINTOCK, J. and STRONG, J. *Cyclopaedia of Biblical, theological and ecclesiastical literature*, 10: 479 (N.Y. 1869–81)

McLOUGHLIN, W. G. *Modern Revivalism: Charles Grandison Finney to Billy Graham.* (Ronald Press Co., 1959)

McCROSSAN, T. J. *Speaking with other Tongues, Sign or Gift, Which ?* (N.Y.: Christian Alliance, 1927)

McGUIGAN, E. J. *Thinking: Studies of Covert Language Processes* (New York, 1966)

MEAD, F. S. *Handbook of Denominations in the United States* 4th edit. (New York, Abingdon Press, 1965)

MELCHER, Marguerite F. *The Shaker Adventure* (Cleveland: The Press of Case Western Reserve University, 1968)

MENZIES, W. W. *Anointed to serve: The Story of the Assemblies of God* 1968) (Springfield, 1971)

MÉTRAUX, A. *Voodoo in Haiti*, (New York, 1959)

MICKLEM, N. *Prophecy and Eschatology* (London, 1926)

MIDDLETON, J. ed. *Magic Witchcraft and Curing* (Garden City, N.Y.: 1967)

MILLER, Ed. *The History and Doctrines of Irvingism or of the so-called Catholic and Apostolic Church*, i, ii. (London: C. K. Paul & Co., 1878)

MILLS, Watson E. 'Reassessing Glossolalia', *Christian Century* 88 (41) (14 Oct. 1970)

MILLS, W. *Understanding Speaking in Tongues* (Grand Rapids, 1972)

MISCHEL, W. and F. 'Psychological Aspects of Spirit possession' in *Amer. Anthro.* 60 (1958), 249 ff.

MOBERG, David O. 'The Encounter of Scientific and Religious Values Pertinent to Man's Spiritual Nature', *Sociological Analysis*, 28 (1) (Spring 1967), 22–23;
'The United States of America' in H. Mol ed. *Western Religion* (The Hague: Mouton, 1972)

MOFFATT, J. *The First Epistle of Paul to the Corinthians* (London, 1938)

MOL, H. ed. *Western Religion: a country by country sociological inquiry* (The Hague: Mouton, 1972)

MONTAGUE, George T. 'Baptism in the Spirit and speaking in tongues: a biblical appraisal', *Theology Digest* 21 (4) (1973), 342–360

MORGAN, J. J. *Dafydd Morgan a Diwygiad '59* (1906)

MOSIMAN, Eddison *Das Zungenreden geschichtlich und psychologisch untersucht.* (Tübingen: Mohr, 1911)

MOULTON, J. H. and MILLINGAN, R. *The Vocabulary of the Greek New Testament* (London, 1930)

MOWINCKEL, S. *Die Erkenntnis Gottes bei den alttestamentlichen Profeten* (Oslo, 1941);
'The "Spirit" and the "Word" in the Pre-Exilic Reforming Prophets' in *J.B.L.* 53 (1934), 199–227; 56 (1937), 261–65;
Psalmenstudien 1 (Kristiana: Dybwad, 1921)

MURPHY, Gardner *Personality: A Bio-Social Approach to Origins and Structure* (New York: Harper, 1947)

MURRAY, R. H. *Group Movements through the Ages* (London, 1935)

NADEL, S. F. 'A Study of shamanism in the Nuba mountains', *Journal of the Royal Anthropological Institute* 76 (1946), 25–37,

259

reprinted in Lessa and Vogt, *Reader in Comparative Religion*, 464–478

NEEDHAM, R.   'Percussion and Transition', *Man* (n.s.) 2 (1967), 606–14

NICHOL, J. T.   *The Pentecostals* (Logos, 1966)

NICKEL, T. R.   *The Amazing Shakarian Story* (Los Angeles: F.G.B.M.F.I. 1964)

NICOLL, W. R. ed.   *The Expositor's Greek Testament 2* (New York: Dodd, Mead and Co., 1901)

NIDA, Eugene A.   'Glossolalia: a case of pseudolinguistic structure'. Unpublished paper delivered at the 39th Annual Meeting of the Linguistic Society of America. New York City, December 28th, 1964

NORBECH, E.   *Religion in Primitive Society* (New York: Harper & Row, 1961)

NORTH, Robert   'Angel Prophet or Satan Prophet' in *Z.A.W.* (82) (1970), 31–67

NOTH, M. and THOMAS, D. W. eds.   *Wisdom in Israel and in the Ancient Near East*, S.V.T. iii (Leiden: Brill, 1955)

O'BRIEN, E.   *Varieties of Mystic Experience* (London: Mentor-Omega, Paper backs, 1965)

O'CONNOR, E. D.   *Pentecost in the Catholic Church* (Dove, 1971)

OESTERREICH, T. K.   *Possession, Demoniacal and Other, among Primitive Races in Antiquity, the Middle Ages and Modern Times* (London and New York: University Books, 1930)

OMAN, J. B.   'On "Speaking in Tongues": A Psychological Analysis', *Pastoral Psychology* 14 (December 1963), 48–51

OMAN, J. C.   *The Mystics Ascetics and Saints of India* (Delhi: Oriental Publishers, 1973)

OSSER, H. A., OSTWALD, P. F., MACWHINNEY, B. and Casey, R. L.   'Glossolalic speech from a psycholinguistic perspective', *Journal of Psycholinguistic Research* 2(1) (1973), 9–19

OTTO, R.   *Aufsätze das Numinose betreffend* (Gotha: L. Klotz, 1929)

PALMA, A. D.   'Glossolalia in the Light of the New Testament and Subsequent History', New York, Biblical Seminary B.S.T. thesis (1960)

PALMER, G.   'Trance and Dissociation: A Cross-cultural study in Psychophysiology'. (University of Minnesota M.Sc. thesis 1966, unpublished)

PARZEN, H.   'The Ruaḥ Hakodesh in Tannaitic Literature' in *Jewish Quarterly Review* n.s. 20 (1929–30), 51–76

PATTISON, E. M.   Behavioral science research on the nature of glossolalia. *J. Amer. Sci. Affil.* 20 (1968), 73–86

PATTISON, E. M. and CASEY, R. L. 'Glossolalia: A Contemporary Mystical Experience' *International Psychiatry Clinics* No. 5 (1969), 133–48

PEDERSEN, Johs *Israel: its life and culture* i–ii E.Tr., A. Möller (Oxford, 1926); iii–iv (1940)

PENN-LEWIS, (Mrs.) Jessie *The Awakening in Wales* (London: Marshall Brothers, 1905)

PENN-LEWIS (Mrs.), Jessie and ROBERTS, Evan, *War on the Saints*, (Leicester: Overcomer Office, London: Marshall Brothers, 1912) 'Pentecostal Churches in Canada' in *World Pentecost* 2 (1971) 14–16

PFISTER, Oskar *Die psychologische Enträtselung der religiosen Glossolalie und der automatischen Kryptographie*, Jahrbuch für Psychoanalytische und Psychopathologische Forschungen (vol. 2) (Leipzig & Vienna: Deuticke, 1912)

PIKE, James A. 'Pastoral Letter Regarding "Speaking in Tongues" ' *Pastoral Psychology* 15 (May 1964), 56–61

PIKE, Kenneth L. *Phonetics, a Critical Analysis of Phonetic Theory and a Technic for the Practical Description of Sounds* (Ann Arbor, 1943)

PILKINGTON, G., *The Unknown Tongues discovered to be English, Spanish and Latin, and the Revd. Edw. Irving proved to be erroneous in attributing their utterance to the influence of the Holy Spirit* (London 1831)

PLOG, S. 'UCLA Conducts research in glossolalia', *Trinity* 3 (1965), 38–39; 'Preliminary analysis of group questionnaires on glossolalia' (Los Angeles: Univ. of California 1966)

PLOWMAN, E. E. 'Catholic Pentecostals: Something New', *Christianity Today* 18, 22 (5 July 1974), 47–48

POLLARD, J. *Seers, Shrines and Sirens* (London, 1965)

PORTEOUS, N. W. 'Prophecy' in H. W. Robinson, ed. *Record and Revelation* (Oxford, 1938)

POSTEL, Guillaume *Le Thrésor des Prophéties de l'Univers* (1969)

PRINCE, Raymond edit. *Trance and Possession States* (Proceedings Second Annual Conference R. M. Buckle Memorial Society 4–6 March 1966) (Montreal, 1968)

RAHMANN, Rudolf 'Shamanistic and Related Phenomena in Northern and Middle India', *Anthropos*, 54 (1959), 681–760

RANAGHAN, Kevin and Dorothy, *Catholic Pentecostals* (New York, Toronto: Paulist Press, Deus Books, 1969)

REES, G. *A Bundle of Sensations* (London, 1960)

RICE, R. 'Charismatic Revival', *Christian Life* 25 (Nov. 1963), 30–32

RICHET, Charles 'Xénoglossie: l'Ecriture Automatique en Langues Étrangères' *P.S.P.R.* 51 vol. 19 (Dec. 1905), 162–194; discussion 195–261

RIGGS, R. M. *The Spirit Himself* (Springfield, Mo.: Gospel Publ. House, 1949)

RIOCH, D. and WEINSTEIN, E. A., eds. *Disorders of Communication* (Baltimore: Williams and Wilkins, 1964)

ROBERTS, Evan and Mrs. PENN-LEWIS, *War on the Saints* (Leicester, 1912)

ROBERTS, Oral *The Baptism with the Holy Spirit and the Value of Speaking In Tongues Today* (Tulsa: Oral Roberts, 1964)

ROBERTS, T. 'Diwygiad '59 a '60 yn Llanbedr a Thalybont, Dyffryn Conwy', *Y Dysgedydd* 86 (1907), 314–17

ROBERTSON, A. and PLUMMER, A., *First Epistle of St. Paul to the Corinthians* (Edinburgh, 1911)

ROBERTSON, Edwin *Tomorrow is a Holiday* (S.C.M. (1959)

ROBINSON, H. W. *The Christian Doctrine of Man* 3rd edit. (Edinburgh, 1926);
'Hebrew Psychology' in A. S. Peake ed. *The People and the Book* (Oxford, 1925);
The Christian Experience of the Holy Spirit 3rd edit. (Nisbet, 1930)

ROBINSON, T. H. 'The Ecstatic Element in Old Testament Prophecy' in *The Expositor* 8th series 21 (1921), 217–38;
Prophecy and the Prophets in Ancient Israel (London: Duckworth, 1923)

ROSAGE, D. E. *Retreats and the Catholic Charismatic Renewal* (Dove, 1971)

ROWLEY, H. H. 'The Nature of Prophecy in the Light of Recent Study' in *H.T.R.* 38 (1945) 1–38;
The Servant of the Lord (London: Lutterworth, 1952);
Studies in Old Testament Prophecy (Edinburgh: T. and T. Clark 1950) ed.

RUNIA, K. 'Speaking in Tongues in the New Testament', 'Speaking in Tongues Today'. *Vox Reformata* 4 (May 1965), 20–29; 38–46.

SADLER, A. W. 'Glossolalia and Possession: An Appeal to the Episcopal Study Commission', *J.S.S.R.* 4 (1) (1964), 84–90

SAMARIN, W. J. *Tongues of Men and Angels*, (Toronto: Collier-Macmillan Canada Ltd., New York: The Macmillan Co., 1972);
'The forms and functions of nonsense language', *Linguistics* 50 (1969), 70–74;
'Glossolalia as Learned Behaviour', *Canadian Journal of Theology* 15 (1969), 60–64;
'Salient and substantive pidginization', D. Hymes ed., *Pidginization and Creolization of Language*, (Cambridge University Press, 1971);

262

'Language in resocialization', *Practical Anthropology* 17 (1970), 269–79;

'The Linguisticality of Glossolalia', *The Hertford Quarterly*, 8 (4) (Summer 1968), 49–75

SARGANT, William 'Some Cultural Group Abreactive Techniques and their Relation to Modern Treatments', *Proceedings of the Royal Society of Medicine* 42 (London: Longmans Green & Co., 1949), 367ff.;

The Mind possessed: a physiology of possession, mysticism and faith healing (London: Pan Books, 1976);

Battle for the Mind (New York: Doubleday, 1957)

SCHAFF, Philip *History of the Christian Church* i chap. iv (New York: Charles Scribners, Sons, 1882–1910)

SCHIMMEL, A. *Mystical Dimensions of Islam* (University of Carolina, 1974)

SCHJELDERUP, H. 'Psychologische Analyse Eines Falles von Zungenreden', *Zeitschrift für Psychologie* 122 (1931), 1–27

SCHOLEM, G. *Major Trends in Jewish Mysticism* (Jerusalem, 1941)

SCHOLLER, L. W. *A chapter of Church History from South Germany* (London, 1894)

SCHUON, Frithjof *The Transcendent Unity of Religions* (Harper and Row, 1953)

SCOTT, R. B. Y. *The Relevance of the Prophets* rev. ed. (Toronto: Collier-Macmillan, 1968);

'The Literary Structure of Isaiah's Oracles' in H. H. Rowley ed., *Studies in Old Testament Prophecy*;

'Isaiah xxi. 1–10; The Inside of a Prophet's Mind, *VT* 11 (3) (1952), 278–81

SEDDON, A.E. 'Edward Irving and unknown tongues', *Homiletic Review*, 57, (1913), 103.

SEDMAN, G. Depersonalization in a Group of Normal Subjects, *Brit. J. Psychiat* 112 (1966), 907–12.

SEIERSTAD, I. P. *Die Offenbarungserlebnisse der Propheten Amos, Jesaja und Jeremia* (Oslo: Dybwad, 1946)

SHERRILL, J. L. *They Speak with Other Tongues* (New York: McGraw Hill, Inc., 1964, London: Hodder and Stoughton, 1965)

SHOEMAKER, W. R. 'The use of *Ruah* in the Old Testament and of *pneuma* in the New Testament: A Lexicographical Study', *J.B.L.* 23 (1904), 13–67

SHOR, R. E. 'Hypnosis and the concept of the Generalised Reality-Orientation' in *American Journal of Psychotherapy* 13 (58) (1959), 582–602

'Signs and Wonders in Rabbath-Ammori' a pamphlet (Milwaukee: Word and Witness Publishing Co., 1934)

SIRKS, G. J. 'The Cinderella of Theology', *H.T.R.* 50 (1957), 77–89

SKINNER, B. F. *Verbal Behavior* (New York, 1957)

SKINNER, J. *Prophecy and Religion* (Cambridge, 1922)

SLOBIN, Dan I. and WELSH, Charles A. 'Elicited imitations as a research tool in developmental psycholinguistics', (University of California; Berkeley, 1968) Language Behavior Research Laboratory Working Paper Number 10.

SPIRO, M. E. 'Religion and the irrational' in *Proceedings of the 1964 annual spring meeting of the American Ethnological Society* (Seattle: University of Washington Press, 1964), 102–115;
edit., *Context and Meaning in Cultural Anthropology* (New York: The Free Press, 1965)

SPOERRI, Th. 'Ekstatische Rede und Glossolalie' in *Beiträge zur Ekstase.* Th. Spoerri, ed. Bibliotheca Psychatrica et Neurologica No. 134 (Basel: S. Karger, 1967)
Sprachphanomene und Psychose (Basel: S. Karger, 1964)

STAGG, F., HINSON, E. G., OATES, W. E. *Glossolalia: Tongue Speaking in Biblical, Historical and Psychological Perspective* (Nashville and New York: Abingdon Press, 1967)

STANLEY, G., BARTLETT, W. K., MOYLE, T. 'Some Characteristics of Charismatic Experience: Glossolalia in Australia' in *J.S.S.R.* 17 (3) (1978), 269–278

STARL, R. 'Psychopathology and religious commitment', *Review of Religious Research* 12 (1971), 165–76

STEAD, W. T. *History of the Welsh Revival* (Boston: Pilgrim Press 1905)

STEVENS, A. *The History of Methodism* (New York: Philips & Hunt, 1858)

STEVENSON, I. Review of M. T. Kelsey, Tongue Speaking, *Journal of the American Society for Psychical Research* 60 (1966), 300–303;
Xenoglossy: A Review and Report of a Case (The University of Virginia Press, 1974)

STOLL, R. F. 'The First Christian Pentecost', *Ecclesiastical Review* 108 (1943), 337–47

STRACK-BILLERBECK, *Kommentar zum Neuen Testament aus Talmud und Midrash* (Munich: Beck, 1926)

Study Commission on Glossolalia Diocese of California, Division of Pastrol Services, *Preliminary Report* (1963).

STURTEVANT, E. H. *An introduction to Linguistic Science* (1947)

STURTEVANT, W. C. 'Categories, percussion and physiology', *Man* n.s. 3 (1968), 133–34

SUENENS, L. J. *A New Pentecost ?* (New York: The Seabury Press, 1974);

'A cardinal looks at Charismatic Renewal' *Dunamis Digest* 7 (Glad Tidings Literature Service, Nagarampalein, India) 12–18

SULLIVAN, F. A. 'Baptism in the Holy Spirit', *Gregorianum* 50 (1974), 49–68

SUNDKLER, B. G. M. *Bantu Prophets in South Africa* 2nd ed. (London: O.U.P., 1961)

SWEET, J. M. P. 'A sign for unbelievers: Paul's Attitude to Glossolalia', *N.T.S.* 13 (1967), 240–57

SYNAN, V. *The Holiness-Pentecostal Movement in the United States* (Grand Rapids: W. B. Eerdmans, 1971).

SYNGE, F. C. 'The Spirit in the Pauline Epistles' *Church Quarterly Review* 119 (1934), 79–93; (1935), 205–17

TABER, Charles R. *French Loan Words in Sango: A statistical analysis of incidence* (Hartford Conn., 1964)

TAMBIAH, S. J. 'The Magical Power of Words' in *Man* 3 (1968), 171–208

TART, C. T. ed. *Altered States of Consciousness, A Book of Readings* (Toronto, 1969)

TAYLOR, R. O. P. 'The Tongues at Pentecost' *E.T.* 40 (1928–9), 300–303

The Acts of the Holy Spirit among the Baptists Today (F.G.B.M.F.I. 1971)

The Acts of the Holy Spirit among the Episcopalians Today (F.G.B.M.F.I. 1973)

The Acts of the Holy Spirit among the Methodists Today (F.G.B.M.F.I. 1971)

The Apostolic Church: its Principles and Practices (1961)

'The Fountain Trust: What it is and What it does' (pamphlet); also 'Fountain Trust: In Christ by the Spirit to the church for the world', (pamphlet) (Fountain Trust, 3a High Street, Esher, Surrey)

'The Unknown Tongues' anon. pamphlet (1831)

'The Work of the Holy Spirit' report adopted by the 1979 General Assembly of the United Presbyterian Church, U.S.A. (obtainable from The Office of the General Assembly U.P.C., US. 510 Witherspoon Building, Philadelphia, Pa. 19107)

THOMAS, W. H. Griffith *The Holy Spirit of God* (Grand Rapids: W. B. Eerdmans Co. 1913)

THOMPSON, L. G. *Chinese Religion: An Introduction* (Dickenson, 1969)

THOMPSON, W. S. 'Tongues at Pentecost, Acts ii' *E.T.* 38 (1926–7), 284–86

TILLICH, P. *Dynamics of Faith* (New York: Harper, 1956)

TIPPETT, A. R. 'Glossolalia as Spirit Possession: A Taxonomy for Cross-Cultural Observation and Description', Paper read to the American Academy of Religion in Los Angeles 1972

TITTERINGTON, E. J. G. 'The Gift of Tongues', *Faith and Thought* (formerly the *Journal of the Transactions of the Victoria Institute*) 90 (1958), p. 65

TOLKIEN, J. R. R. *The Lord of the Rings* (London: George Allen and Unwin Ltd. 1954 and 55); pb. 1968

TOMLINSON, A. J. *God's Twentieth Century Pioneer* (Cleveland, Tenn.: White Wing Publishing House, 1962); *Answering the Call of God* (Cleveland, Tenn.: White Wing Publishing House n.d.)

TOMLINSON, Homer, *The Diary of A. J. Tomlinson* i-iii (N.Y.: The Church of God Headquarters 1953)

TUCCI, G. *The Theory and Practice of the Mandala* E. Tr. A. H. Brodrick (N.Y., Samuel Weiser, 1973)

TULAND, Carl G. 'The Confusion About Tongues', *Christianity Today* 13 (5) (Dec. 1968), 7–9

TURNBULL, T. N. *Brothers in Arms* (Puritan Press, 1963)

UNDERHILL, Evelyn *Mysticism: a study in the nature and development of man's spiritual consciousness* (London: Methuen. 1912)

VAN DER LEEUW, G. *Religion in Essence and Manifestation*, E. Tr. (Allen & Unwin, 1938)

VAN DUSEN, H. P. 'The Third Force in Christianity', *Life* 50 (9 June 1958), 113–124; *Spirit, Son and Father* (New York: Charles Cribners & Sons, 1958)

VAN EDEN, F. 'Account of sittings with Mrs. Thompson' in *Proc. S.P.R.* 17 (1901–3), 75–115

VIVIER, L. M. Van Eetveldt, 'The glossolalic and his personality' in *Beiträge zur Ekstase* edit. Th. Spoerri; Bibliotheca Psychiatrica et Neurologica No. 134 (Basel: S. Karger, 1967); *Glossolalia* (Johannesburg: University of Witwatersrand, Doctor of Medicine dissertation in the Department of Psychiatry and Mental Hygiene 1960)

VON HARNACK, A. *The Acts of the Apostles* (New York: Putnam, 1909)

VON RAD, G. *The Message of the Prophets* E.Tr., D.M.G. Stalker (London S.C.M. 1968)

WACE, H. and SCHAFF, P. eds. *Nicene and Post-Nicene Fathers: Eusebius* (Oxford, 1905)

WADDELL, A. *The Buddhism of Tibet or Lamaism* (London, 1895)

WALKER, D. *The Gift of Tongues and other Essays* (Edinburgh, 1906)

WALTERS, K. 'Wales and the Charismatic Renewal', *Renewal* (1976), 13–15

WEIR, Ruth H. *Language in the Crib*, Janua Linguarum, Series Maior, 14 (The Hague- Mouton and Co., 1962);
'Some questions on the child's learning of phonology', Frank Smith and George A. Miller, eds., *The Genesis of Language* (Cambridge, Mass: MIT Press, 1966), 153–68

WELLINGS, V. The Baptism of the Holy Spirit with signs following (Tenets of the Apostolic Church (5) (1954)

WEPMAN, J. M. and JONES, L. V. 'Five Aphasia: A commentary on aphasia as a regressive linguistic phenomenon' in D. Rioch and E. A. Weinstein, eds. *Disorders of Communication* (Baltimore: Williams and Wilkins, 1964)

WERBLOWSKY, R. J. Zwi 'Mystical and Magical Contemplation: the Kabbalists in Sixteenth Century Safed', *History of Religions* i (1) (1961)
'Structure and Archetype' in *The Journal of the Ancient Near Eastern Society of Columbia University*, Vol. 5 (1973) (=Th. Gaster Festschrift), 435–42

WESLEY J. *Works* vol. v. (N.Y.: Harper, 1826–7)

WESTERMANN, C. *Basic Forms of Prophetic Speech* E.Tr., H. C. White, (Minneapolis: Augsburg Publishing House, 1967)

WHITE, A. *Demons and Tongues* (N.J.: The Pentecostal Union, Round Brook, 1910)

WHITE, Hugh W. *Demonism Verified and Analysed* (Richmond Va.: Printed by Mission Book Co. Shanghai, 1922)

WHITE, Victor *God and the Unconscious* (New York: World Publishing Co., Meridian Books, 1961)

WICKENHAUSER, A. *Die Apostelgeschichte* (Regensburg, 1961)

WILKERSON, David *The Cross and the Switchblade* (New York: Bernard Geis Associates, Random House, 1963)

WILLIAMS, C. G. 'Teulu'r Gors', *Y Dysgedydd* (1957), 258–264; 310–312; 341–343;
'Cymru a'r Mudiad Pentecostaidd', *Y Traethodydd*, cxxx (556) (1975), 180–196;
'Ecstaticism in Hebrew prophecy and Christian glossolalia' in *Sciences Religieuses/Studies in Religion* 3:4 (1974), 320–38;
'Glossolalia as a religious phenomenon: "Tongues" at Corinth and Pentecost', *Religion: Journal of Religion and Religions* 5 (1975), 16–32;
'Selflessness in the Pattern of Salvation', *Religious Studies* 7 (1971), 163–67

WILLIAMS, C. S. C. *A Commentary on the Acts of the Apostles* (London, 1957)

WILLIAMS, J. D. 'The Modern Pentecostal Movement in America: A Brief Sketch of its History and Thought' in *Lexington Theological Quarterly* (1974), 50–59

WILLIAMS, J. R. *The Pentecostal Reality* (Logos, 1972)

WILSON, B. R. 'Speaking in Tongues' in *Man, Myth and Magic* 95, 2649–2653;
Religious Sects (World University Library, 1970);
'Apparition et persistance des sectes dans un milieu social en évolution', in *Archives de sociologie des religions*, Jan-June, 1958), 140–50;
'The Pentecostalist Minister: Role Conflicts and Status Contradictions' *A.J.S.L.* 64 (1958–59), 494–504

WILSON, C. *New Directions in Psychology* (London, 1972)

WILSON, S. G. *The Gentiles and the Gentile Mission in Luke-Acts* (Cambridge, 1973)

WOLFF, H. W. 'Hauptprobleme alttestamentlicher Prophetie', *Evangelische Theologie* (1955), 446–68;
'Die Begrundung, der prophetischen Heils-und Unheils spruche' *Z.A.W.*, 52 (1) (1934), 1ff

WOLFRAM, Walter A. 'The Socio linguistics of Glossolalia' (Hartford Seminary M.A. thesis 1966);
Review of F. D. Goodman, Speaking in tongues: a cross-cultural study of glossolalia in *Language in Society* Vol. 3 (1) (April 1974), 123–126

WOLFSON, H. A. *Philo: foundations of religious philosophy in Judaism, Christianity and Islam* i-ii (Cambridge, Mass.: Harvard Univ. Press 1962)

WOOD, F. H. *This Egyptian Miracle. The Restoration of Lost Speech of Ancient Egypt by Supernormal Means* (London: Rider, 1940);
After Thirty Centuries (London: Rider, 1935)

WOOD, William W. *Culture and Personality Aspects of the Pentecostal Holiness Religion* (Paris: Mouton, 1965)

WORSLEY, P. *The Trumpet Shall Sound: A Study of 'Cargo' cults in Melanesia* (Schocken, 1968)

WRIGHT, A. *Some New Testament Problems* (London: Methuen, 1898);
'Gift of Tongues: a new view', *Theological Monthly* 5, 161, 272

ZANETSKY, I. I. and LEONE, Mark P., *Religious Movements in Contemporary America* (Princeton, 1974)

ZAUGG, E. H. *A genetic study of the spirit phenomena in the New Testament* (Chicago, private edition, 1917)

ZIMMERMAN, T. F. 'Plea for the Pentecostalists', *Christianity Today* (January 4, 1963), 11–12

Yearbook of American Churches (Jacquet, 1967)

INDEX

269

270

272

273

SCRIPTURE REFERENCES

276